Worship

UNDERSTANDING,
PRACTICE,
ECUMENICAL IMPLICATIONS

Today

D0886035

Worship

UNDERSTANDING,
PRACTICE,
ECUMENICAL IMPLICATIONS

Today

Edited by
Thomas F. Best and Dagmar Heller

Faith and Order Paper No. 194

WCC Publications, Geneva

The texts by Michael Ghattas, Sigisbert Kraft, Hans H. Krech and Corinna
Schmidt were translated from German by the WCC Language Service
The text on the Community of Grandchamp was translated from French by
WCC Faith and Order staff

Biblical quotations are taken from the New Revised Standard Version

Cover design: Stephen Raw

ISBN 2-8254-1405-0

© 2004 WCC Publications, World Council of Churches
150 route de Ferney, P.O.Box 2100
1211 Geneva 2, Switzerland
Website: http://www.wcc-coe.org

Printed in Switzerland

Contents

B. TRADITIONS IN SPECIFIC CONTEXTS

C. CROSS-TRADITIONAL MOVEMENTS

D. RELIGIOUS COMMUNITIES

II. Reflections on Worship in Ecumenical Contexts

Introduction

THOMAS F. BEST AND DAGMAR HELLER

Worship today: a new situation in, and among, the churches

This book is a survey of the understanding and practice of worship today in a wide variety of Christian churches, communities and contexts. Our aims in gathering this material are several: (1) to provide information on the understanding and practice of worship in a wide range of churches and Christian contexts; (2) thereby to promote understanding among Christians of their own, and each others', worship lives; (3) to take account of the impact – and implications – of the liturgical renewal and ecumenical movements for worship today; (4) through this to encourage informed reflection and dialogue among Christians about the meaning and practice of worship, both within particular churches and ecumenically; and (5) thus to promote the deepening and renewal of worship within and among the churches.

We believe that the time is ripe for such a survey, and this for several reasons. Christians are recognizing anew that worship lies at the heart of their faith, and that it is foundational and central to the lives and witness of the churches, as well as to the ecumenical movement. The efforts of churches to find new vitality and depth in their own worship through the reappropriation of their own traditions; the rediscovery of common patterns, intentions and values in worship through the movements for liturgical renewal; the growing awareness, through the ecumenical movement, of the worship of other churches and Christian communities; and the growing experience of Christians and churches praying and praising God *together* rather than separately – all these factors have created a new situation within and among the churches. This offers churches the chance to deepen and intensify their own worship life. Equally it calls them to discern the meaning and possibilities of worship with Christians in traditions other than their own. Already the new situation has stimulated much creative work on worship within and among the churches.[1]

But understanding, reflection and discussion on worship are also needed today because, for all their ecumenical progress, the churches remain divided in significant ways. And these divisions are nowhere so clearly visible and painfully felt as in worship – most evidently, though not only, when the churches are unable to gather at the one Table of their one Lord. But also new difficulties in worshipping together have arisen. The fall of the iron curtain in Europe made possible a new and more realistic encounter with the Orthodox churches. Many of these have experienced worship in other churches, and especially in ecumenical contexts, as disturbing and some Orthodox groups would go so far as to say that common prayer between Orthodox and non-Orthodox is not possible.[2] Therefore the Special Commission on Orthodox Participation in the WCC has sought ways to overcome these difficulties, and to further the practice of common prayer.[3] This discussion only affirms that the time for renewed reflection on worship within the churches, and the widest possible dialogue among them, is at hand.

In addition, the difficulties expressed by Orthodox have helped by setting in sharp relief some fundamental differences in the understanding of worship. Among these are: Is worship a service performed by human beings and offered to God? Or is it an act of God, in which human beings are privileged to participate? Is the accent on doxology? What about the pedagogical aspect of worship? Questions such as these find different answers in different traditions. We hope that the sharing on worship in this book will clarify how far these different understandings are actually church dividing and, where necessary, suggest ways of working on the issues which divide us.

Worship Today: contents and contributors

For a host of reasons, then, reflection and discussion on worship is becoming more and more important for the churches today and for the ecumenical movement. We hope to stimulate and support this process – which is ultimately a process of *renewal* – through this book. As a guide and help to readers, we offer the following comments on the structure of this book and on our contributors.

Accounts from churches and Christian contexts: Sections I and II

Section I of our collection includes four sets of articles, all coming from churches and Christian contexts. The first set offers presentations of the understanding and practice of worship today in a wide range of Christian churches. We have tried to arrange these accounts in a way that moves from older to more recent traditions. Thus one proceeds from the ancient foundations, through the churches of the Reformation and the Anglican tradition, through the historic free churches, to the 19th century and later foundations. It is a very diverse collection, including not only the classic ecumenically engaged churches but also, significantly, some whose voices are not so often heard in the ecumenical discussion.

The second set of articles suggests the diversity present *within* the churches as well as across them. In four cases (Lutheran, Anglican, Mennonite, Baptist) the more general account given in the preceding section is complemented by another coming from the same confessional tradition, but emphasizing that tradition's understanding and practice of worship in a specific national and cultural context (indeed, this could have been done for all of the Christian traditions, had space allowed).

The third and fourth sets of articles consist of accounts from a number of new Christian manifestations, all related to the historic Christian churches but in some way cross-traditional. The third set includes the "mega-church" phenomenon in Korea and feminist perspectives on the life and worship of the church today. The fourth set consists of accounts from two widely diverse Christian religious communities, Grandchamp in Switzerland and Iona in Scotland, whose distinctive worship life reflects an authentic and creative interaction between historic traditions of the church and the ecumenical movement.

The author of each article in section I comes from the church or Christian context concerned. Each was asked (1) to explain their church's practice and understanding of worship, focusing on common convictions but reflecting something of the diversity present within the church; (2) to indicate how the worship of their church has been influenced or changed by the liturgical renewal and ecumenical movements; and (3) to indicate other new developments in their church's worship, and how these might help – or hinder – its ecumenical engagement. In addition each author was given three stylistic guidelines, namely: (1) to speak in his or her own voice, while representing the church or Christian community concerned; (2) to write in a style that would be both concise and accessible; and (3) to write so as to be understood by readers *not* coming from the church or Christian community being described.

The authors are as diverse as the churches and Christian contexts from which they come. Many are liturgists; others are liturgically literate theologians, church officials or pastors. They reflect varying degrees of ecumenical experience and engagement. What they have in common is a commitment to the worship life of their own, and the larger, church and a desire to promote understanding and reflection, both within and among the churches, on issues of worship today. To our minds, their accounts provide a substantial and stimulating picture of the diverse and complex reality of worship in the churches today.

We have tried to honour our contributors' diversity by letting them indeed speak in their own voice, and by not imposing a common structure or style on their accounts. This means, inevitably, a considerable diversity among the accounts themselves: some are more academic in tone, others less; some emphasize historical development within their own church and tradition, while others are more theological in orientation, or focus on other aspects of their church or community's worship. We understand this very diversity in presentation as part of the story of "worship today" within and among the churches, reflecting as it does the churches' distinct emphases, histories, cultural settings and self-perceptions.

Section II of this book includes two articles on worship in ecumenical contexts. One is by a theologian and ecumenist with extensive experience in worship in such contexts, and the other is by a liturgist and theologian with extensive ecumenical experience. The first text, from a united church, surveys and evaluates the churches' increasing efforts to worship together rather than separately; the second text offers an evaluation of such common worship from an Orthodox perspective. We feel that these articles offer a sound basis for a constructive discussion in this complex and sensitive area.

Overviews and analyses: section III

Part III of our collection consists of five interpretive surveys. Working from a representative sample of the accounts from churches and Christian contexts, these seek: (1) to discern where the churches, individually and ecumenically, find themselves in relation to worship today; (2) to identify lines of convergence – and continuing divergence – among the churches in their understanding and practice of worship; and (3) to suggest possible future developments in the worship life of the churches, both individually and ecumenically. (It should be noted that the authors were asked not so much to offer detailed comments on particular confessional articles, as to discern the overall situation emerging in the worship life of the churches today, with all its chances and challenges.)

These contributors are all liturgists with substantial ecumenical experience. They come from a broad variety of churches, Orthodox, Roman Catholic and Protestant (Methodist, Baptist and United). Within the framework of their assignment, their articles too reflect a wide diversity of perspective and approach. We believe that their articles model precisely the kind of reflection and discussion on worship today which we hope to encourage and stimulate through this book.

A note on the limitations of this survey

As with any project of this scope and complexity, there are inevitable gaps and inconsistencies in this survey of worship within and among the churches today. Indeed, given the range and diversity of Christian churches and communities, no such collection could pretend to be complete. Regarding the overview and analytical articles in section III we regret in particular that, for editorial and practical reasons, it was not possible for us to provide our five authors with the texts of all of the accounts from churches and Christian contexts.

Worship Today: an invitation to reflection and renewal in the churches

In conclusion, we have the pleasure of extending heartfelt thanks to each of our contributors for their enthusiasm, commitment and, not least, patience at each stage of this lengthy project. We join them in offering this overview of where the churches, both individually and ecumenically, find themselves in their understanding and practice of worship today. May it truly engender a broader understanding of worship within and among the churches; may it encourage reflection and discussion of what unites, and what still divides, us in that worship life which is so central to the whole life of the church; and, most importantly, may it help to deepen and revitalize worship, both within individual churches and in the churches' common praise and prayer.

NOTES

[1] **From Faith and Order** see: *Baptism, Eucharist and Ministry*, Faith and Order Paper no. 111, WCC, 1982; *So We Believe, So We Pray: Towards Koinonia in Worship*, Thomas F. Best and Dagmar Heller eds, Faith and Order Paper no. 171, WCC, 1995; *Eucharistic Worship in Ecumenical Contexts: The Lima Liturgy – and Beyond*, Thomas F. Best and Dagmar Heller eds, WCC, 1998; *Becoming a Christian: The Ecumenical Implications of Our Common Baptism*, Thomas F. Best and Dagmar Heller eds, Faith and Order Paper no. 184, WCC, 1999; "One Baptism: Towards Mutual Recognition of Christian Initiation" [Faverges II, a text-in-progress], FO/2001:24, 2001; and also work being done by the Joint Working Group between the World Council of Churches and the Roman Catholic Church (see "Ecclesiological and Ecumenical Implications of a Common Baptism: A JWG Study", revised draft [provisional, not for publication], Nov. 2003).
In relation to worship in ecumenical contexts: for a representative collection of services from ecumenical contexts see *Worshipping Ecumenically: Orders of Service from Global Meetings with Suggestions for Local Use*, Per Harling ed., WCC, 1995; Per Harling, "The Liturgy of the World: Ecumenical Worship with All Senses", in *Worshipping Ecumenically*, pp.1-26; Janet Crawford and Thomas Best, "Praise the Lord with the Lyre... and the Gamelan? Towards Koinonia in Worship", in *The Ecumenical Review*, 46, 1, 1994, pp.78-96; Teresa Berger, "Worship in the Ecumenical Movement", in *Dictionary of the Ecumenical Movement*, Nicholas Lossky et al. eds, 2nd ed., WCC, 2002, pp.1250-1255; Dagmar Heller, "Ecumenical Worship", in *The New SCM Dictionary of Liturgy and Worship*, Paul F. Bradshaw ed., London, SCM Press, pp.163-65.
[2] See "Evaluation of New Facts in the Relations of Orthodoxy and the Ecumenical Movement: Thessaloniki, Greece, 29 April–2 May 1998", in *Turn to God – Rejoice in Hope: Orthodox Reflections on the Way to Harare*, Thomas FitzGerald and Peter Bouteneff eds, WCC/Orthodox Task Force, 1998, pp.136-38.
[3] See "Final Report of the Special Commission on Orthodox Participation in the WCC", in *The Ecumenical Review*, 55, 1, Jan. 2003, especially "V. Common Prayer" (paras. 36-45), pp.10-12; and "Appendix A: A Framework for Common Prayer at WCC Gatherings", pp.18-26.

Accounts from Churches
and Christian Contexts

Worship in the Armenian Orthodox Church

NAREG ALEMEZIAN

• ORIENTAL ORTHODOX •

Worship is the heart of Christianity, as the response of Christians to the magnificent revelation and aweful omnipresence of the transcendent God. This meeting between God and God's people is not optional and peripheral, but necessary and fundamental as a token of appreciation and acknowledgment of the very fact that God reveals himself to us through God's creation, through the Holy Bible, Jesus Christ and the Holy Spirit. In worship, creatures encounter their Creator and Redeemer. To do so is an authentic and natural desire of the faithful, as stated in Psalm 42:1: "As a deer longs for flowing streams, so my soul longs for you, O God."

Worship and service are essentially one. Through service expectation, encounter and response overflow to penetrate all aspects of a community's daily life, and devotion to God extends into a commitment to serve. Therefore, the worshipping and serving community becomes one body (1 Cor. 12:12ff.), as branches of a living vine (cf. John 15:1ff.).

Our knowledge of God is manifested in numerous expressions of worship, through various normal, festive and aesthetic activities and gestures, for example adoration, devotion, gratitude, honour, joining hands, kneeling, ornaments, piety, praise, prayer, prostration, raising hands, reverence, service, singing, the use of symbols, and thanksgiving.

Without undermining the importance of individual spirituality and personal prayer, corporate ritual and ceremonial acts reflect the social, public, common and organic character of worship, and enable the Christian church to realize itself as a people who worship God "in spirit and truth" (John 4:23).

In worship we confess the greatness of God and adhere to the instruction to worship and serve him only (Ex. 20:1-3; Josh. 24:14-15), with our whole being (Deut. 6:5; Luke 10:27; Rom. 12:1) and guided by the Holy Spirit (Rom. 8:26; Phil. 3:3). The end purpose of worship is to meet God, and to enter into union with him (John 12:26).

The calendar of the Armenian Orthodox Church

The following is a summary of the important features of the calendar of the Armenian Orthodox Church, offered to facilitate the understanding of the *ordo* of worship in various ceremonies and rituals referred to below. The Armenian church has developed a calendar system based on the weekly cycle which includes three types of days: (1) dominical feasts, (2) feasts of the saints, and (3) days of abstinence. All these days are movable except for six: (1) the Theophany and Nativity (6 January); (2) the Presentation of the Lord to the Temple (14 February); (3) the Annunciation (7 April); (4) the Feast of the Birth of Holy Mother of God (8 September); (5) the Presentation of the Holy Mother-of-God (21 November); (6) the Conception of the Virgin St Mary by St Anne (9 December).

The liturgical year of the Armenian Orthodox Church is divided into eight great periods or seasons, namely (1) Theophany and Nativity; (2) Lent; (3) Easter; (4) Pentecost; (5) Transfiguration; (6) Assumption; (7) Exaltation of the Holy Cross; (8) Advent.

CEREMONIES AND RITUALS

In the Armenian Orthodox Church the faithful worship and serve God through the following ceremonies and rituals.

Daily divine office

The Armenian church has seven daily prayer hours based on the exhortation of Psalm 119:164, " Seven times a day I praise you for your righteous ordinances." The seven daily prayer hours are: (1) night hour or vigils or nocturnes; (2) morning hour or matins; (3) sunrise hour or prime; (4) midday hour or sext; (5) evening hour or vespers; (6) peace hour; (7) rest hour or compline. These daily divine offices were originally designed for monastic settings, and presently are held alternatively in the Armenian monasteries and some parishes. They are offered in the nave of the church.

Ecclesiastical feasts

All Sundays are dedicated to our Lord Jesus Christ and are called dominical days. On the Lord's day we affirm our identity as the people of God belonging to God and worshipping him because he is our God, and has been gracious towards us. Every Sunday, during the morning hour, resurrection gospel narratives are read and all the hymns are dedicated to the resurrection of our Saviour. Celebrations of saints' days are prohibited on Sundays.

Ecclesiastical feasts are of two types. The first is further *dominical days*, on which events of the life of our Lord Jesus Christ are celebrated. In addition to this, days appointed in honour of the holy cross, the church, the holy virgin and Pentecost are also considered dominical.

There are about 140 dominical days in the church year, celebrated either on Sundays or other days of the week (except on Wednesdays and Fridays); for example, Theophany and Nativity are celebrated on 6 January; Ascension is celebrated on a Thursday, forty days following Easter.

The second type is *saints' days*. These days are designated for the commemoration of saints who have been recognized by the universal church, and the Armenian church, as being pre-eminent for their holy life lived in piety and virtue, or who have given their life in witness to their Christian faith and for the furtherance of God's kingdom. About 128 days in a year are dedicated to the commemoration of saints. These are not fixed dates, because saints may be commemorated only on Mondays, Tuesdays, Thursdays and Saturdays; if a dominical day falls on any of these days, then the commemoration of the saint will be shifted to some other day. Saints may not be commemorated on any of the days Monday to Friday in a week of liturgical fasting.

Wednesdays and Fridays are days of abstinence. The character of the office during these two days of the week is penitential. Wednesdays are dedicated to the annunciation and incarnation, Fridays to the crucifixion. In addition, there are six dietetic fasting weeks and the period of forty days of fasting of Great Lent. This is a season of intense prayer, fasting, penance, meditation and self-examination. In all, about 150 days in a year are put aside for fasting.[1]

Sacraments

The Armenian Orthodox Church has seven sacraments: (1) baptism; (2) chrismation; (3) repentance; (4) holy communion; (5) holy matrimony; (6) ordination; (7) last anointing. We will speak here especially about holy communion or the eucharist.

Holy Eucharist

Every Sunday, and on other designated dominical days, Armenian faithful gather in churches to celebrate holy eucharist. On very special occasions it is permitted to celebrate holy eucharist outdoors, where an altar is erected and a consecrated rock-stone *(vemkar)* placed, on which the chalice rests during the consecration.

Holy eucharist is the high point of worship in the Armenian Orthodox Church, in the sense that it underlines the Christological character of worship. Holy eucharist is related directly to the events of the salvation history, because Christ gives his life for human beings and brings them to partake of that life by his sacrificial death and his offering of his body and blood. This event does not pertain to the past only, but becomes both a life-generating experience in the present and the foretaste of the kingdom of heaven (Heb. 12:28). William R. Crockett defines this reality in the following statement:

> The eucharist is neither a repetition of the sacrifice of the cross, nor simply a mental recollection of an event that took place 2000 years ago. Through the eucharistic memorial, the sacrifice of the cross is made sacramentally present in order that we may participate in its redemptive reality in the present.[2]

This eschatological hope directs the faithful to have unconditional faith and total trust in Christ, and to offer their gifts as a symbolic response and sacrifice to the self-offering of God. In Armenian, the literal translation of holy eucharist is "holy sacrifice" *(Sourp Badarak)*. Through grace, as the transforming power of the Holy Spirit, we enjoy the heavenly reality in our earthly surroundings and limitations, take part in the communal worship, and relate to the community of faith. Hence, in the presence of Christ, holy eucharist embraces the whole creation and becomes the sacrament of love, thanksgiving, communion, unity and service.

Henry Hill describes the Armenian holy liturgy in these words,

> Armenian beliefs are richly embodied in the holy liturgy which opens with the words, "O mystery deep, inscrutable, without beginning, through the passion of thine holy only-begotten all creation hath been made immortal". Armenian worship takes place within its distinctive conical-topped churches, with the square altar mounted on a high stage or *bema*. The celebrant, wearing impressive and colourful vestments, is assisted by deacons with censers, acolytes and singers. The congregation participate in the liturgy fully, sometimes lifting their hands, sometimes bowing low in reverence.[3]

Occasional pious customs

In the *Book of Rituals* of the Armenian Orthodox Church there are services devised for special occasions and reflecting the piety of the faithful. These include: (1) the blessing of the newborn before baptism; (2) the canon of burial; (3) the requiem service at the graveside; (4) the service of home blessing; (5) the service of hair-cutting of adolescents; (6) the prayer for the sick; (7) the order of confession, and (8) the blessing of the harvest.

Other devotionals

This category includes personal and family prayers, Sunday school and Christian education courses, morning prayers in Armenian schools, home prayer groups, and many other expressions of worship that are not part of the rite of the Armenian Orthodox Church (and do not take place in the churches), but are in line with the teachings of the church.

Characteristics of Armenian worship

The Armenian Orthodox Church's deeply sacramental tradition of worship has ingredients common to all Christians in general, and to the Orthodox church in particular. However, the following basic elements indicate some of the special, distinctive features of Armenian worship – worship which stands at the centre of the church's life and activity.

Worship, theology and doctrine

Its rich worship is founded on the clear theology and doctrine of the Armenian Orthodox Church. This interconnection of worship and dogma is reflected in the creeds and confessions of faith recited during church services, orienting the faithful towards God. It is interesting to note that celebrant bishops proclaim their Orthodox faith at the beginning of the morning service, after denouncing Satan and before publicly confessing their sins. In the context of worship, theological reflection becomes a constant reminder of the dynamic participation and the moving experience of being enriched by the Orthodox faith. Paul Meyendorff rightly notes,

> But Eastern worship, just as Western, expresses the faith, culture and spirituality of a given ecclesial body, its understanding of orders, its approach to tradition.[4]

In his first encyclical St Nerses Shnorhali addresses "the entire Armenian nation whose welfare was entrusted to him by the Lord" as Catholicos, and underlines faith as the prerequisite for Christian worship and service, saying,

> Now the head is primary and most honoured among members of the body because of its elevated position and the existence of the senses in it, and it is succeeded by the other members one by one. In the same way among the faculties of the soul the greatest and primary is the truth of faith which brings forth great and small works of righteousness according to God's commandments. For this reason, first of all, we emphatically place faith before you as the primary good. We are not writing anything new but are making a summary based on the writings of the apostles, prophets and holy fathers. We do this that you may not stray from the truth into the ignorance of the unlearned by listening to words which are not in keeping with the confession of the Orthodox church, but which are outside the holy scriptures and lead to the destruction of the hearer. You should know in whom you believed on the day of baptism, as Paul says, "I know in whom I have believed" (2 Tim. 1:12). It is indeed worthy to hold the confession of faith of the Orthodox Christian, in which we begin in simple and plain words to show the truth of our faith.[5]

Worship and Christian education

Words, music, symbols and movements in worship are tools for Christian formation and discipleship. For Armenians, worship begins at home and extends to the church where we are incorporated into a caring and nurturing community of faith. In order to offer an appropriate worship and to educate its faithful in the tenets of the Christian faith, the Armenian Orthodox Church needs to make worship more practical, pleasant, comprehensive and non-boring. We can be inspired to worship God only if we can fully understand what is happening during our communal worship. To achieve this, the Armenian church needs to be more flexible and spontaneous, to substitute, as much as possible, the use of modern Armenian for classical Armenian, to reduce the duration of services, to take more care for the majesty of the sanctuary and the aesthetic details of the rituals, to make the reading and preaching of the word of God more related to contemporary issues, and to secure the full participation of the believers.

Worship and mystical elements

The ordered, canonical and diverse rituals of the Armenian Orthodox Church reflect the mysterious relationship between human beings and God. A sense of awe, reverence and transcendence in the presence of the triune God and the mysteries of the faith are constantly stressed in the prayers, hymns and gestures of worship, and especially in the celebration of the holy eucharist. In the *Study of Liturgy* this is referred to as "the paschal mystery", and according to New Testament sources it exists on three levels: (1) God "dwelling in light inaccessible" (1 Tim. 6:16), (2) in the historical order, and (3) in the liturgy.[6]

Worship and hymns

Hymns, as songs of praise, adoration and confession in honour of God or a saint, are very significant in the order of worship. The Armenian Orthodox Church is a singing church, and from the 4th century up to this very day the composition of hymns has been a prevalent feature of its life. The Armenian Orthodox Church is distinguished by many hymns dedicated to canonized national heroes. In the preface to the Armenian church hymnbook of 1838, Nerses of Lambron refers to the impact of church music, writing, "(It) awakens all minds to yearn for grace because there is nothing else that can stimulate our will with happiness or sadness except the music of properly sung hymns."[7]

Worship and service

In worship the Armenian faithful feel that they are called to serve, to spread abroad the gospel and to reach out to the needs of their community. Henry Hill sums up this aspect of worship by stating,

At the heart of every Armenian community is the parish church and centre: the focus not only for rites of passage and spiritual sustenance but of social life as well. The Armenian people, whether in the homeland or in the diaspora, are held together as a family by their participation in the activities of the local church.[8]

The worshipper as witness

The Greek word for witness is *martyr*. Martyrs are saints who have sacrificed their lives to bear witness to their Christian faith. The Armenian worshipper is not a spectator but a witness to, and partaker in, salvation history, as well as an active participant in offering himself or herself to God – always remembering that the witness or martyr par excellence remains Jesus Christ. In the words of Aidan Kavanagh,

> By grace, faith and sacrament, the church is the fullness of him who is the fullness of the Godhead bodily. If the incarnation of the Logos was God enhumaned, the church is God in Christ enworlded.[9]

The role of clergy in worship

The established order of worship – scriptural passages, prayers, music, symbols, vestments, movements, fellowship and many other elements – creates the perfect atmosphere for the worshipping church, which gathers under the leadership of the clergy. As consecrated ministers of the church, priests administer the sacraments. God is the source of grace, and priests are only his servants and channels of communication between God and human beings.

* * *

The ecumenical movement enables the churches to come closer to each other and to pursue the visible unity of the one, catholic, apostolic and holy church. According to Malachia Ormanian, worship plays a pivotal role in this respect because " the purpose of ritual is to cultivate the hearts (of the faithful) in an orderly and effectual manner to praise God, ignite their emotions and intensify their services" .[10] He goes on, albeit with some exaggeration,

> From the perspective of worship, church unity lies in the fundamental and basic tenets that the church inherited from the apostolic times. It is understandable that changes occur due to local requirements, but the basics should remain unchanged. Among all the churches, the Armenian church is the most loyal follower of the oldest (order of worship) and rejecter of modernism. In this respect the Armenian church is incomparable to other churches. Therefore the rituals, ceremonies and moral laws of the Armenian church have rightfully been considered models for original orders.[11]

NOTES

[1] In order to avoid the confusion due to the annual total of about 428 days (dominical days, 140; saints days, 128; and days of abstinence 150), we have to remember that the Great Lent and six dietetic fasting weeks overlap the weekly Wednesdays and Fridays.

[2] William R. Crockett, *Eucharist: Symbol of Transformation*, New Year, Pueblo, 1989, p.231.

[3] Henry Hill ed. *Light from the East*, Toronto, Anglican Book Centre, 1988, p.20.

[4] "Liturgy", in *Dictionary of the Ecumenical Movement*, Nicolas Lossky et al. eds, WCC, 2nd ed. 2002, p.705.

[5] St Nerses Snorhali, *General Epistle, Translation and Introduction* by Fr Arakel Aljalian, New Rochelle, New York, St Nerses Armenian Seminary, 1996.

[6] *The Study of Liturgy*, Cheslyn Jones et al. eds, London, SPCK, 1985, pp.11-15,24,28.

[7] Catholicos Babgen, *Armenian Church* [in Armenian], Jerusalem, 1930, pp.78-79.

[8] Hill, *Light from the East*, p.22.

[9] Aidan Kavanagh, *On Liturgical Theology*, New York, Pueblo, 1984, p.15.

[10] Archbishop Malachia Ormanian, *Theology* [in Armenian], Jerusalem, 1985, pp.223-24.

[11] *Ibid.*, p.142.

Worship in the Syriac Orthodox Church of Antioch

MOR CYRIL APHREM KARIM

• ORIENTAL ORTHODOX •

Worship is the *raison d'être* of the church, which is made up of the worshipping sons and daughters of God. It is required to offer worship not because of God's need for worship, but rather due to the sinfulness of the church's members and their constant need for grace. Through worship we are offered the life of grace and spiritual nourishment that is essential for our being as Christians. By opening our hearts to God's word and receiving the divine gifts of the Holy Spirit through the holy sacraments, we are assured of Christ's salvation which was accomplished on the cross.

The Syriac Orthodox Church of Antioch is heir to an ancient tradition of Christian worship which is distinguished by the antiquity and beauty of its prayers and rituals. As recounted in the Acts of the Apostles the early adherents of the Christian faith, fleeing persecution in the Holy Land, reached Antioch, a prominent centre of commerce in the eastern part of the Roman empire. There they were first called "Christians" (Acts 22:26). St Peter is believed to have founded the church in Antioch in CE 39.

Worship and theology

Hymns play a central role in the worship of the Syriac Orthodox Church. They were composed by theologians of early centuries such as St Ephrem (CE 373) and St Jacob of Sarug (CE 521). Early Syriac writers preferred poetry as the mode of theological expression, employing imagery and symbolism basic to all human experience. Mor Ephrem, acclaimed as the "Harp of the Holy Spirit", was the earliest exponent of the poetic genre of the *madroshe*, the teaching songs, in communicating the orthodox faith of the church to a wide audience. Poetry permitted Syriac theologians to avoid static theological definitions and express the subjective spiritual experience of the Creator, whose mysteries the Syriac tradition held to be beyond human comprehension, in a fluid and dynamic fashion. Despite the later Christological controversies of the 4th and 5th centuries, which drew the Syriac tradition along with the rest of Christendom into precise theological positions – and resulting schisms – the poetic form continued to be the preferred mode of theological expression in the Syriac church.

The prolific theologian-poets of the Syriac Orthodox tradition produced volumes of poetry that became the basis of an extensive tradition of liturgical music in the Syriac Orthodox church. Isaac of Antioch, Rabbula, Balai, Shem'un Quqoyo (the potter), Jacob of Sarug, Patriarch Mor Severus and Jacob of Edessa are among those in the ranks of the illustrious poets of the church. They created rich genres of music that survive to this day in Syriac Orthodox liturgical music.

Biblical background

The Syriac liturgy dwells heavily on biblical materials. Characters of both the Old and the New Testaments are frequently invoked. The "saints" of the Old Testament, Abraham, Isaac and Jacob; Moses, David and the prophets; and particularly Job and Daniel and the three holy men in the furnace of Babylon, are as familiar figures as the apostles. They are looked upon as living witnesses to the mystery of Christ always alive within the church. Even more interesting is the frequent reference to "our father Adam and our mother Eve", in a typological contrast to Christ the new Adam and Mary the new Eve. The mystery of salvation is thus connected to the beginning of creation and the first man and woman, who are taken out of Sheol, the place of the dead, when Christ descends to proclaim the good news of the conquest of death by his own death.

Holy eucharist

The eucharistic liturgy of the Syriac Orthodox Church is perhaps the richest in all of Christendom. There are over seventy extant anaphoras, some of which were written as late as the 15th century. The most common ones are about five. The oldest is that of St James, the brother of the Lord and the first bishop of Jerusalem. The usual Syriac word for the eucharistic liturgy is either *qurobo*, meaning "approach", or *qurbono*, "oblation" or "sacrifice". The holy fathers of the Syriac church often refer to the liturgy as the *rozae qadeeshae* (the holy mysteries), signifying the profound mystery of the bread and wine, which become for us the body and blood of our Lord in a manner not comprehensible to the external human senses. Holy eucharist is celebrated on Sundays and major feast days in all churches; many churches also celebrate it on Fridays and Wednesdays.

• The Trisagion or "thrice holy" recalls the vision experienced by the Prophet Isaiah of the Lord's throne and the proclamation of the six-winged seraphim (Isa. 6:1-3): "Holy, holy, holy is the Lord of hosts; the whole earth is full of his glory." Moreover, the tradition of the Syriac Church of Antioch records that at the time of our Lord's crucifixion, the seraphim descended from heaven and encircled the body of Christ, singing the first three verses of the thrice holy (excluding the phrase "who was crucified for us" since Jesus had died for human beings and not for the angels). It is said that Joseph of Arimathea, who was to request the body of Christ from Pilate, was present and was inspired to complete the seraphim's chant, singing forth, "You who were crucified for us, have mercy upon us."

- Lessons are read from the book of Acts, the epistles of St Paul and the gospels according to a lectionary for the whole year. A sermon is also delivered by the celebrant, commenting on the specific feast or event being celebrated.
- The prayer of absolution is an act of repentance offered on behalf of the congregation, asking for mercy and forgiveness.
- Then the Nicene-Constantinopolitan Creed is recited.
- The kiss of peace comes down from the celebrating clergy at the altar and is exchanged among the congregation. It signifies our love and concord with our neighbours, which in itself is a sign of our reconciliation with God through the sacrifice of the cross. The kiss of peace also fulfills the words of our Lord (Matt. 5:23 and 24), "So if you are offering your gift at the altar, and there remember that your brother has something against you, leave your gift there before the altar and go; first be reconciled to your brother, and then come and offer your gift." It likewise recalls the words of St Peter the apostle (1 Pet. 5:14), "Greet one another with the kiss of love."
- At the end of the celebration holy communion is offered to whoever desires and feels spiritually and physically ready to receive it. The body and blood of the Lord Jesus are offered in the forms of bread and wine.

Daily office

In accordance with Psalm 118 (119):164, "Seven times a day I praise You for your judgments, O Righteous One", the Syriac Orthodox Church observes seven periods of prayer each day: evening prayer or *ramsho* (vespers); drawing of the veil (compline) or s*ootoro* (meaning "protection", and based on Psalm 91, which is sung at this hour: "He who sits under the protection of the Most High"); midnight prayer or *lilyo;* morning prayer or *saphror* (matins); the third hour prayer or *tloth sho'in* (9 in the morning); the sixth hour prayer or *sheth sho'ir* (noon); and the ninth hour prayer or *tsha'sho'in* (3 in the afternoon). The midnight prayer consists of three *qawme* ("watches", or literally "standing"). The ecclesiastical day begins in the evening at sunset with the *ramsho*.

Each of the hours has its own particular theme which calls to mind events related to the life and sufferings of Christ. It is the whole mystery of Christ which is presented here in all its majesty, from the creation of the world to his second coming.

The book which contains the hourly prayers is called the *shhimo*, "simple". The *shhimo* has offices for the canonical hours for each of the days of the week except Sundays. Sunday offices are contained in a special book known as the *phanqeetho*, "volume", which is organized according to the church calendar. Each canonical office begins and ends with a *qawmo*, a set of prayers which includes the *Trisagion* and Lord's prayer. At the end of the office, the Nicene Creed is recited and followed by the services for the mother of God and the saints.

At present these prayers are organized into two groups. The first includes the third hour, the evening prayer and the compline, and is held in the early evening. The second, which includes the rest of the prayers, is recited in the morning. These prayers are composed of psalms and poetic hymns. The faithful are encouraged to offer these prayers in their homes; however, in the Middle East, many parishioners go every morning and evening to churches to participate in the prayers.

The church calendar

The Syriac Orthodox Church calendar is organized in cycles of eight Sundays. The first cycle begins with the consecration of the church *(qoodosh 'idto)*, which falls on either the last Sunday of October or the first Sunday of November. The following Sunday is the dedication of the church *(hudoth 'idto)*. The Sundays that follow until Christmas commemorate the chief events preceding the birth of the Word, starting with the annunciation to Zachariah, followed by annunciation to the Virgin Mary, the visitation of the Virgin Mary to Elizabeth, the birth of John the Baptist and the revelation to Joseph. After these Sundays falls the Sunday before Christmas, leading to the feast of the birth of our Lord *(yaldo)* which is celebrated today on 25 December.

The infants of Bethlehem killed by Herod are remembered on 27 December. The circumcision of our Lord is celebrated on 1 January. Epiphany *(denho)*, marking the baptism of our Lord, is commemorated on 6 January.

The next cycle celebrates the Sundays after Epiphany. During this cycle, the presentation of our Lord in the temple of Jerusalem is commemorated on 2 February. The last two Sundays of this cycle are a commemoration of the departed priests and the departed faithful.

The annunciation to the Mother of God *(suboro)* falls on 25 March and is of such significance that the eucharistic liturgy is required to be offered even if it falls on the Good Friday.

The following cycle marks the beginning of the Great Lent. During this period the healing ministry of our Lord is commemorated. The first Sunday commemorates the wedding feast of Cana, marking the beginning of the public ministry of our Lord. The healing of the leper is remembered on the second Sunday, the paralytic on the third, the Canaanite woman on the fourth, the Good Samaritan on the fifth and the blind man on the sixth, leading to Palm Sunday and Holy Week. On the eighth Sunday, the resurrection of our Saviour is celebrated. The Sunday after Easter is called New Sunday.

Three cycles of eight Sundays follow New Sunday, during which the ascension of our Lord is commemorated on the sixth Thursday after Easter. Pentecost falls on the seventh Sunday after Easter. The feast day of Saints Peter and Paul is celebrated on 29 June. The transfiguration of our Lord is commemorated on 6 August. The feast of the assumption of the Mother of God *(shunoyo d-yoldath aloho)* is celebrated on 15 August. The feast of the holy cross is celebrated on 14 September, commemorating the discovery of the holy cross by Helen, mother of the Emperor Constantine.

The last cycle of Sundays is a general commemoration of the Mother of God, the saints, the priests and the departed faithful.

Liturgical language

The church of Antioch employed two liturgical languages: Syriac (Aramaic) and Greek. Aramaic was used in the inner parts of Syria and the dioceses under the jurisdiction of the Catholicos of the East which fell under Persian rule. Greek, on the other hand, was used in Antioch and other major cities falling under the direct jurisdiction of the patriarch. After the division of the 5th century, the non-Chalcedonians adopted Aramaic as their exclusive language (with very few exceptions), while the Chalcedonians continued to use Greek as well as Aramaic.

Translation of the anaphoras and other liturgical books into Arabic began very early on. However, it has only been during the last two centuries that other languages alongside Syriac (such as Turkish, Kurdish, Malayalam and others) started to be used in the liturgy. During the second half of the 20th century bilingual editions of the anaphoras and various other books, such as the baptismal, marriage and funeral rites, were published in Western languages such as English, German, French, Swedish, Spanish and others.

Music in Syriac Orthodox worship

Syriac Christianity has the distinction of having developed one of the earliest musical traditions in all of Christendom.

Today, apart from sermons all prayers are sung in the form of chants and melodies. These melodies were transmitted as oral tradition. As a result a few schools of music emerged, most notably Mardin, Edessa, Tur 'Abdin and Kharput. Thousands of tunes and melodies (most of which have unfortunately been lost) were in use in the past. Nevertheless about seven hundred melodies remain and are preserved in the "Treasury of Melodies", known in Syriac as the *Beth Gazo*. Musicologists have been able to identify different historical stages within the repertory; the oldest of these date back to the earliest Christian centuries.

Based on the eight Sunday cycles of the church calendar, the church fathers used a system of eight melodies. The first mode is used for the first Sunday of the cycle, and so on. During the weekdays the mode will alternate between the first and fifth. The following Sunday would be the second and sixth, then third and seventh and then fourth and eighth. The major feasts also have their own modes. For instance, the canon of the Nativity is composed in the first mode, which is very pleasant and joyful. The second mode, which invokes humbleness, is used for the canon of Epiphany as the Lord condescended to be baptized by a servant. The canon of the Annunciation is composed in the fourth mode, which invokes fear, since the Virgin was frightened when learning what was to happen to her.

Syriac Orthodox liturgical hymns are chanted antiphonally by two choirs *(gudo)*. This is believed to have its roots in a vision of St Ignatius, the third patriarch of Antioch, in which he saw angels worshipping God in two great groups.

Traditionally, the use of musical instruments is avoided in liturgical services. At the synod of 1930, presided over by the late Patriarch Elias III and held at St Matthew's Monastery (near Mosul, Iraq), the use of an organ was permitted. Today the use of musical instruments is becoming increasingly prevalent in Syriac Orthodox parishes.

Early ecumenism – a challenge for today

In the early part of the 8th century, during the time of St Jacob of Edessa and George the bishop of the Arabs, the church adopted canticles called *Qonune Yawnoye* ("the Greek Canons") composed by John of Damascus and his adoptive brother, Cosmas of Mayuma, both of whom belonged to the Chalcedonian part of the church of Antioch. There is definitely a lesson here to be learned by all churches. Though we may not all be in full communion with each other, we should be able to share our resources with each other.[1]

NOTE

[1] In the United States of America, the hierarchs of the Oriental Orthodox churches (Armenian, Coptic, Ethiopian and Syrian) come together annually to celebrate the divine eucharist according to the rite of one of these churches.

BIBLIOGRAPHY

Brock, Sebastian and David G.K. Taylor eds, *The Hidden Pearl: The Syrian Orthodox Church and its Aramaic Heritage*, Rome, Trans World Film Italia, 2001.

Mor Athanasius Y. Samuel, *Anaphora: The Divine Liturgy of Saint James*, Hackensack, 1967.

Patriarch Ignatius Aphram I Barsoum, *The History of Syriac Literature and Sciences*, tr. Matti Mousa, Pueblo CO, Passeggiata Press, 2000.

The Liturgy in the Coptic Orthodox Church

MICHAEL GHATTAS

• ORIENTAL ORTHODOX •

The holy eucharist is the noblest rite, the heart and epicentre of Coptic Orthodox worship: it surpasses all other mysteries. Just as the planets revolve around the sun, all other sacraments revolve around the holy sacrifice. The sacrament and the holy eucharist are the fundamental basis for all the various prayers, liturgies and litanies, rites and sacraments. The fundamental identity of the earthly liturgy lies in its relation to the divine, which it represents by symbolically and mystically embodying the mystery of the sacrifice of Christ. This is done in the knowledge that Christ himself is both the one bringing the offering, and the one being offered. As a realization of God's work it is therefore justly called "the divine liturgy".

The Copts call the celebration of the Lord's supper "the eucharist", "the sacrament of the sacrifice" or "the sacrament of receiving".

The Copts celebrate the eucharist in three different forms: the anaphoras of St Basil, St Cyril (St Mark) or St Gregory. The liturgical language used today is the Bohairic dialect of the Copts, but each of the three liturgies corresponds to an earlier Greek original. The Coptic form of the liturgy is more extensive than the west Syrian texts, interwoven with passages in Greek. In Abul'l-Barakat ibn al-kibt (AD 1324) the use of liturgies is arranged as follows: the anaphora of St Basil is used throughout the year; the anaphora of St Cyril during Lent and in the month of Kyahk (beginning on 10 Dec.); and the anaphora of St Gregory at "festivals of God and of joy", i.e. Christmas, Epiphany, Easter and Pentecost.

The liturgy should be celebrated on Sundays and feast days as well as on Fridays and Wednesdays; in Coptic monasteries it is celebrated on a daily basis. The celebrant and those who wish to receive the eucharist should prepare themselves: this requires sincere confession, fervent faith, complete hope, reverence, humility, purity of heart and body, and fasting. Since the 11th century communal confession and absolution has become customary at the beginning of the celebration of the eucharist, but communal confession has not, to date, managed to supplant individual confession. The obligation to fast has become less strict: in the past it began on the afternoon of the previous day, whereas today fasting should begin nine hours before receiving the eucharist.

The eucharistic bread is baked from wheat and is unsalted, but sour dough is added. The bread is prepared by the sacristan, monk or priest, but under no circumstances by a woman. This is usually done after sunset the previous day, or early on the morning of the day on which the liturgy is to be celebrated. Several loaves are prepared, but only one is chosen for the paten. The wine used is a wine made from grapes; according to church order only wine made from the juice of the fruit of the vine may be used.[1]

The three anaphoras of the Coptic church

As noted above, the Coptic church uses three anaphoras, characterized by St Basil of Caesaria (379 AD), St Gregory of Nyssa (399 AD) and St Mark the Evangelist, as adapted by St Cyril of Alexandria. The latter is therefore also known as the anaphora of St Cyril. In earlier times the Coptic church also used other anaphoras, but Patriarch Gabriel II (1131-45) decreed that only these three anaphoras should be used in future.

The anaphora of St Basil is the most frequently used; that of St Gregory is used at the seven main festivals (Christmas, Epiphany, Palm Sunday, Easter, and other major festivals of Christ); and, finally, the anaphora of St Mark (St Cyril) is used during the month of Kyahk (10 December to 8 January) and during Lent.[2]

The structure of the divine liturgy

The divine liturgy presents itself in three parts, as follows:

1. Preparation of the altar and of the offertory.
2. The liturgy of the catechumens or the liturgy of the word. This part of the eucharistic liturgy focuses on the instruction of believers through readings from the holy scriptures and the homily. Those present follow the lessons very attentively with inner participation. The word of God provides spiritual nourishment and direction on the path to their salvation and eternal destiny.
3. The liturgy of the faithful: This comprises two main parts: (1) the actual anaphora, in which the holy gifts become the body and blood of Christ, and (2) the post-anaphora, which culminates with receiving the body and blood of the Lord.[3]

The spiritual and theological significance of the celebration of the eucharist

In Coptic spirituality the eucharist is understood both as a sacrificial offering and as a gift from God, with the latter being considered the more important. The believers come to church to receive divine benediction; they feel enriched through their closeness to God and his saints. The time people spend in church can be compared with moments spent in the blessedness of heaven. The Coptic sources view the sacrificial offering/remembrance as of secondary importance.[4]

In allusion to the last supper (Luke 22:14-20), in which Christ offered his disciples bread and wine as a sign of his devotion, the believers take on the task of making the *prosphora* (the offertory), that is, they bear the cost of the bread and wine required for the eucharist. During the celebration of the eucharist they receive, in return, the bread which they offered and the wine they gave, transformed into the body and the blood of the Lord, as a gift of God's love. Just as the grains of wheat come together in the bread and the raisins from many vineyards come together in the wine, so also the believers are united with one another and with Christ.

The bread, consecrated by the Spirit of God, and the consecrated wine are transformed into the divine and the life-giving body of the Saviour, and the divine nature of the Logos is in eternal unity with this body. Those who receive the sacrament are thus wholly permeated by the divine, just as fire permeates iron. St Gregory of Nyssa expresses this very clearly when he says that in the divine eucharist Christ unites with our bodies in such a way as to make us immortal and everlasting through his incarnation. He joins with [*vermischt sich*] our mortal human nature which, as a result, is made divine [*vergottet wird*].

Through the divine eucharist the entire Holy Trinity invisibly inhabits the soul of the communicants, satisfying and fulfilling that for which it hungers and thirsts.[5] A certain analogy can be drawn between the real unity of Christ's two natures and the unity between God and humanity in the eucharist. In the case of the eucharist, to be sure, the unity does not exceed the boundaries of a relative, gracious and moral unity. This is, however, credible only on the basis of the unity of the two natures in Christ, which represents the paradigm of the unity realized in the eucharist.

The eucharist, as the moment of truth of the church, is the proper foundation for the church's every act and mission, and for any "ecumenism". Furthermore it overcomes separation, sin, death and "denominationalism". Only in the eucharist will such qualitative catholicity be experienced and prove itself. No ecumenical activity and agreement will justify our striving for unity, unless we can bring all our thoughts and deeds to Christ "eucharistically" (see Col. 2:7; Phil. 4:6; Tim. 4:4). We can no longer deceive ourselves about this.[6]

NOTES

[1] See M. Ghattas, "Theologie und Spiritualität in der Koptisch-Orthodoxen Kirche", in *St. Markus,* Koptisch-Orthodoxes Zentrum, Oct.-Dec., 1991, Waldsolms/Kröffelbach, pp.23-38; M. Ghattas, "Jesus Christus in den Hymnen und im liturgischen Beten der koptischen Kirche", in *Una Sancta,* 2, 1992, pp.130-37; M. Ghattas, "Kopten", in *Religion in Geschichte und Gegenwart,* 4, Tübingen, Mohr, 2001, pp.1670-77; Abu'l Barakat Ibn Kabar (14th century), "Misbah al Zulma – Lampe der Finsternis", ch. 17, partially edited, *Le Muséon,* 1923-25; E. Hammaerschmidt, "Die Koptische Kirche", in *Symbolik der Religionen,* F. Herrmann ed., *X. Symbolik des Orthodoxen und Orientalischen Christentums,* Stuttgart, 1962, pp.170-211; E. W. Crum, "Koptische Kirche", in *RE,* XII, p.812; C. Schneider, "Studien zum Ursprung liturgischer Einzelheiten östlicher Liturgien", in *Kyrios,* 1, 1936, pp.57-63.

[2] See A. Gerhards, "Meine Natur hast Du in Dir gesegnet", in *Die Koptische Kirche: Einführung in das ägyptische Christentum,* A. Gerhards and H. Brakmann eds, Stuttgart/Berlin/Köln, Kohlhammer, 1994, pp.51ff.

[3] See M. Hanna, "La Liturgie Copte", in *Vivante Afrique,* 220, 1962, pp.14-24; R.C. Coquin, "L'anaphore alexandrie de St. Marc", in *Le Muséon,* 82, 1969; O. H. E. Burmester, "Vesting Prayers and Ceremonies in the Coptic Church", in *Orientalia Christiana Periodica,* 1, 1935; J. Madey, "Die eucharistische Liturgie in der Koptischen Kirchen", *Seminarvorträge in der Zeit vom 29.03.-31.03.1985 im Koptisch-Orthodoxen Zentrum mit St. Antonius Kloster e. V.,* Waldsolms/Kröffelbach, pp.14-26.

[4] See O. Casel, "Lieturgia-Munus", in *Oriens Christianus,* 7, 1932, pp.289-302; J. Tyciak, "Die Liturgie des Morgenlandes und die Liturgische Erneuerung unserer Tage", *Ost Studien,* 1, 1952, pp.54-62; S. Bulgakov, "Das eucharistische Dogma", *Kyrios,* 3, 1963, pp.32-57,78-96; *Liturgie, die Göttliche Liturgie der Orthodoxen Kirche,* A. Kallis ed., Mainz, Matthias-Grünewald, 1989, S. XVIIIff.; J. Madey, "Die geistlich-religiöse Bedeutung der Eucharistiefeier für das Leben der Gläubigen", see note 3 above, pp.28-40.

[5] See Gregory of Nyssa, *PG* 45, 39AB-97B; Metropolitan Anba Bischoy, "Die Sakramente in der Koptische-Orthodoxen Kirche", *St Markus,* April-June, 1992, Koptisch-Orthodoxes Zentrum ed., Waldsolms/Kröffelbach, pp.8-10.

[6] See J. Zizioulas, *The Unity of the Church in the Eucharist and its Message during the First Three Centuries [Die Einheit der Kirche in der Eucharistie und ihre Botschaft während der drei ersten Jahrhunderte]* [original in Greek], Athens, 1965; Staniloae, "Towards an Orthodox Ecumenism: Eucharist, Faith, Church – Zu einem Orthodoxen Ökumenismus. Eucharistie-Glauben-Kirche. Das Problem der Inter-Kommunio" [original in Greek], Athens, 1976.

Worship, Rituals and Liturgy in Orthodox Tradition
Insights from Practice and Theology

DIMITRIOS C. PASSAKOS

• EASTERN ORTHODOX •

During the third world conference of the WCC's Faith and Order Commission (Lund, Sweden, 15-19 August 1952), Father G. Florovsky emphasized in an outstanding address that the term *orthodoxia*, as used in Eastern Orthodoxy, does not primarily mean "right opinion"(as usually interpreted in the West), but rather "right glory", that is, precisely, "right *worship*". Accordingly the *lex orandi* has a privileged priority in the life of the church, while the *lex credendi* depends upon the experience and the vision of the church. This fact, the late father suggested, "is the most notable distinctive mark of the Eastern tradition". In this line of thought, the worship of the Eastern church is closely associated with its dogma and ethos. Without the worship, and particularly without the eucharist, which is the basis and the centre of the worship, both the dogmatic and ethical teaching of the church remain hovering in the air. Moreover, the organization of the church, being its third basic means of expressing itself, also has worship as its starting point.

Worship is not primarily an act of piety directed to God. God, being beyond any need, does not have the need of our adoration. Consequently, worship is not primarily the intiative of the human being, but God's redeeming act in Christ through the Spirit. At the same time, it is the way the community understands its nature and its purpose in the world. It is the "labour" of the people of God – thus *leitourgia* – while the community is directed towards the final restoration of all. It becomes obvious, then, that a right understanding of worship has, in an absolute way, everything to do with what kind of ecclesiology the community experiences and expresses.

Basic principles for understanding worship

According to the Orthodox tradition there are basic principles which must be laid down if we are to reach a proper understanding of worship:

1. *The church does not exist for "worship", but worship for the church.* Christ did not found a "worshipping community", but rather the church as a means of salvation, as a new creation for the life of the restored human race. This does not mean that the worship has a secondary position in the church; in fact there is no church without it. Worship is rather the aim of the church, so far as the latter exists not only in *statu viae*, but in *statu patriae* as well. Accordingly, the church is not a sacramental hierarchical "institute" that exists in order to perform the worship as a sacred, everlasting and unchanging "sacrament".

2. *Worship is the "work" (labour) of the people of God.* It finds its fulfilment only in the re-establishment of personal communion among the people, and between them and God. Even when we speak about "personal prayer", this does not mean private or individualistic prayer. The solitary prayer of a single person is still a prayer of a member of the body of Christ. That is why it should be inclusive and universal, otherwise it degenerates into individualistic pietism and emotionalism. Private prayer is a preparation for communal prayer, since the one who prays "in secret" enlarges his or her heart to embrace all needs and sorrows of all of suffering humanity. Worship is, then, an ecclesial act and a participation in the body of Christ.

3. *Worship is centred on the remembrance of the sacrificial act of Jesus Christ for the redemption of all.* It is a process of sanctification. Therefore it refers to the whole human being (as an intellectual, spiritual and physical being). It is a call to the whole human being to take part in the victory of Christ over death. Thus it is actualized as an offering of the body of Christ to God, and has direct consequences for the whole of creation. Ultimately it aims at the redemption and restoration of all.

4. Based on the above-mentioned principle, worship does not exist in order to meet our alleged religious "duties" and "needs". Rather *worship embraces our whole life, the whole space and time, the whole universe.* This is the reason why the Orthodox church sanctifies with its worship every aspect of the personal and social life of its members: worship refers not only to the so-called "transitional stages" of a human being's life (birth, marriage, death) but actually to every moment of the member's life. Moreover, it liturgically articulates space and time (the day, week, year) transforming them in this way as the framework within which the church awaits the coming of Christ, and prepares the whole universe for it. Consequently, the final aim of worship is the transformation of all in the direction of the kingdom of God.

5. *Worship is the proclamation (worship of the preached word of God) of the saving act of God.* This is perceived not only as an invitation to outsiders to believe and share in the salvation which worship affords

to all human beings, but also as a joyful foretaste of the parousia of the Lord. The preached word is an inseparable part of Christian worship and, together with the eucharistic liturgy, constitutes the main elements of the Lord's day – which realizes the kingdom to come but which also is already, here and now, in the world.

6. *Beyond any sacramentalism and liturgical escapism from the world, worship is also a sacrifice and a mission to the world.* It points to the diakonia to which every member is called, following the example of Jesus. Actually the mission of the church is to invite the outside world to participate in the new humanity which is formed as the body of Christ, a humanity of love, unity, equality, justice and freedom. Mainly through its eucharist, the basis of every missionary event, the church brings the marginalized of the world into the foreground and denounces injustice, oppression and every institutionalized evil. Seen from this perspective, the church has a twofold orientation: towards the world, in a movement of diastole (mission), and towards God, in a movement of systole (worship). Although these two orientations should not be confused, the separation of the one from the other leads to a distortion of the ecclesial ethos. With its worship the church is made manifest not only as an experience of the *eschata*, but also as a missionary movement leading in the direction of the *eschata*.

Rediscovering the meaning of liturgy

Although the above-mentioned principles are at the heart of Orthodox worship, there are voices that claim persuasively that we are in the middle of an intense "liturgical crisis", one that can be detected in several practices within our liturgy and ecclesiastical life: the people of God have no voice either in the gathering or in the administration of the church; several liturgical practices, and the very architecture of our churches, emphasize the division between laity and clergy; the language of the service does not facilitate the participation of the people; the eucharist tends to be a sacrament scholastically determined by other sacraments; the bishops are seen – or even worse, act – as ministers of the church exercising their secular power and authority; and the "labour" of the people of God (liturgy) is wasted within the church, without even trying to extend it into the world outside. Theologically speaking, liturgy is no longer the self-revelation of the church for the people of God, and consequently an expression of the church in relation to the world. There is, then, an urgent need to rediscover the meaning of liturgy in accordance with ecclesiology, and to redefine the church in relation to the world.

The insights of cultural anthropology may help us in this regard. One of the most imaginative insights of modern cultural anthropologists is that ritual is a form of communication, a "performative" kind of speech. According to this view, it is rituals which have created the essential categories of human thought. They communicate the fundamental beliefs and values of a community, outlining in this way its "world-view" and its "ethos". Moreover, as the pioneering studies of Mary Douglas on purity have demonstrated, rituals not only transmit culture, but also "create a reality which would be nothing without them. It is not too much to say that ritual is more to society than words are to thought. For it is very possible to know something and then find words for it. But it is impossible to have social relations without symbolic acts."[1]

Rituals and experience

According to this line of thought, rituals not only externalize but also modify experience. This double orientation is expressed in certain general functions which its rituals have for a group. Some of the rituals contribute to the expression, maintenance and transmission of the values and feelings of a given social system; others serve as guardians of these values and feelings, protecting them from doubts and rejections; while yet others contribute to the intensification of solidarity between the participants. Accordingly, one categorization of rituals proposed by the social sciences is the following:

a) rites of passage, which help the participant to accomplish a change of status;
b) rites of deference, which acknowledge superordination, subordination and friendship, thus preserving the existing social structure;
c) rites of intensification, held during periods of crisis in order to increase the solidarity of the group and decrease the tension that exists, thus counterbalancing the crisis.

Keeping in mind, on the one hand, that rituals create a reality – a "world-view" and the "ethos" of a community – and, on the other, the above classification of rituals according to their function, it may be very fruitful to think of liturgy (and consequently ecclesiology) particularly in terms of the above-mentioned rites of passage. This may help to redefine the relation of the church, and its liturgy, to the outside world.

In his classic book *Rites de Passage*[2] the brilliant Belgian sociologist Arnold van Gennep used this term in order to define two types of rituals: those which mark the transition of a person from one social status to another during his or her life (the so-called life-crisis rites), and those connected with specific signs during the course of time (new year, new moon, eclipse of the sun or the moon, solstice or equinox). In short, rites of passage are the rites that accompany every change of place, state, social position and age.

Van Gennep has analyzed these rituals in three successive phases: separation, margin or limen, and aggregation. These signify entering into the neutral zone between social locations or spaces; waiting in it; and leaving from it (e.g., thesis-antithesis-synthesis). The first phase (separation) signifies the person's detachment from an earlier fixed point within the social structure, or from a given set of cultural conditions. During the second phase (the liminal period) the characteristics of the ritual "passenger" are ambiguous, since his or her condition has few, or none, of the attributes of the previous or the following state. Van Gennep and other scholars suggested that in this stage we may differentiate substages such as preliminal, liminal and post-liminal. In the third phase (reaggregation or reincorporation) the individual is in the new, relatively stable state, where he or she is expected to behave according to certain norms and ethical standards. Needless to say, not all stages are discernible in every rite of passage.

It is worth noting that the communal character of liturgy emerges in marginality (liminality), at the edges of structure; and from beneath structure, in inferiority. This observation undergirds a usually neglected principle: the communal character of liturgy presupposes an anti-structural kind of ecclesiology. On a theological level this means the priority of communion over structure; yet on a practical level it does not mean the abolition of every kind of structure in the community. As Victor Turner insightfully claimed, there is a dialectic between structure and communion (or *communitas*): "In *rites de passage*, men are released from structure into *communitas* only to return to structure revitalized by their experience of communitas."[3]

Paul and the mystery of the church

It was undoubtedly Paul the apostle who paved the way for the development of the early Christian ecclesiology into today's Orthodox understanding of the mystery of the church. He presented the church as a body, the body of Christ, the eschatological manifestation of the coming kingdom of God. As a *body*, the community was a historical reality with concrete responsibilities. As the body of *Christ*, it was a reality different from the society and there was a need for the quality of the community's separation from the world outside to be elucidated. As the eschatological manifestation of the kingdom of God, the community should find its full identity through looking towards the eschata, and simultaneously it should manifest this identity in the world. This dual orientation of the community – towards the eschata and towards the world – made the boundaries of the Pauline churches somehow ambiguous. The church was open to outside society, otherwise its members would have had to leave this world (1 Cor. 5:10). But when relations with the unbelievers created problems within the community, then these relations should be questioned. This was the principle according to which Paul faced the problem about eating meat offered to idols in his first epistle to the Corinthians (chs 8 and 10).

For Paul the community was a new social reality, an alternative reality by comparison with the world outside. It was a koinonia of the eschata which, although it had its citizenship in heaven (Phil. 3:20), was at the same time responsible for the evangelization of the world. This principle was crucial for Paul since his communities, with their firm eschatological orientation and the continuous manifestation of spiritual gifts in their gatherings, often tended towards an "enthusiastic" stance of indifference to the world and its everyday problems. One of the most vivid proofs of this was the way in which the eucharist was celebrated in Corinth. This is why the divisions during the Corinthian community's eucharistic meal gave Paul the best opportunity to reaffirm his "eucharistic theology" in a way that could successfully oppose the enthusiastic tendencies of the "strong" within the community. His purpose was to show that during the celebration of the eucharist, where the community was becoming the body of Christ, its eschatological identity and its responsibility towards the world should be manifested simultaneously.

The admission of a member to the church is a process that could be best described as a "state of transition" between two worlds, reminding us of the process analyzed above in relation to rites of passage. Still, it is worth noting that the third stage – of re-aggregation or reintegration into the world – is absent from Paul's thinking. This is absolutely clear in the Pauline baptismal theology and in Paul's eucharistic theology. While for the Hellenistic rites "death" is the necessary path to "life", for the Christian "death" is rather the destination (cf. Rom. 6:1-10; Col. 2:12). This is because what appears in the rites as a limbo-like, interim state between "two worlds" is, for the Christian, the paradoxical enjoyment of God's order of things. If we can speak of re-aggregation or reintegration in the case of the Christian, this is only eschatological: it will take place in the kingdom of God to come.

Similar conclusions could be reached in relation to Pauline eucharistic theology. Paul, facing the disorders occuring during the eucharistic meal in Corinth, restates his theology (which they already well know!) for the benefit of the "strong" in Corinth (1 Cor. 10:16-17). At the same time he makes the eucharist the place for the proclamation of Christ's death. Then, in line with the above analysis, liminality is the appropriate mode of existence for Christians. This is the basis of the anti-structural (or at least *non*-structural) character of the church, which is, in a revolutionary fashion, subversive of the established wordly order (cf. 1 Cor. 6:1-11, 7:21-23,29-31; Phil. 16). The model of such an anti-structural practice is Christ himself who, according to Paul, "though he was rich, yet for our sakes he became poor, so that you through his poverty might become rich" (2 Cor. 8:9), and whose example the apostle follows ("though I am free and belong to no man, I make myself a slave to everyone, to win as many as possible...", 1 Cor. 9:19ff.). This inversion of roles (theologically speaking, this ascetic attitude) is what reveals the church as an alternative – with decisively liminal characteristics – to the world's communal "reality".

Worship: an alternative vision for the life of the world

If rituals communicate the fundamental beliefs and values of a community, outlining in this way its world-view and its ethos, then unless the worship of the church manifests its liminality, it cannot become the church's self-revelation and an expression of the church in relation to the world. To rediscover, then, the meaning of worship means to reaffirm its anti-structural dimension. The ethos of the church and its worship does not comply with any of the structures of the world, rather it contrasts its "anti-structures" to them, offering an alternative vision for the life of the world. These "anti-structures" should never become institutionalized, since the church is looking to the eschata for its identity, and for the time being remains in a state of transition. This is the reason why the worship of the church creates a communion and community rather than an institution; and this experience of community is the starting point for the mission of the church. Although it does not aim at being a social programme for the change of the world, the liturgical experience of communion gradually affects the world outside and its structures from the perspective of the kingdom of God.

NOTES

[1] Mary Douglas, *Purity and Danger: An Analysis of the Concepts of Pollution and Taboo*, London and New York, Ark Paperbacks, 1984 (repr. 1985 and 1988), esp. pp.7-72.
[2] Paris, Nourry, 1909.
[3] Victor Turner, *The Ritual Process: Structure and Anti-Structure*, Ithaca NY, Cornell UP, 1977, esp. pp.94-130.

SELECTED BIBLIOGRAPHY

Georges Florovsky, "The Elements of Liturgy", in *The Orthodox Church in the Ecumenical Movement*, C. Patelos ed., WCC, 1978, pp.172-182.

Nikolaos Nissiotis, "The Church as a Sacramental Vision and the Challenge of Christian Witness", in *Church, Kingdom, World. The Church as Mystery and Prophetic Sign,* G. Limouris ed., WCC, 1986, pp.99-126.

Nikolaos Nissiotis, "Worship, Eucharist and 'Intercommunion': An Orthodox Reflection", *Studia Liturgica,* 2, 1963, pp.193-222.

"Orthodox Liturgical Renewal and Visible Unity", consultation, New Skete Monastery, Cambridge, New York, USA, May 26–June 1, 1998, in *Turn to God – Rejoice in Hope: Orthodox Reflections on the Way to Harare,* Thomas FitzGerald and Peter Bouteneff eds, WCC/Orthodox Task Force, 1999, pp.139-46.

Dimitris Passakos, "Eucharist in First Corinthians: A Sociological Study", *Revue biblique,* 104, 2, 1997, pp.192-210.

Alexander Schmemann, *Introduction to Liturgical Theology,* Crestwood NY, St Vladimir's Seminary Press, 1986.

Petros Vassiliadis, *Eucharist and Witness. Orthodox Perspectives on the Unity and Mission of the Church,* WCC, 1998.

John Zizioulas, *Being as Communion. Studies in Personhood and the Church,* Crestwood NY, St Vladimir's Seminary Press, 1985.

The Roman Catholic Understanding of the Nature and Purpose of Worship

PATRICK LYONS, OSB

• ROMAN CATHOLIC •

The distinctive aspects of Roman Catholic worship

The terminology adopted in the Roman Catholic Church to describe worship emphasizes its public character, firstly by simply annexing the epithet "public" to the term worship, especially in less technical usage, but also by preferring, in all official documents, the term *liturgy*. This is because the Greek etymology of that term conveys the same idea and because, though a term of secular origins, it has nonetheless a long history of Christian usage in the East. The term "liturgy" does not have, however, a long history of use in the West, having been introduced in the Latin form *liturgia* by humanists in the 16th and 17th centuries, probably under the influence of Byzantine texts, and only achieving wider acceptance by the 19th century.

The emphasis on worship's public character implies that it is considered the action of the whole church, where the church is understood primarily as the body of Christ, united with its head. Since the early years of the 20th century, the pioneers of the pastoral or parochial phase of the Roman Catholic liturgical movement have seen liturgy primarily in terms of a close conjunction between the priestly activity of Christ, and the church's participation in it.[1] This view was reflected in the description of liturgy adopted by the constitution *Sacrosanctum Concilium* (SC) of the Second Vatican Council: "Christ, indeed, always associates the church with himself in this great work in which God is perfectly glorified and men are sanctified." The text continues with a definition of liturgy:

> The liturgy, then, is rightly seen as an exercise of the priestly office of Jesus Christ. It involves the presentation of man's sanctification under the guise of signs perceptible by the senses and its accomplishment in ways appropriate to each of these signs. In it full public worship is performed by the mystical body of Jesus Christ, that is by the Head and his members. (SC 7)

The central element in the definition – liturgy as the exercise of the priestly office of Christ – echoes the encyclical *Mediator Dei* (MD) of

Pope Pius XII, which had included the statement, "The liturgy is nothing other than the exercise of this priestly office (of Christ)" (MD 22).

Sanctification and glorification

The conciliar definition says more than that of *Mediator Dei,* however, by teaching that the liturgy operates through signs, perceptible by the senses, through which sanctification is effected. This follows from the fact that all other liturgical actions of the church are either an anticipation or an extension of the eucharistic celebration, the memorial of Christ's sacrifice and the sign *par excellence* of grace conferred. The constitution also represents a change of emphasis in that it speaks first of the "sanctification of man" and then of the "glorification of God" – and in fact does so in more than twenty different places.[2]

Clearly, finding the right relationship between these two elements (of sanctification and glorification, the receptive and active roles) in the church's worship is of great importance. From an ecumenical viewpoint, the tendency in the past to emphasize the church's act of *offering* created the impression of claiming to offer repeatedly the once-for-all sacrifice of Christ. Now, however, the Constitution on the Liturgy seemed to some to present the faithful as mere *beneficiaries* of the action of the church distributing the graces of the sacraments – the church appearing, therefore, as an institution for salvation, incarnated by the hierarchical priesthood, rather than as the community of the faithful.[3]

It is indeed true that the constitution introduces the idea of active participation in the liturgy by quoting St Cyprian on the church as "the holy people united and arranged under their bishops" (SC 26). This is, however, partly because the Council's consideration of the delicate balance between the hierarchical, and the communitarian, nature of the church had yet to come, in the early chapters of the Constitution on the Church *(Lumen Gentium)*. It is also true, however, that all consideration of active participation had to take into consideration the distinction between the common priesthood of the faithful and the ministerial or hierarchical priesthood, which would also be taught by *Lumen Gentium* (10). *This* distinction is much in evidence in *Sacrosanctum Concilium,* in its norms both favouring concelebration and confirming the right to celebrate individually (that is, without an assembly but with a server). Concelebration is rather more the practice today than individual celebration; but it is sometimes questioned in the literature, in that it tends to de-emphasize the common priesthood. While defended by the constitution as manifesting the unity of the ordained priesthood (SC 57), on some occasions, at least, it does little to express the unity of the eucharistic assembly.[4]

Despite such problematic aspects, the church's understanding of liturgy as a twofold action of sanctification and praise (glorification) was well articulated in the principles of reform proposed by *Sacrosanctum Concilium*. The participation of the mystical body in the priestly action of Christ, its ministerial role, was to be expressed in the diversified functions carried out by the members in accordance with their various offices; and it was recognized explicitly that these functions, whether of laity or clergy, pertain to the liturgy (SC 28-29). Such a multiplicity of functions is, however, in practice difficult to coordinate so as to create the impression of liturgy as one focused, objective act, as something "given" in that it is, above all, the action of Christ. Thus it may not always be evident that liturgy is also an *upward* movement, the praise of God. This explains to some extent the nostalgia still obtaining among some members of the church for older liturgical forms.

The post-conciliar reforms endeavoured to maintain the objective character of the liturgy by continuing the tradition of fixed liturgical texts, with the normative version (the *editio typica*) continuing to be in Latin, while vernacular translations and cultural adaptations were to be introduced to foster the active participation of all the faithful (SC 36-40). The plurifomity thus introduced extended also to rubrics in liturgical texts, allowing some possibility (where none had existed before) for a celebrant to use his own words by way of introduction or comment. The outcome cannot always be said to be the happiest; while there is now greater room for creativity without prejudice to the fixed forms, these opportunities have been exploited by some to the extent of introducing a markedly subjective atmosphere in the celebration. However, it must be stressed that this is an *abuse*, going contrary to both the letter and the spirit of the liturgical norms.

Worship: both transcendent and participatory

Various aspects of the conciliar teaching, and of subsequent liturgical reforms, certainly contribute to maintaining the liturgy's transcendent yet participatory character. Of greatest significance, as can be seen from its place in the first paragraphs of *Sacrosanctum Concilium,* is the portrayal of liturgy from the perspective of God's plan of salvation. "The liturgy realizes in the mystery of signs what the Old Testament announced in figures, what Christ accomplished in passing from (the world) to his Father, what will appear in the liturgy of heaven."[5] The post-conciliar reform of the liturgy, especially by its reform of the lectionary, brought the observance of the liturgical year, with its commemoration of the mystery of Christ in all its aspects, historical and eschatological, into greater prominence. The mystery of Christ, celebrated in an intense way in a particular liturgical celebration, extends its presence through the whole year, penetrating and transforming time for those whose lives are regularly influenced by the liturgy.

The celebration of the cycle of Christ's mysteries throughout the year underlines both the representational and the mimetic nature of the liturgy. Catholic liturgists today consider the liturgy as fundamentally representational – in the strong sense, derived from sacraments as perceptible signs of grace conferred – and do not follow exactly O. Casel's theory,[6] which saw in the liturgy an imitation of Christ's mysteries, in the manner in which mystery religions had rites which imitated the story of the gods. But there remains nonetheless an imitative dimension in liturgical celebration, as the liturgical year shows: in the course of the year the cycle of celebration conforms to the pattern of Christ's life. What is true of the whole body is true also of the individual member, insofar as he or she responds to grace: the mysteries of Christ celebrated bring about union with Christ and evoke in the believer, by the indwelling Spirit, the response of a will to conform to him, to imitate him.[7]

The commemoration of the saints, the sanctoral cycle, must be seen in the context of these ontological and moral dimensions of the liturgy. Through the liturgy, communion not only with Christ but also with the saints offers the believer further resources, namely the help of their intercession (as the third eucharistic prayer states) and a moral example inviting imitation (as many euchological texts for saints' commemorations express it). The inclusion of the sanctoral cycle in the liturgy gives rise to a twofold pattern of honour given and aid sought which, because it is derived from the communion between Christ and all his members, reflects in its own way the twofold nature of the liturgy.

The presence of Christ in the liturgy

The twofold action of sanctification and praise, arising from the communion between Christ and his members and thus fundamental to liturgy, implies another truth much emphasized in the liturgy constitution and already present in incomplete form in *Mediator Dei*. This is the presence of Christ in the liturgy. Both documents represent an extraordinary advance on previous thinking, which had restricted the notion of presence to the teaching on Christ's presence in the eucharist; it had been described, especially since the council of Trent, as the "real" presence and effectively there *was* no other conception of Christ's presence when the liturgy was celebrated. In contrast, the Constitution on the Liturgy declared that Christ is present in the minister who celebrates the eucharist, in the eucharistic species, in the other sacraments, in the reading of the scriptures and in the assembly itself. This teaching – which,

when applied to the liturgy of the word, has important ecumenical implications – is the logical consequence of regarding the liturgy as the
priestly action of Christ, in which his body participates: his presence
must pervade the action of the church.

This presence of Christ in the liturgy is mediatorial; it brings about a
presence of God and of the assembly to each other. For this reason the
church follows the ancient pattern of addressing the prayers of the
liturgy to the Father, through Christ, and it does so because of being
empowered by the Spirit. As well as in euchology, this understanding of
liturgy is seen in the ceremonial which includes gestures, vestments, processions, lights and incense (though the attempt to symbolize the presence of heaven and earth to each other is not as marked by architectural
features and divisions as it is in Orthodox liturgy). In fact the *unity* of the
liturgical space, symbolizing the mystical body, is much more marked
than in the past, when the sanctuary was divided from the rest of the
assembly. Nonetheless, the ceremonial elements are not considered *adi-
aphora* but are seen to pertain to the nature of liturgical worship, and
there are norms governing liturgical space.

Liturgy and worship: clarifying our terms

Since various services of a formal ceremonial character, yet with
content indicative of private devotion, were introduced in the centuries
after the council of Trent, the body of formularies and actions making up
the official liturgy has long been in as much need of being *delimited* as
of being *defined*. The constitution *Sacrosanctum Concilium* did much to
define liturgy and circumscribe its limits, but the post-conciliar reforms
were needed as well, so that the extent to which liturgical texts were provided could also indicate what rites might be considered "liturgical".

From the list of books officially so considered and now in use, it is
clear that the liturgy consists primarily in the celebration of the eucharist
(including the liturgy of the word, which draws on a lectionary with a
three-year cycle), and with it the six other traditional sacramental rites,
with the rites of initiation now much more extensive and diversified.
Added to these are related rites: the installation to the liturgical ministries of acolyte and reader (for those who are candidates for the
ordained ministry), the rites of *viaticum* and commendation for those
near death, and the funeral rites. The liturgy of the hours has been
reformed so as to create a certain complementarity between its use of
scripture and that found in the lectionary for the eucharist, thus creating
an important equilibrium between these two daily liturgical celebrations.
In current practice the liturgy of the hours remains largely the province
of religious communities, as well as being of obligation for the ordained

clergy. The rites for the dedication of a church, for eucharistic worship outside the celebration of the mass itself, and for religious profession have all been revised, and there is a book of blessings which provides a wide variety of rites "for gatherings of the Christian people seeking to bring the various aspects of their domestic, social, cultural and devotional lives into clearer relationship with the paschal character of their life in Christ".[8]

The influence of the liturgical and ecumenical movements

From the foregoing it will be clear that the modern conception of liturgy in the Roman Catholic Church has its origins in the liturgical renewal movement, indeed to such an extent that the recent history of its liturgy is identical with the history of that movement. It has come to be realized that, however much credit must be given to the 19th-century pioneers (belonging mostly to the monastic world), the liturgical movement entered a crucial pastoral phase – one capable of affecting the life of the whole church – with the apostolate of Lambert Beauduin, which began in 1909. The movement can be said to have entered on a legislative phase with the Vatican Council and the work of the post-conciliar *Consilium* for the reform of the liturgy and thus, in effect, to have brought about the present official conception of liturgy. It is clear that the liturgical renewal movement was almost entirely a domestic affair, the one ecumenical influence upon it being the stimulus provided by the shared enterprise of biblical studies in this century and, in consequence, the felt need to give a greater place to scripture in the liturgy. Yet the opponents of the liturgical movement, who were never lacking, quite often saw it as a Protestantizing influence.[9] Beauduin, who moved from being a liturgical pioneer to being an ecumenical one, derived inspiration for the later role from the earlier; and given the unsynchronized stages of development of the two movements in the Catholic church, it would appear that the main ecumenical influence in his promotion of the liturgy could only have been his early attraction to the Orthodox world.

Catholic liturgical renewal moved ahead at its own quite surprising pace even during the second world war, and little research has been done on possible links with Protestant liturgical renewal in Europe at the same time, or with the slowly gestating Faith and Order study of liturgy, "Ways of Worship", a process which lasted from 1937 to 1951.[10] Because of the presence of observers from the other churches at the Vatican Council, and the continuance of representation through the five who attended the sessions of the post-conciliar *Consilium* for the reform of the liturgy, it may be asked if ecumenical influence entered by this route. While nothing can be known with certainty about informal contacts, the role of the observers has been clearly described by A. Bugnini, secretary of the *Consilium*. According to him, the only area in which a study group looked to any of the observers for information on the experience of their churches was in regard to the *preces* in the liturgy of the hours – though he also reports a meeting of the lectionary study group with the consultors and observers, at which the views of the observers on lectionary reform were canvassed. The observers in fact encouraged the adoption of the present three-year cycle.[11]

The lectionary which resulted, *Ordo Lectionum Missae* published in 1969, has had an enormous and well-documented effect on lectionary usage in the anglophone Protestant and Anglican world, since the *Revised Common Lectionary,* derived from and very closely related to it, is now in use in many churches and in many countries.[12] In a reciprocal ecumenical gesture, an application was made by the US Catholic Bishops Conference to the Vatican authorities in 1982 for permission to make a trial use of the *Common Lectionary* as a way of helping to prepare a local version of the Catholic lectionary. Permission was refused, and what would seem to have been a very valuable opportunity for ecumenical sharing was lost.[13]

New developments in worship: Are they ecumenically helpful?

The post-conciliar liturgical reforms followed a comprehensive plan over a period of some twenty years, and the resulting renewal of the liturgy has been very thorough and not likely to see serious revision in the near future. Pastoral conditions continue to change, however, and so possibilities of adaptation already provided for need always to be examined, and sometimes urgently. This is true, for example, of liturgical practice in parts of the world where ordained ministers are no longer – or never were – available. An official document of 1988, *Sunday Worship in the Absence of a Priest,*[14] regulates the form and content of these communion services. From these it is clear that the thinking in the document proceeds from the ordained ministry[15] and thus the likelihood is, as such services proliferate, that a debate will arise on the relationship between ordained and non-ordained ministries – in effect, on the need to understand lay ministry in something more than a derived sense, and to arrive at a deeper understanding of the baptismal or common priesthood. Clearly there could be a gain for all traditions in making this an ecumenical discussion.

In the constitution *Sacrosanctum Concilium,* the Vatican Council acknowledged officially for the first time the importance of liturgical inculturation (37-40). This process, described as "a dialogue between culture and Christian worship,"[16] is today the concern of all the Christian churches. Inculturation in any Christian tradition brings about a pluriformity which may express, better than does uniformity, the unity of that tradition; but it may also be a disintegrating force and the Catholic church tends, in practice, to be cautious in allowing processes of liturgical inculturation. Other traditions have similar concerns but it is clear that a refined and shared idea of unity – and even unity itself – could in fact emerge from an acceptance by all of the pluriformity which sound liturgical inculturation would bring.

A development which is very slow in coming in Roman Catholic parish liturgy is the celebration of the liturgy of the hours. The constitution did present this as the particular concern of clerics and religious communities, but turned finally to the duty of pastors "to see to it that the principal hours, especially vespers, are celebrated in church in common on Sundays and on the more solemn feasts" (SC 100). The ecumenical possibilities here are obvious, and the celebration of the liturgy of the hours is in fact the principal liturgical sharing recommended by the current Roman Catholic *Directory on Ecumenism*.[17]

NOTES

[1] See, for example L. Beauduin OSB, "Essai de manuel fondamental de liturgie", *Les Questions Liturgiques [et Paroissiales]*, 3, 1913, pp.56-66, and the same author's *La piété d'Église,* Louvain, Abbaye de Mont César, 1914.

[2] Cf G. Diekmann OSB, *Personal Prayer and the Liturgy*, London, Chapman, 1969, p.57.

[3] See, for example, P. Vanbergen, "The Constitution on the Liturgy and the Faith and Order Reports", *Studia Liturgica,* 5, 1966, p.13.

[4] See, for example, J. Baldovin, "Concelebration: A Problem of Symbolic Roles in the Church", *Worship,* 59, 1, 1985, pp.32-47.

[5] A. G. Martimort, "Preliminary Concepts", in A. G. Martimort ed., *The Church at Prayer: Introduction to the Liturgy,* English translation of first edition, New York, Desclée, 1968, p.5.

[6] O. Casel, *The Mystery of Christian Worship,* Westminster, Newman, 1962; for a critique, see, for example, D. Power, *Unsearchable Riches: The Symbolic Nature of Liturgy,* New York, Pueblo, 1984, p.117.

[7] The Roman Catholic position on the liturgical year is in accord with that of Thomas J. Talley, who rejects Carel Deddens' conclusion that "the liturgical year represents a deviation from the purity of the spirituality of the early church". Talley claims instead that all the seasonal phenomena of our worship have grown "out of the imaginative and affective response of the people of God in generation after generation to the proclamation of this one story of one life and one death that became the story of their lives as it is the story of ours". T. J. Talley, *Reforming the Tradition,* Washington, Pastoral Press, 1990, p.139.

[8] M. Collins OSB, "Liturgy", in J. Komonchak, M. Collins, D. Lane, eds., *The New Dictionary of Theology,* New York, Glazier, 1987, p.593.

[9] Cf. L. Beauduin, OSB, "L'Encyclique *Mediator Dei*", *La Maison Dieu*, 13, 1948, pp.7-25.

[10] Reference is occasionally made to Christians of other traditions being influenced by the Roman Catholic movement. See, for example, J. Srawley, *The Liturgical Movement. Its Origins and Growth,* Alcuin Club Tracts XXVH, London, Mowbray, 1954, 7: "The Liturgical movement in the Roman Communion... has awakened considerable interest and appreciation among Christians of other communions." Also, W. Franklin, "The Nineteenth

Century Liturgical Movement," *Worship*, 53, 1, 1979, p.34, notes that "Protestant students" attended the liturgy courses offered by the Abbey of Maria Laach in Germany "from 1922". Cf. P. Lyons, OSB, "Liturgy and Ecumenism" in A. Chupungco OSB ed., *Handbook for Liturgical Studies*, I, Collegeville, Pueblo, 1997, p.86.

[11] A. Bugnini, *The Reform of the Liturgy, 1948-1975*, Collegeville, Liturgical Press, 1990, p.201n, p.417. Bugnini also denied that there was any basis for the claim that the third eucharistic prayer had been composed in collaboration with Protestants: p.201n.

[12] See, for example, H. Allen, "Lectionaries – Principles and Problems: a Comparative Analysis", *Studia Liturgica*, 22, 1992, pp.68-83. The relationship is comprehensively documented in S. P. Kyambadde, *The Catholic Lectionary and the Revised Common Lectionary in Ecumenical Perspective.* Pontificium Institutum Liturgicum, Dissertatio ad Doctoratum in Sacra Liturgia consequendam. Roma, Ateneo S. Anselmo, 1998.

[13] Cf "Notiziario", *Rivista Liturgica*, 70, 1983, p.758; A. Tegels, "Common Lectionary", *Worship*, 58, 1984, pp.536-39.

[14] Pope Paul VI, *Christi Ecclesia* (2.6.1988) in *Enchiridion Vaticanum* II, Bologna, EDB, 1991, pp.442-69.

[15] The ministry of lay people in these circumstances is described as of a supplementary or substitutional nature – *"indoles suppletiva"*, 21; it is not their "proper role", no. 31.

[16] A. Chupungco OSB, "Liturgical Inculturation and the Search for Unity", in Thomas F. Best and Dagmar Heller, eds., *So We Believe, So We Pray: Towards Koinonia in Worship*, Faith and Order Paper no. 171, WCC, 1995, p.57.

[17] Pontifical Council for Christian Unity, *Directory for the Application of Principles and Norms on Ecumenism*, Vatican Press, 1993, nos. 116-119.

Worship in the Mar Thoma Syrian Church of Malabar

ABRAHAM KURUVILLA

• MAR THOMA •

The Mar Thoma Syrian Church of Malabar is part of the ancient church on the south-western coast of India, believed to have been founded by the apostle Thomas. The present-day Mar Thoma Syrian Church of Malabar is that segment of this ancient church which was reformed in the early 19th century under its great leader, Abraham Malpan. The reform movement was inspired by the availability of the Bible in Malayalam through the efforts of the CMS missionaries, who were actively involved with this ancient church during the first part of the 19th century. The fellowship with the missionaries, and the availability of the Bible for the common believer, created the climate for reformation. Today the Mar Thoma Church is spread throughout India. The church also has a significant presence in North America, the Persian Gulf, the UK, Malaysia, Singapore and Australia.

In order to understand worship in the Mar Thoma church, two dominant elements in the heritage of the church must be taken into account. Firstly, the forms of worship are of the West Syrian liturgical family. This link was established in the 17th century, nearly two hundred years before the reformation of the 19th century. The second dominant factor is the principles of reform accepted by Abraham Malpan and his associates in the 19th century, as received through the CMS missionaries early in that century. The first of these principles of reform was acceptance of the Bible as the authority on all matters of faith and practice. A second major principle was the understanding of salvation as a gift of God appropriated through faith. The West Syrian liturgies were translated for the first time into Malayalam in accordance with the principles of reform. The result was that the essential form and spirit of the West Syrian liturgies were retained, while elements without scriptural warrant were trimmed out.

Features of worship in the Mar Thoma church

Integration of the sacrament and the word of God

In the days before its reformation, the worship life of our church was dominated by a one-sided emphasis on the sacrament. The exposition of scripture was neglected, or absent altogether. Our reformation made it possible to have the gospel heard in the local tongue and expounded meaningfully by the celebrant. At the same time "sharing" in the eucharist (as distinct from "seeing" the eucharist, watching it "being done") was emphasized. Participating in the eucharist in one's own language, and sharing in the eucharist in faith, only enhanced the spiritual meaning of the eucharist. What is worthy of special notice is the fact that the word of God gaining its rightful place in the eucharistic liturgy did not take away from the meaning of the sacrament, but added to it.

Increased involvement of laity in worship

The West Syrian liturgy has, by nature, much space for the involvement of laity. The reformation in our church further enhanced this. This happened in the form of the laity – both male and female – being allowed to preach the word of God and to lead in extempore prayers. Moreover, responses made by the people in the eucharistic service offer a high level of participation for the laity in the celebration of the eucharist itself. The thanksgiving prayer itself is not one long prayer said by the celebrant; at several points the laity join in with responses. Even the words of institution, and the epiclesis, are said responsively by the celebrant and the people.

Worship as an act in communion with the whole creation

The eucharist, the central act of worship in the Mar Thoma church, is an act of thanksgiving to God the Father for his marvels in creation and salvation. This is not a private act of an individual believer; it is an act of the local community of believers in communion with the church catholic in space and time. It is also an act in communion with the rest of creation and the heavenly court. Significantly, the eucharist is offered not on an "altar" but on the "thronos" of God. The church is gathered before the throne of God in eschatological anticipation, recalling the past and giving thanks for the past, present and future. It may further be observed that, while the Mar Thoma church does not pray for the departed and does not invoke the saints, it affirms strongly the belief that the communion of saints is the communion of the believers – both living and dead. The church in history is in communion with the church triumphant in giving thanks to God, that is, in offering the eucharist. There are no prayers for the dead, as their struggles on earth are over and they are already with the Lord sharing his peace. The departed saints are remembered and given thanks for.

The richness of symbolism

The worship of the Mar Thoma church is rich in symbolism. Candles are placed on the "thronos", and the censer is used. The celebrant repeat-

edly blesses the people with the sign of the cross and the people recip-
rocate, acknowledging their reception of the blessing. However, icons
are not used. The sign of peace is exchanged; the emphasis is on the
peace of God being received by the community of believers. Notably, the
sharing of peace among the believers is a sharing in the heavenly peace
mediated through the celebrant.

The celebrant and the people alike face the thronos during the eucharistic prayer. This has symbolic significance as an assembly before the throne
of God. It is only during the readings from the scripture, and during the
proclamation of the word of God, that the celebrant faces the people.

The Holy Spirit in the liturgy

The prayer for the descent of the Holy Spirit (epiclesis) is very
prominent in the liturgies of baptism, anointing with "muron", the
eucharist and ordination. The eucharistic epiclesis prays for the descent
of the Holy Spirit on the believers as well as the elements. The material
elements – bread, wine, water, and so on – become channels of grace
through the operation of the Holy Spirit. However, this is not understood
at a material level. The Mar Thoma church explicitly rejects the doctrine
of transubstantiation yet it is affirmed that, in the context of the prayers
of the believing community, the material elements come to stand in a
new relationship, within which they become channels of grace.

The Mar Thoma church approves the use of the word "mystery" to
explain the manner in which material things become channels of grace.
The manner in which the material things become channels of grace in a
sacrament symbolizes the possibility of nature itself, by the operation of
the Holy Spirit, becoming a channel of divine grace. The elements of
nature such as air, water, food, trees and the earth all have within them
the possibility of being sanctified, and becoming an effective channel of
divine grace. The church, which participates in the eucharistic "mystery", discerns the "mystery" in the whole creation and works for the
sanctification of the whole creation in the power of the same Holy Spirit.

Elements of worship

The worship of the Mar Thoma church has all the elements of a
developed Eastern form of liturgy. The elements of the eucharistic
liturgy are outlined below:

PRE-ANAPHORA
– the opening prayer
– the kyrie eleison (sixfold, three by the celebrant with three responses
  by the people)

- the epistle (this is preceded by a prayer and a chant)
- the gospel (this is preceded by a prayer and succeeded by a chant)
- the promeon (an extended doxology praising Christ)
- a prayer for the sanctification of the celebrant and the people
- the sedra (a lengthy prayer containing supplications and intercessions)
- the liturgy of incense
- the creed
- the sermon
- the confession and absolution

THE ANAPHORA
- the offertory (only the gifts of the people are offered; the elements are pre-prepared on the "thronos")
- the kiss of peace
- the introductory dialogue between the celebrant and the people (the initial greeting by the celebrant is trinitarian)
- the preface (the people respond with the sanctus and benedictus)
- the words of institution
- the anamnesis
- the epiclesis
- the great intercession for the church and the world
- the second blessing and the fraction (while the celebrant breaks bread the congregation joins in a chant or the deacon leads a litany)
- intercession for current and specific needs of the world and the worshipping community
- the Lord's prayer
- the third blessing
- the elevation of the elements *(sancta sanctis)*
- communion of the clergy
- communion of the people
- fourth and final blessing

The prayers of the eucharistic liturgy are fixed and the clergy celebrating has no freedom to alter them. However, there are several anaphora approved by the church, any one of which may be used on a particular Sunday at the discretion of the priest. Although there are eight different anaphora, the liturgy of St James is considered the principal one, with the others patterned after it structurally. The responses of the people remain the same.

The non-eucharistic worship usually consists of adoration, confession, responsive readings of psalms, the prayers for the Holy Spirit, the intercessions and the creeds. These services may be led by the laity, either male or female. However, in practice it is only on special occasions that women lead the worship.

From the time of reformation the liturgical life of the church, as outlined above, has been complemented by gatherings in homes or other convenient places – that is, places other than the church. These are unstructured meetings of believers. Here there would be singing, reading of psalms, extempore prayers, preaching and witnessing. The character of these gatherings is essentially that of "free church" or charismatic groups. The special feature of the internal life of the Mar Thoma church is that its members value the formal, highly structured Eastern liturgy as well as the house gatherings which give room for spontaneous liturgical expressions. Some of these gatherings also encourage *glossolalia*. The unstructured liturgy has another expression in the "conventions". Most parishes would have an annual convention. The house gatherings and the conventions attract interdenominational attendance, and the preachers may also be drawn from other denominations.

Influence of the ecumenical movement on worship in the Mar Thoma church

The worship forms of the Mar Thoma church have not undergone any significant change in the last fifty years or so. In fact this has been a period of liturgical conservatism; and neither the ecumenical movement nor any other movement has made an impact on the prevailing conservative mood.

In terms of the content of the liturgy it may be mentioned that, as a sequel to the formation of the joint council in 1978 with the Church of South India and the Church of North India, the heads of churches are included in each other's intercessory prayers. The liturgies of the three churches have also been published under one cover.

Although the forms of worship have not been affected much by the liturgical or ecumenical movements, interchurch relations have improved a great deal. For example, episcopal churches permit pastors from sister churches to preach during the eucharist.

New developments in worship

As mentioned earlier, there are hardly any new developments as far as liturgical forms are concerned. However, this fact itself has serious implications for the life of the church. There are two forms of protest against the liturgical stagnation. Firstly, the second- and third-generation migrants are becoming disenchanted with the church. This is evident in the urban centres of India as well as among the migrant (diaspora) communities of the west. Secondly, within the villages of Kerala state, the home ground of the Mar Thoma church, people who bear the burdens of stress arising from social change find the fully structured worship of the church less fulfilling than before. There is a significant formation of para-church groups which gather at the same time as the regular worship of the parishes, and a significant number of people who are choosing to give up the worship of their parish for the sake of para-church liturgies.

Within the history of the Mar Thoma church, reform of the liturgy has been associated with divisions in the church. Consequently, rigidity in liturgical form has come to be equated with preserving the unity of the church. The pain of past division seems to haunt the church even now. But the unity of the church needs to be discovered in addressing unitedly the spiritual challenges posed by the post-modern world. If we take those challenges more seriously, the need will emerge for forms of worship which will facilitate sharing our common pain before God, hearing God's word relevant to this situation, and giving thanks to God for his continuing guidance. Being challenged by God for common mission is inextricably linked to the search for the unity of the church and unity in worship. It is, I believe, the reluctance to hear this challenge that lies at the root of the prevailing crisis in ecumenism and ecumenical prayer.

Worship in the Evangelical Lutheran Church in Germany

HANS H. KRECH

• LUTHERAN •

The basic understanding of worship

In the Lutheran understanding the church has its inexhaustible source in worship. This is where the church is most recognizably the *church*. Our confession defines the church in terms of what happens in worship: the "pure preaching" of the gospel and the "right celebration" of the sacraments (that is, according to the words of institution). Why is this so?

The decisive redemptive event in an unredeemed world is that human beings "become righteous before God by grace, for Christ's sake, through faith" (*Confessio Augustana* [CA], IV). This happens through the gospel and the sacraments, the means through which God gives the Holy Spirit, who works faith *ubi et quando visum est Deo* ["when and where God pleases"] (CA V). In this the church has what it is, what it has to do, and what it has to give. Many other things make up the picture of the church; it is beautiful, attractive, interesting, great or small, magnificent or modest, meaningful and even important – but the only *essential* thing is that God himself, through preaching and sacraments, gives the Spirit who awakens, nourishes, renews the faith through which we partake of Christ – and does so in *God's* own time.

The Augsburg confession offers an extraordinarily concise and exact summary of worldwide Christianity's confession of the faith as rooted in scripture and Tradition. What it says is this: worship is first of all service of God through the means of word and sacrament in the communion of the saints. Through his word, and in the celebration of the sacraments, the Lord bestows on us the salvation that redeems, sets free and leads to eternal life. The community is thus prepared for acceptance, prayer and praise as well as for loving deeds in the world. Sacrament and sacrifice permeate all that happens in worship. In worship the gathered congregation thus finds its identity.

To be sure, the "essential" referred to above happens within this world, and in forms that have developed from a particular way of life in a given region at a given time. The outward form grows out of the life and faith of the particular gathered, worshipping congregation, set within the universal fellowship of the one church of Jesus Christ on earth.

Christian worship has, from the beginning, been the memorial of the cross and resurrection. The risen Christ enters into the circle of his own, and through his greeting of peace binds them to himself, and with one another. They recognize themselves as *his* people: he is their God, and they are his people. In this the whole history of salvation recounted by scripture becomes an immediate, present reality, into which people enter when they come to worship. That which has happened from ancient times becomes tangible through Christ. That which is promised for the most distant future can already be glimpsed in him:

> See, the home of God is among mortals. He will dwell with them as their God; they will be his peoples, and God himself will be with them; he will wipe away every tear from their eyes. Death will be no more; mourning and crying and pain will be no more, for the first things have passed away. And the one who was seated on the throne said, "See, I am making all things new" (Rev. 21:3-5.)

In the here and now of worship we enter into this redemptive event of the past and the future, bringing with us our faith, our questions, our doubts and our hopes. And we may be sure that this is, in truth, our *own* past and our *own* future. Worship cannot be anything less than this, nor can it seek to serve any other purpose.

The Christian church, which is dependent on the risen Christ in its midst, gathers for worship especially on the *day of resurrection*. It comes together in the confidence that the risen One is there in its midst, that he gives his Spirit and sends his church out into the world. It expects that he will share with those who are gathered – share his sending, his meal, his care for the weak, his praise of the Father, his heavenward gaze, his love for the world as the Father's world. In all its great undertakings and perplexity, its plans and its down-heartedness, its successes and failures, the church expects no less than that the Lord, in its midst, will put things right, will forgive, make new beginnings, reconcile and thus serve his people. Because it is essential to life: *that* is why the people are called together on the day of resurrection. Remembrance of the resurrection is the primary theme, the essential reason for Sunday worship. And it must be public – that is why the bells are rung. These things must be recalled ever anew, for they are being lost as the sense of God's presence disappears from everyday life.

Characteristics of the understanding of worship in the Evangelical Lutheran Church in Germany (VELKD)

In the course of its history, the church has learned from experience that this "essential" constitutes the very centre of worship and that, in the midst of all changes, this centre remains: God *speaks* seriously and compassionately with us, and *he shares the meal* with those whom he wants to send out into the world. In this way he imparts salvation. Worship is thus the event of salvation in the midst of the unredeemed world. In the course of centuries, these two things have been firmly established at the centre of worship, and even in the most far-reaching adaptation of worship to a particular age and its culture this centre is still recognizable. To do justice to it the gathered community must look away from themselves, and towards God. When they do so the secret of worship, the "treasure in earthen vessels" (2 Cor. 4:7), is opened to them. Then they can look beyond the immediately obvious to depths that are not humanly feasible. Then a vast "space" will open up to them, enabling each one of them to participate, in his or her own way, in the experience of God's presence – *ubi et quando visum est Deo.*

For the sake of this experience, the congregation holds to this centre of worship as the very core of its life. Anything that is added or altered, anything adapted to a particular time or place, any renewal or innovation must serve this core, making it still more clearly recognizable; otherwise it is superfluous. In this regard, the most recent surveys on what is expected of the church by secular society have produced a surprising result: precisely those who practise their faith without any close church connection expect worship to be designed in a way that corresponds to this essential core. This finding shows how relevantly the church acts today, when it places the emphasis in its worship on that which is *foundational* to it.

Martin Luther left much of the existing form of the mass as the basis of the worship service (*Formula missae*, 1523, *Deutsche Messe*, 1526) – though focusing the mass on the central elements which he considered important, namely *preaching and the Lord's supper,* in order "that nothing else... shall happen than that our dear Lord himself shall talk with us through his holy word and we in turn may talk with him through prayer and praise" (I cite the consecration of the *Schlosskirche* at Torgau). This definition has shaped the Lutheran church in the most decisive way. Under the "word", Luther himself subsumed the sacrament as *verbum visibile*. In the following centuries, however, the Lord's supper was celebrated only rarely in the course of the year. This was due to the special honour accorded to the Lord's supper, which should not be lessened by regular Sunday usage. Not until the liturgical renewal movement in the 20th century, and the beginning of the ecumenical awakening, was the ancient church's tradition of worship including proclamation *and* the celebration of the Lord's supper reintroduced. The *Erneuerte Agende* [revised service book] (draft of 1998) gives this as the standard practice for Lutheran churches.

The preaching of the word, celebration of the sacraments and common prayer are constitutive for Evangelical Lutheran churches and are thus the irreplaceable core of their worship. Worship is public; and the invitation is addressed to all those for whom Christ came, died and rose again and who want to turn to God for Christ's sake.

The ecumenical dimension of Lutheran worship

The Evangelical Lutheran Church knows that in its worship it is incorporated into the worshipping life of the worldwide church of Christ. In this it is ecumenical in its orientation. It is especially linked to the worship tradition of the West, and it places particular emphasis on the central importance of preaching and the celebration of the Lord's supper, as well as the participation of the whole congregation in the liturgy.

The individual congregation, and the association of congregations in a regional or national church, seem at first sight to be simply faith communities. They are made up of people with compatible faith convictions, and are engaged in common diaconal and public services. They appear as the church of Jesus Christ only when, gathered for worship, they join in the one universal adoration of God at all times and in all places, and join in the eternal praise of the heavenly hosts. Then they truly become part of the *una sancta ecclesia* spoken about in the creed, the *communio sanctorum*.

Worship is crucial for the church. In all that happens in it and through it, the church is only the church to the extent that it allows itself to be built up through the presence of the Lord in worship, that it seeks worship and lives for, and from, worship. Accordingly, "church fellowship" among the churches is expressed adequately only if it is practised as a "fellowship of worship"; it can – and should – include more, but it must be a fellowship of *worship* if it is to exist at all.

The Evangelical Lutheran Church's experience in the ecumenical movement has been particularly enriching in this respect. Direct encounters with other churches, and the results of ecumenical dialogues (especially the WCC Faith and Order document *Baptism, Eucharist and Ministry* and the Lima liturgy) have enriched our worship. This is reflected in, amongst other things, a new diversity in prayer and associated gestures, in the restoration of the eucharistic prayer in the celebration of the Lord's supper, and in the inclusion of the creation in the composition of worship in general. Traditionally, Lutheran worship is above all Christocentric in character. Nowadays, through the influence of the ecumenical fellowship and also movements of a charismatic nature, the confession of God the Creator and God the Holy Spirit comes much more clearly to expression, and gains new creative force.

Lutheran worship is the gathering of all baptized believers around their Lord Jesus Christ. It is open for all to participate. In this sense it is oriented towards being a "folk church". The invitation to holy communion is, in principle, addressed to all baptized believers who accept that Christ is really present in the bread and the wine (Christ's "real presence"), and gives himself for our salvation at his table. Church fellowship, that is, unlimited fellowship in worship in word and sacrament, exists with the Lutheran churches in the Lutheran World Federation and with other Reformation churches participating in the Leuenberg agreement *(Konkordie)*. Eucharistic hospitality is practised officially with the Old Catholic Church in Germany as well as with the Association of Mennonite Congregations and the Methodists. Even though there are continuing differences in doctrine and church order, common practice has contributed to convergences in worship. It has also led to a respect for distinctive elements in one's partner churches, as shown in the way one does liturgy in one's *own* church. (An example in Lutheran worship would be the care for the consecrated elements of the Lord's supper following the celebration, in consideration of Orthodox and Roman Catholic spirituality.)

The *Erneute Agenda* of the Lutheran and United churches in Germany contains a series of criteria for ordering worship including, among other things, the "ecumenical dimension of worship". The service book, like the German Evangelical hymn book before it, includes a large number of prayers and songs from all over the Christian world. The liturgical work for the Lutheran *Agende II* (special services), on worship services from the common tradition of the ancient Church (Easter night and other vigils, stations, hours and so on), is being done systematically in cooperation with other churches, especially the Roman Catholic Church.

The study on "Worship and Culture in Dialogue",[1] initiated and carried out by the Lutheran World Federation, has had an important and lasting influence on the liturgical work of the Evangelical Lutheran churches. This study project likewise crosses traditional confessional boundaries, and is bringing the churches closer to one another and deepening their fellowship in worship. There are plans to continue work on the study in the regions once it has been concluded at the international level. As far as Europe is concerned, this is a promising venture. Following the successful start to Europe-wide cooperation among Lutheran churches at the consultation on "Lutheran Worship Today" (5-8 March 1998) in Augsburg, this cooperation will be developed in future in Europe. Experience so far shows that, even where all the issues surrounding church communion have not yet been clarified, common celebration of worship is possible. Bearing in mind the importance and place of worship in the churches, this represents a great opportunity for promoting the ecumenical movement.

New developments in shaping Lutheran worship

The renewal of worship is on the agenda of most churches. The circumstances of life have changed considerably in many places. Traditions are being overturned. Some of the inherited traditions still work well, but there are signs that their days are numbered: low church attendance, falling interest among the younger generation, declining importance of worship in the eyes of the general public. There is no prospect of a return to the "good old days". The world in which Christians live has moved on. Above all: *God* has moved on with his people, with those who believe. God is opening doors. We note interest in new forms, in questions about the meaning of worship as being together in God's presence. Awareness of the wonders of creation is growing, and the redemptive wind of the Spirit is breaking new ground. Tangible results are expected.

Within the Western life-style, in the bustle of a way of life symbolized by TV-spots, in a "world of outward appearances", and the unrealistic expectations fomented by advertising and consumerism – worship represents a powerful corrective on behalf of *life*. Worship is an effective alternative to isolation, and the related anonymity of modern society, an alternative that promotes personal life and community in Christ. The word does not *scatter*, it *gathers*. To those who are *excluded* from celebrating, the eucharist extends an invitation to *enter in*.

This situation is affecting liturgical developments. Reflecting the longing for tangible, binding signs, personal blessings are taking an increasingly important place in church services and at watersheds in people's lives. The VELKD acknowledged this with its service booklet "Service for the Sick", first published in 1993, offering blessing of the sick, with anointing, as a liturgical act. This is an innovation for Lutheran churches in Germany, but it has met with surprising and lasting acceptance. The booklet quickly reached a wide public. The same can be said of the "Thomas Mass" (a contemporary, "accessible" eucharistic service) which was started in Finland, and has been adapted to the German context.

Innovations are also taking place in regard to the worship space, music, gestures (including dance) and liturgical dress (for example, an alb with stole in the liturgical colour appropriate to the church calendar). These are essentially ideas from the ecumenical fellowship that have been willingly taken up and integrated into our own context. The traditionally austere Lutheran service has thus been given a noticeably more festive form, which is widely welcomed.

Last (but not least), a new branch of liturgical development is beginning to take shape thanks to the efforts of women's groups in creating worship services. Liturgies showing a feminist influence are used especially by women's groups themselves; they are most often prepared for used in more limited situations. Proposals are given in the *Erneuerte Agende,* as "examples of worship using an open form". They employ structures that depart from the traditional ones, for example circular structures; and in particular they emphasize concrete experience. So far, however, such models have not been successfully linked with the tradition and universality of the church.

Because the church of Jesus Christ is alive, and worship is the expression of its life, the issue of worship is constantly shifting, dynamic – and directed towards Christ.

NOTE

[1] See S. Anita Stauffer, ed. *Worship and Culture in Dialogue,* 1994; *Christian Worship: Unity in Cultural Diversity,* 1996; *Baptism, Rites of Passage, and Culture,* 1998; all Geneva, Lutheran World Federation, Department for Theology and Studies.

Worship in the Church of Scotland

PETER DONALD

• REFORMED •

The Church of Scotland has been and still is a major force in the lives
of Scottish people. It is the church by law established, and so exercises
a territorial ministry across the whole of Scotland. Public worship is
offered every Sunday in every parish in the land. Beyond the lives of
those who are counted members by profession of faith, through the conduct of weddings and funerals it has contact with a high proportion of the
population at large. It has a recognized role in the public life of Scotland,
and of the United Kingdom as a whole. In terms of active membership
the other major church in Scotland is the Roman Catholic Church; the
various other denominations in Scotland are comparatively small.

The modern establishment of the Church of Scotland (the "church"),
dating to a statute of 1921, guards the spiritual independence of the presbyterian government of the church. The general assembly, which meets
annually, is the sole authority and judge of the life of the church – a
notable exception then, in British constitutional terms, to the sovereignty
of the Queen-in-parliament. The achievement of this establishment followed a long struggle which can be dated back to the Reformation of
1560. However, within this long period of history (and of course also
since) there is a complicated narrative which deserves attention beyond
the scope of this paper. Understandings of church government, and
approaches to worship, within the Church of Scotland have been con-
tested. This explains the existence nowadays of the Episcopal Church of
Scotland and the Free Church of Scotland, not to mention other smaller
breakaway churches and independently formed churches which are alive
today in Scotland. Moreover, processes of reunion and reform – owned
to varying degrees within the Church of Scotland – have left their mark.
It is important to mention also that one may see broad lines of difference,
in the historical development of the church, between the highlands and
the lowlands of Scotland.

"The Church of Scotland is part of the holy catholic or universal
church: worshipping one God, Almighty, all-wise, and all-loving, in the
Trinity of the Father, the Son and the Holy Ghost, the same in substance,
equal in power and glory." Beyond this statement in the Articles Declara-

tory of the Church of Scotland (1921), the contemporary church presents a varied picture of worship. Reflection on the renewal of worship is expressed at general assembly level. Beyond that, however, the subject of worship is entrusted to the direction of the minister(s) of the parish. It is certainly possible in Scotland to see the influences of the liturgical renewal and ecumenical movements, but not necessarily everywhere. Personal interpretations count for much. What follows, therefore, is an attempt to portray general movements in the understanding of worship in the Church of Scotland, but with due recognition of where the issues of diversity and unity fit.

A description of contemporary experiences of worship

The word of God preached

"The Church of Scotland acknowledges the word of God, which is contained in the scriptures of the Old and New Testaments, to be the supreme rule of faith and life." The standard diet of worship focuses around the reading of the scriptures and preaching, the proclamation of the word which commands a response. It is only very rarely that there is not preaching, although forms of preaching have undoubtedly been changing (see "accessibility", below). In many congregations, the sermon comes towards the end of the service; elsewhere it is located closer to the readings, in common with the standard eucharistic order of service. The most obvious expectation of an ordained minister is that he or she is a *preacher*. For a minister to be called to a charge, the last and decisive test is to lead worship for the congregation, and this conduct hinges around the delivery of a sermon. The sermon is central to the Christian education of adults who, beyond the time of their profession of faith, tend to participate very little in small group learning. Children are generally not expected to be present for the sermon; a Sunday school system, or something equivalent, is deemed more educationally suitable. And indeed "education" seems the right term, just as, occasionally, the minister is referred to as the "teaching elder". That is not to deny, however, other elements within preaching – such as exhortation, comment on contemporary issues and so on – which regularly have their place. Purely exegetical preaching is rare.

Psalms, songs and hymns

Standing to sing plays a major part in the church. The congregation will usually sing four or five times, and most often a combination of psalms, songs and hymns. There is a church hymnary authorized by the general assembly (together with general assemblies of other Presbyter-

ian churches in the United Kingdom), and plans are in motion for
another revision of this (that is, to make the fourth edition). There is a
strong tradition of metrical psalm singing, which in some places is supplemented by psalms in other versions, some more modern. There is a
plethora of songs open to use by congregations, and more and more are
picking and choosing. A particular Scottish contribution comes, on the
one hand, from the Iona Community, and on the other from the Church
of Scotland *Songs of God's People* which has just this year been added
to by a collaborative effort with other churches in Scotland, including the
Roman Catholic Church, called *Common Ground.*

All together there is a great variety of congregational worship
singing, appealing to different tastes – but not necessarily to everyone at
once! In addition to congregational singing some, but not all, congregations honour the choral tradition with introits and anthems and elements
of sung liturgy. The organ is still the common instrument of accompaniment, except in parts of the highlands where unaccompanied singing is
preferred, but in some congregations the use of guitars and keyboards
and other instruments significantly displaces the tradition of the past.

Prayers

Worship is animated by prayer, and several "slots" of prayer will
occur in the course of a Church of Scotland service. As there is no obligation to follow a fixed liturgy, these are led or delegated by the minister.
Some are extemporary, others draw on written forms ancient and modern. The congregation sits, with heads bowed, for prayer; responsive participation has been introduced in some congregations in recent years, but
the norm is silently to join with the person leading the prayers. The one
exception to this is the Lord's prayer, which is said aloud together. The
tradition of prayer in the home is encouraged, but given again its lack of
set forms it may be observed less consistently than is desirable. In very
recent years the general assembly panel on worship has published its
own aid for private devotions to try to help this situation. Family prayers
are perhaps even more a rarity, though the situation is possibly a little
better in the highlands. A vestige of these prayers, in the saying of grace
before meals, seems not to be very common either.

The sacraments

Since the Reformation the right administration of the two sacraments
of baptism and the Lord's supper or holy communion has been seen,
alongside preaching, as the function of the ordained minister. In most situations (although perhaps not all) a set liturgy, authorized for use by the
general assembly, is followed on these occasions, but which version of

the liturgy is at the discretion of the minister. The baptismal ceremony does not normally involve immersion, either for infants or adults, rather water on the head in the name of the Trinity. A question is put to the parents or sponsors of infants as to their Christian faith; there is also a question asking them to undertake a Christian upbringing for the child. An adult bringing a child for baptism should be a professed member or adherent of the church. Baptisms are normally performed before the congregation on a Sunday, during which occasion the whole congregation is often asked to join in saying the Apostles' Creed.

In most parishes holy communion is comparatively rare, with four times a year being average, though in some parishes it is celebrated weekly and in some only once or twice a year (the latter being more the case in the highlands). In parts of the highlands there continues the tradition of the communion season, which may begin with fasting on the Thursday and end with thanksgiving on the Monday; in the lowlands the historical emphasis on preparation survives only in the visits of elders to communicant members in advance of the service (though here the emphasis on catechesis and "fencing the tables" has largely died away). At the communion service itself, the elements of bread and wine are usually received by people where they sit, in some congregations by people moving to sit at tables set lengthways in the church – and also, nowadays, in some congregations by people coming to stand around the communion table. By tradition the elders distribute the bread and wine to the people, in silence. The use of a common cup, as opposed to individual glasses, varies according to the congregation. Ordinary bread is "set apart for this holy use and mystery". By grace through faith, Christ is seen to be present as baptism is administered and the elements of bread and wine are shared in remembrance of him. The creed, either the Apostles' or the Nicene, is said or sung in some congregations on these sacramental occasions; likewise the *sursum corda*, the *sanctus* and the *agnus Dei* (in English! – see "accessibility" below).

The offering

At public worship the people are expected to offer a donation for the work of the church, and sometimes there are other offerings for "outside" causes. Such money received finances the entire work of the church. In addition, the participation of the people is valued whether in the leading of worship or in church organizations and mission.

Leaders and people

As will already be clear, the ordained minister has a pivotal role in the conduct of public worship. Often members of the congregation assist in doing readings and leading prayers and music; in this context, the elders' distinctive role is to be an example in attendance at worship and, as already mentioned, to help serve at communion. Members of the diaconate, and ministers in training or auxiliary ministers, are involved as appropriate. The average congregation will include not only professed members but also adherents and visitors.

Language

Services are held in English or, where appropriate, in Gaelic. The actual language of English services, however, varies greatly. The Bible is available in translations old and new; the language of prayer and song runs likewise. It can be said, however, that in general a congregation will keep to its appointed linguistic emphasis (as opposed to mixing and matching) – at least until the minister changes! Liturgical revision authorized by the general assembly has provided services in contemporary English, but these are used entirely at the discretion of the minister.

Accessibility

Given the prominence in worship of receiving and responding to the word, reflection on the accessibility of worship services has pushed in certain directions. In most places the length of the sermon (now 15-20 minutes?) is less now than it was earlier; and there is something of a trend towards having all-age services or other experimental worship, where music and drama and visuals are given space in preference to a monologue from the pulpit. In some congregations this is even extending to the use of video as a means to prompt reflection and prayer. The interest in *accessibility* may also be partly behind the adoption of aspects of liturgical renewal. In fact printed service-sheets, and vocal congregational participation, are viewed as much on these grounds as in terms of ecumenical change. For similar reasons, the use of the historic creeds is not overly favoured (this is not much taken as a theological issue).

The Christian year

Since up to this century the Church of Scotland, in its presbyterian manifestation, distanced itself from observing the Christian year, it is worth noting that there has been a turn-around on this – at least with regard to Christmas and Easter. There are lectionaries approved by the general assembly which acknowledge major feasts of the Roman calendar, though not saints' days, and these are used to an extent (although not universally). At Christmas the churches are busier, but not so much at Easter, this reflecting views in the general population which spill over, to some extent, into the membership of the church. Fasting and abstinence are rare as disciplines.

Architecture

With comparatively few pre-Reformation buildings surviving, the architecture of Scotland's churches bears witness to a general preference for plainness in the setting of worship. Good acoustics for the spoken word dominated many years of church architecture, and there was (and still is, in some places) a positive antipathy to colour and decoration. Consequently church exteriors are often more impressive than their interiors. This said, the forces for liturgical renewal have had a major influence in Scotland from the late 19th century – with what benefit is open to discussion – and nowadays (following various influences) both new church design and art for interiors receive heightened attention. The pulpit continues to this day to be a prominent piece of furniture, together with the lectern. The font and communion table are generally placed where they can be seen by the sitting congregation. Only rarely is it expected that a congregation should move physically during their participation in worship.

Ecumenical worship

The church is fully committed ecumenically at national and international level, and its members have fairly widespread opportunities to worship with those of other church traditions, in the Week of Prayer for Christian Unity and on other occasions through the year. Some close partnerships exist, including with the (Anglican) Scottish Episcopal Church; joint services take place with Roman Catholics. A good awareness of the world church has been fostered by exchanges in both directions and by the Iona Community, in particular, making songs and hymns from far afield widely known. This said, the ecumenical movement with respect to the other presbyterian churches in Scotland is far from satisfactory, even – or especially? – in parts of the highlands, where forms of worship are nearly indistinguishable between the denominations.

The ordinances of religion

The parish minister frequently conducts marriages and funerals for those who may or may not be baptized, and who are not professed members of the church. It is almost always the case that some of those who share in these services of worship of course are members of the church, or of some other church. In the case of weddings, there will have been preparation of the couple and, in most cases, participation in the worshipping life of the congregation in advance of the wedding. Civic offices (where prayers are offered, say, for the good conduct of government) are also conducted in churches by ministers of the church. Worship services are likewise held for school communities, as appropriate to their needs. In all of these situations – in contrast to the will of the large majority present for Sunday morning worship – there is an offering of Christian worship in which a number of those present will not wish actively to share. Evangelical hope is nevertheless affirmed on such occasions.

Reflections on contemporary experiences of worship

Worship is offered to the glory of God. In the Reformed tradition as adopted by the Church of Scotland, the prevailing emphasis is on a reverential and learning approach, largely free from physical gestures, yet feeding those who attend in mind and in spirit. Sunday is the settled day for the worship of the church, and this takes place in a single gathering so that all people can come together, young and old, at the same time. The communal life of the church is served through other gatherings more social in nature, though not excluding prayer, and indeed through prayer meetings and Sunday evening worship in some places; but the heart of the life of the church is focused on the Sunday morning congregation. In our worship practice there is a fundamental expectation of unity in Christ.

With the conduct of worship entrusted to the minister ordained to word and sacrament, who has liberty, within the terms of the ordination vows, to interpret the church tradition, the presence of the risen Christ is therefore anticipated as the word is preached and the sacraments administered. Whatever the variants, the liturgy of the word is clearly the staple diet of the worshipping people. But on set, very special occasions, the liturgy of the sacrament of holy communion is upheld as the best worship that can be offered to God the Father, through the Lord Jesus Christ and in the power of the Holy Spirit. Whereas attendance on – so to speak – "ordinary" Sundays is hoped for, on communion Sundays it is expected. In parts of the highlands the common practice is that not everyone is personally prepared to consume the bread and wine; elsewhere the participation is more universal amongst those who have publicly professed faith (and in some cases, according to local circumstances, baptized children desiring and prepared to participate). The minister therefore, as the one given episcope (oversight, supervision) joins with his or her people in what can be understood to be holy, catholic and apostolic worship.

Worship in a changing social situation

Worship in the church is not untouched by social change. For example with regard to baptism, the sacrament of entrance into the life of the church, falling numbers of children being brought for baptism reflects the falling estimation of the place of the church generally in Scotland today. Children attending worship and Sunday school, or its equivalent, are mostly the children of active adults in the congregation – a definite change in social patterns of the last thirty years. Likewise Sunday attendance, and the falling numbers of those prepared to take on membership through profession of faith, is symptomatic of the church losing its draw on the people of Scotland. More and more the services for burgh (that is, for civic events) or school, or for the dead, are conducted, as has already been noticed, with a mixed constituency present.

The drop in the size of the church causes much concern. Of course it can be said more confidently now than before that the regular worshipping community is present on a Sunday out of choice, and not due to social custom. However, worries about the effectiveness of mission prompt discussions on the understandings of worship. Some will argue that a crucial challenge for the church is to make its worship appealing, accessible, attractive. This has been a major part of the impetus for the adoption of new music and media such as video. Here it has not always been clear that theological considerations have been to the fore – though there are notable exceptions to that comment! That said, at the other end of the spectrum there has been a conservative, even straitjacketed, holding on to past tradition with no greater theological justification.

Nonetheless the question *is* raised: What worship can draw us near to God? In Scotland earnest theological engagement with the question, not least ecumenically, is accompanied by less considered movements. In an establishment where the input of the individual minister is so significant, the dangers are all too apparent. At the same time, nevertheless, the beauty of a fairly free and open tradition of worship is that it allows enriching experiment, contemporary attentiveness to the real needs of the worshipping community, and a potential freshness to accompany the rhythm of our approach in worship to our living God. In current church union discussions, the Reformed churches resist being obliged to use fixed liturgical forms.

Liturgical renewal and ecumenical exchange

Liturgical renewal has had its influence on the church since the late 19th century and, to an extent, has thus prepared the ground for ecumenical exchange in worship. There has been recovery or, more accurately, a reopening to the wider catholic tradition to which the church insists it belongs. Although in certain quarters this innovation has been resisted, the possibilities before today's church lie in drawing from whatever is rich in traditions both Scottish and global. For many, variation and diversity is highly acceptable and accepted. What effect does this have on the unity of the church? Bonds of common styles of worship cross the denominations. To some extent, people shift their membership to the church where the form of worship suits them best. Ministers, meanwhile, labour to craft weekly orders of worship appropriate to their congregations and fitting for the glorifying of God, all in the context of so many differing expectations. A sharing in prayer and praise must help in creating ecumenical openness. Despite the challenges clearly being raised in all these developments to ecclesiastical discipline, the sharing may make its own contribution to the search for unity over ministry and sacraments. The connections to the ministry of the whole people of God are very much on the agenda, not least because of the celebration of diversity in worship.

Scottish history teaches us that differences in forms of worship push people apart, making for the disunity of the church. Some historic differences have arguably had their day (even though some doubt it!), for example the question of the use of musical instruments in worship. Other differences clearly continue to matter; not least, in today's Scotland, debate about the interpretation of the scriptures and the continuing Protestant-Catholic issues of contention.

A final word of hope

However, a final word of hopefulness might be sounded. Without claiming there are no problems involved, experiences of worshipping together under various forms, and with various leaders, give members of the Church of Scotland and others good reason to believe that we are indeed one in Christ. For we are one in being drawn to glorify God. It is indeed as human beings our "chief end and purpose". There is every reason to continue worrying away at those remaining obstacles to visible unity through diversity.

Anglican Worship: An Evolution from Imperialism to Ecumenism

DAVID R. HOLETON

• ANGLICAN •

Worship at the heart of Anglicanism

Worship plays a central role in Anglicanism and has done so since the Reformation of the 16th century. It is largely in the context of worship that Anglicans have formed their self-identity. Perhaps more than any other church issuing from the Reformation, Anglicans have looked more to the liturgical texts contained in the *Book of Common Prayer* as expressions of their belief than they have to any conciliar statement, particular theologian or confessional statement. While, in its beginnings, this weight was also shared by the *Thirty-Nine Articles*[1] and the *Book of Homilies*,[2] these documents have effectively fallen into complete desuetude, leaving the entire weight to be borne by the liturgical texts. Thus, for Anglicans, the maxim *lex orandi, lex credendi* plays a very particular role in their sense of who they are as a Christian community: if one wishes to understand how Anglicans understand themselves in their relationship to God, to one another, to other Christians and to the world, one must look at the way they express themselves in their liturgies.

Patterns of worship

The prayer book rubrics direct that the offices of morning and evening prayer (matins and evensong) will be sung or said each day, and that the eucharist will be celebrated on Sundays and holy days. In the daily offices, praise is offered to God (in the appointed psalms and canticles), two passages of scripture are read (one from the Old Testament or the Apocrypha and one from the New Testament), and prayer is made for the church and the world. Except on a Sunday, preaching at the office would be unusual. In the eucharist, following the classical shape of the Western liturgy, the community gathers to hear the word of God in scripture and preaching, to pray for the church and the life of the world, to give thanks (make *eucharistia*) for God's mighty acts of salvation in creation and redemption, and to share in Christ's self-giving of his body and blood at the eucharistic table.

Every act of worship, for Anglicans, is to the praise and glory of God and is, thus, doxological. At the same time, it takes place in the context of the gathered community whose members bring with them their own particular cares, concerns and thanksgivings which are earthed in an incarnational theology which is typical of Anglicanism. Thus Anglican worship depends on a careful balance and integration of heart and mind, of word and sacrament and of text and ceremonial. Prayers (and hymns) are addressed to God, not the congregation, and the scripture readings and preaching are addressed to the community; the sacraments convey God's saving grace and are moments of personal encounter between Christ and the community – the divine meeting the human. As God is praised and glorified in all these things so, too, the community is nurtured.

> The eucharistic action models the way in which God as redeemer comes into the world in the Word made flesh, to which the people of God respond by offering themselves – broken individuals – to be made one body in Christ's risen life. This continual process of transformation is enacted in each celebration.[3]

While from 1549 the prayer book has provided for the weekly celebration of the Sunday eucharist, the practice was at first observed mainly in the cathedrals and larger collegiate and parish churches, where there was the minimum required number of communicants to receive communion along with the priest. Beginning in the 19th century, this pattern of infrequent reception of communion changed dramatically so that, today, the weekly celebration of the eucharist and reception of communion (increasingly by all the baptized, regardless of age[4]) has become the usual Sunday pattern in Anglican parishes.

The historic prayer books and the churches: one-way ecumenism
From the time of the imposition of the first *Book of Common Prayer* at Pentecost 1549 there has, until the last century, been only one legal liturgical text at any given time. While there has always been some diversity of liturgical "style" in which the prayer book was used (often depending upon the nature of the community in which the liturgy was being celebrated), historically there has been little desire to deviate from the printed text itself. The effect of this has been to form Anglicans, regardless of theological differences, by the same liturgical texts. Because there was so little real change in the texts over the centuries, the words of the prayer book were deeply rooted in the memory of the faithful.

The text of the *Book of Common Prayer*, along with the authorized (or King James) version of the English Bible, became foundational in the evolution of the English language. The particular beauty of the English language of this formative period of Anglican liturgical life has given Anglicans a strong sense not only of the importance of the "beauty of holiness", but also of the "holiness of beauty" as fundamental in the way Anglicans have conceived of the role played by worship in their lives.

Because of the established position of the Church of England and the disproportionate influence of Anglicanism (in terms of the number of individuals who were actually Anglicans) on most parts of the English-speaking world, the texts of Anglican worship found themselves quoted in classic English literature and in the general use of the English language itself. As such, the "ecumenical" influence of Anglican worship was very much one way: other churches adopted Anglican texts. Sometimes this was done officially as, for example, the historic *Sunday Service of the Methodists,* or the *Book of Common Prayer reformed...* of the Unitarians; sometimes it was a less direct borrowing of prayer book texts along with a slavish faithfulness to the use of the Tudor (or pseudo-Tudor) English of the prayer books as the "appropriate" language for prayer, even though this was no longer the language of common speech.

The ecumenical influence of other churches on Anglicanism was rarely textual but rather musical, ritual or ceremonial. The hymnody of the Methodists, at first rejected by mainstream Anglicans, was eventually incorporated into Anglicanism and helped make it a "singing church". Similarly, the 19th century "catholic revival" in Anglicanism saw the gradual restoration of "catholic" usages in Anglicanism which was sometimes based on mediaeval English liturgical models, sometimes on contemporary Roman Catholic models.

Anglican worship and the ecumenical movement

The 20th century saw a massive reversal of some of this largely uni-directional model. Beginning with the Anglican liturgical movement (which has been shown to have been as much an indigenous movement as it was a borrowing from other traditions), Anglicanism has seen a renewal of almost every aspect of its worship life. The historic Tudor-language prayer books play an increasingly marginalized role in Anglicanism as a whole. Where they continue to be used as the only or pre-dominant liturgical text, it is usually in a translation into an indigenous language in Africa. In their place, throughout the Anglican world, there are new prayer books or books of alternative services which are used by the vast majority of worshipping Anglicans. In the creation of these books the ecumenical movement has played a major role.

While, historically, the ecumenical influence of the liturgy may have been very one-way (the influence of the *Book of Common Prayer* on the liturgical texts of other churches), the present liturgical renewal has seen the emergence of a genuine ecumenical dialogue. This is true at a variety of levels including those of academic research, multilateral ecumenical dialogue, as well as the practical level.

Academic research on the origins and evolution of Christian worship has played a major role in the renewal of patterns of worship in the churches today. This has not been a mere "fad" in which one tradition simply copied the work of another, but often reflects scholars working within their own traditions yet coming to similar conclusions. Academic cross-fertilization has also played an important role in this process. This has led to a growing consensus on the basic shape (or *ordo*) of baptism and eucharist; and it is this shape that has become the pattern on which modern liturgies are built across the ecumenical spectrum. Anglican scholars have certainly carried their share of the load in these studies, and have made significant contributions which have influenced the emerging consensus on questions of Christian initiation, the role of confirmation in the life of the churches, the development of the eucharistic prayer and the shape of the liturgical year, among other matters.

At the level of formal ecumenical dialogue, Anglicans have also had the sense that worship was a way towards unity among the churches. While at the first world conference on Faith and Order (Lausanne 1927) worship was generally considered to be a barrier, rather than a means, towards unity, at the second world conference on Faith and Order (Edinburgh 1937) the first formal initiatives were taken to enter into an "understanding of one another's ways of worship". William Temple, then archbishop of Canterbury, expressed the urgency of the matter when, in his conference sermon, he called for the study of the doctrinal questions involved in what he called "the greatest of all scandals in the face of the world" – the maintenance of barriers against completeness of union at the Table of the Lord.[5] Since that time, worship has never ceased to be on the agenda of Faith and Order, and has demonstrated itself to be an important dimension in the way to Christian unity.

A moment of particular importance in this process was the production of the WCC Faith and Order document *Baptism, Eucharist and Ministry* (the Lima statement), which remains the most important multilateral document on worship of our age. It is of some significance that another archbishop of Canterbury, Robert Runcie, presided at a celebration of the eucharist using the Lima liturgy at the assembly of the World Council of Churches held in Vancouver in 1983. There, the worship tent attracted thousands of worshippers daily and gave an important impetus to the role worship can play in creating ecumenical convergence – affirming the point made by Archbishop Temple over forty years earlier. Throughout this process Anglicans have been involved, both contributing and benefitting from it.

Anglican worship within the emerging ecumenical consensus on worship

Ecumenical liturgical work as normative

Over the last forty years, ecumenical work in the renewal of the liturgy has become normative. Since the time of Vatican II, liturgists have been involved in the task of preparing common ecumenical liturgical texts. For example, in 1964, an unofficial group of Roman Catholic, Anglican, Lutheran and Reformed liturgists began to meet in North America. This informal gathering eventually became the Consultation on Common Texts (CCT) which by 2002 included 22 churches or agencies among its membership. The CCT has produced a number of ecumenical liturgical texts such as *A Liturgical Psalter for the Christian Year*, *A Christian Celebration of Marriage*, *A Celebration of Baptism* and *Services of Prayer*.

At about the same time as the formation of the CCT, a similar group, the Joint Liturgical Group (JLG), was formed in Great Britain and presently contains eight member churches. Like the CCT, the JLG has produced a number of ecumenical liturgical texts including a daily office and liturgical material for holy week, as well as a variety of books directed towards the liturgical renewal of the churches. The liturgical texts have found their way into use within a number of churches in the British Isles, and have been important in creating an atmosphere of ecumenical convergence.

In more recent years, other national ecumenical working groups have been established including the Australian Consultation on Liturgy (ACOL), the Joint Liturgical Consultation within New Zealand (JLCNZ), the Liturgical Committee, South African Church Unity Commission (CUC), and the Association of Irish Liturgists.

Working together with the Roman Catholic Bishops International Commission on English in the Liturgy (ICEL), the CCT and JLG formed the International Consultation on English Texts (ICET) which was responsible for the creation of modern language liturgical translations of the gloria in excelsis, creeds, sanctus, our Father, Gloria Patri, magnificat, benedictus, Te Deum, etc. used by the English-speaking churches. These were published as *Prayers We Have in Common*. The work of ICET is presently carried on by the English Language

Liturgical Consultation (ELLC), which also includes the ecumenical liturgical consultations from Australia, New Zealand, Ireland and South Africa. In 1989 a revised version of the ELLC texts was published by ELLC as *Praying Together*. Presently ELLC is examining other liturgical possibilities such as a collection of common eucharistic prayers.[6]

Common lectionaries: an important ecumenical witness

In addition to common liturgical texts, English-speaking churches have enjoyed common liturgical lectionaries. The publication of the Roman Catholic *Ordo Lectionum Missae* (OLM) in 1969 attracted widespread ecumenical attention. A variety of North American churches began publishing their own recensions of OLM, and in 1974 the Consultation on Church Union (COCU) produced its own version. A working group of the CCT – the North American Committee on Calendar and Lectionary – produced a common version of OLM which was published in 1982 as the *Common Lectionary*: the lectionary proposed by the Consultation on Common Texts was revised and republished in 1992 as the *Revised Common Lectionary*. This lectionary has found widespread use in the English-speaking churches of North America and overseas.

Anglicans have been instrumental in the foundation and the work of all these ecumenical liturgical groups, and the work of these groups has found its way into the renewed liturgical texts of provinces throughout the Anglican world. A glance at the acknowledgments pages of any contemporary Anglican liturgical book – *Common Worship* (England 2001); *A Prayer Book for Australia* (1995), *A New Zealand Prayer Book* (1989), *An Anglican Prayer Book* (South Africa 1989) or *The Book of Alternative Services* (Canada 1985) – will quickly show how the work of these ecumenical groups has been incorporated into the liturgical life of Anglicanism.

Thus, the *shape* of the liturgy is one example of an emerging liturgical consensus. Most of the basic *texts* (gloria, creed, sanctus, Lord's prayer and so on) are common texts produced ecumenically. Some of the *eucharistic prayers* are either the work of informal ecumenical working groups (e.g. an ecumenical English translation of the oldest version of the anaphora of Basil the Great) or based on a common ancient text (e.g., the prayer from the *Apostolic Tradition* attributed to Hippolytus). The *readings* are from the *Common Lectionary,* and commentaries written on the lectionary have an ecumenical dimension which, in turn, can create a new ecumenical openness in preaching.

Other elements of liturgical celebration also witness to a remarkable convergence. Contemporary hymn books, for instance, reflect a sharing of musical resources. Reforms in liturgical space are pursued in common. The alb, once a distinctly "catholic" liturgical garment, has emerged as the quasi-ecumenical garb of liturgical ministers in many Western traditions and has become the standard basic garment worn by Anglicans in eucharistic worship. The overall effect of this on Anglicanism has been of tremendous significance. While modern Anglican liturgical books are unmistakably Anglican in character, they are also unmistakably ecumenical. Anglicans remain bound to one another around the world through their common liturgical heritage of the *Book of Common Prayer*, but they are also increasingly bound to other churches by the emerging ecumenical liturgical consensus.

The renewal of worship and an emerging ecumenical culture

Anglicans, like Christians in general, are increasingly exposed to one another's liturgical celebrations through both direct attendance at services and television. When they visit or watch the liturgical celebrations of other churches (particularly baptism and eucharist) there is a feeling of "being at home". Parish clergy often report how parishioners, on returning from travels during which they worshipped with friends in churches of other traditions, express the sense of familiarity with the liturgical shape, texts and music they have experienced when away. Increasingly, Bible study groups meet locally and include members of various churches. As these groups study the Sunday pericopes from the *Common Lectionary*, they rediscover scripture as a common inheritance, and are often struck by the similarity of interpretation of the pericopes by the previous Sunday's preacher. Thus biblical preaching has become a uniting element. Pastors, too, often meet weekly to discuss the Sunday pericopes and, thus, a certain ecumenical insight is brought to bear on the biblical text.

The overall effect of this is one which has created a sense of ecumenical culture and presses afresh Archbishop Temple's concern that division at the Lord's table is "the greatest of all scandals in the face of the world". The past few decades have witnessed an increasingly open attitude towards eucharistic hospitality, and a growing conviction that eucharistic sharing is the common fare of Christians as they work towards Christian unity. An increasing commitment to a baptismal ecclesiology, which has been fundamental to the three statements of the International Anglican Liturgical Consultation on baptism, eucharist and ministry, has heightened the awareness that baptism is complete admission into the church catholic which, in turn, renews its baptismal faith at the weekly celebration of the Sunday eucharist.

NOTES

[1] Articles which sought to set down, within the mid-16th century context, as much as was necessary to secure catholic faith and order in the Church of England. Historically, candidates for ordination were required to assent to the Articles before their ordination to the diaconate.

[2] A collection of sermons first published in 1547, and subsequently expanded and revised, which was required to be owned by all parishes and used as a basis for reading, studying, and preaching from scripture.

[3] Fifth International Anglican Liturgical Consultation, Dublin 1995, principle no. 3.

[4] Successive meetings of the International Anglican Liturgical Consultation (IALC) have affirmed that baptism admits to the eucharist and that all the baptized, regardless of age, are communicants. The first IALC (Boston 1985) recommended "that the general communion of all the baptized assume a significant place in all ecumenical dialogues in which Anglicans are engaged", *Children and Communion*, Grove Books, Bramcote, Nottingham, UK, 1985, IV, viii. The Boston Principles and Recommendations were incorporated into "Walk in Newness of Life," the statement of IALC-5 (Toronto 1991) which was devoted to Christian initiation. See also *Christian Initiation in the Anglican Communion*, David R. Holeton ed., Grove Books, Bramcott, Nottingham, UK, 1991, and *Growing in Newness of Life: Christian Initiation in Anglicanism Today*, David R. Holeton ed., Anglican Book Centre, Toronto, 1993.

[5] See *The Second World Conference on Faith and Order Held at Edinburgh, August 3-18, 1937*, Leonard Hodgson ed., New York, MacMillan, 1938, p.19 ; also printed under the title "Christian Unity" in *Religious Experience and Other Essays and Addresses by William Temple*, Canon A.E. Baker ed., London, James Clarke, 1958, p.156.

[6] With the publication of the instruction *Liturgiam Authenticam*, ICEL formally withdrew its participation in ELLC. Roman Catholic participation in the Consultation continues through the various regional/national groups which include RC participation. Many parties hope that the present difficulties are temporary and ELLC looks forward to the day when ICEL will again be able to participate formally in its meetings.

Worship in the Mennonite Tradition in Germany

CORINNA SCHMIDT

• MENNONITE •

Before saying something about our Mennonite understanding of worship, I should like first to make a few remarks concerning the constitution of our community. I speak on behalf of the fifty or so congregations which are grouped together in the *Arbeitsgemeinschaft mennonitischer Gemeinden* (council of Mennonite congregations). Besides these there are also Russian migrant congregations and the *Bund Taufgesinnter Gemeinden* (federation of baptismally linked congregations), for which I cannot speak.

Moreover, in the Mennonite understanding each congregation is autonomous, which means that its character, activities, and hence also its celebration of worship are shaped by its own particular tradition and development at any given time. This in turn depends on the people who are active in the work of the congregation. There is therefore no "order book" for general use in worship, and no uniform liturgy. Many congregations also have both full-time preachers, male and female, and lay preachers who set different emphases in worship. So there is no such thing as "the Mennonite service".

The fundamental understanding, for our tradition, of the nature and purpose of worship

Worship is understood as the ministry of the word. It is about listening to God's word, so preaching or proclamation play a central role. This is visually expressed in many churches by the position of the pulpit, which is placed in the centre of the chancel. The spoken word, including prayers, is said facing the congregation. Preachers never stand with their backs to the congregation.

The sense of community is central in worship and this is reflected differently in different congregations:
- there may be a "sing-in" in preparation for worship;
- there may be moments of free prayer in worship;
- there is a place for detailed announcements, for instance about people who are sick, or about the different activities of the congregation.

Community is also expressed in the preparation of the service, which is seldom organized by only one person. Communion services in particular involve many people.

In this connection, it may also be interesting to mention that the places where we meet for worship are generally not church buildings, but rooms of various kinds. Worship services may also be held in someone's living room, and people are brought much closer together by this "intimate" atmosphere where there is no space between the worshippers and preachers. The congregation may also sit in a circle. As many congregations are very scattered, the coffee hour which follows the service is also part of the worship fellowship. The Sunday service is the meeting place for the community.

Distinctive aspects and qualities of our worship

Different as the congregations are, there are still certain essential elements of worship: the sermon, prayers (of thanksgiving and intercession), hymns, announcements and blessing.

Prayer is generally a prepared element of the liturgy, but some congregations traditionally have times of silent prayer or forms of free prayer. In most congregations the Lord's prayer is said every Sunday.

As regards hymns, we have a common *Mennonite Hymn Book*, but each congregation has other resources as well – song folders, perhaps, or songsheets. The Aaronite blessing (Num. 6:24-26) may be used as the spoken blessing, but this is not uniformly the case.

There are variable elements in the service, depending on the situation of each congregation.

The Lord's supper is generally celebrated four times a year. On some occasions a different aspect of the meal is emphasized – in the Hamburg congregation, for instance, a harvest thanksgiving service is held sitting at tables and the emphasis is strongly on the community aspect of the Lord's supper.

One element in worship can be testimonies, when people tell the congregation about their experience with God, and where they have clearly felt God at work within them. Finally, since we have no fixed liturgy, great freedom is left to whoever is preaching to shape the service.

Ecumenical influences on our worship life

Here again the ecumenical influence varies greatly depending on the nature of the congregation. One common feature in all our congregations is the fact that we have many interconfessional marriages. As Mennonites try to practise the priesthood of all believers, elements from other confessions are naturally introduced: for example, the responsive reading of a psalm, music from Taizé, or the tradition of pilgrimage.

Another influence is certainly also the long-established common ecumenical services, such as the World Day of Prayer. The experience of these, for example, the practice of rituals such as anointing, gives our own congregations new ideas for Sunday worship. A few courageous women have also tried to introduce some of the elements of the World Day of Prayer tradition into Sunday worship.

New developments in our worship life

There are some Mennonite communities which are very missionary or evangelical in their approach. In their services they place a strong emphasis on free prayer, testimonies and praise and adoration. They are very free in style and largely reject set prayers as not being "genuine" enough.

A new development in the last few years, mainly in southern Germany, is evening services for young people. These are very charismatic in style and draw a large attendance. A completely different set of songs is used at these services. Some of our sisters and brothers are sceptical about this development because it is moving away from a community celebration of worship. It also raises theological questions, because these services convey a very specific image of God, focusing solely on God as King and Ruler. However, these new developments also challenge our very "plain" preaching services. In the ecumenical context these forms are no doubt something of a hindrance, especially in traditions for which this kind of worship experience is entirely foreign.

One or two special types of service should also be mentioned. We have what are called discussion services, based on a Bible study. Then there are issue-related services picking up concerns and questions from the congregation, and regular family services by which we try to bring even the youngest children into the community. In these services there is no sermon in the traditional sense.

Finally, I think it is important to say that in many places we try on different occasions to hold ecumenical services with neighbouring congregations. We do this at a Sunday service so that everyone comes together under the one roof, leaving the other church empty. In other words, ecumenical fellowship is not confined to the ecumenical Bible week, the World Day of Prayer or other "special" occasions.

Baptist Worship in Ecumenical Perspective[1]

NATHAN NETTLETON

• BAPTIST •

Any attempt to write in general terms about Baptist theology and practice of worship must commence with an acknowledgment of the fraught nature of the attempt. Baptists have historically been committed to the autonomy of the local congregation in most areas of theology and practice, including worship. Contrary to popular opinion, this conviction is not just a belief that each congregation should be free to get things wrong in its own unique way, but one that God leads each congregation in differing ways, taking into account their unique context, culture and giftedness. It is, you might say, the principle of liturgical inculturation pushed to its logical limit. Baptists then, do not usually seek to express or symbolize their unity by agreeing on texts or patterns of worship that will be common to many congregations. Rather they have seen liturgical diversity as an inevitable consequence of each congregation discerning and faithfully responding to a God who values and utilizes their particularity. Historically they have tended to rally round the cause of common mission, rather than common prayer.

Influences: theological and historical

The beginnings of Baptist worship

Questions about worship were significant in the disputes which saw the first Baptists take the separatist path in the early 17th century, but they were concerned not so much with form or style as with authority. By what authority does the church determine its liturgical practice? Their answer was that scripture is the sole external authority. From this conviction came two distinctive liturgical stances: baptism for believers only, and non-conformity.

Although the early Baptists were best known, and indeed named, for a liturgical distinctive, the limitation of baptism to believers only and the preference for immersion as its mode does not presuppose a general liturgical style. Indeed, most Christian traditions today affirm immersion as the preferred mode, and the baptism of conscious converts as the normative model, but these convictions are expressed across the full spectrum of Christian liturgical styles.

The same is true of non-conformity. Liturgical non-conformity is the refusal to conform to a pattern of worship dictated by an earthly authority. The Puritan movement was committed to taking its liturgical cues from scripture alone and was thus unwilling to conform to any pattern of worship not mandated by the Bible. One thing that distinguished the Baptists as they emerged from the Puritan movement was that they were non-conformist in principle rather than simply in the particulars – many Puritans were no less willing to impose liturgical conformity than was the Church of England; they merely disagreed over what should be imposed. The Baptists, by contrast, held that the interpretation of the scriptural witness could not be imposed either, and that each congregation was responsible for discerning how God, through the scriptures, was calling them to order their worship.

It can be seen, then, that the reasons Baptists took their separatist path included the desire to escape a particular liturgical conformity, but not a desire to create an alternative conformity. Indeed, openness to changes of practice as "more light and truth broke forth from God's word"[2] was frequently affirmed in the early Baptist writings and confessions of faith. These starting points meant that Baptist liturgical practice was always likely to be responsive to new liturgical trends, but unlikely to be uniformly influenced in any one direction. Indeed, most of the significant shifts have been either derivative or reactionary, and have led to more diversity, not less.[3]

The liturgical style of the first Baptist congregations was simply a continuation of what had been taking place within their particular sector of the Puritan movement. The extreme rejection of prepared materials that characterized the first congregation (led by John Smyth in 1608) was not common to all Puritans, but neither was it unique to those who became Baptists. Within half a century there was such a significant move "backwards" – towards prepared patterns in the interests of order and dignity – that by 1691 prominent Baptist leaders such as Benjamin Keach could openly advocate the careful composition of hymns, sermons and prayers.[4]

Revivalist developments

During the latter part of the 18th century, the Evangelical revival swept across British Protestantism and had a massive impact on the Baptists. Studies of this have mostly focused on the movement's impact on the Baptists' mission, evangelism and sense of identity, but less attention has been given to its impact on their worship. This was, however, significant, generating the beginnings of a shift in the understanding of the purpose of worship: the revivalist passion for procuring conversions led to the worship service being seen as an instrument to be employed for this task. This shift influenced Baptist worship in Britain, but its biggest impact was on the American frontier. American revivalism, expressed most clearly in the form of the "camp meeting", developed a liturgical pattern that was oriented almost entirely to the "harvest" of souls.[5] The change can be traced in the increasing anthropocentricity of American hymnody, and it produced a "shift from subtlety to straightforwardness" in liturgical language, imagery and architecture.[6] However, these changes were neither universal among Baptists nor unique to them, for frontier revivalism reshaped virtually all Protestant traditions in the USA.[7]

The ecumenical and liturgical renewal movements

This same pattern of evolution continued in the 20th century, as sectors of the Baptist communion embraced major liturgical changes in response to patterns encountered in broader movements. The influence of the ecumenical movement has been widespread, but low key, apparent mainly in a more frequent borrowing of resources, especially for occasions such as weddings and funerals. Because Baptist ecumenical engagement has occurred primarily at the local level, this pattern of borrowing has further diversified Baptist practice.

The influence of the liturgical renewal movement has not been widespread among Baptists, but it has been profound among some and can be clearly seen in many of the liturgical resources being produced by and for Baptists.[8] It is something of a paradox that Baptists have been so slow to connect with this movement, since so much of its work has involved recovering some of the earliest layers of Christian worship practice — a quest for which Baptists have often strongly avowed their affinity.

The charismatic and church growth movements

The instinct for fidelity to early church patterns is greatly counteracted in much Baptist thinking and practice about worship by the revivalist tendency to view worship as an evangelistic tool, and a consequent willingness to reshape that tool in the interests of maintaining its effectiveness in a changing world and in disparate contexts. This is apparent in the influence of two other movements. The charismatic renewal movement has had a very widespread influence, especially when one notes the number of churches which, though not embracing the public use of gifts such as glossolalia, have been greatly influenced by the movement's liturgical patterns and music.

The church growth movement has also had considerable influence. Seeing congregational size as the indisputable measure of God's blessing, it has produced "mega-churches" with big-production, performance-oriented liturgies.[9] The "seeker sensitive service" has also emerged from this movement. If churches had heeded the argument of the movement's leaders that (since this is not a worship service but an evangelistic event) they need to have another occasion in the week to meet for worship, this could have generated a renewed understanding of worship as the community's praise of God. However, this has not occurred on any noticeable scale; and where it has been attempted, the pattern of the seeker event seems also to be the governing form for the worship service.[10] Although this movement may claim Baptist origins, it is neither confined to Baptist churches nor developing as a natural expression of something avowedly "Baptist". Instead it may simply represent a marriage between evangelical revivalism and the growth principles of modern business culture.

This history suggests that Baptist liturgical practice has never developed a unique pattern of its own. Although in particular eras or areas there has been the "familiar paradox" of virtual uniformity in free-church worship,[11] when read over four centuries and several continents, the most notable feature of Baptist liturgical history has been its openness to change. As is the case in several denominations, the diversity is greater now than ever before; but it is nevertheless still possible to identify some dominant types.

Dominant patterns in Baptist worship

The *reformed service of the word* has been the most prevalent liturgical form among Baptists for much of their history, and outside America it has remained so until recent decades. Incorporating hymn singing, prayers, scripture and preaching, it is essentially the historic fourfold order without the liturgy of the Table. In some places the fourfold movement has still been clearly evident, with the intercessions, offering and prayers of thanksgiving following the sermon; but as the sermon came to be seen as the climax of worship, these elements were more frequently to be found preceding it. Intercessions and thanksgivings are commonly combined into one extended "pastoral prayer", led from the pulpit or lectern. Usually the only books in use were the Bible and the hymnbook – but many Baptist hymnbooks contained liturgical settings of psalms, canticles and prayers for congregations to chant in unison or read responsively. Baptist sources, though, have always provided such material in forms which, like the hymns, assumed the occasional selection of material rather than its ordinary usage within a fixed liturgical form.

The Lord's supper has been celebrated with varying levels of frequency. Weekly observance has been rare, quarterly more common, and monthly probably the most prevalent, although observing it in different weeks in morning and evening services has often allowed fortnightly communion. Until a generation ago, the observance of the Table was often appended to the main service, after the dismissal; and although this originated for reasons similar to those behind the ancient dismissal of the catechumens before the eucharist, in many places it led to communion being seen as an optional "extra". Memorialism has tended to be the dominant understanding of the eucharist, often leading to an almost funereal tone. A recent variant on this service, influenced by the charismatic movement, has seen the hymns (which previously were interspersed through the service) replaced by a contemporary genre of praise songs, grouped into an extended "worship time" at the beginning of the service. The retention of other formal elements, such as scripture readings and intercessory prayer, still distinguish this variant from the contemporary praise-and-worship form described below.

The *revivalist service*, as has already been noted, came to prominence in the evangelical revivals of the late 18th and 19th centuries. It quickly became the dominant pattern in the USA and, more gradually, elsewhere as well. The service has a threefold pattern based on the order of the evangelistic rally.[12] The first part, often simply called the "preliminaries", consists of rousing singing and testimonies. The second and longest part is the preaching, which is oriented towards securing a response of repentance and dedication. The third part, once commonly known as the "harvest" or the "altar call", is the calling of penitents to express their decision by coming forth to pray and be prayed over; in some places, this part included immediate baptism.

Scripture reading and intercessory prayer have tended to diminish in prominence over time, with scripture often being reduced to an introduction or illustrations in the sermon, and intercession for the world outside often disappearing altogether. Observance of the Lord's supper varied. In some places it continued as an addendum after the main service. In others it became a token inclusion in the "preliminaries" before the sermon. Generally in revivalist services it became less frequent, and in some places disappeared almost entirely.

The *contemporary praise-and-worship service* emerged in the latter part of the 20th century under the influence of the charismatic movement and has become the dominant form in much of the Baptist world, either in a pure form or hybridized with the reformed service of the word as described above. It has much in common with the revivalist service, and indeed grew from it, but via a detour through Pentecostalism. Essentially it employs the order and music of Pentecostalism but removes, or downplays, the spontaneous prophetic input from the congregation (including glossolalia). Often the order of the service is identical to the revivalist form but the first part, now frequently known as the "worship time", is given greater prominence and understood not just as a warm-up, but as a journey into an intimate worshipful encounter with God. The metaphor of moving through the courts of the Tabernacle towards the Holy of Holies is often employed to explain this action. The congregational singing which dominates this first part is led from the front by a "praise band", and employs a light rock musical genre with the words of the songs invariably projected on screens for the people to see. Some use of responsive prayers is reappearing within these services, but rebadged as "praise shouts" with the words projected, and a strong percussion accompaniment setting the rhythm. The third part of the service, now known as the "ministry time", is less focused on the conversion of the unchurched, and includes prayers for healing and sanctification, or for a deeper experience of God and an intensified commitment to God.

In some places, especially under the influence of prosperity doctrines, this form is now being seen as a two-part order. The first part, known as the "act of worship", is an extended bracket of songs, beginning with upbeat praise and moving into a more intimate worship mode; this is followed by an exhortation to sacrificial giving (with the promise of God's blessing in return), and the collection of the tithes and offerings. The second part, the "act of commitment", consists of the sermon, usually oriented towards securing a commitment to faithful Christian living (with a promise of earthly blessings for those who do so), and then the "ministry time" during which people come forward to express their response in fervent prayer for themselves and one another.

Worship in the *African-American Baptist* churches is structurally similar to that of the revivalist and praise-and-worship styles, but it is distinct enough in ethos and expression to be identified separately. It is almost without parallel in the extent to which the people's identity and experience (including, especially, their suffering) are fully and redemptively expressed in the worship event.

The *ancient-future worship service* has emerged in the Baptist scene only recently, and it will be interesting to see whether it fulfils the claims that some are making for it.[13] Essentially it is an evangelical reappropriation of the classical fourfold shape of worship, complete with scripted participatory liturgies and "high-church" multi-sensory symbolism. What sets this movement apart from the established liturgical churches is a very free-church attitude to the authorization of liturgical practices and texts, and often a more playful approach to the linguistic forms used in worship, and to the use of space and action.

Family resemblances

Despite the extraordinary diversity represented in the above descriptions of worship, some features can be identified as constituting some identifiable Baptist "family traits".

The first would be the importance ascribed to personal sincerity and individual experience. Baptists have generally understood worship as the outpouring of the believing heart, and so tend to value the sincerity with which each individual enters into the liturgy above the content, structure or aesthetic quality of the corporate action of the liturgical event. Similarly they will be less likely to judge the success of the liturgical event by its overall correctness or profundity, than by the depth of the experience which the individual worshippers have within it.

A second characteristic trait of Baptist worship is the centrality of preaching. While Baptist preaching has ranged from carefully crafted, sober expositions of scripture, to emotional extempore pleadings for conversion, it has always been regarded as a central and essential ingredient of the worship service. Indeed, in some places Baptists have been known to speak of attending a sermon rather than attending worship, and the sermon has sometimes occupied as much as three quarters of the total service time.

Another characteristic trait of Baptist worship is the prominence of singing. Although the early Baptists argued over whether it was acceptable to sing texts other than biblical psalms and canticles, spirited singing has always been a feature of Baptist worship. The early debates were quickly settled, and Baptists were the first churches to introduce congregational hymn singing in 17th-century England. The 20th century has seen a rapid expansion in the range of material for congregational singing, as well as a proliferation of new musical styles and accompanying instruments. In the contemporary praise-and-worship services in particular, with their light rock music and band, singing has come to occupy an even more prominent place in the worship. In fact, to many Baptists the word "worship" has come to refer to the time the congregation spends in song.

Extempore prayer is another notable characteristic of Baptist worship. Arising from the emphasis on personal sincerity noted above, Baptists have generally valued the prayer that flows spontaneously from the heart above that which has been crafted by others for congregational use. In some places and times, Baptists have frowned even on pastors writing out their own prayers for use in public worship – let alone using a prayer from a book. However, there have also been many Baptists who have recognized that the Holy Spirit can inspire pastors at least as well in their studies as in the pulpit, and that prayer can have an impressive as well as an expressive function.[14] Well-crafted prayers can serve to impress both the truth of the gospel and the language and rhythms of prayer on the heart and mind. However, even in the recent contemporary praise-and-worship and ancient-future styles (which are more dependent on pre-composed texts than any previous form of Baptist worship) it would be very unusual to find no opportunity provided for extempore prayer, either from the worship leader or with congregational participation.

This though leads us to the final characteristic trait: the widespread Baptist ambivalence towards written liturgical texts. Since their beginnings, the significance Baptists have ascribed to personal sincerity and extempore prayer has frequently expressed itself in a distrust (and even outright rejection) of pre-composed liturgical materials. At the same time, however, the steady increase in the amount of singing in Baptist worship has meant that more and more of that worship is dependent on the use of written liturgical texts. Indeed, the widespread use of hymnals as a source of spiritual writings to aid personal devotion is evidence of how Baptists have valued the impressive function of written texts – even if they have usually not recognized its correlation with the use of prayer books in other traditions. Clearly most Baptists have failed to note that what they do in song, and what other traditions do in chant or spoken word, are functionally the same. Thus there continues to be a widespread dissonance between what Baptists think they do and what they actually do in their worship.[15]

Ecumenical issues

When considering the implications of present-day Baptist liturgical thinking and practice for ecumenical participation and engagement, and for the search for Christian unity, a number of issues stand out.

Common liturgical texts

The first concerns the emphasis, in ecumenical dialogue, on the quest for common liturgical texts as a pathway to greater unity. This quest is essentially foreign to the Baptist mindset. While it is recognized that things such as a common hymnal have sometimes fostered a greater sense of familial bond between Baptist congregations, Baptists have never seen differences in worship language, style or structure as an obstacle to unity, even among themselves. Conversely, however, the quest for common patterns and texts in worship may well prove, in itself, to be an obstacle to unity for Baptists. The belief that God's call to each congregation is particular, and the consequent insistence on protecting each congregation's right to discern and obey the details of that call without external human interference, mean that Baptists do not begin with the assumption that greater homogeneity in worship is a desirable objective. Rather, they would tend to suspect that the quest for common worship might come at the expense of the Spirit's mission of incarnating the body of Christ in each community in ways which are truly indigenous to it.

The "ecumenical consensus" on the structure of worship

A second issue relates to where the majority of Baptists stand with regard to the so-called "ecumenical consensus" on worship. It could justifiably be argued that the biggest divides between churches no longer follow denominational lines, but are between churches whose worship conforms to the traditional fourfold structure of the "ecumenical consensus", and those whose worship follows the three- or twofold structures identified above in the descriptions of revivalist and contemporary praise-and-worship styles. There is considerable conversation and cooperation among congregations from different denominations on each side of this divide, but very little *across* the divide, even among congregations of the same denominational affiliation. The responsibility for this divide is mutual; but it is apparent that the very language of "consensus", or even of "convergence", serves to exclude those who do not subscribe to it.

This is not a specifically Baptist issue, but since the majority of them do not identify with the liturgical "consensus" they more readily find partners for conversation and cooperation among those whose worship forms they share, including the Pentecostals and those of the traditional denominations who have adopted revivalist and pentecostal worship structures. Until real progress is made in promoting significant understanding and respect across this divide, most Baptists will not see much relevance in the "ecumenical" endeavours taking place on the other side. If the ancient-future worship movement grows as rapidly among Baptists as some are predicting, this is likely to bring more Baptists into conversation with those on the "consensus" side – but only through a switching of sides, not a healing of the rift.

Ordination and liturgical presidency

A third issue, or rather group of issues, surrounds Baptist understandings of the relationship between ordination and liturgical presidency. There have been eras in Baptist history when the leadership of worship has been largely the exclusive preserve of the ordained pastors, but this is increasingly rare today. In some of those eras sacramental presidency was reserved to the clergy, but even then it seems probable that this was done for the sake of decency and public image, rather than because of any widespread conviction that the sacraments would other-wise be rendered invalid.[16]

Baptists in general do not think of the church in institutional, but rather in congregational, terms and so they would assert that where a group of believers congregate and bind themselves to one another to offer themselves as the body of Christ, there is the church and the full-ness thereof.[17] They will not regard their celebration of eucharist as being dependent on the validation of the congregation, or its presider, by any outside body. While most Baptists would argue this simply on grounds of congregational autonomy, a case can be made that the most intrinsically Baptist position on this matter locates sacramental priest-hood in the baptized status of the gathered congregation, rather than the ordained status of any individual within it.[18] This is not simply a "lay presidency" position, but a view of presidency as being congregational. This view would hold that where two or three gather in his name, there is Christ, embodied in them, presiding at his own Table. Because bap-tism is thus seen as ordination for ministry and the religious life, it can be argued that far from abolishing the clergy, Baptists have instead abol-ished the laity![19]

In practice this is not to dispense with the ordained ministry, but it does make clear that ordained ministry is delegated from the congrega-tion. Commitment to the threefold ordering of ministry, and episcopal succession, is extremely rare among Baptists; and since they usually order their ministry at the local level, there is little likelihood of this changing in a widespread way. While it is true that Baptist understand-ings of ordination are another issue on which Baptists have never man-aged to achieve any solid consensus, it is also true that they would not usually see the lack of consensus as an obstacle to unity. To many other churches, though, the Baptist practices are likely to be a significant obstacle.

Conclusion

The most notable feature of Baptist worship practice, especially when looked at across the centuries as well as around the globe, is its diversity. Neither their history nor their theology has wedded Baptists to any one liturgical pattern or style and, far from being an accident or oversight, this diversity is actually something which Baptists have a the-ological commitment to protecting. They hold that God values and utilizes the particularity of their giftedness and their context, and calls them to develop patterns of worship and discipleship which will best serve the cause of God's reign in their own lives and locality. Historically then, they have tended to rally round the cause of common mission rather than common worship.

Tragically, large sectors of the Baptist communion have abandoned this historic expectation of diversity, and sought to secure a conformity which both isolates them from the rest of the Christian church and fundamentally transgresses the heritage of their Baptist forebears. However, for the rest of the Baptist family it remains paradoxically true that it may be precisely the diversity of theology and practice which they are unwilling to eliminate from their own ranks – and which they would consider to be a model for unity – that ends up being the biggest obstacle to their involvement in the quests for a fuller visible unity in the Christian church.

NOTES

[1] Some parts of this chapter first appeared in a thesis entitled *The Liturgical Expression of Baptist Identity* submitted by the author in 2001 in partial fulfilment of the requirements for the degree of master of theology from the Melbourne College of Divinity.

[2] The saying itself is attributed to John Robinson, a Pilgrim father, in 1620.

[3] Ernest Payne's historical survey bears this out: "The Free Church Tradition and Worship", *The Baptist Quarterly*, 21, 1965, pp.51-63.

[4] *The Breach Repaired in God's Worship,* London, John Hancock, 1691, pp.138-39.

[5] David T. Priestly, "The Impact of Revivalism on Baptists in North America", in *Baptist Faith and Witness: The Papers of the Study and Research Division of the Baptist World Alliance – 1990-1995*, William H. Brackney and L. A. (Tony) Cupit eds, Birmingham, Alabama, Samford UP, 1995, pp.69-70.

[6] Thomas R. McKibbens, Jr, "Our Baptist Heritage in Worship", *Review and Expositor,* 80, 1983, pp.63-65.

[7] James White, "The Classification of Protestant Traditions of Worship", *Studia Liturgica,* 17, 1987, p.271.

[8] Michael Walker, "Baptist Worship in the Twentieth Century", in *Baptists in the Twentieth Century*, K. W. Clements ed., London, Baptist Historical Society, 1983, pp.23-25.

[9] Raymond Bailey, "The Changing Face of Baptist Worship", *Review and Expositor*, 95, 1998, pp.49-50.

[10] Donald P. Hustad, *True Worship: Reclaiming the Wonder and Majesty,* Carol Stream IL, Hope Publishing and Wheaton IL, Harold Shaw, 1998, pp.230-31.

[11] Ken Manley, "The Way We Were – Worship in Australian Churches in 1900 – The Baptists", *Australian Journal of Liturgy*, 1, 1988, p.156.

[12] It is, however, arguable that this pattern did not begin with the evangelistic camp meetings, but with Zwingli's service of the word in which the confession of sins immediately after the sermon became the concluding act of worship.

[13] Robert Webber, who popularized the phrase, suggests that it may become the dominant pattern among post-modern evangelicals. See, for example, his ancientfutureworship.com website or his books, notably *Ancient-Future Faith*, Grand Rapids MI, Baker, 1999.

[14] Christopher Ellis, "Baptist Worship", in *The New SCM Dictionary of Liturgy and Worship*, Paul Bradshaw ed., London, SCM Press, 2002, p.55.

[15] It is also worth noting that in the last half century there have been some Baptists making significant contributions to the production of liturgical texts. Stephan Winward, Neville Clark, Alec Gilmore and Paul Sheppy in the UK and John Skoglund in the USA have been especially prominent.

[16] Marjorie Warkentin, *Ordination: A Biblical-Historical View*, Grand Rapids MI, Eerdmans, 1982, pp.78-84.

[17] Baptist World Alliance, "Towards A Baptist Identity: A Statement Ratified by the Baptist Heritage Commission in Zagreb, Yugoslavia, July 1989", reproduced in Walter Shurden, *The Baptist Identity: Four Fragile Freedoms*, Macon GA, Smyth & Helwys, 1993, p.64.

[18] Nathan Nettleton, "Eucharistic Celebration – A Baptist Perspective" in *Eucharist: Experience & Testimony*, Tom Knowles ed., Melbourne, David Lovell, 2001, pp.180-85.

[19] Paul Bradshaw, "Patterns of Ministry", *Studia Liturgica*, 15, 1981, pp.57-58.

Worship in the Religious Society of Friends (Quakers)

JANET SCOTT

• QUAKER •

Worship is at the heart of Quaker experience. For God is met in the gathered meeting and, through the Spirit, leads us into ways of life and understandings of truth which we recognize as "Quaker". As we follow these leadings in our community and in the wider world we are enabled to reflect on their meaning, testing our vision within our discipline and tradition.[1]

The diversity within the Quaker tradition

The Quaker movement began in Britain during the mid-17th century. It was part of the religious ferment of the period of the civil war and the commonwealth, and incorporated influences from puritanism and anabaptism. Initially, it appears to have been millenarian as well as charismatic. It challenged many accepted religious practices of its time, and established practices of equality between men and women, rich and poor, adults and children, based on an understanding that authority belongs to Christ, who has "come to teach his people himself".

In the period of the Restoration, which brought much persecution, Quaker theology changed from being millenarian to being a realized eschatology, to an understanding that Christ has redeemed his people and it is possible now to live in the redeemed and restored life. In the late 1660s, George Fox brought the sometimes-undisciplined charismatic behaviour of Quakers into a structure of meetings, a "gospel-order", which provided a way of organizing and disciplining the church and of making decisions.

The fundamental character of the worship established during this period was of waiting upon God and speaking only that which was directly inspired by the Holy Spirit. This inspiration could come through anyone who was present. On occasions, when adults were in prison for their faith, children kept the public meetings for worship open. Essentially worship was inward, and needed no outward forms or rituals.

There has been much variation in the interpretation of this fundamental Quaker understanding of worship. At the time of George Fox, Quakers expected long meetings for worship, perhaps up to three hours; and they expected Friends like Fox to speak at length when so moved. Later Quakers were affected by the Enlightenment and by Quietism, and 18th-century worship was characterized by an increase in the reliance on silence. There was, however, a system of recording ministers – that is, those whose vocal ministry was considered to be helpful, and spiritually grounded, were so recognized by their local meeting and could be given the authority of a "travelling minute", enabling them to travel to other meetings and to be recognized there. This practice of "travelling" in the ministry preserved many contacts between meetings, and helped in the preservation of common understandings of faith and practice among Quakers. It was such ministers who most frequently attended Yearly Meetings.

In the 19th century Quakers in Britain, Ireland and the United States – then the main centres of Quakerism – became increasingly "evangelical". In the United States there were splits within Quaker meetings. These had complex causes, but resulted in there being some meetings with a more evangelical, and some with a more liberal, theology. Initially worship was largely the same in these different strands of the Quaker tradition. But for some of the more evangelical Friends (as they moved westwards and came under the influence of the revival movement) a more "programmed"[2] or semi-"programmed" form of worship was found desirable. During the 1880s, some of these meetings adapted the system of "recorded ministers" to a pastoral system. This reflected an important shift: whereas ministers were not paid for their ministry, pastors were seen as being "released" from some, or all, of their need to earn a living in order to provide support for the programmed worship (and perhaps for the pastoral care) of the community. However, neither ministers nor pastors were regarded as being "ordained" in the sense used in other churches.

During the 20th century British Quakerism, along with the small European and Australasian meetings which have been established or influenced from Britain, has moved from an evangelical to a more liberal theology, and has given up the recording of ministers. Ireland remains largely evangelical in theology, and unprogrammed in worship. The United States has both liberal and evangelical strands, the latter including both those with the traditional unprogrammed worship and those whose worship is programmed. Missionaries from the United States have established the Quaker tradition in parts of Africa (especially Kenya) and in South and Central America (especially Bolivia and Guatemala), and these meetings are programmed and pastored.

There is increasing contact among the different strands of the Quaker tradition, and attempts to understand and to recognize one another. Nevertheless it must be admitted that, at different ends of the Quaker spectrum, there are churches which are so similar to Protestant churches that their Quakerism seems to be only historic; and meetings with such a universalist or humanist slant that their Christianity seems to be only historic. However, despite this variety and complexity, there are distinctive Quaker understandings of worship, and these are firmly rooted in a distinctive Quaker understanding of Christianity.

The Quaker distinctives

The first – and perhaps defining – aspect of Quakerism is the experience of, and belief in, direct access to God without any human intermediary. Although this access to God is understood by Quakers as being available to all of humanity, this is a Christian understanding because of the Quaker experience, and understanding, of the God to whom this access is available. God is experienced as more than a creator, and the experience of God is described in the tradition in ways which relate to Christ (as for example, the Inward Teacher, the Light, the Priest), and in ways which relate to the Holy Spirit. The experience within worship of being taught, of being moved to speak, of being called into a ministry of word or action, are all experiences which are only explicable within a Christian and biblical tradition and language.

A second, closely related aspect is the emphasis on the inward rather than the outward. This is shown in the rejection of the outward elements of sacraments such as water and bread and wine, in favour of the understanding of sacramental living as a transforming process of the activity of the Holy Spirit in the whole of life. Allied to this is the rejection of creeds as a way of indicating belief, in favour of the integrity required when faith is carried out in life. Here again, though, it is aspects of Christian practice which are rejected; Quakerism itself is Christian. It depends on Christian understandings of sacrament as a way in which God operates within individuals and communities and, through them, within the world. And it depends on Christian and biblical understandings of how the activity of the Holy Spirit is able to be recognized in human lives.

A third distinctive aspect of Quakerism is in the testimonies. Quakers are not alone in seeing that religion is a way of life; in fact this view is common to most religions. Quaker ethics are, in general, Christian, and the particular testimonies to truth, simplicity, equality and peace cannot be claimed exclusively by Quakers. What may be distinctive is that they are based on an understanding that since God has already acted to redeem the world, the redeemed life may be lived here and now. These testimonies are witness to the characteristics of a life lived under God. They provide, when lived out, the evidence for the truth of Quaker claims to be a Spirit-led community, and the criteria by which Quakers may recognize the Spirit at work in each other and in others.

A fourth distinctive aspect is in the method of conducting meetings for church affairs. Though many religious groups may seek the will of God, the Quaker business meeting depends on being led into unity through the Holy Spirit, which is understood to lead into truth and holiness. The presence of Christ as president and shepherd means that all human leadership is subordinated. Authority is regarded as resting in Christ, as being recognized in the gathered meeting, and as being recorded in the minutes.

The fifth distinctive aspect is the understanding of the Bible as inspired by the same Spirit which teaches the community how to read it. The character of the Holy Spirit thus provides the criteria by which the contents of the Bible are judged; the text will be understood best by those who "walk in the light". Thus Quakers are part of Christianity in recognizing that the Bible has authority, but distinct in subordinating the Bible to the "Spirit which gave it forth".

These distinctives are part of what Quakers mean when we talk of ourselves as "church" and when we claim the characteristics of church: "one, holy, catholic and apostolic". One way of expressing this is to talk of our experience of the Light. The Light is *one* Light. Whether we call it the Light of Christ, or the Inward Light, or the Holy Spirit, it is one and it leads us to unity with itself and so with each other, so that we "know one another in that which is eternal". The Light is *catholic*, worldwide, for it "enlightens everyone that comes into the world"; whether or not, or however, people respond, there is that of God in and for everyone. The Light is *holy* – awesome and ungraspable – it works within us if we let it, showing us our faults, transforming our lives, making us more like itself, and thus more able to join in its work of transforming the world. The Light is *apostolic*, for it is the same Light which the apostles knew, which inspired them in their lives and in their writings and in their decisions; and we too are apostolic if we live in, and are guided by, that same Light.

These characteristics may be found in a Friends church, where the worship includes the singing of hymns, reading from the Bible, vocal prayer led by a member of the church who has thought about the needs of the community and has prepared prayers, a prepared message or sermon given by a pastor or another Friend, and music from a choir. Such programmed worship will also include a period of "open worship" lasting perhaps for twenty minutes, when members of the church will be free to contribute as led by the Spirit. There is usually some flexibility in the worship so that the open worship may be extended if that seems right, and part of the programme left out. The characteristics will also be found in an unprogrammed meeting, lasting for about an hour, which may, in complete silence, experience gathering and centring into the presence of God and which may – or may not – be moved to singing, prayer, teaching or other spoken ministry.

"The validity of worship lies not in its form but in its power."[3] It is the power within the worship that enables Friends to recognize each other. Whether the power is named as God, as Christ or as the Holy Spirit, it is experienced as a Real Presence with the power to transform lives, and through them to transform the world.

Quaker worship

Quaker worship is a process of transformation, one which takes a life-time. The metaphor of the Light helps us to describe it. One of the favourite Quaker metaphors, this is used both of God and of Christ, and describes an active presence. In silent worship, the worshipper can be described as "turning towards the Light". Like spring sunshine coming through a window, revealing the dust and dirt that are waiting to be cleaned away, the Light shows where changes have to be made. But it is also a healing Light, able itself – if permitted – to make the changes which it reveals as being needed. So the Light strengthens and directs and calls, slowly drawing the worshipper towards the realization of what action has to follow. Such action might be the speaking of a word, in worship or afterwards; it might be the call to a deeper life of prayer, or a call to a particular ministry in the meeting or in the world; it can result in child care or peace marches, for there are many different tasks which contribute to the transformation of the world. The essential is faithfulness. Every call which is ignored lessens the ability to hear. But faithful listening and responding, in even the smallest matter, leads to an increased ability to respond to the Light. So worship and action are not separate: the action which is prompted in worship is itself part of the worship.

So also for the words. Quakers have always resisted particular forms of words such as creeds, because the Holy Spirit and its activity cannot be restricted to human words – however accurate a description of the faith they may be. For Quakers, the words also should spring from worship and feed back into the worship. For Fox, before one could speak one had to walk in the Light: "What thou speakest is it inwardly from God?" This gives words both an authority and a provisionality. The authority comes in the recognition, in worship, of the power of the Holy Spirit speaking through a person; the words are "given", not crafted. But they also are provisional for they come through a human vessel, and are given for a particular time and place. The words themselves are a vessel; their function is to turn people to the Word which they find within themselves in their own hearts. Sometimes this happens best through words which are themselves imperfect, broken, so that their beauty or their wisdom does not form a barrier. The Quaker has the task of reaching through the words to the Silence, to that silence of the spirit which is the place where the word of God is spoken, and to bring that word, in fear and trembling, to where it can confront us.

Quakers therefore look for words of prophecy, for the words which come from God and which are effective. These words may bring comfort or offence, hope or brokenness; but they will, in the traditional phrase, "speak to one's condition" and be recognized, deep in the heart, as the words of truth with the power to lead, guide, direct and transform.

It would be foolish to suggest that every meeting for worship, or every Friends church service, reaches this depth or that every word spoken in worship is a word of God. Quakers come to worship as ordinary human beings, albeit with extraordinary expectations. We are as prone to self-centredness, to shallowness, to superficiality, to putting our own thoughts, feelings and worries at the top of our agenda, as anyone else. In the unprogrammed meetings we face a particular temptation to consider that what we deeply feel, or what we are thinking, is necessarily a message to be shared with the meeting. We have to learn what is of the Holy Spirit and what is of the human spirit – and how to tell them apart. But when a gathered meeting, or a church, is open to the Holy Spirit moving within and amongst it, it comes to recognize when, and how, the same Spirit is at work in an individual. At the simplest level, it enables those present to know whether or not a piece of spoken ministry is truly from the Source; at another level, the church can sense, in a Friend, obedience to God and integrity between word and life. It recognizes the Friend it can trust, because it recognizes the Spirit in whom the Friend trusts.

Quakers and the ecumenical movement

Quaker experience of, and interest in, the ecumenical movement varies considerably. Evangelical Friends in general, like those in many evangelical churches, can feel alienated from a movement which they perceive as being too "political" and not sufficiently concerned with spreading the good news of salvation. In some parts of the world, there is little that is ecumenical. Friends in Burundi are deeply concerned about developing forgiveness between rival groups, and in doing so are reaching out to other churches. Where there is more local ecumenical activity, for example in Britain, some Friends have taken an active part.

There is now a much kinder attitude towards other churches than was held in the 17th century, when others were held to be "in the Fall". We recognize the Holy Spirit at work in the lives and worship of other Christians.

At the same time, there is no desire to be so much like other Christians that we lose our distinctiveness. We may, from time to time, worship with other Christians in their way; but our motivation is from fellowship rather than from the expectation of depth and power. We can, of course, be surprised by what we experience in the worship of other Christians. But we can also be irritated by what seems to be "busyness" in liturgy and ritual. In particular we feel that our silence, and the understanding on which it is based, is one of our gifts and treasures which we hold in trust for the whole church. We would point out that our form of worship is open to everyone, and that no one is excluded from any part of it. We therefore offer the whole church a way of worship which is *eucharistic*, and in which all can join together. Let me explain what I mean in using this central Christian term.

An important aspect of the ecumenical movement is the way in which it has encouraged us to think about our worship in common Christian language, rather than only in our own terms. It is this which leads us to see how and when our worship is "eucharistic". Without going into a full description of the eucharist, it might be enough to say that in our silent worship the worshippers offer themselves, and their whole lives, to be joined to the sacrifice of Christ; that they feel the power that cleanses and reconciles them to God and to each other; that they know the real presence of Christ amongst them as teacher, shepherd and priest; and that they are strengthened by the Holy Spirit as a loving and forgiven community and are empowered to go out to do the work of God in the world. In programmed worship also, the aim of the programming is to help the church to reach the same spiritual state, one in which worship is offered "in spirit and in truth". In Paul's words (Rom. 12:1-2), Friends offer ourselves to God as a "living sacrifice", dedicated and fit for God's acceptance, the worship of mind and heart. In letting our minds be remade, and our whole nature transformed, we become able to discern the will of God and to know what is good, acceptable and perfect.

Quakers and renewal from within

Perhaps the newest developments within Quaker worship are coming as we learn from each other, rather than from other churches. With more contact between Friends, some programmed Friends are learning the value of silence, and some unprogrammed Friends are learning the value of planned preparation for worship. We are more prepared to experiment with different forms of Quaker worship than with borrowings from other churches. We are conscious of a need to model, within our own movement, the unity and diversity which we desire for the whole church. We see the importance of reclaiming the meaning of our own name: "Friends". Whilst "Quakers" was a name given to us in about 1650 by others "in scorn" (but is a name which we bear proudly), "Friends" has been our own chosen name since about 1654. It reminds us of the command of Jesus in John 15:12-17: we are his Friends if we love one another as he has loved us.

A world conference of Young Friends from all our traditions met in 1985, and wrote as part of its epistle (message):

> We have often wondered whether there is anything Quakers today can say as one. After much struggle we have discovered that we can proclaim this: there is a living God at the centre of all, who is available to each of us as a Present Teacher at the very heart of our lives. We seek as people of God to be worthy vessels to deliver the Lord's transforming word, to be prophets of joy...We must let our lives mirror what is written on our hearts – to be so full of God's love that we can do no other than to live out our corporate testimonies to the world of honesty, simplicity, equality and peace, whatever the consequences… We have no illusions about the fact that to truly live a Christian life in these cataclysmic times means to live a life of great risk.[4]

That is the essence of Quaker worship: to hear and obey the living God.

NOTES

[1] *Quaker Faith and Practice*, Great Britain, Yearly Meeting of the Religious Society of Friends, 1995, p. 15.

[2] That is, including previously prescribed elements such as hymns or pre-composed prayers (eds note).

[3] *To Lima with Love: The Response from the Religious Society of Friends in Great Britain to the World Council of Churches document "Baptism, Eucharist and Ministry"*, London, Quaker Home Service on behalf of London Yearly Meeting of the Religious Society of Friends (Quakers), 1987.

[4] Paul Anderson, report of the world gathering of Young Friends, 1985, the full text of the epistle is available at www.wgyf.org/1985epistle.asp

The Nature and Purpose of Worship
A Church of the Brethren Perspective

JEFF CARTER

• BRETHREN •

Our fundamental understanding of the nature and purpose of worship

As the Reformation was a call upon the Catholic church to reform and re-establish the apostolic purity of the church, the Radical Reformation was a reaction to the Protestant church's establishment of state churches and a call to greater sincerity in both personal and corporate piety. Two radical reformed groups, Anabaptist and Pietist, drew upon a primitive interpretation of scripture as they sought to restore the New Testament church and deepen their Christ-centred discipleship.

The *Anabaptists*, a 16th-century reform movement in Europe, chose baptism as their defining ordinance both in reaction to the state church and in their literal imitation of Jesus. In polity and structure, the Anabaptists sought to create a visible and disciplined church that conformed to the standards of the New Testament and rejected the conforming spirit of the world. Sectarian by necessity, the Anabaptists often were seen as a threat to the state church in both their belief, centred on a non-credalism, and their practice of believer's baptism.[1]

The *Pietists*, a 17th-century religious movement, focused devotion on the inward call of the Spirit. In its pursuit of individual and corporate renewal, pietism "tended to elevate practice above doctrine, spirit above form, piety above orthodoxy, active engagement above mere consent, and fellowship above ecclesiastical or socio-cultural barriers".[2]

Owing much to the Anabaptists, the Radical Pietists, a contra-distinction to classical Pietism, advanced the notion of the New Testament apostolic church by establishing acts of obedience – ordinances – to include the more radical trine (threefold) immersion form of baptism, feet-washing, anointing of the sick, and church discipline.[3] The Radical Pietists (with their commitment to nonviolence and emphasis on a church of voluntary disciples), as well as the Pietists (with their emphasis upon the Spirit), greatly influenced the separatist notions of the emerging Brethren in the Palatinate region of Germany.

In 1708 five men and three women, in response to their felt-call to imitate Jesus, were led to the river Eder in Schwarzenau, Germany, and were baptized by trine immersion. An unnamed person baptized Alexander Mack, the "founder" of the movement, and Mack then baptized the other seven. This single act marks the beginning of a faith tradition which includes the Church of the Brethren but whose founding rests in the Anabaptist, Pietist and Radical Pietist movements of central Europe.

As a reform movement, the early Brethren fashioned their worship in response to what they perceived to be the coldness and dogmatism of the state church. Their public worship was simple, without formal liturgy, and included Bible study, prayer and singing. It was a time for biblical instruction and practical interpretation. As Schwarzenau Brethren gathered, they did so in homes, emphasizing their fellowship and shared call to obedience in Christ. As the movement grew, so did the attention it attracted from the authorities. Seen as a separatist movement, the early Brethren were forced to leave Schwarzenau, to sojourn through Europe seeking places of religious tolerance, and eventually to leave Europe for the New World and the religious freedom which William Penn offered near Philadelphia. As the waters of baptism birthed the Brethren movement in Europe, so the first baptism on Christmas day 1723 signified the beginning of the church in the New World. Within thirty years of its founding, the Schwarzenau Brethren movement was almost exclusively a North American religious movement.

It is key that it was services of *baptism* which inaugurated both the European and New World establishment of the Brethren movement, because it is in baptism that we understand the nature and purpose of worship. Worship is, first and foremost, the recognition of God and God's continued action upon creation. Worship is, second, a personal act of obedience and acknowledgment of our personal relationship with God; and third, a corporate response to God's call and an awareness of the community. In the ordinance of baptism, candidates confess their belief in God, their trust in Christ Jesus, and their faith in the continued work of the Spirit through the church. The commitment of faith, as well as the act of baptism, is done in the presence of the community. At the close of the ordinance, those officiating participate in a laying-on of hands, signifying the charge of obedience and service. All three actions are in imitation of Jesus as his baptism is recorded in the New Testament, and they signify a personal commitment made to God, consecrated by the church leadership, and witnessed by the community. With baptism comes church membership. Therefore it is through an act of worship that one becomes part of the community, participates in community, and affirms the community.

Distinctive aspects and qualities of our worship

Brethren values expressed in worship

From a non-credal, non-liturgical perspective it may be more helpful to speak of Church of the Brethren *values* as one seeks to define worship, because worship is an extension of daily piety. At the centre of Brethren[4] belief and practice is the understanding of "radical discipleship" – a practical, applicable and existential understanding of the New Testament, and specifically the Sermon on the Mount.[5] To be identified as "Christian" means to identify oneself with the mind and spirit of Jesus, and to live that understanding through an imitation of Christ *(imitatio Christi)* by both word and deed. Community, *Gemeinschaft,* can be defined as a closely-knit family feeling within the church where fellowship with God and each other is vital.[6] From a familial understanding of community springs forth an egalitarian ecclesiology defined by the *priesthood of all believers*, and practised through an equality of clergy and laity. The role of the community is to build up each believer and to provide a place for mutual cooperation and belonging.

From its sectarian beginning, the community is also the visible church set against the values of the world. Consequently the community respects individual conscience and supports a life convicted in the way of Christ, knowing that those who choose this radical discipleship will be seen as peculiar from the perspective of the "world".

Alexander Mack was once asked, "How will we know these Brethren?" Mack's response was, "By the manner of their living." It is through the fruit we bear that our faith is known. For the Brethren, worship is a time to instruct the community in the areas of service, evangelism, defenceless love, integrity, simplicity in living, purity, industry and stewardship.[7] Brethren have spent little time in developing a systematic theology; hence, the heart of worship is relational and practical. Even today, there is little patience for the homiletical abstract: Brethren want to know *how* they should live in relationship to God, to themselves, and to their brother and sister.

The latest edition of the Church of the Brethren minister's manual, *For All Who Minister,* begins the section on worship with the following introduction:

> Brethren have always been a worshipping people... A definition of worship, from the Old English word *weorthscipe*, is "giving God the worth due God". Worship is a meaningful and genuine meeting with God and Christian sisters and brothers. It is a time in which we together celebrate and affirm the good news of Jesus Christ. As God comes to us, we respond to God by participating in a rehearsal of our faith, followed by the enactment of that faith in the

world. God is the one we worship. We come to worship expectantly: to praise God, to give thanks to God, to confess to God, and to proclaim God's wondrous acts. We then go back into the world as transformed people.[8]

This introduction is followed by an admonition that acts of worship should be related but are not prescribed. Therefore, worship resources are offered in the manual as guidelines that speak to commonly held beliefs and values.

Key aspects and variations within the worship experience

From the perspective of the free-church tradition, liturgy is understood on the basis of the New Testament usage of the word – "which denotes not only the style of worship of the Christian community but also encompasses good works and acts of charity".[9] Broadly speaking, in the Church of the Brethren liturgy is *implicit* and *decentralized*. Some communities are highly liturgical and others non-liturgical; consequently, it is nearly impossible to categorize "the" liturgy of our tradition. What is possible is enumeration of key aspects, and known variations, within the worship experience.

Typically there is a gathering when announcements, a call to worship, invocation, prelude and opening statement may be shared. In keeping with the importance of stewardship, there is often a time for the returning of gifts, both of money and of self. Each worship service ends with a sending, blessing or benediction. Although worship leaders have freedom to rearrange the order of worship, Brethren worship emphasizes the following: God's presence in the midst of the gathered people; the centrality of Jesus Christ; the works and activity of the Holy Spirit; a sense of the community as the body of Christ; a bond as the priesthood of believers; congregational participation in worship; and the interplay of worship and service, with service being both an act of worship and a result of worship.[10]

First and foremost, worship is word-centred. At the centre of worship is the scripture reading, most often followed by a sermon. The scripture reading is of the preacher's selection, both verse and version, with some preachers selecting the appropriate lectionary text from *The Revised Common Lectionary*. Currently, the lectionary readings coincide with the bulletin series offered by the denominational publishing house. Bulletins with the printed order of worship are common – but not consistent throughout the denomination. When the scripture is read, it is read plainly and without additional liturgical movement such as the congregation standing, or the necessity of the presiding pastor reading the gospel text. In many, but not all, Brethren meeting houses the pulpit is the place from which the scripture is read so that the word and the preached word are not divided. Historically, this is an accurate depiction of the relatedness of the gospel reading to the sermon. The sermon may take many forms, but typically it is a practical application of the scripture lesson.

Another mainstay in most Church of the Brethren worship experiences is music. Music may be "performance" based, or shared hymnody. As noted in the church minister's manual, "Long before instruments were permitted in the sanctuary, four-part singing of hymns was a regular expression of the congregation's faith. Chorales, gospel songs, psalm tunes, and classical hymns have made up a large part of the singing style."[11] During the last half-century, the piano and the organ have been the accompanying instruments in most churches.[12] With the addition of musical instruments, music programmes were developed and choirs added. These choirs may be adult-, youth-, children- or gender-based. It is important to note that the choirs assist in interpreting the scripture through music; it is the choir speaking on behalf of the congregation rather than "performing" for the congregation in worship.

In our worship, prayer is often and varied. As most Brethren services have some type of community sharing time, so the prayers reflect the joys and concerns of the community gathered. Prayers often incorporate reference to those in need as well as the world beyond the church, and are offered by those who lead in worship. Prayers can be free in both form and function, or they may be scripted for purpose and prose. The form used is less important than the fact that prayers are offered for the community, on behalf of the community. Prayers are typically of one voice, and historically that voice would not be discerned until the moment of prayer.

Ordinances and ritual life

Concerning ordinances, Church of the Brethren theologian Dale Brown sums up the Brethren understanding as follows,

> The Brethren departed from sacramental terminology to speak of ordinances in referring to their many covenantal acts. This may have resulted from their attempt to follow the New Testament, which does not use the words sacrament or *means of grace*, but which does refer to acts instituted by Christ and commended by the apostles.[13]

Therefore the ritual life of Brethren is understood to be in obedience to Christ and hence is symbolized in agreed-upon ordinances: baptism by trine immersion, Love Feast and communion (feet-washing, agape meal, bread and cup communion), anointing for healing and the strengthening of faith, and the laying-on of hands. Each ordinance has a role in both the community and in the individual's faith experience. Each ordinance is ritualized, either during corporate worship or at an appointed time when representatives of the congregation can be of witness and support. The ordinances not only serve a symbolic role; they also have a pedagogical function: one learns service and humility by washing another person's feet; one learns hospitality by eating a common meal together; one learns his or her place in community when one is asked to bless a brother or sister with the laying-on of hands. With each of these practices there is no extensive teaching or preparatory sermons; those who learn how, learn by doing.

Children within the worship life of the church
The pedagogical value of worship, and specifically of the ordinances, means that there is an implicit need for children to be part of congregational life. While the entire worship experience is not necessarily developed with children in mind, sections and moments of worship are often designed to recognize and affirm the presence of children in congregational life. As Jesus drew the children into his arms, so the church is asked to form a space for regular and intentional ministry to children. This noted importance of children, coupled with the obvious age required for the practice of believer's baptism, have caused some churches to create rituals of child dedication so that children are seen as vital to a congregation and so that a congregation has the opportunity to pledge support and nurture to parents at a time of dedication. For such reasons rituals exist outside of the agreed-upon ordinances, and many of these rituals form part of the unique character, or identity, of a particular congregation or geographical area.

The influence of the ecumenical and liturgical renewal movements

The ecumenical movement
In the late 19th and early 20th centuries the Church of the Brethren began to break with its sectarian past, and started to adopt some of the religious conventions of mainstream North American Protestant Christianity. By the middle of the 20th century it had engaged the ecumenical movement, transitioned from free ministry to the paid pastorate, placed an emphasis on seminary-educated pastors and, for the most part, changed the architecture of its meeting houses to mirror the steepled churches of mainline America. With these leadership changes and structural alterations came changes in programme.

In many meeting houses the pulpit was divided into a raised pulpit and lectern. The communion table (which historically sat on the floor, on the level of the congregation) was elevated, and placed in a chancel area as an altar backed by a dossal cloth. Many sanctuaries gained stained glass windows, and worship elements such as Christ candles and bronze crosses were added from neighbouring traditions. Professional ministry brought with it broader understandings of worship, as well as awareness of what worship elements were being used in other Brethren congregations and other Christian communities. The *Common Lectionary* was introduced, and both music and worship aids were collected from other Protestant traditions. Writing thirty years ago Brethren theologian Dale Brown surmised,

> Today, one finds a wide appropriation of resources from other denominations and a freedom to use books of prayers and liturgical manuals from many sources. The most consistent characteristic of Brethren worship today is its growing variety. It is true that some congregations may be enslaved by the necessity to maintain the typical Protestant style of worship of several decades ago. Others may be faddish in the compulsion to experiment with [the] new. For the most part, however, there is a growing freedom to appropriate from others, and to experiment with new forms.[14]

As the membership of the Church of the Brethren grew in the mid-20th century, the theological background of its membership broadened. Consequently, liturgical elements such as bread and cup communion (offered outside of the twice-a-year Love Feast service), acolytes, robed choirs, worship leaders and ushers were added to worship. With these additions came an implicit understanding that the Church of the Brethren was moving from sect to mainstream denomination – albeit not universally. Although many of the more rural congregations retained older patterns of worship and leadership, both smaller rural and larger urban congregations formalized their worship and moved away from the spontaneity of earlier days.

The worship renewal movement
The worship renewal movement has also had a broad influence upon Church of the Brethren worship. While some churches refuse innovation, many congregations are either (1) blending worship influences, so that the overall traditional structure of worship is maintained but with the addition of elements such as praise choruses, guitar/percussion, drama and visual displays; (2) starting an additional worship service devoted to contemporary "seeker" worship (a path chosen by many larger churches); or (3) transforming current worship into a contemporary structure (this is often done by recently started congregations or younger churches). Elements most utilized in contemporary "seeker" worship are

music, drama, audiovisuals, informality, "therapeutic" hermeneutic, and liturgical dance. In addition to modern multi-modal worship elements, recent interest has also focused on monastic practice and liturgy.

As a denomination the Church of the Brethren focuses on worship each year at their annual conference, the highlight of which is community worship. Each worship service is a blend of the old and the new and, if annual conference is any indication of the denomination's worship experiences, the liturgical renewal movement has introduced many new innovations for worship. However, the Brethren are struggling to find the right combination, balance, and authentic spirit within this blending. One issue intrinsic to the current conversation is the focus on the act of worship. So much contemporary worship seeks to speak to the individual, and enhance the individual's relationship with God. Because Brethren see worship as an act not only of personal piety but also of communal encounter, there is widespread criticism that the theology of praise choruses, and the "therapeutic" hermeneutic of the homily, speak too much to the individual and not enough about the relatedness of the community and the community's relationship to God.

New developments in worship

A relatively new development in worship, related to the liturgical renewal movement and Brethren overseas mission work, is the inclusion of multicultural hymnody. Over the past hundred years Brethren have been involved with mission activity in Scandinavia, Turkey, Switzerland, France, India, China, Korea, Nigeria, Brazil, Ecuador, the Dominican Republic, Indonesia, and many of the Central American countries.[15] Due to a great emphasis upon indigenous forms of faith and worship, Brethren missionaries are moving away from instructing other peoples in codified sectarian practices. As this happens, the effect on worship (both in the mission field and back home) is dramatic. Worship celebrated at the mission church is an extension of the indigenous population's daily lives and culture, frequently being expressive and energetic. With great enthusiasm, missionaries return from the mission field ready to share Brethren worship as they have experienced it there. Yet when elements from "mission worship" are shared with American Brethren, these elements are either embraced as a refreshing – but only occasional – interruption of the routine, or they are criticized as "chaotic" and "too emotional". Therefore integration of such worship elements from the mission field has been sporadic.

In an effort to bring more multicultural influence and greater variety to North American worship, and to do so in a consistent fashion, the Church of the Brethren's most recent hymnal[16] (produced by members of the Anabaptist tradition) incorporates worship elements such as cultural instrumentation and hymns. The inclusion of multicultural elements has broadened the variety of worship and has engaged the wider Christian church symbolically.

A closing statement

Without creed or formal liturgy, worship for the Church of the Brethren is a contextualized extension of personal piety celebrated within the fellowship of community. The expressed purpose of worship is that worship calls one to service, and that service should be done as an act of worship.

NOTES

[1] Donald F. Durnbaugh ed., *The Brethren Encyclopedia,* Philadelphia and Oak Brook IL, Brethren Encyclopedia, 1983-1994, 1:28.

[2] *Ibid.*, 2:1022.

[3] *Ibid.*, 2:1079.

[4] Hereafter "Brethren" denotes the Church of the Brethren.

[5] Vernard Eller, "Beliefs," Donald F. Durnbaugh ed., *The Church of the Brethren Past and Present,* Elgin IL, Brethren Press, 1971, p.39.

[6] Durnbaugh, *The Brethren Encyclopedia,* 1:534.

[7] Vernard Eller, "Beliefs", in Durnbaugh, *The Church of the Brethren Past and Present,* p.40.

[8] Earle Fike, Jr, *For All Who Minister,* Elgin IL, Brethren Press, 1993, p.3.

[9] Dale W. Brown, "Liturgy", in Durnbaugh, *The Church of the Brethren Past and Present,* p.53.

[10] Fike, *For All Who Minister,* p.10.

[11] *Ibid.*

[12] *Ibid.*

[13] Brown, "Liturgy", in Durnbauch, *The Church of the Brethren Past and Present,* p.54.

[14] *Ibid.*, p.64.

[15] Merle Crouse, "Missions", in Durnbaugh, *The Church of the Brethren Past and Present,* p.109.

[16] *Hymnal: A Worship Book, Prepared by Churches in the Believers Church Tradition,* Elgin IL, Brethren/Faith and Life/Mennonite Publ. House, 1992.

Worship from the United Methodist [USA] Perspective

LAWRENCE HULL STOOKEY

• METHODIST •

The historical development of our church

In order to understand the liturgical stance of the United Methodist Church, the historical development of that church must be considered. In late colonial and early post-colonial America, a renewal movement started among Anglicans in England (most notably by the Anglican priests John and Charles Wesley) and spread rapidly. In 1784 – after the revolution, when anything "British" was considered deeply suspect – these American reformists founded The Methodist Episcopal Church. In the 1830s, a group known as The Methodist Protestant Church broke away, insisting on a church without bishops, and in which the laity had an equal voice with clergy.

The remaining Methodists subsequently split into two groups over the issue of slavery and "states rights", with the southern group taking the name The Methodist Episcopal Church, South. None of these divisions had to do with major disagreements about worship; and while some liturgical variations developed between them, basically the three groups had a common practice of worship. In 1939 these three groups reunited to form The Methodist Church.

Meanwhile, in the early United States the English-speaking Methodists had theological influence among certain German-speaking immigrants. One group (which grew primarily out of the Reformed church tradition and, specifically, strains of Puritan pietism) began, in 1800, to organize itself along Methodist lines as The Church of the United Brethren in Christ. Another group, more strongly influenced by pietistic Lutheranism, formed The Evangelical Association in 1803. The differences between the two groups had primarily to do not with fundamental issues of doctrine or liturgy, but with issues related to voting rights and the role of bishops. In 1946 these two groups – which had long since ceased to use German as their primary language – merged to form The Evangelical United Brethren Church, commonly known as The EUB Church.

In 1968, The EUB Church and The Methodist Church united to create The United Methodist Church. The statements of faith of both of the uniting churches stand today side by side as doctrinal standards for the united church. These statements contain important affirmations about worship. (1) Both statements affirm the centrality of the canonical scriptures (66 books) and their careful interpretation in the church. (2) Both affirm that baptism and the Lord's supper are sacraments (signs and means of grace from God to us) as well as ordinances (our pledges of faith to God, ordained by Christ). (3) Both state that baptism is open to children. (4) Both insist on the importance of the public worship of God, but (5) further indicate that latitude with respect to the exact forms of worship is to be allowed: these forms may be modified according to particular needs. (6) Both the uniting, and the resulting united, church "set aside" clergy authorized, by ordination, to preach the word and administer the sacraments.

The fifth point – respecting latitude in the forms of worship – has allowed liturgical differences to proliferate within The United Methodist Church. These often reflect the regional, ethnic, socio-economic, political and theological variety that exists within our very large and diverse denomination. (Here it should be noted that we are an international body, not a national church.) While there is a central core of commonality, at the "outer fringes" it is possible on Sunday morning to find a few United Methodist congregations whose worship is almost indistinguishable from (on the one hand) the eucharist of an Anglo-Catholic parish within Anglicanism, and (on the other hand) the exuberance and spontaneity of a Pentecostal congregation. Sometimes worship practice ignores official teaching: there are United Methodists, both lay and clergy, who reject the baptism of infants despite the clear statements on this issue by the denomination (including material in our ordination vows).

Sources for understanding our worship

In a statement of this limited length it is impossible to cover all forms of worship found within United Methodism. Hence the basis of my statement will be the two official liturgical books published by the united church:

1) the *United Methodist Hymnal* (authorized by the general conference of 1988, and published in 1989 by the United Methodist Publishing House);
2) the *United Methodist Book of Worship* (authorized by the general conference of 1992, and published in the same year by the United Methodist Publishing House).

The *Hymnal* includes the full orders for the Sunday service (with and without the eucharist), services of the baptismal covenant (including confirmation and reaffirmation), wedding and funeral, and the Psalter, creeds, acts of praise and selected prayers. The *Book of Worship* expands on this collection and offers alternative forms in many cases. It also includes the revised common lectionary, ample resources for the liturgical year, and many additional prayers and rites, including acts of dedication, consecration and ordination.

The United Methodist Church can be characterized as "a free prayer book church". The two volumes noted above include ample resources for any congregation which wishes to follow prescribed rites. The use of neither book is absolutely mandated; the *Hymnal* has, nevertheless, been adopted overwhelmingly by congregations. The extent of use of the *Book of Worship* is more difficult to assess, since it is not a "pew book" but intended for use only by those who plan and conduct worship. It is clear, however, that it is being widely used. It also must be noted that, even when United Methodists conscientiously follow a prescribed text, they do not hesitate to make local adaptations and emendations; nor have they ever been disciplined by the church courts or hierarchy for so doing – even if they have slipped over into what, in other churches, might be deemed heresy!

It is important to note that United Methodists share much of what they do in worship with other members of the Wesleyan family (including the African Methodist Episcopal Church; the African Methodist Episcopal Zion Church; the Christian Methodist Episcopal Church; the Free Methodist Church; the Wesleyan Church; and the several branches of British Methodism). In what follows, this pan-Wesleyan commonality is implied wherever the general terms "Methodist" or "Methodism" are used (rather than the more limited name of "United Methodist".)

The fundamental understanding of the nature and purpose of worship

In the traditional debate over whether worship is *sacrificium* (our offering of praise to God) or *beneficium* (God's gift of blessing to us), United Methodists assert "both". This stance flows from a basic sacramental perspective. The "articles of religion" of The [former] Methodist Church assert that the two sacraments

> are not only badges or tokens of Christian men's professions, but rather are certain signs of grace, and God's good will towards us, by which he doth work invisibly in us, and doth not only quicken, but also strengthen and confirm, our faith in him (art. XVI).

The former EUB "Confession of Faith" affirms that the sacraments

> are symbols and pledges of the Christian's profession and of God's love towards us. They are means of grace by which God works invisibly in us, quickening, strengthening, and confirming our faith in him (art. VI).

Thus in worship we praise God and offer up ourselves, giving testimony before the world of the graciousness of God "in order that the world might believe". At the same time, the faith we express is thereby strengthened by the very God whom we bless. Contrary to Kierkegaard's analogy, the God we worship is not an audience who passively views the performance given on stage by the laity (coached by the liturgical leaders). Rather, God is the author, producer and director of the drama. The "audience" is the world to whom we give witness that God is the One who is worthy (a word closely related to the Anglo-Saxon term "worship") "to receive power and wealth and wisdom and might and honour and glory and blessing!" (Rev. 5:12b). Worship is thus both the duty and the joy of the Christian. Indeed, it is in the assembly of worship that the church is constituted and reconstituted week by week. Methodism began and continues as a worshipping people.

If a choice must be made as to which takes priority – *beneficium* or *sacrificium* – United Methodists will, most likely, solve it on the basis of the covenantal theology which undergirds contemporary baptismal practice: God is the initiator of the covenantal grace revealed most prominently in the work of Christ. *Sacrificium* is our response, which is facilitated by (and never apart from) *beneficium*. But this does not mean that worship can be seen primarily as instrumental: we do not worship mainly because we can thereby receive a blessing. We worship because God is worthy.

Apart from the reading of scripture and its interpretation in a sermon, all in the context of prayer and praise, together with the administration of the sacraments, United Methodists have few absolutes as to the irreducible elements of a worship service. Indeed this skeletal framework constitutes "The Basic Pattern of Worship", given here in full:

> *Entrance:* The people come together in the Lord's name. There may be greetings, music and song, prayer and praise.
> *Proclamation and response:* The scriptures are opened to the people through the reading of lessons, preaching, witnessing, music, or other arts and media. Interspersed may be psalms, anthems and hymns. Responses to God's word include acts of commitment and faith with offerings of concerns, prayers, gifts, and service for the world and one another.
> *Thanksgiving and communion:* In services with communion, the actions of Jesus in the upper room are re-enacted: taking the bread and cup, giving thanks over the bread and cup, breaking the bread, and giving the bread and cup. In

services without communion, thanks are given for God's mighty acts in Jesus Christ.

Sending forth: The people are sent into ministry with the Lord's blessing. This pattern is found both in at the beginning of the *Hymnal* and the *Book of Worship*. It forms the outline not only for more fully articulated forms of the Sunday service but also for other rites including the wedding, funeral and other occasional services.

The distinctive aspects and qualities of worship in our tradition

For Methodists generally the worthiness of God that undergirds worship is an experiential as well as a doctrinal reality. Not only can we believe in the worthiness of God, but we know in our own *experience* the personal God revealed in Jesus Christ. One distinctive Methodist mark (though we do not claim to be the only ones who have it) is the role of personal experience. Indeed, United Methodists seek to test all things by four measures: scripture, Tradition, reason and experience.

The centrality of experiential theology is evident in the hymns of John and Charles Wesley. Hymn singing was not invented in England by them, but it was certainly introduced by them into Anglican circles. For in their time, Anglican worship followed the Reformed pattern – and not the Lutheran pattern – in singing only versified psalms. The Presbyterian and free-church innovation of new hymn texts was viewed with great suspicion. Those suspicions were intensified by words in Wesley hymns such as "I know and feel" in relation to basic Christian doctrine. Many Wesley texts assert that those who sing them can "prove" what is being affirmed in the words. The meaning of this is obscure to us today; for "prove" then meant "to experience", and did not imply scientifically verifiable demonstration. Indeed, shouts of joy and tears of repentance or compassion are familiar in much experiential Methodist worship.

Most forms of worship (the sacramental rites, weddings, funerals, confirmation, preaching services, morning and evening prayer, ordination, services of healing, and various acts of dedication and consecration) are shared by many denominations. Two services to which, however, Methodists make some more exclusive claim are the love feast and the covenant renewal service.

The *love feast*, which is the less popular of these two, is essentially an adaptation of Moravian rites known to John Wesley – though practice today among Moravians and Methodists is rather divergent, with the Methodist order being far less formal and more infrequent.

The *service of covenant renewal* has had more widespread and consistent use, often being observed on the first Sunday of the calendar year, or at some other regular time designated locally. Adapted by John Wesley from Puritan models, the service can be closely related theologically to a reaffirmation of the baptismal covenant, though Wesley himself did not make this theological connection clear. Indeed, as explicit rites of baptismal renewal have emerged within United Methodism in recent years, there seems to be a certain redundancy between these and the Wesleyan covenant service.

One other practice to which Methodists lay a particular claim is less a service than an action which can be used in a variety of services, or independently of liturgical occasions. This is the *testimony meeting* in which individuals give personal witness to the power and grace of God within their lives. Sometimes such testimonies are given as a part of corporate worship, or immediately preceding it; but at other times they may find a place within study groups or classes. Historically, testimony was an integral part of the covenant renewal service discussed above. An interesting adaptation of the testimony practice has emerged recently within the funeral service, as those who attend may be invited to give testimony to the grace of God as revealed in the life of the deceased.

How our worship has been influenced by the ecumenical and liturgical renewal movements

United Methodism has been greatly influenced in its liturgical renewal by the ecumenical movement. Ecumenical studies and practices in baptism have produced a new examination of baptismal theology and practice, such that within the last several years a denominational study paper has been produced on this long-neglected subject. Ecumenical study and reform of eucharistic practice has emboldened United Methodists to rediscover the rich eucharistic theology set forth by the Wesleys, and largely lost until recently. While not observed weekly in most congregations, the frequency of holy communion has increased notably within recent decades, as has our understanding that the sacrament is a corporate and eschatological feast, and not merely a historical re-creation of the upper room meal for the benefit of individual believers. We have been full participants in the process of producing, and responding to, the Faith and Order convergence text *Baptism, Eucharist and Ministry* and have gained much from that process.

So also, the recovery of the liturgical calendar has been the result of ecumenical contacts and interaction with renewal efforts. The provision for daily prayer hours (morning, midday, evening and night prayer) within United Methodist worship orders is a further sign of ecumenical and renewal influences. Services of healing (with provision for anointing), and the imposition of ashes at the beginning of Lent, also reflect a recovery of practices lost to earlier Methodists, but preserved in other churches until they could be reappropriated by us. The use of current

English (rather than archaic forms), and the search for language that is inclusive of all persons and less gender-defining for God, also reflects ecumenical interaction and the intent for renewal – though we are bold enough to hope that, in this regard, we have been more the leaders than the followers of other Christian bodies.

A careful study of the recent *United Methodist Hymnal* and *Book of Worship* reveals a great indebtedness to the Presbyterian, Lutheran and Episcopal liturgical books (as well as others) which immediately preceded it in publication. While Methodist hymnody has always had something of a pan-Protestant character, the scope of that hymnody has recently been broadened and it now includes a significant number of selections from the Roman Catholic tradition. But beyond that, United Methodist thinking about the theology of worship has been indebted to the Vatican II documents on the liturgy and the Roman Catholic thinking that flowed therefrom, and also to Orthodox liturgical theology, particularly that of Alexander Schmemann.

Finally, ecumenical contacts and practices, and renewal movements, have helped to de-clericalize United Methodist worship. While the ordained are rightly seen as those who preside at the sacraments and who regularly preach, the consistent active liturgical participation of the laity – which is rooted in the identity given to the whole community – is expected. Particular lay members may read the scriptures during services, help to lead in the offering of prayers, take distinctive roles in the sacramental rites (possibly including the distribution of holy communion both in the corporate service and in homes and hospitals afterwards), and take a larger part than previously in planning and evaluating services of worship, and in setting liturgical policy. This is not intended, however, to be a substitute for the participation of all present.

New developments in united Methodism, as these help or hinder Christian unity

As implied in the previous section, most of the recent official reforms of United Methodist worship reflect ecumenical dialogue and, to that extent, promote the cause of Christian unity.

One problem for Methodists, however, is the closed communion table of some of the churches. Methodism had an *open table* long before many other Protestant groups did and Methodists tend to be mystified – and indeed insulted – at being turned away from the Lord's table in churches that require more than baptism for admission to the supper of the Lord.

A likely problem for other churches is United Methodism's extension of sacramental presiding roles (within particular parishes, not universally) to lay pastors who are assigned to serve those specific congregations. Such extraordinary sacramental powers have long characterized a denomination that – literally – has more congregations than there are post offices in the United States, some of them quite small and incapable of financially supporting ordained clergy. The coexistence of ordained clergy and unordained lay pastors, particularly as presiders at the eucharist, is a conundrum for United Methodists as well as a potential problem for ecumenical relationships in the search for intercommunion.

At an unofficial level, a style of worship usually called "the seekers' service" has become popular in certain parts of United Methodism (and many other Protestant churches in the United States). Beyond simply using more contemporary styles of music, such services usually neglect any consistent sacramental practice, and often diminish the biblical content of worship services. Congregational participation tends to be minimal, or is limited to the repeated singing of "praise choruses" rather than longer hymn texts that embody doctrinal and mystagogical content. To the extent that this type of service attracts non-church people and prepares them gradually to participate in the full worship of word and sacraments, it causes no problem either within United Methodism or to other churches. But to the extent that such reductionist forms constitute an alternative to, or a substitute for, services of word and sacraments, they create perplexing problems and raise serious questions about the integrity of worship, in light of both the official worship materials of United Methodism and its relationships with sister churches.

While not a recent development, an obstacle to ecumenical understanding lies in the failure to adhere to official baptismal practice. Contrary to church teaching, some United Methodists practise "rebaptism" because (1) they reject their own church's affirmations about the baptism of infants; or (2) they believe only a certain mode is to be used, again contrary to official teaching which allows sprinkling, pouring or immersion; or (3) they value experience to such an extent that a spiritual awakening may be deemed an occasion for rebaptism (without necessarily disputing a prior baptism due to the age of the candidate, or the mode of administration). In other words, what is actually a *reaffirmation* of baptism may be administered in such a way as to be indistinguishable from baptism itself. Other churches rightly object to such violations of the principle of one baptism and, while United Methodism is seeking to reform itself in this matter, change comes slowly.

"Under Our Own Vine and Fig Tree"

Sunday Morning Worship in the African Methodist Episcopal Church

VINTON R. ANDERSON

• METHODIST •

The African Methodist Episcopal Church heritage

On a Sunday morning in November 1787 at St George's Methodist Episcopal Church in Philadelphia, Richard Allen and other black Methodists who had been pulled from their knees while at prayer walked out in protest, declaring, "We will worship God under our own vine and fig tree." That experience triggered a movement which subsequently led to the formation of the first national African American institution in the new world.[1] The founding of Mother Bethel in Philadelphia, the sacred citadel of faith and freedom for African Methodists,[2] established a place where former slaves could exercise social and political authority based on their understanding of the gospel. They had heard the itinerant preachers proclaim that "God shows no partiality, but... anyone who fears him and does what is right is acceptable to him" (Acts 10:34-35), and that "there is no longer slave or free... for all of you are one in Christ Jesus" (Gal. 3:28). A tradition of inclusiveness in worship began, for black Christians had now removed the wall of separation and affirmed in practice the gospel imperative to "go into all the world... to every creature".

Worship in the African Methodist Episcopal Church has its basis in a theology of liberation which springs from the event of 1787.[3] To talk of worship in the African Methodist Episcopal (AME) context is to reflect on a history of oppressed people who for more than two centuries have fostered a philosophy of self-help and self-determination. Out of their peculiar struggle they have crafted a theology of liberation which affirms freedom for the total person. There can be no spirituality for AMEs that excludes the well-being of body, mind and soul. Therefore, we continue

• This text was published as chapter 9 in *The Sunday Service of the Methodists. Twentieth-Century Worship in Worldwide Methodism – Studies in Honor of James F. White*, Karen B. Westerfield Tucker ed., Nashville TN, Kingswood, 1996. Used by permission.

to testify, "I looked at my hands, and they looked new. I looked at my feet, and they did too." Our worship on Sunday morning centres on Jesus, the anointed one, who "bring[s] good news to the poor... proclaim[s] release to the captives and recovery of sight to the blind,... let[s] the oppressed go free,... proclaim[s] the year of the Lord's favour" (Luke 4:18).

In attempting to catch the essence of the African Methodist Episcopal heritage and to convey that legacy to their constituency, the bishops in 1976 included the following statement in the Episcopal salutation: "The liturgy and worship forms must reflect the peculiar content of our religious experience, therefore reinforcing and reaffirming our authenticity and legitimacy as African Methodist Christians."[4] Obviously the bishops intended to be clear about their position to incorporate African American cultural elements into corporate worship. This inclination would be a corrective to those who tended towards a Euro-American mind-set and would somewhat run counter to the view of Daniel A. Payne and others who strongly embraced the Euro-American Methodist form. Payne, elected a bishop in 1852 and greatly revered by his denomination as the apostle of education, had resisted the use of spirituals, calling them cornfield ditties. In Payne's autobiography, *Recollections of Seventy Years,* he labels those who participate in slave songs and the ring shouts as "ridiculous and heathenist".[5]

It should not be thought, however, that AME bishops a hundred years later are diametrically opposed to Payne's judgment for his own day. There still remains a respect and appreciation for the Euro-American heritage, and it is coupled with a sense of black pride and the determination for an identity with one's African roots. The 1976 Episcopal salutation further avers,

> That the AME Church must be committed to identify itself with a value system which has grown out of the black experience with God, and not the adoption of another culture imposed on black people. That value system should interpret the intervention of God within the black context and the historical pilgrimage of black people. Our church must be in the role of enabler, and free people from the false values which make them ashamed of themselves and their heritage, and equip them with the understanding and freedom to deal with their life-conditions and decision-making process.[6]

It must be understood, then, that worship on Sunday morning in an African Methodist Episcopal church is a response of praise and thanksgiving to a powerful God who has brought black people from a mighty long way, whose journey towards freedom is placed alongside the exodus from Egypt and the *via dolorosa.* Worship celebrates a faith learned in the crucible of adversity. It remembers the biblical story and recognizes the more recent past of a particular people: the Middle Passage, the blacksmith shop, the plantations and the cotton fields. So we sing, "My soul looks back and wonders how we got over."

What must it have been like when the time came to walk out of St George's sanctuary? What courage must have been required? The black Methodists were a people who had been trapped by a system which had dictated their very existence, had directed their every move and controlled their destiny. Now they were set free to pursue their Christian pilgrim journey in an environment of their own choosing. What must it have been like in the blacksmith shop, transformed into the "house of God" at that first worship service in 1794? We, who are African Methodists, can imagine what it was like for them by acknowledging our own exuberance and relief when we tread on holy ground each Sunday morning, ground which represents our own place of refuge from an unfriendly world.

While it was clear that the Allenites could now say about their place of worship, "This land is our land", Richard Allen had no intention of breaking away from the Methodism which had so greatly affected his life. In fact, he said in his journal,

> We were in favour of being attached to the Methodist connection; for I was confident that there was no religious sect or denomination [that] would suit the capacity of the coloured people as well as the Methodist; for the plain and simple gospel suits best for any people; for the unlearned can understand, and the learned are sure to understand; and the reason that the Methodist is so successful in the awakening and conversion of the coloured people, [is] the plain doctrine and having a good discipline.[7]

Richard Allen was, in fact, keeping with the tradition of Methodism as defined by John Wesley in his appeal to common people, his commitment to social change, his fervour in evangelism, and his opting for freedom and spontaneity in worship. Allen may have been affected by the tradition of "a heart strangely warmed" and Wesley's contention that to be an "altogether Christian" required both a love of God that "engrosses the whole heart" and a love for the neighbour.[8] These images of Christian virtue and behaviour, taken from the father of Methodism and coupled with Allen's African heritage characterized by attentiveness to spiritual matters and a quest for freedom learned in the slave environment, provided the necessary ingredients for the formulation of Sunday worship in an African Methodist Episcopal church.

As early as 1801 Richard Allen had published A *Collection of Hymns and Spiritual Songs* for use in the fledgling society now set on a course to proclaim God's salvation, liberation and reconciliation.[9] That work, along with Allen's directive in 1817 (following the Methodist Episcopal Church *Discipline*), "Let the morning worship consist of singing, prayer, reading of a chapter out of the Old Testament and another out of the New Testament, and preaching", shaped the sum, substance and style of Sunday worship for the generations of AMEs which followed. This informal order of service was the seed for the more formal order which grew to become the solid trunk for Sunday worship in AME churches.

For more than a century, AMEs have gathered for worship heralded by the words, "I was glad when they said unto me, let us go into the house of the Lord. Our feet shall stand within thy gates, O Jerusalem." The suggestion of gladness, announcing our presence in God's house to worship God, indicates that joy and praise are two predictable expressions related to the worship experience. Gathered as the people of God, we become fully aware of the multiplexity of social and personal issues which surround us, and we seek to reconnect with God and each other as we rediscover gladness despite the difficult journey.

AMEs hardly congregate without remembering the great distance God has brought black people, and without celebrating social and political victories which intertwine with present struggles for personhood and self-esteem. Just as sure as we come to meet our God at our holy meeting-place, believing in God's power to change the world and therefore advancing the concept of "justice and equality for all", we come also to each other in our vulnerability, risking ridicule and seeking approval. We come singing, "Nobody knows the trouble I see; nobody knows but Jesus."

James Cone, in *For My People,* describes how on Sunday morning theological, social and economic realities converge over a period of several hours as worship, and states that,

> Worship, therefore, is not primarily an expression of the individual's private relationship with God. It is rather a community happening, an eschatological invasion of God into the gathered community of victims, empowering them with "the divine Spirit from on high", "to keep on keeping on" even though the odds might appear to be against them. In the collective presence of the poor at worship, God re-creates them as a liberated community that must bring freedom to the oppressed of the land.[10]

Worship styles

It is generally felt by AMEs that there is a common thread which weaves together the peculiar content of our worship, and allows African Methodists to be at home wherever they worship in faithfulness to the Christ-event and the Wesley-Allen legacy. It cannot, however, be said that worship in general in our context is monolithic.

There is a quality of connectedness among AME churches, but the flavour of worship may differ from setting to setting. No single picture describes our Sunday worship, yet there is order in what we do. Worship may be explosive, unpredictable, joyous or doleful, formal or spontaneous, contagious or sterile, or a combination or variation of all the above. For example, in one congregation the worshippers may be quiet and meditative, the music subdued; in another, worship may be more spirited and up-tempo. A third congregation may worship in the highly spirited charismatic style with lots of instruments and loud joyful sounds. But in each case the congregation always knows what follows. The gamut can run from traditional to ultra-contemporary, but in some mysterious way a formal structure gives shape to the unpredictable moments. By the grace of God, the Sunday worship experience in an AME church may empower persons and the congregation. The community's gathering provides the setting, attitude and the substance for the Spirit of God to indwell and to energize so that the work of Christ may be continued in both individual and community.

A colourful array of worship styles exists in the African Methodist Episcopal Church family. In Bermuda, the British influence is merged with the American as worshippers lustily sing hymns from the Anglican tradition and gospel songs of American origin. The order of worship is distinctly African Methodist and there is an appreciation and use of classical anthems as well as spirituals and contemporary choruses. Spontaneity is by no means squelched but congregations want and expect a well-planned service with sermons that appeal to their hearts and minds. Many churches broadcast over the radio and during the week it is common to hear parishioners discussing aspects of a particular sermon.

In South Africa, where African Methodism is flourishing and where the AME Church has been present for one hundred years, the order of worship serves as a guide, for spontaneity is natural and uninhibited. Rich vocal tones swell as South Africans sing hymns and anthems. One may hear a children's choir render an *a capella* version of "Cast Thy Burdens Upon the Lord" from Handel's oratorio *Elijah* or listen to an entire congregation joyfully harmonize their version of "Guide Me, O Thou Great Jehovah". Several languages may be sung at one time, but all in beautiful harmony and often without instruments. With the singing there is always body movement, and the dancing is joyful and unfeigned. In extreme cases younger people may jump several inches from the floor in continuous rhythm to the music. Dance frequently attends the offering of money, which is regarded as a time of celebration: worshippers may dance to the table, put their money down, and dance back to their seats, sometimes going to the table more than once. The offering, then, can take an unplanned amount of time, but it is clearly one of the high points of the service.

Regional differences can be found in worship styles within the United States. In South Carolina, a "hotbed" of African Methodism, the members of the churches in the "low country" are known to have a style all their own. A common practice is the syncopated clapping which accompanies the music and is used as a response to the sermon when it has hit home. Dancing in the aisles with intricate steps even by someone who may look too old and unsteady to move can set the onlooker to wondering how it is possible. AME worship in Alabama still includes the mournful tones of the call and response songs and of many old spirituals and songs that may not be heard elsewhere. In some areas it is not uncommon to see someone "get happy" and "walk the benches". The latter is a practice in which a person seems to float on air while walking on the back of each pew as if in a trance. Deep in the coal mine areas of West Virginia, African Methodism has another flavour. Worshippers still follow the order of service, but their music is what many of us call "hillbilly" with banjo accompaniment and country-style singing. Churches in urban centres with their magnificent pipe organs and large choirs still have space for gospel singing and for testimonies and emotional outbursts called "shouting". Many worshippers bring with them to the city remnants of their religious upbringing from the rural South.

Despite a variety of worship styles, such as those found among AMEs in Canada, West Africa or the Caribbean (with its calypso beat and local colour), the churches honour an AME order of worship.[11] Whether east or west, north or south, Sunday AME worship should be identifiable because it generally follows a prescribed order of service. Thus local expressions and an established worship pattern define who we are as children of God and as spiritual descendants of Richard Allen.

Those who prefer a freer or a non-structured style of worship may not perceive what AMEs cherish about uniformity and linkage with our history and the early church. For while we revere our own uniqueness, we can never forget that we as a communion are one member of the body of Christ, and consequently yoked with other communions whose history and worship, like ours, has its roots in the first-century church. As is true for other Christians throughout the world, AMEs share in biblical traditions and the ancient liturgies of the church. Consequently, worship is not detached and unrelated to what other Christians do. Proclaiming the word of God and administering the sacraments are central to our life and witness. We have been deliberate about embracing elements of worship which celebrate our ecumenicity and have been intentional about engaging in worship that has liturgical integrity and theological relevance. Hence, worship is seen as purposeful movement towards a goal which is intensely spiritual and fulfilling. Albert W. Palmer may lend support to our notion of order and discipline in worship, pointing to the sixth chapter of Isaiah as a pattern for public worship.[12] Even in our own denomination, when some argue that worship is too controlled and the Spirit often muzzled in periods of rejoicing, there is also agreement that a fine line exists between allowing for spontaneity and maintaining order.

I have found a helpful response to the concern expressed for freedom and structure in the imagery of Ezekiel's vision of the valley of dry bones:

> And as I prophesied, suddenly there was a noise, a rattling, and the bones came together, bone to its bone. I looked, and there were sinews on them, and flesh had come upon them, and skin had covered them; but there was no breath in them.... I prophesied as He commanded me, and the breath came into them, and they lived (Ezek. 37:7,8,10).

The passage shows the essential relationship of structure to substance. Until breath, the *ruach* of God, enters our frames, there is no life. Likewise, a framework is necessary to receive God's *dunamis* or power, namely, the Holy Spirit.

The AME Church seeks to be authentic to Christian tradition and its own heritage through a diversity of forms and styles of music, its prayer, preaching and fellowship. The *AME Bicentennial Hymnal* (1984),[13] and the amended version, the *AME Hymnal* (1986)[14] along with the *Book of Worship* (1984),[15] were intended to be faithful to universal principles of worship and yet perpetuate the tradition unique to our own worshipping congregations. They include the three-year lectionary adopted by the Consultation on Church Union (Cocu) and other liturgical services developed within the Cocu family.

The AME commission on worship and liturgy, in its preface to the *Book of Worship,* refers to the denomination as constituting a "liberating and reconciling people". In response to the perceived assault on what had been essential in worship, the preface stated,

> [We] must be open to explore new styles without dismantling all that is old...
>
> It should provide both clergy and lay persons with a meaningful worship guide in the dual task of nurturing the community of faith and calling Christ to the attention of the unbeliever...
>
> It is our deepest hope that this instrument... will stimulate liturgical renewal and worship integrity, as well as a measure of uniformity amongst worshipping African Methodists. It is our prayer that from its use a fresh movement of the Spirit will move upon our Zion.[16]

The order of worship

Primary, in both the *Hymnal* and the *Book of Worship,* is the Sunday morning order of worship. In a typical worshipping congregation, the order of worship would be as follows:[17]

- The prelude
- The introit (if desired)
- The processional
- The doxology
- The call to worship
- The hymn of praise
- The prayer and choral response
- The anthem or song by choir
- The scripture lessons
- The choral preface to the decalogue
- The decalogue (often abridged or summarized)
- The gloria patri
- The choral selection
- The benevolent offering
- The announcements and parish concerns and recognition of visitors
- The sermonic selection or hymn
- The sermon
- Prayer (the Lord's prayer chanted, all kneeling)
- The invitation to Christian discipleship
- The affirmation of faith
- The offering and choral offertory
- The doxology or hymn
- The benediction
- The recessional
- The postlude

A few aspects of the Sunday order of worship that are firmly held by African Methodists must be mentioned. It should be noted that the doxology (the text by Thomas Ken) is twice sung in the service, at the beginning and at the end, but using alternate tunes (often the Old Hundredth and a gospel tune). Perhaps its placement in both locations symbolizes the parameters of the celebration event. The in-between time, which may be substantially extended depending on the Spirit's energizing, validates the observation that, for black people, linear time is not important – experience is. For some worshippers, as long as the Spirit is high, "church" goes on and they are content. Yet for others, the extended duration of the worship service is a bone of contention. The tension exists around the notion that the Holy Spirit is an agent of order, and therefore constrains as well as excites. What must be admitted is that congregations, too, have personalities, and that variable very much pre-scribes the character and model of the service.

The call to worship normally used is a standardized compilation of passages from the Old Testament and is as follows (here M refers to the minister, P to the people or congregation):

M: I was glad when they said to me, "Let us go to the house of the Lord!" Our feet shall stand within Thy gates, O Jerusalem!

P: For a day in thy courts is better than a thousand. I had rather be a door-keeper in the house of my God than dwell in the tents of wickedness.

M: Because of the house of the Lord our God, I will seek thy good.

P: Those that be planted in the house of the Lord, shall flourish in the courts of our God.

M: Blessed are they that dwell in thy house. Lord, I have loved thy habitation, the place where thy glory dwelleth.

P: For the Lord is in his holy temple, let all the earth keep silence before him.

M: Let the words of my mouth, and the meditation of my heart, be acceptable in thy sight, O Lord, my strength and my Redeemer.

P: O sing unto the Lord a new song, for he has done marvellous things! Make a joyful noise unto the Lord, all the earth, sing praises!

Alternative calls to worship are encouraged for special days, but they often supplement the regular opening sentences.

In many of the smaller congregations a lay member is often asked, without warning, to offer the morning prayer extemporaneously, and with reverent pride the petitioner lifts the congregation to the throne of grace. In that prayer might be heard a familiar expression which predates the emancipation of black slaves in America and is a recognition of God's inclusive nature: "He is a father to the fatherless, and a mother to the motherless." Lay leadership in morning worship is highly acceptable in all of our congregations. In addition, there are designated special days for full lay leadership, such as men's day, women's day, missionary day, children's day, youth day, and lay witness day.

The decalogue or ten commandments with choral responses, ending with the greatest commandment in the words of Jesus (Matt. 22:37-40), has long usage among AMEs. Two short versions are also utilized, an abridged text and the summary of the law. It is placed in the order of service after the reading of the Old and New Testaments. In some liturgical circles, the recital of the law would be considered ill-placed following the reading of the gospel, but in AME worship it fits. The use of the decalogue has promoted moral fortitude and ethical principles easily understood by a two-thirds world people in a first-world context who need a set of religious rules to guide their progress.

The altar call which has become prevalent in our second century is a significant component of Sunday worship. While not done on a regular basis in all of our congregations, this period of contrition and gratitude is for us a liberating act, reminding us of our former bondage, and rein-forcing in us a determination to be inwardly and outwardly free. During the altar call, the congregation kneels and lays before the altar (commu-nion rail) those needs and situations which plague both individuals and community, thereby functioning as an occasion to search for wholeness and to find healing. This element of worship is placed to meet the par-ticular emphases and needs that arise from the Sunday service.

Our congregations have continued the practice of an invitation to discipleship, during which the unsaved and the unchurched are pre-sented the opportunity to respond to God's good news of salvation in Jesus Christ. It is sometimes referred to as "opening the doors of the church". At this time in the service, persons are welcomed into the gath-ered community of those who have said "yes" to Jesus, and the invita-tion is issued to others to unite with the congregation to do kingdom work. There are three categories of candidates for membership into the body of Christ in African Methodism: (1) confession of faith/new con-verts; (2) Christian experience/baptized Christians from other churches; and (3) letter of transfer/Christians from other AME churches. Those who confess Christ for the first time and choose membership in the AME Church, after completing a course of instruction, are baptized as a sign of new life through Jesus Christ. After baptism, there is a three-month probationary period during which the candidate attends new membership training classes. The culmination of the process is the order for receiving persons into full membership which includes "the right hand of fellowship", a lively ritual which welcomes and introduces new members into the local church.

Another aspect which cannot be overstressed is the time of announcements and congregational concerns. For the AME Church, as in other historic black churches, the major forum for sharing community concerns is the local church. It is a time which affirms, perhaps more than any other, that the sacred and the secular are indivisible. Critical issues are always laid before the congregation. The church is *the* arena for disseminating information whether it be regarding social unrest, a display of racism, criticism of unfair economic policies, the identifica-tion of community representatives for public office, the advancement of the cause of young people, the preservation of the black male and fam-ily solidarity, the HIV/AIDS crisis, or the promotion of ecumenical rela-tions. So, the announcements, congregational and community concerns, and even the acknowledgment of visitors are by no means incidental to worship. Those segments become the focus around which the gathered community seeks God's corporate blessing and engages each worshipper in mission and ministry. It may be at this time or following the sacraments that the church is led into an act of fellowship and celebration which can be a powerful manifestation of *koinonia*. The act of fellowship in some settings is called "passing the peace".

The sacraments

In all that we do at Sunday morning worship, nothing diminishes the centrality of the sacraments. In the vernacular of our church community, one might be heard to say, "Chile (child), you know I can't miss my communion."

The eucharist, referred to in most of our churches as holy communion or the Lord's supper, is usually administered on the first Sunday of each month (and on other occasions) to commemorate, with great thanksgiving, what God has offered to us through the life, death, and resurrection of Jesus Christ. In observance of the Lord's supper, our foreparents composed the well-known spiritual "Let us break bread together on our knees".

The elements of unleavened bread and unfermented juice of the vine (in some cases sacramental wine) are administered by ordained clergy, offered to all baptized believers, and received by persons kneeling at the altar rail. If persons are unable to kneel, they receive communion while either sitting in the pews or standing at the altar. There is meticulous care of the table exercised by the women whom we have designated as stewardesses. The altar rail and the table are dressed in white linen, spotlessly clean, creating an aura of reverence.

In the *Book of Worship* there are two orders for holy communion. One is the "traditional" order when the sacrament is administered at the conclusion of prayer, scripture and the preached word. The other order is called the service of word and sacrament; it is more clearly conceived of as a unit.

The AME Church baptizes infants, children and professing believers; all are believed to be biblically authenticated. In no wise is rebaptism allowed. The sacraments are a response to the word and a sign of our new freedom in Christ Jesus. Those persons who are of age and have not been baptized may choose one of three modes: sprinkling, pouring or immersion. Sprinkling and pouring are done at the altar rail. Immersion may take place in a heated pool which is a part of the architecture of the local church, or it may be done in a borrowed pool at a sister church, in a rented pool, in a river or lake, or at the seashore. Sometimes it becomes an occasion for an afternoon service.

The setting for worship

The place dedicated for the worship of God in the AME tradition can be a rather unpretentious and tiny facility with few furnishings and con-

veniences, or it may be a spectacular edifice – gothic or contemporary –
with seating capacity up to three thousand and decorated with accou-
trements. It may be a simple frame or cinderblock structure laid out and
built by members of the congregation, or it could be a structure of concrete, steel, brick or stone carefully designed by an architect and built by
the finest craftspersons. The space also may be an acquired facility pur-
chased as the result of an open occupancy housing market after the
majority community has taken flight to new suburbs and blacks have
moved in. The sanctuary may be a converted Jewish synagogue, or it
may be a building formerly occupied by a white congregation. A transformed supermarket, office building or movie theatre might also become
a place for worship. In each and every location, whether small or large,
decorated or plain, AME people "come into God's house, to magnify the
Lord, and to worship him".

The arrangement of Sunday morning worship is affected by a number
of different factors: a distinct understanding of time is found in black cultures; yet there are also the pressures of the clock in Western societies;
and each worshipping community has its space needs and logistical considerations. Some of the larger congregations may hold as many as three
Sunday morning services on a regular basis. Other congregations hold at
least two morning services. In at least one of our mega-churches, the third
service begins at noon. In still other congregations, the worship day is
completed with an evening service. It is also true that the spiritual fervour
of Sunday morning services may carry over into afternoon fellowship
services, which are a characteristic phenomenon of the black church.
These fellowship services may be either inter- or intra-denominational.

The ethos of worship

This ordered spiritual journey, called the order of service, is carefully
planned and executed by committed and inspired persons, both clergy
and lay, and rekindles the worshipping community with a spirit that runs
"from heart to heart and breast to breast". Together, clergy, choir, ushers,
altar pages or acolytes, and other appointed worship leaders do their work
in the presence of Jesus and under the inspiration of the Holy Spirit. The
hopes and dreams of the gathered community are reborn in worship, and
they depart to be the church scattered, often as a lone voice in the struggle for social identity and for true citizenship as children of God.

Even with all of the sublime euphoria penetrating the abject frustra-
tion of a minority people, there is still an air of expectancy as the worship service begins. The clergy may vest in a pulpit gown trimmed with
kente cloth of Africa design, in cassock and surplice, or in an alb and
wear either a kente stole or a stole in the colour of the particular liturgi-

cal season. The clergy, choirs and acolytes in process, the ushers strutting about, and the stewards and trustees, deaconesses and stewardesses all filing in with faces aglow, announce the grandeur of the occasion. The congregation waits: a diverse people from all stations of life, from common labourer to corporation executive, artisan or professional, all equalized in their "Sunday-go-to-meeting" clothes. They've come to praise the Lord, often with hung-down heads, or heads "bloody but unbowed", seeking solace for the soul, food for thought, direction for life decisions, something to hold on to in the week to come.

From this description of worship on Sunday morning, with its praise and proclamation, with the combination of head and foot worship (hand clapping and foot patting) as a demonstration of collective pathos, the questions to be asked are: Have they worshipped God "in spirit and in truth"? Have the people been stirred and stretched? Has the service been inclusive and multigenerational in its appeal? Have the defined goals for a planned celebration of authentic and indigenous expression of the faith been met? Have the people been nurtured?

In order to reflect on this reality from the AME perspective, attention is drawn to three prominent symbols: the cross, the pulpit and the anvil. The cross is for those who struggle for survival with dignity, an inexorable sign of God's loving care in Jesus Christ – the Jesus who understands all about us because Calvary is no strange place. The pulpit and the anvil might indeed be synonymous. Together they symbolize the strength of the word, the place where God's word is pounded out in tuneful, stentorian tones, and sometimes with whooping and dynamic gestures. Because the pulpit is central in AME worship, preaching is central, and the preacher who is sent by the bishop knows full well that, above all else, he or she is expected to preach the word. No matter that the preacher's theology may be fundamentalist, conservative, neo-orthodox, or liberal, there must be in his or her preaching some validation in the existential situation. Exhortation without logic is unacceptable; preaching without practise is inconsistent and therefore not believable.

As in other communions, AMEs debate the effectiveness of Sunday morning worship on the basis that preaching lacks quality. Sometimes it is argued that worship is not nurturing: there is too much performance; there are too many clichés; and it is without empathy. It might also be contended that the service is too preacher-centred, and that the style is too manipulative with a bent towards eliciting applause or creating a "feel-good" syndrome. Or the opposite may be the case: that the preacher is not sufficiently involved and is dry and insipid.

The criticism may also refer to the music: that it lacks sufficient variety or is too loud, or the tune is too worldly, or the lyrics are inappropriate. Nevertheless, numerous types of choirs sing with exhilaration, though with varying degrees of proficiency and employing a variety of musical genres. Some find reason to criticize how and when the offering is received or simply complain about whatever is uncomfortable, saying, "It is not the way we have always done things."

What cannot be contradicted is that when there is a well-prepared and balanced AME order of worship, where there is a synchronizing of the sacred and the secular, when thought and action are merged, when there is an emphasis on a faith that never doubts, then all the people of God are embraced and fed by the Holy Spirit. When such an event is held, spontaneity is not pre-empted by formalism. Animation does not negate genuine vitality, and a climate of bliss does not circumvent the sharing of legitimate emotions, such as pain, emptiness, sorrow, disappointment and anger.

Sunday morning AME worship is "a foretaste of glory divine". It takes seriously the needs of the human family, and it understands that all the answers are not determined by human effort, and that salvation depends on our God. The well-known cliché "after a while and by and by" is not irrelevant. For while we are convinced that there must be some respect due us in this world, we cannot allow our vision of a home "beyond this place of wrath and tears" to vanish. Not all of our dreams and hopes and aspirations will be consummated this side of the Jordan; there will always be one more river to cross.

The African Methodist Episcopal Church has at its masthead the motto, "God Our Father, Christ Our Redeemer, Man Our Brother". In 1992 there was an amendment to the third phrase, so that it now reads "Humankind One Family". Sunday morning worship, though designed, implemented, financed and supported by black people, is in actuality the body of Christ proclaiming the universality of the church's mission and ministry. We pray without ceasing Jesus' high priestly prayer, "that [we] all may be one" (John 17:20). We adhere to the Pauline passage that we are "neither male nor female" by honouring the presence of ordained men and women who preach and preside at the Lord's table. We follow the doctrine and discipline of the AME Church as a rule of faith and life. Above all else, we invite and embrace all of God's children. Although our worship together on Sunday morning is always a reminder of that oneness in Jesus Christ, it is unequivocally a celebration of the culture of black people and of the God who has called us to be.

NOTES

[1] The history of the African Methodist Episcopal Church is recounted in Charles Spencer Smith, *A History of the African Methodist Episcopal Church*, Philadelphia, Book Concern

of the AME Church, 1922; Harry V. Richardson, *Dark Salvation: The Story of Methodism as It Developed among Blacks in America*, Garden City NY, Anchor/Doubleday, 1976; and C. Eric Lincoln and Lawrence H. Mamiya, *The Black Church in the African American Experience*, Durham NC, Duke UP, 1990.

[2] Throughout this chapter, "African Methodist" will refer to those Christians of the African Methodist Episcopal Church.

[3] AME worship and worship in the African American tradition is discussed in such writings as James H. Cone, "Sanctification and Liberation in the Black Religious Tradition with Special Reference to Black Worship", *The AME Church Review*, 100, Jan.-March 1985, pp.18-31; Harold Dean Trulear, "The Lord Will Make a Way Somehow: Black Worship and the Afro-American Story", *Journal of the Interdenominational Theological Center*, 13, fall 1985, pp.87-104; Melva Wilson Costen and Darius Leander Swann eds, "The Black Christian Worship Experience: A Consultation", *Journal of the Interdenominational Theological Center*, 14, fall 1986 and spring 1987; and Melva Wilson Costen, *African American Christian Worship*, Nashville, Abingdon, 1993.

[4] *The Book of Discipline of the African Methodist Episcopal Church, 1976*, Nashville, AME Sunday School Union, 1976, p.11.

[5] Daniel A. Payne, *Recollections of Seventy Years*, New York, Arno and *The New York Times*, 1968, pp.253-56.

[6] *Discipline*, p.12.

[7] *The Life Experience and Gospel Labors of the Rt. Rev. Richard Allen*, Nashville, Abingdon, 1960, p.29.

[8] Sermon 2, "The Almost Christian", II.1-2, *Works*, 1:137-38.

[9] Richard Allen, *A Collection of Hymns and Spiritual Songs, from Various Authors*, Philadelphia, printed by T.L. Plowman, 1801, repr. Nashville, AMEC Sunday School Union, 1987.

[10] James Cone, *For My People*, Maryknoll NY, Orbis, 1984, p.150.

[11] For a study of AME worship in Zambia, see Walton R. Johnson, *Worship and Freedom: A Black American Church in Zambia*, New York, Africana Publ. for the International African Institute, 1977, pp.75-79.

[12] Albert W. Palmer, *The Art of Conducting Public Worship*, New York, Macmillan, 1939, pp.49-52.

[13] *The African Methodist Episcopal Church Bicentennial Hymnal*, Nashville, AME Publ. House, 1984.

[14] *The African Episcopal Church Hymnal*, Nashville, AME Publ. House, 1986.

[15] *The Book of Worship*, Nashville, AME Publ. House, 1984.

[16] Preface, *The Book of Worship*, n.p.

[17] *The AMEC Hymnal*, pp.xiv-xxii; and *The Book of Worship*, pp.9-22.

Worship as Understood and Practised by the Christian Church (Disciples of Christ)

KEITH WATKINS

• DISCIPLES OF CHRIST •

The Christian Church (Disciples of Christ) stands in the Reformed tradition as it was mediated by English-speaking Presbyterians, Congregationalists and Baptists in the United States in the early 19th century. This historical grounding has provided several characteristics that are also found in other church traditions with a similar heritage: a strong focus upon the transcendence of God and the need to obey the divine will; emphasis upon the importance of scripture as the word of God and primary source of information about God's intentions for human life and for the church; a stronger interest in questions relating to salvation than in questions relating to doctrines about the nature of God; a strong interest in reasonableness in theology and worship; a distrust of clergy and confidence in the ministry of all Christians; and a preference for extemporaneity rather than fixed texts in worship.

Distinctive characteristics of Disciples worship

Disciples have gradually developed a distinctive approach to worship that can be described under four headings. First, the Lord's supper is celebrated every Sunday as the normal service for the congregation. Indeed, Disciples believe that the remembrance of Christ's death and resurrection at the table is the one action that distinguishes Sunday from the other days of the week. The Lord's day and the Lord's supper are inseparable. The Sunday service ordinarily includes hymns and prayers, scripture readings and a sermon, an offering, and an invitation to people to become Christians and members of the congregation. The defining act, however, is the celebration of the Lord's supper. From their beginnings in the early 19th century, Disciples have assigned responsibility for developing the order of the Sunday service to congregations. Although each congregation, under the leadership of elders and their pastor, develops the pattern for its own use, two outlines are widespread. One is similar to the classic " shape of the liturgy" – introductory praise, readings from the Bible, sermon, prayers, offertory and eucharist; while the other is derived from customs that were widespread when congregations conducted the Lord's supper every Sunday even though there was preaching only occasionally. This second pattern reverses the order of sermon and eucharist.

Second, "the breaking of the loaf", as Disciples once called the supper, is presided over by local elders whom the congregation chooses from its own membership. In their earliest years, Disciples understood these local elders to be their ministry, fully responsible for the oversight of the congregation. This understanding has largely disappeared and today Disciples are not sure whether these elders should be considered laity or clergy; but there is rarely any doubt concerning the importance of this locally authorized presidency over a congregation's sacramental life. Disciples have, from the early years of the movement, ordained people with appropriate character and education to the office of ministry; and the general oversight of congregations and responsibility for worship ordinarily rests with these pastors. In most congregations today the pastor shares in leading the Lord's supper; but in nearly every church the voicing of the eucharistic prayers remains the responsibility of the congregation's elders.

Third, the prayers offered at the communion table are prepared by these local elders, often at the very moment that the service is taking place. The preparation of these prayers varies from one elder to another – some write their prayers in advance, while others speak them impromptu – but the personal character of these eucharistic prayers continues to mark Disciples practice. It has been the custom to have two prayers at the table, one said over the bread and the other over the cup. Their focus is usually devotional more than theological, expressing some aspect of the experience of salvation rather than articulating a doctrine of salvation or of the presence of Christ in the eucharist.

Fourth, Disciples hold a high doctrine of baptism as the act in which God acts to forgive sins, establish the new life of grace, and commission the new believer to live the Christian life. Baptism is performed in the name of the triune God, when people are old enough to speak for themselves, and by immersion; it is followed by admission to the table. Ordinarily, children of church families are welcomed by the congregation in a service of blessing, but their baptism and admission to the eucharist are delayed until they make their own confession of faith in Jesus Christ. Even so, Disciples welcome Christians baptized in other ways to the eucharistic table; and the majority of Disciples congregations are ready to receive these persons into membership even though the form of their baptism has differed from that practised by Disciples.

Other church traditions possess one or two of these characteristics, but no group outside the Disciples family of churches holds all four of these elements together. Churches in the catholic traditions also maintain the practice of eucharistic worship as the normal Sunday service. They differ sharply from Disciples, however, because the communion prayers in Orthodox, Roman Catholic and Anglican churches are developed and adopted by the general synods of these church bodies and published in books for pastors and others to use; and services of holy communion are always to be presided over and the prayers offered by ordained ministers. While some other Protestant churches also practise extemporaneous prayer, they rarely do so at the eucharist; and they ordinarily assign responsibility for administering the sacraments to ordained ministers.

Influence of the ecumenical and liturgical movements upon Disciples worship

One of the strongest convictions of Disciples is that there is only one church of Christ, even though that one church exists in multiple historical forms; and they have also believed that every congregation and larger church body is obliged to form its life according to the essential characteristics of the church universal. Their insistence upon the weekly eucharist and believer's baptism expresses two of these characteristics, as understood by Disciples. This church has been active in the ecumenical-liturgical movement of the 20th century, and especially in the Consultation on Church Union (now Churches Uniting in Christ) in the United States. They believe that recent developments in the ecumenical-liturgical movement confirm the eucharistic character of worship that Disciples long have held; and Disciples rejoice to see the way that other church traditions are recovering the practice of weekly eucharistic worship. They see in developments such as the [Roman Catholic] rite of Christian initiation of adults a renewed interest in believer's baptism, and they believe that here too their own understandings of normative Christianity are confirmed.

Their participation in the ecumenical-liturgical movement, however, has also brought important questions to Disciples. Much of their own development has been in isolation from other liturgical traditions, with the result that Disciples have developed idiosyncratic ways of conducting the eucharist and performing baptism. They have valued simplicity in form and an informal, popular style. As viewed by many observers from other traditions, however, Disciples liturgies appear truncated, their ceremonies abbreviated, and their theological understandings not well developed. Their participation in the Faith and Order processes, in the Consultation on Church Union, and in the North American Consultation on Common Texts has stimulated significant new work among Disciples aimed at strengthening their liturgical practice.

At the same time, Disciples have been affected by the dramatic changes in American culture that began in the 1960s and continue today. Along with other mainstream Protestant churches, Disciples have declined in membership and grown older in average age of constituents. During these years churches with charismatic and non-sacramental worship, and conservative theology, have grown rapidly. Some Disciples find themselves drawn to this contrasting pattern of convergence, with the result that they reduce even more their practice and theology of the Lord's supper. The contrast between Disciples with an ecumenical interest, and those developing according to "evangelical" principles, is one of the most important factors in contemporary liturgical practice among Disciples.

Liturgical questions facing Disciples today

The most important liturgical question for Disciples is stimulated by their participation in the ecumenical-liturgical movement: How should Disciples modify their traditional patterns in order to express more fully the ecumenical norms for celebrating the Lord's supper? This broadly stated question can be divided into several others: How can the extemporaneous prayer tradition be made stronger, both liturgically and theologically? How should the office of local elder be understood in the light of ecumenical understandings of ministry and sacramental practice? What guidelines should shape local decisions concerning the order of worship and related matters? How should sacramental and liturgical theology be expressed so that it is consistent with both ecumenical convictions and with Disciples customs?

A second question for Disciples concerns the relationship between baptism and the Lord's supper. Through most of the history of the whole church, and also of the Disciples, baptism has been understood as a prerequisite for admission to the Lord's table. In mainstream Protestant churches, in which the normal custom was to baptize the infants of church families, admission to the table was deferred until the late preadolescent years – the same age when children ordinarily were baptized in Disciples congregations. Increasingly, churches that practise infant baptism encourage communion at a much earlier age; and at the same time a growing number of Disciples are questioning the practice of denying their own – admittedly unbaptized – children from participating in the church's family table. Although the topic has only recently moved to a public arena, some Disciples are questioning the theological tradition and disciplinary practice that requires baptism before communion.

A third question focused by participation in the ecumenical-liturgical movement concerns baptism – at what time of life it should be undergone, and its form, meaning and repeatability. Disciples face a dilemma. On the one side, their doctrine of baptism – that God is at work for the remission of sins – connects them with Catholic, Lutheran, Anglican and Reformed understandings of baptism. Yet the pastoral norm in all of these church traditions, in contrast to Disciples practice, is infant baptism by affusion, and with a strong rejection of rebaptism. The more Disciples associate with the churches in these traditions, the more they find themselves acknowledging the legitimacy of infant baptism, with some slight tendency to begin practising it themselves. On the other side, the Disciples practice of believer's baptism by immersion connects them with Baptists and other evangelical church traditions, most of which hold a non-sacramental understanding of baptism and are ready to rebaptize as a pastoral practice. Many of the rapidly growing churches are in these traditions. The impact upon some Disciples is that they find themselves moving away from their own classic understandings of baptism and instead developing non-sacramental, evangelical doctrines and practices.

Conclusion

Perhaps the most important challenge facing Disciples as they participate in the ecumenical-liturgical movement is to become stronger contributors to the theological and pastoral discussion about worship. Despite the fact that the two sacraments have always been at the centre of Disciples identity, the scholars in this church have contributed relatively little to the scholarly literature concerning worship, the eucharist or baptism. At a time like this, when liturgical practice and sacramental theology are being reconsidered, the opportunity is present for Disciples – representing as they do a non-catholic sacramental understanding of worship – to speak helpfully to other portions of the body of Christ.

Liturgical Renewal
in the Old Catholic Church
Its Basis, Progress and Purpose

SIGISBERT KRAFT

• OLD CATHOLIC •

The Old Catholic Church: a brief introduction

After the promulgation of the decree on the infallibility and supreme
jurisdiction of the pope at the First Vatican Council in 1870, a number of
distinguished theologians, headed by the Munich church historian Ignaz
von Dölliger, as well as many priests and lay people – chiefly in Germany, Switzerland and Austria – were unable in good conscience to recognize these new dogmas and were consequently excommunicated. To
preserve a worshipping community for themselves and their children,
they therefore had to form their own congregations and local churches.

Because of their appeal to the faith of the ancient church they were
called Old Catholics. They quickly formed ties with the church of
Utrecht where, in 1702, a break had come about between Rome and the
local Catholic church. The Vatican had accused the Catholics of the
Netherlands of being Jansenists. The Archbishop of Utrecht, Petrus
Codde, was deposed from office and the cathedral chapter, which had the
right to elect bishops, was dissolved. Bishops, clergy and people saw
these unwonted centralizing measures as an infringement of the rights
which were theirs within the ancient church. In 1723, after Codde's
death, the chapter elected a new archbishop, Cornelius Steenhoven. The
Vatican was informed of this election, like that of all his successors; but
in each case until after Vatican II, the response was excommunication.

After the election of the first Old Catholic bishop in Germany by a
synod of priests and laity in 1873, the bishop of Deventer, Hermanus
Heykamp, consecrated the former Breslau professor, Joseph Hubert
Reinkens, as bishop. In 1889 the union of Utrecht, the association of Old
Catholic bishops and their sees, was founded and the common confession of faith was set out in the declaration of Utrecht. Today, Old
Catholic churches are to be found in the Netherlands, Germany, Switzerland, Austria, the Czech Republic, Poland, the USA and Canada, and
there are also communities in France, Italy, Scandinavia, Slovakia and

Croatia. The local churches have an episcopal-synodal constitution; they are autonomous and establish their own canon.[1]

Preserving the tradition of worship

Utrecht has always upheld its membership of the Catholic church. So it is not surprising that the Tridentine liturgy was maintained unaltered – and even in Latin – in the Netherlands until the first decade of the 20th century.

After 1870, in the Old Catholic movement too, powerful voices were raised against any changes. The liturgical tradition was to remain untouched, not least in order to counter the accusation that the "Old Catholics" were really "New Protestants"! In fact they saw themselves as being just as Catholic as they had been before 1870, so introducing change was by no means easy.

One paragraph in the declaration of Utrecht was to take on particular significance for later liturgical reform. Picking up one thesis from the first union conference in Bonn in 1874, it states,

> Considering that the holy eucharist has always been the true central point of Catholic worship, we consider it our duty to declare that we maintain with perfect fidelity the ancient Catholic doctrine concerning the sacrament of the altar, by believing that we receive the body and the blood of our Saviour Jesus Christ in the form of bread and wine. The eucharistic celebration in the church is neither a continual repetition nor a renewal of the expiatory sacrifice which Jesus offered once for all upon the cross; but it is a sacrifice because it is the perpetual commemoration of the sacrifice offered upon the cross, and it is the act by which we represent upon earth and appropriate to ourselves the one offering which Jesus Christ makes in heaven, according to the Epistle to the Hebrews 9:11,12, for the salvation of redeemed humanity, by appearing for us in the presence of God (Heb. 9:24).[2]

Then, referring to 1 Corinthians 10:17, it emphasizes that

> ...it is, at the same time, a sacrificial feast, by means of which the faithful, in receiving the body and blood of our Saviour, enter into communion with one another.

The first reforms in worship

As early as 1873 a student and close collaborator of Ignaz von Döllinger, the Munich church historian Johannes Friedrich (1836-1917), published a *Christkatholisches Andachtsbuch* [Old Catholic Prayer Book].[3] Only about a sixth of the book offers private prayers; the greater part contains texts and introductions on the celebration of the mass, the sacraments and sacramentals. Friedrich is concerned to show how the church worshipped in earlier times. He pleads for a liturgy which involves the whole congregation in the celebration:

> For there can be no greater debasement of congregational life than the separation of priest and people that now exists in the Roman Catholic tradition, so that each seems to be praying and acting for himself.[4]

The reforms that were essential, not least finding a language that could be understood by everyone, could only be drawn and developed from the sources of the early church. Friedrich begins his prayer book with an introduction to the celebration of the mass in the early church. Then comes a presentation of the "order of worship in the eigth book of the Apostolic Constitutions, otherwise known as the Clementine liturgy". In the order of the mass, Friedrich compares the Roman canon synoptically with an "Ethiopian liturgy", in this case the eucharistic prayer of Hippolytus, so that the differences and desired changes of which he speaks can be clearly seen. He refers to the collection *Die Hauptliturgieen der alten Kirche in wortgetreuer Übersetzung nebst Einleitung* [The Great Liturgies of the Ancient Church in Faithful Translation, with Introduction] by Joh. Ludwig König, a pastor in Wolkwitz, of the Pomeranian church in the (as it was called) Old Prussian Union.[5] König speaks in the introduction of the "great disfavour with which the ancient liturgies are regarded, especially in the Protestant churches".[6] No doubt it was partly for this reason that his book soon fell into oblivion and did not come to the notice of the Old Catholic authors who soon started to produce new, theologically grounded liturgical outlines.

At the first synod of the catholic see of the Old Catholics in Germany in 1874, it was stated that it was "desirable that in public worship and in the administration of the sacraments the language of the people should be used as the language of the liturgy". The second synod in 1875 instigated the preparation of a rite in German. This was drafted by Heinrich Reusch and sent to the parishes by the following year. It contains German texts for the administration of all the sacraments, including ordination to the priesthood, accompaniment of the dying, burials and blessings. Besides individual confession, it also provides for collective sacramental acts of repentance with absolution. By decision of the fourth synod in 1877, an order of service for Sunday worship conducted by lay persons was introduced. On Sundays and Feast days when no priest can be present to celebrate the eucharist, the congregation should still gather for worship.

In Switzerland, Bishop Eduard Herzog of Bern published a *Christkatholisches Gebetbuch für den gemeinsamen Gottesdienst* [Old Catholic Prayer Book for Common Worship] in German in 1879-80.

When it first appeared, as we read in the introduction, it did not yet "enjoy official status" and was simply "recommended to congregations wishing to celebrate the mass in German". Adolf Thürlings[7] – then the Old Catholic priest in Kempten, and as from 1887 professor of pastoral theology and liturgics at the Old Catholic faculty of the University of Bern – prepared a *Liturgisches Gebetbuch nebst einem Liederbuch als Anhang* [Liturgical Prayer Book with Hymn Book Attached], which was published in 1885. It contains the *Ordinarium* and the *Proprium* of the mass as well as orders for "matins and evensong" (the morning and evening hours of the congregation), following the example of the *Book of Common Prayer*. The Roman canon is preceded by a first order of the mass, maintaining its structure but making alterations in the content. Much greater changes are to be found in Herzog's work, especially quotations from the Letter to the Hebrews and the displacement of the *Communicantes* and the commemorations of the living and the departed to the end of the prayer, immediately before the great doxology.

In the works of Herzog and Thürlings the German prayers and readings are constitutive liturgical texts and not simply aids to understanding the service in Latin, like the Roman Catholic popular missals that appeared about the same time. The above-mentioned understanding of sacrifice contained in the declaration of Utrecht is clearly present in both books.

Both Herzog and Thürlings restore the epiclesis, but contrary to the models of the ancient church they insert it before the words of institution. As compared to the Roman canon of the mass they alter the words of the offertory to "We present him to thee as our pure, holy, unspotted sacrifice..." Herzog places the post-sanctus, the epiclesis and words of institution under the heading "consecration" and calls the anamnesis "prayer of sacrifice"; in Thürlings's rendering it is called "memorial". In his first order, the epiclesis is called "invocation" and the account of the institution is called "consecration". In both liturgies, the words "For this is my body...For this cup is my blood..." are highlighted in capital letters as a moment of transformation, as in the Latin missals of the time.

Thürlings's second order adheres more closely to the familiar text from the *Missale Romanum*, but likewise includes the theologically founded alterations in the words of the memorial and offertory. In place of the petition *ut nobis Corpus et Sanguis fiant dilectissimi Filii tui Domini nostri Jesu Christi* in the Roman canon, the text says: "...that in these gifts we may partake of the communion of the body and blood of your beloved Son, our Lord Jesus Christ". The content of the prayers of thanksgiving, notably the concluding prayer of the preparation of the elements *[Secret]* has likewise been altered, but space does not permit us to go into that in greater detail. Initially, Thürlings's liturgy for the mass was likewise simply "recommended for use", but by 1888 it was approved by the bishop and synod representatives and printed by their own publishing house.[8] Both authors start from the assumption that the "silent mass" no longer exists, and that the priest speaks or sings the whole liturgy loudly and clearly, with the congregation also responding aloud.

The liturgical orders prepared by Herzog and Thürlings were soon adopted by all German-speaking Old Catholic parishes and were in regular use up to the middle of the 20th century.[9] In Germany the fourth synod in 1877 had already added a second lectionary to the pericope of the *Missale Romanum* for Sundays and feast days.

Further developments in worship

The churches in Poland itself, and the churches of Polish emigrants in the USA and Canada which developed around the turn of the century and after 1918 and joined the union of Utrecht at a later date, did not spring from the theological opposition to the First Vatican Council. In their liturgy and popular piety they have retained Roman Catholic traditions.[10]

The structure and specific aspects of worship

After the second world war the German Old Catholic Church accepted the results and desiderata of the (Roman) Catholic liturgical reform movement. This, of course, was concerned not so much with alterations and reform of content as with a better understanding of the traditional liturgy as a basis for active participation. The German altar book of 1959,[11] for which Kurt Pursch was largely responsible, follows this line of thinking. Pursch places the eucharistic prayer under the headings "offertory and consecration" and gives preference to the second high prayer which is closer to the Roman canon; a third order following Hippolytus, added a decade later – without reference to the liturgical commission of the episcopal see – considerably shortened and altered the text of the outline. At the end of the anamnesis, just before the short invocation of the gifts that follows, the change made by Thürlings and Herzog is reversed in the words... "we offer to thee in him the bread of life and the cup of salvation". However, this altar book also includes a fourfold lectionary.

Discussing the theme "the theology of the eucharistic prayer", the international conference of Old Catholic theologians, meeting in Altenberg near Cologne, 24-28 September 1979, was to be crucial in setting the direction for the further work of liturgical renewal.[12] At the conference, the then archbishop of Utrecht, Marinus Kok, had urged that a common eucharistic prayer for the union of Utrecht should be composed. One year later, the International Old Catholic Liturgical Commission set up by the conference of bishops was able to present a text which was sent initially to the churches for their consideration. In its theology and structure – in keeping with the consensus of opinion at the theological conference[13] – the Utrecht eucharistic prayer follows the order of the ancient church more consistently than the high prayer of the Roman missal of 1969-70, the Lima liturgy of 1982 and the many Anglican and Protestant adaptations of the Hippolytus text from the time after the Second Vatican Council. Herwig Aldenhoven, the liturgical scholar from Bern, had already done important work which paved the way for this in his study "Darbringung und Epiklese im Eucharistiegebet" [Offertory and Epiclesis in the Eucharistic Prayer].[14]

Like the 1978 Old Catholic liturgy for the mass, the gradual renewal in Germany (trial versions in 1979 and 1986), the "Kerkboek van de Oud-Katholieke kerk van Nederland" of 1993 and finally *Die Feier der Eucharistie im Katholischen Bistum der Alt-Katholiken in Deutschland* [The Celebration of the Eucharist in the Catholic Diocese of the Old Catholics in Germany] of 1995 (2nd ed., 1997) re-established the link with Johannes Friedrich and the liturgical tradition of the early church.[15] This work drew on many insights gained from the state of full communion which was established in 1931 with the Anglican communion.

The new German missal includes a faithful translation of the Hippolytus text with, naturally, the eucharistic prayer of the Utrecht union, as well as some texts from the Old Catholic churches in the Netherlands and Switzerland. But it also includes eucharistic prayers from the Lima liturgy, from Taizé, the Roman Catholic Church in Switzerland, the new Anglican prayer books, the Lutheran World Federation and two Protestant provincial churches in Germany. The eucharistic prayer for the commemoration of the departed follows an outline prepared by the Roman Catholic liturgical scholar Heinrich Rennings, and there are also new texts – 23 versions of the eucharistic prayer in all. The church year maintains – as does the Anglican communion but contrary to the new Roman order – the season of Epiphany up to 2 February (Candlemas) with the Sundays of the baptism of Jesus and the marriage at Cana. Collects have been prepared for Sundays throughout the year, picking up the theme of the readings in the three lectionaries proposed in each case. This largely follows the *Ordo Lectionum Missae*.

In 1999 a new *Oud-Katholik Gezangboek* was published in the Netherlands, followed three years later by a "Lectionarium", intended for use in parishes, and the *Kerkboek van de Oud-Katholieke Kerk van*

Nederland. This includes the *Ordinarium Missae* with 12 versions of the eucharistic prayer and the *Proprium* for the church year, the administration of the sacraments, blessings and burials, as well as the liturgy of the hours. New hymn books were published in Switzerland and in Germany in 2003.[16]

The liturgical commission in Germany has issued individual booklets for the celebration of the sacraments and burials, the most recent being unction for the sick and the marriage ceremony.[17] As an alternative to the blessing pronounced on the couple, the latter includes prayers of epiclesis preceding the vows of betrothal and exchange of rings. For confessionally mixed couples a prayer of blessing from the Lutheran *Agenda* is also included. A particular eucharistic prayer for marriage can also be used on the Sunday of the marriage at Cana and on wedding anniversaries.

Celebrating in community

Until after the second world war little changed, compared to the Roman Catholic service, in the congregation's participation in the celebration. The congregation took part chiefly through the singing of the hymns and normally also in the liturgical responses. In many places the congregation received communion together only once a month. Easter night had been replaced by a celebration of the resurrection on the evening before Easter.

The priest celebrated at the high altar, distanced from the congregation and with his back towards them, and did the readings himself. On special occasions there was a solemn high mass *[levitiertes Hochamt]* with "deacon" and "sub-deacon", in which priests assumed also the roles of deacon and sub-deacon.

This did not change until the 1960s. Nowadays in the European sees of the union of Utrecht, the celebration of the eucharist with the priest facing the congregation; the regular receiving of communion; the readings and intercessions being done by members of the congregation (who also bring the elements to the altar) – all this is accepted as quite normal. In small groups the eucharist is celebrated as a table mass, often with a discussion sermon and free prayers. The sign of the cross and genuflection during the eucharistic prayer have gone. In many places the whole congregation joins in the great doxology, holds hands during the Lord's prayer and gives one another the peace with great warmth. Attendance is high during the three days of Easter, and especially on Easter night.

Despite the diaspora situation of the congregations almost everywhere, and the long distances that have to be travelled, many congregations also hold weekday services.

A new ordination liturgy

After 1980, at the request of the international bishops conference of the union of Utrecht, the International Old Catholic Liturgical Commission worked on a new version of the orders for ordination services.[18] Here too the aim was to bear witness in the *lex orandi* to the *lex credendi*, the basis of faith of the ancient church and hence of the Old Catholic faith. Each local church and its bishop are basically in communion with all the local *ecclesiae* of the one holy, catholic and apostolic church. As the full communion of all the churches no longer exists and because divisions must be healed, the bishop has the special task of ministry of unity beyond the bounds of his own church. In the ordination of deacons and priests, emphasis is laid on the fact that that ministry is subordinate to the bishop and the local church. The shared responsibility of the whole church is expressed through the agreement pronounced by the congregation, not unlike the *Axios* of the Orthodox ordination liturgy. This is intended to counter unwanted developments such as nomination or presentation only "from above" instead of by synod vote, or practices in which all that matters is the "ordaining power" of the ordainer who is himself validly ordained. These are chiefly to be found in the case of *episcopi vagantes* and, most recently, the "progressive" demands for ordination from Roman Catholic women outside their own church's orders.

Previously the orders used in the union of Utrecht were close to those of the *Pontificale Romanum,* even using the Latin formula *accipe spiritum sanctum* in the German language liturgy for the consecration of bishops – as, for instance, was still the case at the consecration of Josef Brinkhues in Mannheim in 1966. Even when Old Catholic bishops were invited to co-officiate at Anglican consecration services, they used these words at the laying-on of hands – such was the concern to ensure that Rome cannot deny the validity of Old Catholic ordination.

In the new order for the ordination of deacons, variations are provided for the prayer of consecration. If men are being ordained reference is made, as always, to the seven deacons in Acts 6. When women are being ordained deacon, the words used instead are, "Together with the apostles, women accompanied the work of your Son and were the first to meet the Risen One." For the first time two women were ordained as priests in Germany on Whit Monday (Pentecost) 1996, and in the years since then women have also been ordained in Old Catholic dioceses in Austria, Switzerland and the Netherlands. In this case the words, "He appointed Mary Magdalene to announce the resurrection to her brethren. Ever since that time men and women have borne witness to the good news of Jesus Christ" are inserted into the prayer of consecration.[19]

Summary and outlook

The reference to the faith and teaching of the early church has also led to a reform of worship in the Old Catholic churches in Western Europe in recent decades. The established results of liturgical research have been helpful here, as have the results of relevant ecumenical consultations. The episcopal-synodal constitution of the local churches has helped to shorten the road from the preparation of liturgical outlines to their practical use in parishes.

The celebration of the eucharist is at the centre of church life. If partaking of the one bread draws the many into the communion of the body of Christ and makes them one body (1 Cor. 10:16-17), then this celebration makes the concern for Christian unity a duty for all of us. The common reference to the Jewish roots of Jesus' institution, and the *lex orandi et credendi* which grew out of it in early times, is essential here.

If the separated churches of today were to take to themselves the witness of faith and worship which once bound all Christian communities in East and West, they would be on the path to unity. No one could reasonably say that to do this is not enough, or that it contradicts the basic statements of the faith and is hence "invalid". Even the divisive questions concerning the understanding of the ordained ministry can be overcome on the basis of the common *lex celebrandi* and the ancient church's understanding of the *berakah*/eucharist and the epiclesis. For this reason the churches' conversation on eucharistic fellowship and ministry should move beyond its present excessive focus on the accounts of the institution of the eucharist, taken in isolation.

NOTES

[1] Cf. in general Thaddeus A. Schnitker, "Old Catholic Worship", in *The New SCM Dictionary of Liturgy and Worship*, Paul Bradshaw ed., London, SCM Press, 2002, pp.339-40.
[2] On von Döllinger's initative, the conference was attended by Old Catholic, Anglican, Orthodox and Protestant theologians. See Urs Küry, *Die altkatholische Kirche, Ihre Geschichte, Ihre Lehre, Ihr Anliegen*, Stuttgart, Evangelisches Verlagswerk, 1966, pp. 103-106. Cf. Heinrich Reusch ed., *Bericht über die 1874 and 1875 zu Bonn gehaltenen Unions-Conferenzen*, Bonn, 2002.
[3] J. Friedrich, *Gott meine einzige Hoffnung, Christkatholisches Andachtsbuch*, Leipzig, B. Honer, 1873.
[4] *Ibid.,* Introduction, V.
[5] Neustrelitz, Verlag der Hofbuchhandlung von G. Barnewitz, 1865. König presents 18 eucharistic prayers which he allocates to seven liturgical families (Alexandrian-Ethiopian, Mesopotamian, Jerusalem-Antioch-Constantinople, Gallican-Mostarabic *(sic)*, Milan, Rome, Carthage). In the introduction he expressly emphasizes that his work is meant to aid the renewal of worship. He refers chiefly to earlier works by his contemporary Christian Karl Josias von Bunsen who, in turn, names as his sources the works of the founder of Ethiopian studies in Europe, Hiob Ludolf (1624-1704), the collection of Oriental liturgies by the French Catholic theologian Eusèbe Renaudot, the works of the Anglican

Joseph Bingham (1668-1723), the Bonn Protestant theologian and archaeologist, Johann Christian Wilhelm Augusti (1771-1841) and the Catholic theologian Anton Josef Binterim (1779-1841). A *Collection of the Principal Liturgies ...particularly the ancient...* by the Anglican bishop Thomas Brett (1667-1743) had already appeared in England in 1720.

[6] *Die Hauptliturgieen der alten Kirche in wortgetreuer Übersetzung nebst Einleitung*, IV.

[7] See Sigisbert Kraft, "Adolf Thürlings – ein Wegbereiter der Liturgiewissenschaft und der Erneuerung des Gemeindegottesdienstes", in *Internationale kirchliche Zeitschrift (IKZ)*, 74, 1984, pp.193-236.

[8] *Das Heilige Amt auf die Feste und Zeiten des Jahres*, Bonn, 1888.

[9] To be sure, at the suggestion of Bishop Adolf Küry of Bern the former Benedictine Ludwig Winterswyl, after his conversion to the Old Catholic Church, produced already in 1934 a comparative study "Das eucharistische Hochgebet der altkatholischen Liturgien". This made a synoptic comparison between the corresponding texts from The Netherlands, Switzerland and Germany as well as the *Book of Common Prayer*, and the canon of the *Missale Romanum,* which was regarded as witness to the common liturgical heritage.

[10] The missal "The Celebration of the Holy Sacrifice of the Mass", published by the National Commission on Liturgy of the Polish National Church in the USA (PNCC) in 1990, adopted the eucharistic prayer of the Utrecht union with considerable alterations in theology and wording. As in the other eucharistic prayers of the PNCC, the words of Jesus in the account of the institution of the eucharist are explicitly described as a moment of consecration. The offertory verse "Wir bringen mit Lobpreis und Dank diese Zeichen seines Opfers vor dein Angesicht" is altered to "We offer this sacrifice of your Son before you, Father, with praise and thanksgiving and ask you that you accept this oblation". The literally translated epiclesis of the gifts which follows thus comes out of context.

[11] *Altarbuch für die Feier der Heiligen Eucharistie im Katholischen Bistum der Alt-Katholiken in Deutschland*, published on behalf of the bishop by the [Old Catholic] Liturgical Commission, Bonn, 1959.

[12] The papers and the deliberations can be found in *IKZ*, 70, 3, 1980.

[13] *Ibid.*, p.226.

[14] In *IKZ*, 61, 1971, pp.79-117; 62, 1972, pp.29-73,89.

[15] Munich, Bremberger Verlagsgesellschaft. More on the sources of the early Christian anaphora and work being done on them today in Sigisbert Kraft, "Ist Eucharistische Gemeinschaft möglich? Überlegungen 20 Jahre nach Lima", in *Liturgisches Jahrbuch*, 2, 2002, pp.101-10.

[16] On the history of the hymnbook, cf. the study by Sigisbert Kraft, *Der deutsche Gemeindegesang in der alt-katholischen Kirche: Kirchenlied – Messegesang. Ein Beitrag zur Gesangbuchforschung – eine Hilfe für die Praxis von heute*, Universität Bern, Christkatholische Theologische Fakultät, dissertation, 1976.

[17] *Die Feier der Trauung im Katholischen Bistum der Alt-Katholiken in Deutschland*, Bonn, 2001.

[18] Cf. Sigisbert Kraft, "Die neugefasste Weiheliturgie der altkatholischen Kirchen und ihre ekklesiologische Bedeutung", in *IKZ,* 79, 3, 1989, pp. 192-203. The texts of the commissionings and the prayers of consecration are also documented here.

[19] It should be noted that the Polish National Catholic Church in the USA and Canada is as strict as the Roman Catholic Church in rejecting the ordination of women.

Variations on Themes in Worship
Pentecostal Rites and Improvisations

DANIEL ALBRECHT

• PENTECOSTAL •

The nature and purpose of worship

A GENERAL UNDERSTANDING

To consider the nature and purpose of worship from a Pentecostal perspective,[1] it would be good in this first section to offer a general definition of worship. In this paper "worship" means the human expressions directed to God, expressions that signify appreciation, reverence, devotion, profound love and other human affections that believers deem appropriate and authentic in their response to their understanding of divine revelation. Worship is normally contextualized by a faith community that over time has developed particular forms and styles of worship expressions (that is, acts, practices, rites), which function in part to make a "public witness to the union of God and humanity", and to call attention of the believers to God's character, actions, presence and provisions as recognized in the believing community's history and present moment.[2]

"Because it is God who always takes the initiative, Christian worship is best discussed in the terms of *response*."[3] So, in a real sense all worship is "responsive". Within the Pentecostal tradition a particular kind of responsiveness marks the understanding and practice of worship. A worship service is a kind of dramatic "conversation", a responsive interaction, a communion between the worshippers and their God. It is seen by Pentecostals as an *experience* wherein they express loving devotion and praise while encountering the presence of God. Such an experience of God signifies to Pentecostals God's loving concern and it helps to nurture, call, transform and commission them as people of God.

A PARTICULAR PENTECOSTAL PERSPECTIVE

The term "worship" itself represents a set of meanings to Pentecostals. Amid this set, Pentecostals understand worship as having at least three main connotations: (1) worship as *a way of Christian life,* particularly outside of the church services and activities: all of life is seen as worship – as an expression, a gift, offered to God; (2) worship as *the entire liturgy*, the whole of the Pentecostal service; and (3) worship as a *specific* portion, aspect or *rite* within the overall liturgy. Considering a Pentecostal understanding of worship within the context of their liturgy may be instructive. Within a Pentecostal worship service one might speak of dimensions of worship as experiential/experimental in the following ways: worship as encounter with God, as attentiveness to God, and as yielding a sensitivity to human need.

Worship as encounter[4]

Among Pentecostal congregants, saying "worship" is sometimes another way of saying "presence of God". "Worship" functions as a code term. It refers to the encounter with the divine as mediated by a sense of the divine presence and/or power. Pentecostals believe strongly in the manifest presence of God. Their experience of the holy presence shapes them spiritually. In the liturgy, the heightened awareness of this presence occurs often within a particular rite or phase of the service, for example during the rite "worship and praise".[5]

The Pentecostal attitude towards worship is essential to understanding their practice of it. For Pentecostals, worship is not strictly a human activity. Worship involves a deep communion between divinity and humanity, an encountering, a mutual experiencing. An attitude of expectancy shapes the practice of this communion. Believers expect God to come and meet with his people. Pentecostals believe that God alone inaugurates such a meeting by God's gracious acts and presence. Believers can only prepare themselves. The worshippers cannot force God's presence and movings. They can, however, prepare and wait for God's actions in and among them, and then respond to the "flow of the Spirit" when God's "promptings" or "stirrings" occur. Although pastoral or liturgical leadership is exerted, Pentecostals look to the Spirit who ultimately initiates, guides, facilitates and leads the worship. Because they fundamentally believe that God "desires to meet with his people", the Pentecostals approach worship with an attitude of expectancy. God will encounter God's people. This perspective moulds the style and structure of the liturgy and informs the understanding of worship as a type of encounter with God's presence and power.

Worship as attentiveness to God

While the goals of encounter may predominate, the worship service reflects a kind of performance, one that *attends* closely to the divine. Particularly in the praise and worship rites of the service, Pentecostals see themselves engaged in serving or performing for the divine. God is

the audience and the congregation performs the drama of praise. For as
they say, "God inhabits the praises of his people." This performance, for
the congregants, represents a way of attending to or focusing on the
Divine. It is a way of "ministering to God". Here the English word "service" informs. Attentive worship is adoration that focuses upon and is
seen as service directed unto God.

Worship as yielding sensitivity to human need
Pentecostals believe that serving God with attentive adoration will
result in an orientation that sensitizes them to the need of humanity. Service or ministry unto God both differs from and connects with other
aspects of ministry/service in the Pentecostal worship economy. To perform heartfelt authentic acts directed towards God is understood as the
ultimate in human expression. Truly worshipping God by God's grace,
they believe, allows them a subsequent awareness of human needs. In
the midst of their worship Pentecostals often report an emerging empathy towards the needs of others, and a motivation to minister to the
needs of others. God, they believe, "desires to minister to peoples'
needs" through God's faithful and gifted (graced) people. While much of
such ministry to others should eventuate outside of the worship service
context, Pentecostals believe that some such ministry should occur during the liturgy itself.

The pattern is understood as: in worship the believers minister to God
and then God, in turn, ministers in and through the believers to others.
For example, in many Pentecostal church services it is customary to
engage in some form of healing rite during the worship service. Congregants may form circles of prayer, praying for one another's needs. Or the
pastor may call those who desire prayer for a need to come to the altar
to be prayed for by the elders. At other times worshippers may simply be
asked to stand to signify a prayer request. Other worshippers will then
come to pray with them. In each case, congregants reflect a sensitivity to
human needs, a sensitivity founded on their belief that God is concerned
with human condition in all of its manifestations and that God calls and
gifts his people to minister to human needs.[6]

Distinctive aspects and qualities of worship: values, expressions and sensibilities

In this second section, we will attempt to illuminate some of the "distinctive aspects and qualities" of Pentecostal worship. Three categories
overlap and interact with each other: primary values that support and
inform Pentecostal worship; rites – acts of worship or worship expressions and practices that characterize Pentecostal "liturgy"; and liturgical

sensibilities or embodied attitudes that orient and animate the rites and practices of Pentecostal worship.[7]

VALUES THAT SUSTAIN AND INFORM WORSHIP[8]

Fundamental to Pentecostal worship are certain *values* that not only seek expression, but that support and inform both the worship *acts* and the *sensibilities* inherent and common to a Pentecostal form of Christian worship. Let us begin by identifying six of these implicit primary values.

Experience

First, there is little doubt that the value that most informs and supports Pentecostal worship and spirituality is experience. From what we have said above concerning the nature of worship as encounter, no one will be surprised by this assertion concerning the value of experience. Personal experience of God by the Holy Spirit not only lays at the core of the worship service for Pentecostals, it is for them the realm of authentic and vital religion. While doctrinal belief, liturgical participation, and ethical actions are valued and emphasized among Pentecostals, it is their experience of God that contextualizes their understanding of doctrine, liturgy and morality.[9] As a Christian group that emphasizes the experience of God, it might be expected that Pentecostals would emphasize the role of the Holy Spirit – the Spirit's presence and actions. As we have indicated, worship means an encounter with the Holy Spirit. Such an encounter is oriented and facilitated by a variety of modes of sensibility (see below), and interpreted, even corrected by scripture and doctrine. It is challenged and shaped by an ethical understanding of Christian love and mutual edification and by participation in liturgical action and praxis. But foundationally the personal encounter with the Holy Spirit remains at the centre of Pentecostal spirituality and worship. Pentecostals believe that God "comes" to meet with God's people, that God listens and responds to worshippers. They act on the belief that God has initiated the divine-human relationship and has invited people to enter into the presence of God. The particular order of rites or the configuration of a liturgy seems secondary to the *gestalt* or the entirety of the experience to Pentecostals. For the fundamental fact (belief) that God is present and that the faithful are called to attend to God's presence and to respond appropriately to that reality in worship (and praise) informs and gives meaning to all their liturgical practices. This "meeting with God" is understood as an experiencing of the divine.

Word of God and biblical authority

A second and all important Pentecostal value is represented in the symbol of "word of God" which complements and helps to balance the value of experience. The value of word of God can in part be thought of in terms of biblical authority and in the belief that God has spoken and still speaks. The importance of biblical authority to the Pentecostal tradition can be seen in a portion of an early Pentecostal official statement of faith: "The Bible is the inspired word of God, a revelation from God to man, the infallible rule of faith and conduct, and is superior to conscience and reason but not contrary to reason (2 Tim. 3:15,16; 1 Pet. 2:2)."[10]

Beyond official doctrinal statements, Pentecostals speak about and from the Bible frequently – not only in their worship services but in daily conversation. According to New Testament scholar Russell Spittler, to understand some of the unique practices and beliefs of Pentecostals is to understand their high regard for biblical authority "coupled with an inclination to take the words of scripture at face value". For example,

> if speaking in tongues is described in scripture as an acknowledged and approved part of Christianity, Pentecostals can see no good reason to eliminate it from contemporary spirituality.[11]

When Pentecostals employ the term "the word of God" they may be referring to the Bible. On the other hand, the terms "the word" or "the word of God" also symbolize the belief that God has spoken not only in the past but that God still speaks in and through the Bible and that God confirms the truth of the Bible in other ways, other "words". In the worship setting, Pentecostals hear the word of God in at least three primary ways: proclamation of the biblical messages, narrative testimonies and charismatic words or utterances. Each of these has a place in the worship service, but only as they are discerned to be authentically representing God's truth. Pentecostals insist that all words, including sermons, testimonials and charismatic words, must be measured by the Bible.

Oral aspects of liturgy

A third value that supports and informs worship in the Pentecostal tradition is its appreciation for orality. Even in Western countries the Pentecostal worship tradition is carried on largely as an oral culture. Ecumenical scholar Walter Hollenweger has recognized the centrality and importance of "oral liturgy" to Pentecostals worldwide.[12] Their oral liturgy not only reflects the type of liturgy that early Christians enacted but, according to Hollenweger, Pentecostal orality helps to make their liturgy accessible to a wide range of people and people groups globally. This raises an important issue. One of the most significant functional elements of a Pentecostal, oral liturgy is the active participation of all the members of the congregation.[13] The oral liturgy allows for broad participation for at least three reasons.[14] First, its basic contours and structure are easily memorized by the congregation. Second, it is continually "in the making", i.e. it is a dynamically emerging liturgy. This oral dynamic reflects and requires the people's participation, their engagement with one another and God in the moment and movement of the liturgy.[15] Third, it is the people and not merely the experts who exert liturgical leadership in the formation and performance of the worship service.[16] For example, narrative forms, such as testimony, which are highly valued by Pentecostals, allow the people to participate in the emerging liturgy and in a developing understanding and ethos of their spirituality as well.[17]

Spontaneity

Fourth, spontaneity, another value of the tradition, emerges within the oral and narrative forms of worship. As we have noted, Pentecostals believe that the Holy Spirit is ultimately the liturgical leader. It is the Spirit who guides the worship and the Spirit moves unpredictably (John 3:8). Pentecostal spontaneity has been portrayed as "liturgical improvisation" analogous to the dynamics of improvisation in music or acting.[18] In music, jazz especially, a scored or "scripted" melody is well known, or memorized, yet the musicians are free spontaneously to adapt, invent, expand and embellish improvisationally. The Pentecostal worship service or portions of it attempt to interact with and follow the Spirit by spontaneous improvisation. There is an underlying liturgical "script" (i.e. foundational rites, see below) and as with a melodic theme this Pentecostal "script" is well known if not written, but the script anticipates improvisation. Such improvisational enactment of the rites is one of the ways Pentecostals infuse their worship forms with new life. They believe that their interaction with the Spirit requires not only forms but freedom to respond with authentic heartfelt expressions.

Spiritual gifts

Fifth: of course, such improvisation under the impulse of the Spirit is akin to another valued dimension of Pentecostal worship, spiritual gifts (the *charismata*). Within the Pentecostal tradition "the gifts" function as a fundamental symbol inherent to the tradition's spirituality and worship. The charismata continue, as they have historically, to distinguish Pentecostal ritual from other Christian liturgies and to serve as a trademark of the overall spirituality. The manifestations of the gifts (especially the Pauline charismata) may be understood in part as reflections of a Pentecostal experience of Spirit baptism, sanctification, empowerment and edification. Elsewhere, we have described these as symbols contextualized by the Pentecostal liturgy.[19]

Ministry and mission(s)

Sixth, the Pentecostal tradition has always valued *ministry and mission(s)*. Within the framework of Pentecostal spirituality, ministry is often spoken of in three dimensions: ministry to God in worship, an edification ministry directed with the "body of Christ", and ministry to the world, called mission(s). Edifying ministry is prominent in the Pentecostal worship services. It consists of the actions, prayers and other rites in which believers share and serve the needs of one another in "the body". Pentecostalism has tended to democratize the category of ministry and that of mission too. While ordained ministry is normally recognized for its role of leadership, Pentecostals see all of God's people as called and gifted in some way in order to minister. As a result, Pentecostals seek opportunities to serve. The recognition of the exigencies in the human condition, coupled with their view of the biblical Jesus who sought to minister to people in need and called his followers to do likewise, has influenced the Pentecostal tradition. Consequently, the tradition takes ministry seriously. As we have indicated, the worship service becomes a natural setting in which ministry occurs. It also serves as a kind of launching pad for other ministries, particularly those directed towards "the world" beyond the faith community. Pentecostals call this type of ministry "missions".

While clearly there are other significant implicit values – for example, a certain other-worldliness, or particular awareness of eschatological realities, or others – that influence Pentecostal worship, the six above suggest the supportive, informative, interactive role that these values play within Pentecostal worship tradition.

RITES: ACTS AND EXPRESSIONS OF WORSHIP

With some of the fundamental values which undergird the Pentecostal tradition and its understanding of worship in view, we turn to consider the acts of worship as distinctive elements of the worship service. By rites or acts of worship we mean those actions, sets of actions, enactments and practices that characterize and express the values of worship in Pentecostal Christianity.[20] Hollenweger has argued that Pentecostal liturgy includes most elements of historical liturgies. "Yet", he says, "these parts are hardly ever named [by the participants] and for most observers are not recognizable as such."[21] Here, we will not attempt to prove the historicity of Pentecostal acts of worship, but will seek to identify the basic elements of a Pentecostal worship service as Pentecostals themselves conceive of and experience them.

When considering a Pentecostal service phenomenologically, certain patterns of acts and rites become clear, spontaneity notwithstanding.

Often there appears a certain fourfold pattern, which elsewhere we have described as the foundational rites and the microrites.[22] Essentially, there are three foundational rites which appear as separate "clusters" of acts of worship. Each of these clusters represents an adaptable pattern that potentially consists of several individual acts, or microrites. Together this cluster or pattern of microrites make up a foundational rite. There are three such foundational clusters or rites – the worship and praise rite which generally initiates the service, the sermon or biblical-pastoral message rite, and the altar response rite, which often indicates the climax of the liturgy. These three rites form a fundamental framework for many Pentecostal services.

The aggregate of microrites can be thought of as a fourth category of rites. Not that they represent a cohesive group; rather, they are individually moveable. They often do not depend on a particular sequence or pattern, though one microrite may emerge as a part of a pattern (e.g. a microrite may emerge within a foundational rite and then become integral to that foundational rite, or a microrite may emerge within a foundational rite and then become integral to that foundational rite, or a microrite may "season" the foundational rite in some way). Certain microrites also serve to assist in patterns of gathering and dispersing the people. They also function in transitions between foundational rites. The microrites are often recognized as characteristically Pentecostal, either in their particularity or the way they are expressed within the larger Pentecostal liturgical frame.[23]

Here, we can only identify but not explain some of the characteristic micro-rites and worship practices of the Pentecostal tradition. Enthusiastic, heartfelt, contagious music remains a hallmark of Pentecostal services. The foundational rite, "worship and praise", is largely structured by and infused with Pentecostal singing often with the local popular instrumentation. Clapping and other kinesthetic actions normally are expressed with the music. Raising of hands is common. Movement such as swaying or dancing in the Spirit, falling under the power of the Spirit or a Jericho march can emerge. Music and movement are quite normal in the tradition.

Other microrites are more oral or verbal. Sacred expletives, happy exclamation, such as "Hallelujah", "Thank you, Jesus", "Glory", may be in response during the sermon, or may erupt during other moments of the service. Testimonials of God's grace and assistance bring awareness of God "at work" in the everyday life of the common person. They serve as encouragement and stimuli to hope in divine intervention.

Many forms of prayer are notably oral and/or kinesthetic. We have mentioned collective oral prayer as concert prayer. Prayer often involves movement and can involve the tactile as well. Worshippers often move together, hold one another's hands, or reach out and touch another, perhaps, laying a hand on a shoulder and praying with or for a fellow worshipper. Divine healing is believed in and participated in at all levels of the congregation. Prayers for inner healing and exorcisms may also be practised. If a person is not present, proxy prayer might take place. It may even include the anointing of a prayer cloth, subsequently sent to a sick but absent believer, as token of the community's prayers and faith in God's healing provisions.[24]

We have already mentioned the role of charismata. Some Pentecostals experience and testify to the place of visions and dreams as well. But even more characteristic of Pentecostal worship and ethos is the time of believers' fellowship. Of course, during the gathering and dispersing rites such "fellowshipping" flows as a trademark of the connection and interdependence of the faith community. Worshippers may come early to fellowship and pray together, they may remain long after the benediction to visit, share and/or pray. The genuine love and sense of fellowship in the Spirit is obvious in the best of Pentecostal worship.

SENSIBILITIES IN WORSHIP

To understand Pentecostal worship, however, is not merely to identify rites (foundational or micro). Even the most characteristic practices do not in themselves describe worship in the Pentecostal tradition. To explain Pentecostal worship, one must take account of its rites and the values they express, as we have, and in addition must seek to identify and understand the sensibilities with which Pentecostal rites are enacted and experienced.

So the last of the three categories to be considered here is the category of the modes of sensibility in the worship service.[25] As embodied attitudes, the modes of worship sensibility help orient and animate each of the various Pentecostal acts of worship, i.e. rites, actions and characteristic practices, including the charismata, within the Pentecostal service. As a part of the worship services, the acts of worship, the rites, help to provide a dimension of organizational design – the structural and processual aspects – to the liturgy. However, the embodied attitudes, that is, the worship sensibilities, work by helping to animate the rites. Through the various modes of sensibility within the worship service, the Pentecostal practices are expressed and experienced.

Worship sensibilities then are a dimension of the worship experience dynamically related to, though not necessarily contained within, the structure of the rites. The modes of liturgical sensibility interact with the rites; that is, a "dynamic affect" mediates between the acts of worship (the rites) on the one hand, and the attitudes of worship. There are at least seven modes, or ideal types, of sensibility[26] that pervade Pentecostal services: celebration, contemplation, transcendental efficacy, penitence, ecstasy, improvisation (ritualization) and ceremony.[27]

A close look at any Pentecostal worship service would reveal at least some of these seven modes of sensibility and possibly others. Recognizing these sensibilities helps to provide a better understanding of an essential affective component of Pentecostal spirituality and worship. These modes seldom emerge as unmixed, or as ideal types. For instance, a sensibility of contemplation may coincide with a penitent/purgative mode of sensibility or the mode of celebration might mix with a more ecstatic mode.

Sensibilities do not exist in isolation. Neither are they merely emotions. They are affective ways of experiencing and expressing the Pentecostal rites framed by the worshipping context. As we have said, various sensibilities may arise in the midst of a particular act of worship. In fact it seems theoretically possible that any rite or practice could be matched with any of the sensibilities, though some modes of sensibility certainly seem more appropriate to particular rites or actions of worship than do other sensibilities.

RITES AND SENSIBILITIES: TWO AXES

We are portraying our understanding of the relationship between the modes of sensibility and rites of the Pentecostal worship as two dimensions, each on its own axis. To illustrate these two axes and thereby to show a relational dynamic within a Pentecostal service, let us briefly consider one simple gesture very common during the Pentecostal liturgy – the raising of hands.[28] We employ this example to help show how this and other gestures, as well as more complex microrites, within the Pentecostal service may potentially be enacted with, and oriented by, a variety of modes of sensibility. It also may suggest that the meaning of a particular rite, action or physical gesture changes in accord with the mode of sensibility.

In the liturgies of Pentecostal churches outstretched arms with lifted hands can express a broad range of experiences.[29] Such breadth is supported by a range of ritual sensibilities. Thus, one gesture (the raising of hands) has the ability to express numerous and differing experiences, and it can have varied meanings, each one animated by at least one liturgical mode of sensibility. Individuals, for example, often extend hands high to express praise to God in a celebrative mode. Sometimes in a more ecstatic sensibility, hands are lifted and waved as an expression of the ecstasy. Lifting hands, with palm up, often expresses an openness to

God, a vulnerability and receptivity, and is frequently accompanied by a sensibility of contemplation. The lifted hands and bowed head as an act of contrition may express the penitent mode. The mode of transcendental efficacy also animates hands to be lifted. For instance, in healing rites typically a pastor, elder or congregant places one hand on the person being prayed for and lifts his or her own other hand heavenward. This can express a reaching out to God while touching one in need, an offering of oneself as a conduit for healing power, an "instrument for God's work". Of course, the liturgical leaders at times lift their hands as a sign of blessing and this happens in a more ceremonial mode of sensibility. Hopefully these examples make clearer how a simple act or gesture may be employed variously and with many possible modes of sensibility. And it suggests that other more complex acts of worship and rites are also oriented and animated by a similar variety of sensibilities, resulting in a potentially rich array of worship expressions and a multifaceted worship experience.

Let us summarize. In this second section we have attempted to discuss some of the distinctive aspects and qualities of worship from a Pentecostal perspective. We have done this by considering the main categories (or variables) of primary values, expressive acts (rites) and sensibilities. These three basic elements are inter-related (as variables) in a worship experience. The dynamic relationship among them determines (at least in part) the process and contours of the worship service. Briefly stated, the relational process consists of the following. The primary values support and inform both the rites and the sensibilities. The rites express or dramatize the values in acts that symbolize the values and beliefs. Also, the rites enact the sensibilities, disclosing and communicating the embodying attitudes through acts; rites give a human face and voice to the values and sensibilities, they incarnate and provide the values and sensibilities with action. The sensibilities orient and animate the rites and facilitate the appropriation of the values.

Worship and Christian unity[30]

In this third and final section we turn to consider the Pentecostal worship tradition in light of the liturgical renewal and ecumenical movements and the search for Christian unity. Here we shall address two basic questions in a preliminary fashion: (1) How have the liturgical and ecumenical movements influenced the worship tradition? (2) What developments in the Pentecostal traditions may help (or hinder) the search for Christian unity?

Before we address these questions directly, a word about the Pentecostal worship tradition is appropriate.

Although Pentecostalism has roots in the historic church and several renewal movements, the modern Pentecostal movement emerged at the beginning of the 20th century. This early movement and its descendants have been named "classical Pentecostals". A second phase of Pentecostal-like worship appeared in the middle of the century within mainline churches as a kind of "neo-Pentecostalism". It came to be called "charismatic renewal". These two currents, while different, have many similarities including aspects of spirituality, forms of prayer, and elements of renewed worship. With these similarities in mind, it may be helpful in this section to speak of the Pentecostal-charismatic movement as one stream – albeit with two currents. By classifying the two together we might be better able to consider briefly some relational qualities between the topics under discussion. For often what has affected the one, i.e., the charismatic, has impacted the other, i.e. the Pentecostal. For example, sometimes charismatic renewal has been affected by developments in the larger church and has then mediated some of that effect to the classical Pentecostals. On the other hand, the impact of Pentecostals upon mainline churches has often first been conveyed through the charismatic renewal. We turn now to look at how the church at large has influenced the Pentecostal-charismatic worship tradition, particularly via the liturgical and ecumenical movements.

PENTECOSTAL-CHARISMATIC WORSHIP AND THE LITURGICAL AND ECUMENICAL MOVEMENTS

Liturgical renewal as seedbed for charismatic renewal
Liturgical renewal provided a seedbed for the charismatic movement and it helped to create the conditions within which the charismatic renewal could germinate and grow. In their book Worship in Transition: The Liturgical Movement in the Twentieth Century, Fenwick and Spinks assert that "it is undoubtedly the case that the charismatic renewal and charismatic movement and the liturgical movement are related".[31] The question is, of course, in what ways are they related? The two have numerous similarities including both having an interest in the early church, both stressing the faith community and participation in and accessibility for worshippers in the worship, and both having sought to re-emphasize the role of the Bible in liturgy and life. These similarities aside, the two movements are not coterminous. Fenwick and Spinks speak of a symbiotic relationship between the two. In their view, the liturgical movement originally served as a seedbed for charismatic renewal. That is to say: the liturgical renewal helped to prepare the way for the charismatic renewal, and then renewed members worked for liturgical renewal.[32]

Cardinal Suenens, whose name has been so closely linked with
Catholic charismatic renewal, sounded a similar theme when he noted
the charismatic renewal's indebtedness to the liturgical movement which
helped to stimulate and shape the emerging charismatic renewal.[33]
Again, members of charismatic renewal engaged in the ecumenical
movement, seeing their renewal in the Spirit as a force for Christian
unity. Fenwick and Spink recognized this dynamic. An

> important feature of the charismatic movement has been the way in which it
> has helped to erode denominational boundaries. Catholics and Protestants, for
> example, have been forced to take each other seriously as fellow Christians in
> the light of a common experience of the Holy Spirit.[34]

So, one could say that the Pentecostal-charismatic worship tradition
was influenced by liturgical renewal, in that the liturgical renewal func-
tioned to create a more flexible and sympathetic environment, a seedbed,
in which another phase of the Pentecostal-charismatic movement,
charismatic renewal, might develop.

*The ecumenical and liturgical movements: fostering contact between
worship traditions*

Another form of influence on Pentecostal-charismatic worship
brought about by both the liturgical renewal and the ecumenical movements can be seen in the contact encouraged between worship traditions.
Such contact has cultivated a process of cross-fertilization and borrowing between worship traditions, that in turn has produced what theological and liturgical scholar Robert Webber has identified as "convergence". Webber classifies four worship traditions – liturgical, traditional
Protestant, creative/contemporary model, and the Pentecostal-charismatic – that he claims are presently borrowing significantly from one
another. The mutual influence that results from such borrowing he calls
the "convergence of worship traditions". In large part, this convergence
is the result of the movements and dynamics exerted within the contemporary ecumenical and liturgical realms. Webber believes that the liturgical renewal movement is responsible for "the spiritual stimulation
which comes with borrowing from various worship communities".[35]
Although some observers have argued that more has been borrowed *from*
the Pentecostal-charismatic worship tradition (we shall return to this
below) than *by* them in recent years,[36] the sharing seems to be moving in
both directions.

In fact, the current contact and borrowing between the Pentecostal-
charismatic worship and other worship traditions seems to have nurtured
an increasing openness among Pentecostals towards other ways of wor-

ship. Webber cites several examples of Pentecostal openness. He notes an openness among many Pentecostal leaders to learn from others, an interest in the potential contribution of others towards a fuller experience of worship. Such interests coupled with a "felt-need", has led some Pentecostal pastors to begin to restructure their worship services to include elements from the broader Christian worship tradition while remaining faithful to their own Pentecostal values. Webber is "convinced that borrowing, done intelligently and with spiritual sensitivity and then wisely integrated into worship, can have a powerful positive effect on a congregation's life" – and, we would add, foster the goals of Christian unity.[37] Let us now look briefly at some other developments within the Pentecostal-charismatic worship tradition that may suggest potential for (or resistance to) the search for Christian unity.

HELPS (AND HINDRANCES) IN THE SEARCH FOR CHRISTIAN UNITY

When we speak of developments that help (or hinder) the search for Christian unity, we imply an acceptance of University of Notre Dame professor of liturgy James White's assertion that "worship traditions are never static". When White refers to the Pentecostal-charismatic tradition he extends his assertion that traditions are dynamic and developing with the emphasis: "especially when dominated by the Holy Spirit!" Here, we will mention only three developments within the Pentecostal-charismatic worship tradition which may prove to be helpful in the search for Christian unity (we will also note some elements which might hinder the same).

First, the Pentecostal-charismatic tradition has shown native impulses and vision (at least periodically) for Christian unity. Others have documented the early Pentecostal envisioning of unity. And it is clear that the charismatic renewal brought with it a hope and impetus for ecumenism.[38] At the same time, it must be admitted that there have also been hesitancies and fears which have slowed ecumenical endeavours especially among classical Pentecostals.[39] It may be that one of the main problems is that Pentecostal visions of Christian unity are different from the visions of many in the ecumenical movement, or at least they are perceived to be different. Nonetheless, a native impulse towards unity persists. Towards that end, Pentecostals have consistently been a people who believe in and actually practise crossing boundaries.[40] Rooted in Pentecostal values (see above), and believing that "the experience of the Holy Spirit is the one importance force which sweeps away all denominational, racial, educational, and social divides", Pentecostals do reach across boundaries towards a unity.

A second element that may help the search for Christian unity is related to the influences that we have noted above, particularly as mediated through what we called mutual borrowing of worship practices. As we have indicated, classical Pentecostals have in recent decades moved away from the isolation that once characterized them. The resulting interaction has helped ecumenical relations.[41] While we noted (above) the influence of the liturgical movement on the Pentecostal-charismatic tradition, and the borrowing by Pentecostals of more historical forms of worship, it is also quite clear that Pentecostal-charismatic worship has had a significant impact on the worship of the wider church.[42]

This impact, seen in part in the aspects of Pentecostal-charismatic worship adopted by non-Pentecostal faith communities, may forecast an increased openness of Pentecostals to ecumenical dynamics. Perhaps the development of increased mutual borrowing may serve as a stimulus for Christian unity. Why? Pentecostals may recognize the willingness of others to adopt some of their worship practices as a symbol of respect and sympathetic understanding. Such attitudes might reduce suspicious fears that often hinder our ecumenical goals. Also, due to the recent development of mutual borrowing, Pentecostals can more easily recognize something familiar in other traditions of worship. This recognition in turn may help Pentecostals to affirm more quickly (at least something of) the nature of the other's tradition, discerning the Spirit's work in sister traditions. This may then help us to build bridges, a concept with which we will conclude.

A third development that may help in our search for Christian unity is the emergence of what the late Jerry Sandidge called "bridge people", individuals and groups that will build and become themselves ecumenical bridges.[43] Bridge people seek to address the hindrances – the fears, misunderstandings or misperceptions, and apathy – that plague authentic ecumenism, and use the "helps" as a foundation from which to build. Sandidge identified the need for bridge people more than a decade ago. While his call must still be heard and heeded, there are some signs of bridge people among us. Two prime examples of such people are Walter Hollenweger and Cecil (Mel) Robeck, Jr.[44] Hollenweger and Robeck know and love the potential in Pentecostal-charismatic tradition, yet both are troubled by its shortcomings. And both believe in the Spirit's call to true Christian unity. Their analyses, critiques and hard work model the bridge person's role and they are signs among us of hope in our search for unity.

Summary

In this paper we have attempted to describe the nature of worship from a Pentecostal perspective. We have discussed and briefly analyzed some of the characteristic aspects of Pentecostal worship and the relational dynamics among them. Also, we have considered the interaction among contemporary movements – all with an eye towards Christian unity. Our aim in discussing (perhaps even affirming) particular distinctive qualities of a Pentecostal type of worship is not to produce more divisions among Christians. Rather our aim is to appreciate, and even to encourage, the variety found both within and among worship traditions. And our aim is, in the midst of this greater appreciation, to seek to comprehend, to move towards, and to experience the unity in Christianity, especially as mediated in forms of Christian worship.

NOTES

[1] While this descriptive analysis seeks to be a general introduction to worship from a Pentecostal perspective, the inherent problems of such an endeavour are all too obvious. Pentecostal worship is expressed by widely divergent people and people groups around the world and within a great variety of denominational families as well as independent-type Pentecostals. No one description can do justice to all of these peoples and their experience of worship. I admit that I am a North American, white and male. And I am a member of a particular Pentecostal tradition, the Assemblies of God. These few traits alone, though not entirely limiting, do contextualize my perspective. While in this paper I attempt to transcend my own idiosyncrasies and give voice to other Pentecostal perspectives, I am aware that this cannot ever be fully realized.

[2] See "Worship" by J. W. Sheppard, in S. Burgess, J. McGee and P. Alexander eds, *Dictionary of Pentecostal and Charismatic Movements [DPCM]*, Grand Rapids MI, Regency/Zondervan, 1988, p.903.

[3] J. D. Crichton, "A Theology of Worship", in *The Study of Liturgy*, Cheslyn Jones, Geoffrey Wainwright and Edward Yarnold eds, New York, Oxford UP, 1978, p.7.

[4] Of course, Pentecostals believe in encountering and relating to their God outside of this particlar dimension. They often encourage each other with the verse "we walk by faith and not by sight" (1 Cor. 5:7). To the Pentecostals this verse means that the Christian life is not based on "sight" of manifestations of the divine. It is rather founded on faith in God. Nonetheless, a kind of dimension akin to hierophany or epiphany is appreciated as facilitating worship, particularly within the ritual worship setting.

[5] See D. Albrecht, *Rites in the Spirit: A Ritual Approach to Pentecostal-Charismatic Spirituality*, Sheffield, UK, Sheffield Academic Press, 1999; and Albrecht, "Pentecostal/Charismatic Spirituality: Looking through the Lens of Ritual", PhD diss., Graduate Theological Union, Berkeley CA, 1993.

[6] In connection with the theological nature of worship as understood by Pentecostals, and the purpose inherent in that nature as described in this section, let us briefly note what might be thought of as "pastoral purposes" (or perhaps "pastoral functions" or roles) related to the worship service. These include the functions of developing an environment that supports and nurtures the worship experience. Also included in the pastoral purposes of worship is teaching attitudes and forms of worship. Through instruction and practice within the worship service worshippers learn that a wide range of expression may become worship. Encouraging the corporate nature of worship is another pastoral purpose of the worship service. While Pentecostals enjoy and practise private devotions, they also seek and appreciate the "opportunity to be part of the uniqueness that happens in corporate praise and adoration". It is often described with the metaphor of a symphony. Many and varied instruments play individual parts to produce a multifaceted performance. And of course, proclaiming the gospel and calling for an authentic response to the gospel are central pastoral purposes of nearly any Pentecostal worship service. These and other pastoral

functions are addressed by Allen Groff, a Pentecostal writer, counsellor and long-time pastor, in a private communiqué, "Nature and Purposes of Worship".
[7] In addition to orienting and animating rites, the sensibilities to some extent facilitate the appropriation of the values or beliefs.
[8] Russell Spittler has identified implicit values that support Pentecostal/charismatic spirituality in his article "Spirituality", *DPCM*, 804-809.
[9] On the centrality of experience see Harvey Cox, *Fire from Heaven*, New York, Addison-Wesley, 1995, where he recognizes the experiential nature of Pentecostal worship in claiming that for Pentecostals "the experience of God is absolutely primary". As a result, he altered his approach in order better to study Pentecostals, p.71. Also see his description of experience, pp.300ff. For differing Christian approaches to Christianity, Spittler in his "Spirituality" cites Lesslie Newbigin, *The Household of God: Lectures on the Nature of the Church*, London, SCM Press, 1953, where Newbigin describes three basic approaches: a view that emphasizes the intellect, seeing it as belief and doctrinal assent; an approach that regards obedience, participation and religious actions as the primary realm of religion; and thirdly, that which recognizes personal experience as foundational. Pentecostals are clearly represented in the third approach.
[10] From the American Assemblies of God's 1916 formulation as quoted by Spittler, "Spirituality", 805-806. The statement has subsequently been revised.
[11] *Ibid.*
[12] Walter J. Hollenweger, *Pentecostalism: Origins and Developments Worldwide*, Peabody MA, Hendrickson, 1997, pp.269-72.
[13] *Ibid.*, p.271.
[14] *Ibid.*, p.270.
[15] Ronald Grimes, noted ritologist (ritual studies expert), identifies this dynamic as "ritualizing". By this he means the activity of cultivating or inventing rites; it is a process, a quality of nascence or emergence; see his *Ritual Criticism*, Univ. of South Carolina Press, 1990, pp.9-10.
[16] Hollenweger argues that such an oral liturgy should not be thought of as only for preliterate peoples. In fact the majority of people in the world today are "oral people", and a liturgy that is not sensitive to them might be exclusive in some ways. He also suggests that today many "middle-class... highly trained intellectuals find the 'oral order' more satisfying" than the strictly written one. He notes the great attracting power of the charismatic movement within the mainline churches as one evidence of this; see *Pentecostalism*, p.271.
[17] Testimonies and narratives are fundamental to Pentecostal worship and spirituality as Steven Land among others had argued; see his *Pentecostal Spirituality*, Sheffield, UK, Sheffield Academic Press, 1993, esp. ch. 2 and his "Pentecostal Spirituality", p.485. "Such narratives place daily life as well as 'spiritual experience' within a biblical/faith framework. These 'sharings' may occur in speech or song; they may take on a formal aim or be informally related. But authentic testimony which speaks out of human experience seeks to discern the works of God in the life of the faith community and world. Functioning in this way, testimony narratives provide a way of doing theology. Thus, the narratives both interpret the works of God and give voice to the words of God"; see Albrecht, *Rites*, ch. 7, the section "testimonial narrative".
[18] See Albrecht, *Rites*, ch. 5; Cox, *Fire from Heaven*, ch. 8; Land, *Pentecostal Spirituality*.
[19] See Albrecht, *Rites*, ch. 7 and "Pentecostal/Charismatic Spirituality", pp.306-308.
[20] We use the term rite (or foundational rite) when referring to a portion or phase of the worship service (e.g. the sermon, the song service), or a set of actions (e.g. various types of altar/responses). Rite (or microrite) is also used when speaking of a particular practice or specific act or enactment (e.g. laying on of hands and prayer, taking an offering, receiving water or Spirit baptism) recognized by Pentecostals as a legitimate part of their overall ritual.
[21] Hollenweger, *Pentecostalism*, p.271.
[22] See Albrecht, *Rites*, ch. 4; also Albrecht, "Pentecostal Spirituality: Looking through the Lens of Ritual", *Pneuma*, 14, 2, fall 1992, pp.107-25.
[23] See Spittler's description of "characteristic practices" in his "Spirituality", *DPCM*, 806-808; see also for a fuller list of "microrites", i.e. Pentecostal worship expressions, Albrecht, *Rites*, appendix B.

[24] Such rites point to the dynamic and creative potential inherent in the Pentecostal practices and understanding of worship. The potential has both positive and negative possibilities. Positively, Pentecostal/charismatic worship can allow for enthusiastic, vital participation of all congregants. It encourages each person to enter into a dramatic conversation with God mediated through a faith community, wherein worshipping Pentecostals become a people, a family, an interconnected, supportive, transformative community. The community seeks to reorder itself within its understanding of divine guidance, guidance from the Holy Spirit as understood in the worship context.

But there are, of course, potentially negative possibilities inherent in the Pentecostal practice and understanding of worship, as well. One danger of a Pentecostal understanding of worship is that it can become too narrow. Pentecostals have in the past been intolerant of other forms of worship. Or Pentecostals can become fixated on their own rites and practices, revealing little appreciation for other possible symbolizations from historic Christianity or contemporary spiritualities. These potentially negative attitudes may work together to produce a form of Christian elitism (an oxymoron). Finally, the Pentecostal conception of worship is also filled with the danger of self-deception. In the affectively charged dimension that Pentecostals call worship, human sensations and emotions are encouraged and believed to help in the communicative process with the divine. The need to rightly discern an authentic "move" of the Spirit is opposed to self-deceiving impulses. The danger of assigning divine origins to neurotic impulses and behaviour always threatens in the absence of rigorous discerning practices. In general Pentecostals seem aware of these potentials, positive and negative, and apparently believe the risk is worth taking. The benefits outweigh the negative possibilities.

[25] By "sensibility" we mean an embodied attitude which is the result of abilities to feel or perceive, as in a receptiveness to impression or an affective responsiveness towards something. Our understanding of sensibility overlaps Steven Land's category of "Pentecostal Affections"; see his *Pentecostal Spirituality*, esp. ch. 3.

[26] Although examples of an "ideal type" (a singular, unmixed sensibility) of a Pentecostal ritual mode of sensibility may be uncommon in the actual practice of the rites (most often the modes co-exist, and even mix), the "ideal" or "pure" category can fulfill a heuristic function.

[27] We think of these seven modes of sensibility in Pentecostal worship as follows. The celebrative mode embodies an attitude characterized by expressiveness and spontaneity; it roots in the actions an attitude of playfulness which enjoys the experiencing of the religious symbols. The mode of transcendental efficacy occupies the other end of the spectrum of liturgical altitudes from celebration, it refers to an attitude that participates in pragmatic ritual work particularly in relationship to a transcendental reality – God, and the power of God to produce an effect. Transcendental efficacy functions with practical goals. It is more concerned with consequence than meaning. The contemplative mode is marked by a deep receptivity and a sense of openness to, and docility before, God. The penitent/purgative mode of sensibility is characterized by contrition, repentance, remorse, sorrow, lamenting or grieving. The mode of (transcendental) ecstasy is the sense that one is directly influenced by God, a sense of being inspired or moved to act, possibly even the sense of being acted upon or seized by the divine, a sense of a direct experience of the divine; while the ceremonial mode shows more intentionality than the other sensibilities and requires some suppression of individuality in favour of a larger liturgical task. See Albrecht, Rites, for a fuller description of these sensibilities.

See also Ronald Grimes, who identifies a series of modes of sensibility. Although his categories are not meant to apply to Pentecostal ritual (they are broad and seek to encompass types of sensibilities in varied – even universal – ritual settings), his general insight suggests application for Pentecostal ritual. In the identification, description and analysis of Pentecostal sensibilities, we have used Grimes's foundational insight. However, our set of seven modes of ritual sensibilities reflects an extension, a significant rearrangement and conceptual adaptation of Grimes's categories, in order to make them specifically applicable to the Pentecostal rites. For Ronald Grimes's categorization of modes present in ritual see his *Beginnings in Ritual Studies,* London/New York, Univ. Press of America, 1982, pp.35-51; for examples of his modal conception used as a framework for interpreting particular rituals see *Beginnings,* pp.101-13,221-31 and in the case studies of his *Ritual Criticism,* pp.7-144.

[28] For an excellent discussion of religious ritual gestures see Ann Hawthorne, "Introduction – Method and Spirit: Studying the Diversity of Gestures in Religion" in *Diversities of Gifts: Field Studies in Southern Religion*, Ruel Tyson, Jr, James L. Peacock and Daniel W. Patterson eds, Urbana and Chicago, Univ. of Illinois Press, 1988, pp.3-20.

[29] It seems clear that ritual gestures are quite important to Pentecostal worship, particularly those gestures made with the use of the congregants' hands. Not only the lifting of arms and hands wide spread, but the laying-on of hands in healing rites, holding hands in prayer, reaching out, extending a hand towards another in need, signing in songs (sign language-like) and other hand gestures are prevalent.

[30] See D. Albrecht, "Ecumenical Potential and Pentecostal Spirituality", in *Pentecostal-Charismatic Theological Inquiry International: Cyberjournal for Pentecostal-Charismatic Research*, fall 1997.

[31] John Fenwick and Bryan Spinks, *Worship in Transition: The Liturgical Movement in the Twentieth Century*, New York, Continuum, 1995, p.111.

[32] *Ibid.*, pp.111-12.

[33] *Ibid.*, p.109.

[34] *Ibid.*, p.110.

[35] Robert Webber, *Signs of Wonder: The Phenomenon of Convergence in Modern Liturgical and Charismatic Churches*, Nashville, Abbott Martyn, 1992, pp.54-56.

[36] James White, *Protestant Worship: Traditions in Transition*, Louisville KY, Westminster/John Knox, 1989, p.205.

[37] Webber, *Signs of Wonder*, p.56.

[38] Cecil Robeck has written extensively on ecumenical issues from a Pentecostal perspective. Among his works see esp. "Pentecostals and Ecumenism: An Expanding Frontier", paper presented at the Pentecostal Research Conference, Kappel, Switzerland, 1991; "Pentecostal Perspectives and the Ecumenical Challenge", an unpublished paper, available from the author; "Revisioning the Unity we Seek: The Calling of Faith and Order", an unpublished paper presented at a theological symposium sponsored by the Ecumenical Development Initiative, Atlanta, USA, 1995. See also Hollenweger, *Pentecostalism*, pp.334-88, on what he calls "the ecumenical root" of Pentecostalism's history and development.

[39] Robeck sees "fear as a key issue" in ecumenism; quoted in Hollenweger, *Pentecostalism*, p.372.

[40] See Hollenweger, *Pentecostalism*, p.355. While Pentecostals do not always live this out, it is fundamental to their history and ethos. Hollenweger sees this radical reaching out (crossing boundaries) mostly in the initial phase of the movement's development. In its initial phase, the charismatic renewal also portrayed an optimism for ecumenism and the potential role the charismatic movement might play in the search for Christian unity. See Hollenweger on K. McDonnell, *Pentecostalism*, pp.362 ff., and Hollenweger's *The Pentecostals*, London, SCM Press, 1972, pp.424-56; also Albrecht, "Ecumenical Potential".

[41] Hollenweger gives some examples of the move from isolation, including some Latin American Pentecostal churches joining WCC. For other examples see "Pentecostalism", pp. 367-88, also Hollenweger's *The Pentecostals*, London, SCM Press, 1972, pp.424-56.

[42] White and Webber, for example, argue that the "borrowing" from, and impact of, Pentecostals and their worship elements has been extensive in recent times. See White, *Protestant Worship*, ch. 11, and Webber, *Signs of Wonder*, chs 5-6.

[43] Jerry Sandidge, "Consultation Summary: A Pentecostal Perspective", *Pneuma*, 9, 1, spring 1987, pp.96-98.

[44] While several names of individuals and groups could be cited as emerging bridge people, we wish to mention three more: David Du Plessis, who as a classical Pentecostal "blazed the trail" in the 20th century for ecumenical activities among Pentecostals, and Kilian McDonnell and Peter Hocken, who represent the *ecumenical* vision as bridge people with the charismatic renewal.

Worship and Unity
in the Church of South India

M. THOMAS THANGARAJ

• UNITED •

The Church of South India: the beginnings

The Church of South India came into being on 27 September 1947 as an organic union of the Anglican, Presbyterian, Methodist (British) and Congregational churches in South India. These four ecclesial traditions each had their own understandings about the nature and purpose of worship. Therefore, when the union was achieved, the Church of South India (CSI) formulated the following "governing principle" with regard to worship, as recorded in article 12 of the CSI constitution:

> The Church of South India will aim at conserving for the common benefit whatever of good has been gained in the separate history of those churches from which it has been formed, and therefore in its public worship will retain for its congregations freedom either to use historic forms or not to do so as may best conduce to edification and to the worship of God in spirit and in truth.[1]

Based on this governing principle, the CSI proceeded to formulate rules for the worship of the church. These included the power of the synod to "issue forms of worship to be used on special occasions, and regulations with regard to the essential elements or constituent parts of other services".[2] The church saw a common liturgy for the service of holy communion as a distinctive stage in the journey towards fuller unity, and the constitution mentions this specifically:

> As the Church of South India grows in unity of mind and spirit and experiences closer fellowship in worship, it may develop a common form or forms of the service of holy communion adapted to the special needs and religious experience of South India.[3]

Initial directions

One can detect here two major directions. First, the CSI was hoping that a common form (or forms) of holy communion would be an outcome of a growing sense of unity. That is, the need for a common form, or forms, of worship will develop as people in the CSI begin to experience being together in the various elements of the church's life. Second, the unity of the church will be nurtured and strengthened precisely as a common form of eucharistic worship is developed and used by the congregations. This common form might be introduced experimentally first; hopefully it would then be accepted by the whole church as representing its official form of eucharistic worship. Through participation in this common form of worship the people would – over time – experience a strengthening of, and growing in, unity.

When the CSI was founded great hopes were placed on the generations of Christians to come who, being born, baptized and nurtured in the CSI, would not bear the burden of the history of the earlier constituent denominations – rather, their piety would be shaped by the *common* form of worship which they would experience in the CSI. These two directions (the experience of unity leading to common forms of worship, and common forms of worship strengthening unity) are not mutually exclusive, but complementary. One can see how in the first few decades of the history of CSI the second direction has been in the forefront; today, the first direction is really the motivating force for liturgical renewals within the church.

Two major commitments

The two directions described above were propelled by two important commitments.

A commitment to unity

With its concern for unity, the CSI in its very constitution listed nine elements as mandatory for every eucharistic worship. They are the following:

1. Introductory prayers.
2. The ministry of the word, including readings from the scriptures, which may be accompanied by preaching.
3. The preparation of the communicants by confession of their sins, and the declaration of God's mercy to penitent sinners, whether in the form of an absolution or otherwise, and such a prayer as the "prayer of humble access".
4. The offering to God of gifts of the people.
5. The thanksgiving for God's glory and goodness and the redemptive work of Christ in his birth, life, death, resurrection and ascension, leading to a reference to his institution of the sacrament, in which his own words are rehearsed, and to the setting apart of the bread and wine to be used for the purpose of the sacrament with prayer that we may receive that which our Lord intends to give us in this sacrament.

6. An intercession for the whole church, for whom and with whom we ask God's mercy and goodness through the merits of the death of his Son.
7. The Lord's prayer, as the central act of prayer, in which we unite with the whole church of Christ to pray for the fulfilment of God's gracious purposes and to present our needs before the throne of grace.
8. The administration of the communion, with words conformable to scripture indicating the nature of the action.
9. A thanksgiving for the grace received in the communion, with which should be joined the offering and dedication of ourselves to God.[4]

Having outlined these as necessary elements of eucharistic worship the CSI, in its first synod, appointed a liturgy committee which sought to frame a common form of worship to symbolize, actualize and nurture the unity of the church.[5]

The liturgy committee envisaged expressing the unity of the church in three specific ways. First, it wished to express the unity by incorporating some ancient liturgical forms in the new liturgy. The liturgy and worship was to embody the historic unity of the church through the ages. For example, the use of the *Trisagion* in the eucharistic liturgy was precisely to nurture a sense of the historic unity, the *Trisagion* being seen as "the constant praise of the Jacobite church".[6] Similarly the preparatory prayer before the consecration of the elements, "Be present, Be present, O Jesus", comes "from the Mozarabic liturgy, a Gallician form of the Western rite which had its origin in Spain".[7]

Second, being united at worship meant the inclusion of the various forms, prayers and practices from the four constituent denominations of the church (Anglican, Presbyterian, Methodist and Congregational). Liturgies were organized with multiple choices at each step in the liturgical movement. There was a conscious endeavour "to preserve features perhaps peculiar to one tradition but dear to people brought up in that way".[8] For example, the confession of sins may be done either using the prayer given in the worship book, or extempore prayer. Another important illustration is the way in which the CSI combines the centrality of word and sacrament in its eucharistic liturgy.

Third, unity was clearly distinguished from uniformity; therefore the common orders of worship, including the eucharist, were allowed to take local form and shape. By choosing different options given in the common liturgy, two congregations using the same liturgy can make their worship significantly different. Moreover, congregations were free to choose particular parts of the common liturgy, as seemed appropriate for their particular situation.

A commitment to being an Indian church

It should be borne in mind that the inauguration of the Church of South India took place only one month after the independence of the country of India: the nation gained its independence on 15 August 1947 and the inauguration of the CSI was celebrated in Madras (Chennai) on 27 September 1947. Thus the union efforts went alongside the struggle for national independence. Therefore, the commitment to being an *Indian* church was central to the new church. Yet the liturgy committee did not greatly succeed in incorporating Indian elements in the common liturgy. In replying to a Swiss Reformed theologian's complaint that the CSI liturgy did not contain any distinctly Indian features, L.W. Brown, the chair of the liturgy committee, had this to say:

> We realize the force of this criticism but our church has not become unified enough in three years of life to be able to speak with a single voice. It is an Indian church and it will develop its own theology and know exactly what it wishes to say in its praise of God.[9]

The leaders of the church were right in assuming that the Indian character of the liturgy will develop as there is growth into fuller unity: over the years the CSI has gained a voice of its own when it comes to liturgical renewal. The *Book of Common Worship* has included several Indian elements in the liturgies. For example the singing of Psalm 128 during the wedding service can be accompanied by the ceremony of seven steps which is peculiar to Indian culture. Even when the written liturgy does not suggest any particular Indian expressions, people in local situations appropriate the liturgy in their own ways and make it "Indian". As J.R. Chandran writes,

> It is true that over the years Christians in India have become quite open to adopting local cultural elements. We have been adopting Indian music and dance for liturgical use. Several external symbols like the use of *Kolam* or *rangoli* [decorative drawings on the floor], and the use of *pottu* [a coloured mark], on the forehead by women have become quite common among Christians. We have also included the well-known prayer from the *Brhadaranyaka* Upanishad [Hindu scripture] in the CSI service of baptism... The question is whether we can go further and see to own as our religious and cultural heritage all that we recognize as true, beautiful and good in the other religious traditions of India.[10]

The commitment to Indian culture is expressed much more self-consciously in the most recent eucharistic liturgy of 1985. The general rubric for this liturgy expresses the indigenous voice of the church. It reads,

> In that this service attempts to express an understanding of worship that is more Indian than our traditional Christian worship forms, people are encour-

aged to conduct the service in as authentic an Indian style as possible, and should feel free to adapt the service to fit local conditions and customs.[11]

The alternate version is organized under Indian categories such as *pravesa* (entry), *prabodha* (awakening), *smarana-samarpana* (recalling and offering), and *samabhaktva* or *prasada* (sharing). The lighting of the lamp and singing a *bhajan* are explicitly made a part of the liturgy.

Complexities and challenges

The journey towards making worship both to express the growing unity of the church and to nurture the church towards fuller unity has not been an easy one. The road has been paved with many complexities and challenges; let us look at a few of these.

Language

The Church of South India includes within its fold people who speak one of four major languages of South India: Tamil, Telugu, Kannada and Malayalam. Though these four languages come from the same Dravidian roots, they each have a different script. Therefore, when the CSI meets as a whole church the language that unites all these is English. That is why *The Book of Common Worship* was first done in English, and then translated into all the four languages. For a common liturgy to express a sense of unity it needs a common language, and English has played that role until now. But in local and regional situations the unity is expressed through performing the liturgy in one of the four languages. There are dioceses and other places within the CSI where for a diocesan or parish meeting and worship one has to operate with two or more languages. At this point, creative ways of doing the liturgy in two or more languages have been found. As far as the singing of hymns is concerned, the people of the CSI can sing Western hymns together, each in his or her own mother-tongue, because most Western hymns are available in translation. But when it comes to singing indigenous hymns it is not easy, because the local hymns are very local indeed. In recent years there have been attempts to collect indigenous hymns common to all the four language areas and to compile them, in the four languages, in a hymnbook which can be used when the CSI meets as a whole. Bishop Amirtham has been involved in the publication of such a hymnbook.

In addition to the *Book of Common Worship,* other liturgies have been written in local languages with local musical arrangements. The seminaries have been in the forefront in creating such liturgies. To give one example from the Tamil region, the Tamilnadu theological college in Tirumaraiyur had a liturgy for the service of the word which was written in the local idiom and music. This was popularized by the seminary

through its students. When that seminary joined with the Lutheran seminary at Tranquebar to form a new seminary at Madurai, four new liturgies
were created and popularized, and these liturgies are very "Indian" in
their character. Similar leadership has been offered by the seminaries in
other language areas. While these liturgies are "Indian", they fail to function as an expression of the unity of the church because they have not yet
been used on occasions when CSI is at worship *as a whole church*.
Respecting the language traditions of each of the areas within the church,
while finding ways to worship in unity, is quite a challenging task.

Denominational differences

Due to the earlier missionary decisions on the issue of comity, the
denominations which came together to form the CSI were separated not
only in their doctrine and polity, but also by geographical boundaries.
For example, the diocese of Tirunelveli was entirely Anglican before the
union; similarly, the diocese of Kanyakumari consisted only of Congregational parishes. In such a situation, a new common form of worship
seemed unwarranted. The people in these dioceses did not see the need
for a new, common form of worship to express their new unity; indeed,
the unity achieved was not "real" to them because there were no other
denominations in their geographical area – they had, as it were, no one
to unite *with*. Therefore the liturgy of the united church had to become
an "educator" for the people on unity and its meaning. It is interesting
that an early publication after the union discussed the various liturgies
then available in India, and how one is enriched by using some of those
in one's own worship life.[12] In the introduction to this book we read,

> The booklet arises out of a practical need of the Church of South India. Before
> the union was inaugurated, the members of the uniting denominations natu-
> rally concentrated their attention to what they held in common. Since then, as
> naturally, they have thought more of what is distinctive in their own heritages,
> anxious to bring to the new church all the good things they can.[13]

Thus there was a need to educate the people on the unity that has come
about, and worship was one avenue for such an ecumenical education.

This meant, then, that the reception of the common liturgy in local
congregations and dioceses was not going to be evenly experienced, nor
would it be always easy. For example, the congregations which belonged
to the Anglican tradition before the union had the greatest difficulty in
accepting the new sense of unity in worship. Some of these congregations were still using the 1662 order of worship found in the Anglican
Book of Common Prayer, and it was very difficult for them to use the
Book of Common Worship of the Church of South India. Bishops and

presbyters had to find creative ways to convince people to use the new liturgy – for example, a few bishops had the policy of insisting on the CSI liturgy whenever the bishop was visiting a parish!

And it worked! Over the years these parishes have begun to use the CSI liturgy regularly, though not always. While it has been a difficult and challenging task for Anglican dioceses, dioceses and parishes with Presbyterian and Congregational backgrounds had less difficulty in using the new liturgy. Their earlier understanding of freedom in liturgy enabled them to accept the new liturgy without any trauma or pain. In most cases, the reception of the new liturgy has been made easy through the work of creative musicians in each language area who arranged the CSI liturgy in local musical forms and made them accessible, acceptable, and attractive. To give an example from Tamilnadu, the musical setting of the eucharistic liturgy by M.S. Jesudason, Honest Chinniah, and Messieurs Thavapandian and Dhanapandian has helped CSI congregations to enjoy the new liturgy. The fifty-year history of CSI has clearly shown how people on the whole have come to understand their unity, to value it immensely, and to cherish the CSI liturgy which undergirds and expresses it.

Identity and solidarity

Worship and liturgy has, for most South Indian Christians, been an important way of defining their Christian identity. Therefore they would like their worship to be distinctive and different from Hindu or Muslim worship. As Alexander John writes,

> Because of the church architecture, art, music and worship which are different from the traditional modes in use in India, many have felt that the Indian church has repudiated the Indian culture. It is not a rejection, but just being different from the Hindu forms.[14]

Being a minority community within the much larger Hindu population, Christians have seen their worship patterns as distinctive mark of their Christian identity. This fact should be respected and valued. At the same time, however, being Christians in India implies being responsible Indians who, in their life and worship, express their solidarity with all the people of India. At this point, the CSI cannot just be concerned about its internal unity; it has to operate with the unity of the people of India as its goal and purpose. How the CSI worship can celebrate people's distinctive Christian identity, and at the same time inspire a larger vision of the unity of India as a whole, is a challenge which is both complex and difficult.

The future

There are two areas in which the CSI will be challenged in the coming years. First, during the last five years some congregations in the CSI which belonged to the earlier Anglican tradition have separated from the CSI to form the Anglican Church of India. Though some major reasons for this division are political, the issue of worship and liturgy has been an important factor as well, since these are congregations which use the 1662 order of worship of the Church of England. It is a sad development. The CSI faces a large challenge in negotiating with these congregations and welcoming them back into the CSI.

Second, Dalit Christians (Christians who belong to the so-called Untouchable castes) are demanding, and securing, leadership roles in the CSI. Not all of these Christians have been part of the liturgical renewal movements; rather, they have shaped in their piety and worship by the rural and folk traditions of South India. As they assume leadership roles within the CSI they would – and do already – question present liturgical forms. They would see the unity of the church more in the folk traditions of music and worship. The CSI needs to prepare itself for this welcome challenge: for example the most recent version of the CSI eucharistic liturgy is shaped by the "classical" traditions of Indian culture rather than those of the Dalit Christians. How one negotiates this without losing the ecumenical vision is quite a challenging task.

NOTES

[1] *The Constitution of the Church of South India*, Madras, CLS, 1952, p.11.
[2] *Ibid.*, p.50.
[3] *Ibid.*
[4] *Ibid.*, pp.5f.
[5] See Marcus Ward, *The Pilgrim Church: An Account of the First Five Years in the Life of the Church of South India*, London, Epworth, 1953, ch. 7, "Liturgical Developments".
[6] T. S. Garrett, *Worship in the Church of South India*, Richmond VA, John Knox, 1958, p.21.
[7] *Ibid.*, p.29; see also H. Boone Porter, "Be Present, Be Present", *Studia Liturgica*, 21, 2, 1991, pp.155-64.
[8] L. W. Brown, "The Making of a Liturgy", *Scottish Journal of Theology*, 4, 1951, p.56.
[9] *Ibid.*, p.57.
[10] "Relation between Gospel and Culture", *The South India Churchman: The Magazine of the Church of South India*, April 1986, p.5.
[11] *Church of South India Liturgy: The Holy Eucharist (An Alternate Version)*, Madras, CLS, 1985, p.1.
[12] *Ways of Worship: How the Holy Communion is Celebrated by Different Branches of the Church of South India*, Madras, CLS, 1950.
[13] *Ibid.*, p.vii.
[14] "Has the Indian Church Repudiated the Indian Culture?", *The South India Churchman*, March 1960, p.3.

A Seventh-day Adventist Perspective on Worship

DENIS FORTIN

• SEVENTH-DAY ADVENTIST •

[The angel] said with a loud voice: "Fear God and give him glory, for the hour of his judgment has come, and worship him who made heaven and earth, the sea and the fountains of water" (Rev. 14:7).

The nature and purpose of worship

For Seventh-day Adventists these prophetic words from the book of Revelation are an invitation to all people on earth to worship God, the Creator of all that exists, and to experience God's salvation and God's presence in one's life. Worship is a high point in an individual's Christian experience. Of a personal nature, worship is one's response of faith to God; hence worship begins in the heart and is private. Genuine worship is characterized by an attitude of respect and awe towards God because of our realization of God's greatness, an attitude of adoration since God alone is worthy of our devotion, and an attitude of joy and thanksgiving for God's love as manifested in Jesus Christ.

Worship occurs also at the social and communal level, where it consists of a fellowship of believers who present to God praises for the life and purpose God brings to their community; here corporate worship emphasizes both the transcendence and the immanence of God. There are many reasons for corporate worship. We worship God in heartfelt response to God's creative work and for all the benefits of God's salvation; we gather together to learn from God's word and to understand God's teachings and purposes for our lives, to fellowship with one another in faith and love, and to witness to our personal faith in Christ's atoning sacrifice on the cross. In addition to all this, worship is a manner in which God manifests himself.

Congregational worship

Acts of worship are important expressions of our religious commitment to God. For Seventh-day Adventists, formalism and ritualism are to be avoided as distortions of worship, since simply "going through the motions" brings little meaning to worship. The opposing distortion of informality is also to be avoided, since it reflects an inadequate commitment to worship and trivializes both religion and our relationship with God.

The weekly worship service followed by Seventh-day Adventists is non-liturgical, in the sense that it does not follow a prescribed yearly calendar of readings and litanies – although local congregations will mark important events such as the birth and resurrection of Christ – and is similar to worship in Protestant churches within restorationist and revivalist traditions. The following example of a simple order of worship is typical of that followed by the majority of Adventist congregations:

- prelude (music)
- introit
- call to worship
- doxology
- prayer of invocation
- hymn of praise
- scripture reading
- pastoral prayer
- special music
- offering
- hymn of preparation
- sermon
- hymn of consecration
- benediction
- postlude (music)

Normally, a minister or elder is responsible for the preparation of the worship service and its various parts. This person usually selects the hymns and the scripture reading, attempting to make these selections in accordance with the theme of the sermon. The sermon is the dominant part of this worship experience, and is presented by the minister or the church elder. In some cases, a non-ordained lay person may preach the sermon. The choice of the theme addressed in the sermon is left with the preacher, who prayerfully selects a subject, under the guidance of the Holy Spirit, to edify the congregation.

Lay members participate in various aspects of the worship service, such as prayers and scripture readings. Prayers are a basic act of worship, and are usually free and extemporaneous. The Lord's prayer is not a usual part of Adventist worship, but is considered a model prayer given to us by Christ.

The sabbath as day of worship

Especially important for Seventh-day Adventists is the day of worship. The biblical sabbath was instituted as a day of rest and worship, and as an eternal and universal memorial of the acts of God at creation (Gen. 2:1-3; Ex. 20:8-11) and in the redemption of humanity (Deut. 5:12-15). A proper observance of the sabbath, as commanded by God and exemplified in the life of Jesus and the apostles, is an integral part of an attitude of worship and reflects a genuine reverence for God.

Seventh-day Adventists also see an eschatological dimension to worship and sabbath-keeping. They understand the prophetic messages of the book of Revelation (particularly chs 12-14) as describing an endtime conflict between the forces of good and evil, with both competing for the allegiance and worship of human beings. While the unredeemed inhabitants of the earth worship the dragon-like beast and follow the religious confusion it promotes (Rev. 13:8,12), the people of God are described as being faithful to the commandments of God (Rev. 12:17,14:12) and worshipping the Creator God (Rev. 14:7). Seventh-day Adventists understand faithfulness to God's will and the sabbath as the outward demonstration of one's inner commitment of love to God.

Ordinances and worship

For Seventh-day Adventists other acts of worship include the ordinances of baptism, foot-washing, and the Lord's supper. These rites of the Christian church, as instituted (or "ordained") by Christ, serve as reminders of God's works of grace in the salvation of humanity and proclaim the deep significance of Christ's acts of redemption.

The ordinance of baptism is often performed during worship services as an act of worship to God, and serves as a reminder to all worshippers of God's gift of redemption in Christ. Baptism is also understood as a symbol of one's consecration to Christ's service, and of entrance into the people of God, the church. As the worshipping congregation witnesses such a confession of faith and baptism, and welcomes this new believer in Christ, it praises God for his gift of redemption offered to all humanity.

Seventh-day Adventists perform the Lord's supper as a memorial of Christ's once-for-all sacrifice on the cross and as commemorating our deliverance from sin. This service is a proclamation of the meaning of Christ's death for the church, and anticipates his second coming when all redeemed humanity will assemble at Christ's banquet table (Matt. 26:29; Rev. 19:9). As such, the Lord's supper is a fellowship of worshipping Christians who, in spiritual communion with Christ, acknowledge their dependence on Christ and recommit their lives to his service. In a world filled with strife and divisiveness, our corporate participation in the Lord's supper contributes to the unity and stability of the church, demonstrating one true communion, both with Christ and with one another.

As part of the celebration of the Lord's supper, and preceding it, Adventists practise a foot-washing service as a memorial of Christ's condescension and incarnation to save humanity. Following Jesus' example and instruction (John 13:1-17), this service is understood as an ordinance of Christian humility and service, and as a fellowship of forgiveness and cleansing among brothers and sisters. The spiritual experience that lies at the heart of foot-washing conveys a message of forgiveness, acceptance, assurance and solidarity, primarily from Christ to the believer, but also between believers. This service expresses our willingness to serve others, and prepares our hearts for the communion of the Lord's supper that follows.

The influence of the ecumenical and worship renewal movements

Since its origin, the Seventh-day Adventist church has been concerned with the lack of unity within Christianity and has advocated a unity based upon the teachings of the Bible. It has also endeavoured to foster good relations with other denominations. But it has refused to join various ecumenical bodies for fear of losing its independence, and of compromising its missionary and evangelistic spirit.

Nonetheless other denominations, particularly mainline Protestant denominations, and the liturgical renewal movement have had an impact – albeit indirect – upon the Adventist church and its style of worship. The fear of formalism and ritualism is not as prominent among us as it used to be, and the traditional simplicity of our worship services is slowly being replaced with more elaborate forms of worship, especially in larger congregations and on Adventist college or university campuses. Responsive readings, litanies, written prayers of confession, and other more formal elements are being introduced as attempts to make worship services more meaningful.

On the other hand a worship renewal movement, in which a contemporary worship style and contemporary Christian music have been adopted, is also impacting many Adventist congregations. Although traditional hymns and a simple order of worship are not entirely discarded, this style is another attempt at making worship services more meaningful. While a more formal Protestant worship style is favoured by the older generations, the contemporary style is more readily accepted by the younger generations.

BIBLIOGRAPHY

Handbook of Seventh-day Adventist Theology, Commentary Reference Series, Vol. 12, Hagerstown MD, Review & Herald Publishing Assoc., 2000.

C. Raymond Holmes, *Sing a New Song*, Berrien Springs MI, Andrews UP, 1984.

Ministry, special issue on worship, Oct. 1991.

Norval Pease, *And Worship Him*, Nashville, Southern Publishing Assoc., 1967.

Richard Rice, *Reign of God: An Introduction to Christian Theology from a Seventh-day Adventist Perspective*, 2nd ed., Berrien Springs MI, Andrews UP, 1997, pp.367-90.

George W. Reid, "Toward an Adventist Theology of Worship", web page: http://biblicalresearch.gc.adventist.org

Seventh-day Adventist Church Manual, 16th ed., Hagerstown MD, Review and Herald Publishing Assoc., 2000, pp.67-77.

Seventh-day Adventist Minister's Manual, Silver Spring MD, Ministerial Association, General Conference of Seventh-day Adventists, 1992, pp.133-45.

Worship within the Salvation Army

EARL ROBINSON

with The Salvation Army International Doctrine Council

• SALVATION ARMY •

The Salvation Army's fundamental understanding of the nature and purpose of worship

We are called to live our whole lives as an act of worship

The Salvation Army's fundamental understanding of the nature and purpose of worship begins with a belief that God calls us to live our whole lives as an act of worship. Worship is an encounter with God in which we meet him through a variety of languages and through all our senses. Our whole life is an act of worship, a continuing encounter with God where we turn our attention to God to the extent that each of us can say, "I am a prayer."

In Romans 12:1-2 Paul urges us to enter into an act of worship in view of the mercy of God. This worship encompasses both body and mind, and is truly holistic. We surrender our body with all its senses, with all its life – this is an unconditional gift, a holy gift pleasing to God. Instead of conforming to the spirit of the time we are being transformed by a renewal of our minds (cf. Rom. 12:2) to rethink and repent. Through this act of worship and renewal we can judge what is the will of God.

This is a strong description of our whole life lived as an act of worship. It rejects the division of life into different compartments – one for work, one for pleasure, one for family and friends, one for religious activities, and so on. Such compartmentalization disconnects us. It reduces worship to an entity of its own instead of allowing it to be a natural part of our whole life.

The text in Romans encourages us to surrender our daily life (symbolized by our body) as a gift and to let our minds, or our common sense, be renewed and transformed. When we do this we experience the all-encompassing renewal which alters our thinking and makes us powerful tools in the hands of God.

Worship is an act and an expression of love

We believe that worship is in essence an act of love, an expression of love. The greatest commandment is, "Love the Lord your God with all your heart and with all your soul and with all your mind and with all your strength" (Mark 12:30).

This commandment shows the intensity and depth of the love to which God calls us. It is a love which involves our total being with our full strength. God calls forth our strength because he knows it is there, and he wants to activate it into a full life of love.

To express this love we do not constantly try to feel love or assess our capacity for love. We simply get on with living. By the grace of God we have been given this life to live. The sheer joy of life and love of life can be worship. It can be a form of praise to God, the Creator of all. God wants us to love to live. Viewing our whole life and being as an act of worship is the cornerstone of our life with God. But in the context of that vision we recognize the need for both individual, more formal expressions of worship and the need to come together as the people of God for corporate acts of worship.

Distinctive aspects and qualities of worship in Salvation Army tradition

Acts of worship are supported by that which is visible and concrete

In those individual and corporate expressions of worship, we need to create visible and concrete acts of worship. We need to find places where we worship as individuals and places where we share fellowship in worship, places where we have our sight sharpened because we consciously seek the presence of God.

"Seeing" is a powerful act of worship which has had some distinctive accompaniments in The Salvation Army – seeing joy in the Lord in the clapping of hands during our singing; seeing the giving of one's life in worship to God in coming to the front of the meeting place, to what is referred to as the "mercy seat" as a witness to that commitment; in an earlier era, seeing dances of praise to God as Salvationists would participate in "glory marches" around the meeting place and behind The Salvation Army flag. Other visible supports to worship have sometimes been underestimated in our tradition. To see a candle burning, to let the eye rest on beautiful flowers or pieces of art or religious icons, can facilitate worship and close encounters with God. When we join each other in worship, the arrangement of the room is vital. If it is ugly, or not well prepared, we have to set this important sense of seeing aside, we have to close our eyes or try to focus on other senses and miss the visual dimension of worship. Our buildings, furniture, colours and material can all support our worship through seeing.

The visual parts of worship are important in action as well. Dance, drama, movements, kneeling – all these visual expressions strengthen our worship.

Corporate worship presents many opportunities for sharpening our sight. This worship in community requires openness towards God and each other, a willingness to share, to be vulnerable and to be challenged. It requires a love for the people of God and for the fellowship God has given, a love for the world which is lost, and an urgent desire to be in the presence of God as part of his people. With such an attitude we enter into a genuine fellowship, and here have our eyes opened so that we can see.

Worship involves hearing God in sounds

We worship through the words of the scriptures, of the sermon, of the prayers, of the songs and of the testimonies. We are blessed when these means of grace bear the marks of a genuine encounter with God, and when they are perfected to his glory through his presence.

There is a significance to the spoken word which we must never forget. To read the scriptures, to reflect upon them and relate the message to our situation is crucial for our worship. We need this for spiritual growth and nourishment. This has been a vital element of Christian worship through the centuries, one with its roots in synagogue tradition, as is reflected in the way Jesus expounded the scriptures in Nazareth (see Luke 4:16-21). The apostles preached the word and their letters were read by the young churches for teaching and nourishment. To Titus Paul writes, "He must hold firmly to the trustworthy message as it has been taught, so that he can encourage others by sound doctrine and refute those who oppose it" (Titus 1:9). We believe that, as the scriptures are inspired by God, so we will be assisted by the Holy Spirit when listening to and proclaiming the message.

Music has become one of The Salvation Army's most cherished tools of worship – a joyful expression of words put to music in congregational singing; the music of the brass band in accompanying that singing and presenting their own musical selections of worship; the music of the songster brigade; more recently, the more contemporary music of worship teams. It unites us. Many of our songs reflect worship as a corporate act. God's greatness deserves countless multitudes singing to his glory: "O for a thousand tongues to sing my great redeemer's praise" (Charles Wesley). When we join in the singing we worship with our whole being; and when we listen to the music we "hear" the testimonies from past and present, we hear the voice of God calling us.

Worship is engaged in through personal, spontaneous prayer

Everything in worship is brought into the presence of God through prayer. The Salvation Army has a strong tradition of personal, spontaneous prayers in its worship – often to the exclusion of written, liturgical prayers. We believe that this tradition is of great value and should be nourished in the teaching of our people from early childhood or early Christian life, as it is a spring of power and new life. Even though that priority should be kept, written and liturgical prayers can give an immense impact in worship and be a means of blessing as well as a teaching tool in the quest for a dynamic prayer life. We can draw upon prayers from church history, as well as writing prayers ourselves under the inspiration of the Holy Spirit.

In a novel by the Swedish writer Sven Delblanc, *The Daughters of Samuel,* the poor widow Cecilie receives a much-needed pair of glasses from her children as her birthday present. These glasses become both a joy and a pain to Cecilie. Her sight improves and her work becomes easier; but now she is also able to see the bitterness and poverty in the faces of her children, and notices the hopelessness around her. She turns this experience into a prayer: "Don't make the world so cruel that I want blindness as a gift! That is all I dare to pray, Thou good and merciful God!"

Her prayer is like the old biblical prayers which contain cries for help *and* for a more just world. She doesn't ask for liberation from the "sharp sight" that notices both joy and pain. She asks that she will never reach the point where the pain and cruelty become her whole horizon.

We believe that our prayer life could be illustrated by such a pair of glasses. Through prayer we get a sharp and clear sight of our own reality and the reality of the world around us. We bring everything into God's presence when we praise God for all he is and all he does. We bring to God our pain and the sharpness of our protest as we pray, "Deliver us from evil". We come with our petitions (the most natural part of prayer) and with our intercessions, our open acts of love for others. Prayer sharpens our sight and our hearing, and fills our silence with God's rest and peace.

Worship is expressed in discipleship

What may be the most distinctive aspect of worship in Salvation Army tradition is our emphasis on ways in which worship is expressed in discipleship. The biblical words for worship are, at their roots, words for service. This implies a deep connection between Christian worship and service: they are essentially one.

The most common Hebrew words for worship have *ebed*, which means "servant", as their root. This root word describes all sorts of service. In the New Testament the two words used for worship are *latreia*, which means "service" and "worship" (see Rom. 12:1), and *leitourgia*, which was used in everyday language to mean service to the community or state, usually without pay (see Heb. 10:11).

Our life as an act of worship directs us towards true discipleship. In Isaiah 58:6-7 we are given directions for this life:

> Is not this the kind of fasting I have chosen: to loose the chains of injustice and untie the cords of the yoke, to set the oppressed free and break every yoke? Is it not to share your food with the hungry and to provide the poor wanderer with shelter – when you see the naked, to clothe him, and not to turn away from your own flesh and blood?

Jesus told the story of the good Samaritan to illustrate the truth that love for God demands unconditional love for our neighbours (Luke 10:25-37). The true disciple does not separate worship from compassionate service, nor fails to see the holy in the everyday.

Ecumenical and liturgical renewal influences on Salvation Army worship

Visual emphases and written and liturgical prayers in worship

There are a number of ways in which The Salvation Army's ecumenical involvement in worship services, and its exposure to the liturgical renewal movement, may have indirectly – and perhaps unconsciously – had an influence on our worship. Two of those ways have been alluded to above.

The first way has to do with the admission that there are visible supports to worship whose value has been somewhat underestimated in our tradition. Mentioned above were the ways in which worship may be facilitated by seeing a candle burning, or letting the eye rest on beautiful flowers or pieces of art or religious icons. Having beautiful flowers before us in worship has been common for a number of decades. And, although still not common practice in our worship settings, there is now the occasional use of candles and art and religious icons, which is not considered out of place in Salvation Army worship.

The second way has to do with the admission that written and liturgical prayers can give an immense impact in worship, and can be a means of blessing as well as a teaching tool in the quest for a dynamic prayer life. Personal, spontaneous praying is still a priority in Salvation Army worship, but it is also generally accepted that it is important to be able to draw upon prayers from church history, and to write out prayers of our own, for use in worship.

Silence in worship

Even more highly valued in contemporary Salvation Army worship is the importance of listening to God in worshipful silence. Salvationists are not as well trained in hearing God in the silence as in hearing him in the sounds. With many other people today – and perhaps partly because of our exposure to ecumenical and liturgical renewal worship services – we are also rediscovering the wonder of worship in silence.

The Orthodox church calls itself the church of silence. Silence is seen as an expression of awe because God can come in the silence (1 Kings 19:11-12) more than in the mighty manifestations. The Quaker tradition is built on silence in worship. The silence is a condition for listening to God. The essence of prayer is not so much our words, but an offering of ourselves and a willingness to listen.

We recognize that we need times of silence in which we step back, reflect and refrain from "filling up" time with our activities and words. This is a vital act of worship, a fountain of new life and strength. Silence can be frightening unless we discipline ourselves for it and learn to live with it. In the silence, our whole being turns into prayer because we are in the presence of God in our nakedness of spirit, our poverty, our sins and our broken words. Here we are given rest, healing and peace. For Jesus said, "Come to me, all you who are weary and burdened, and I will give you rest" (Matt. 11:28).

Worship – yesterday, today and tomorrow – in the search for Christian unity

Salvationists sometimes sing the chorus, "This is the day that the Lord has made", and by this we point to the fact that, when we worship, the present tense is all-important. We are meeting God now – *today*. The Holy Spirit is contemporary and present today. But to the "today" of our worship belong yesterday and tomorrow. The salvation story's "then" is the foundation for our celebration today, and at the centre of the message is the Christian hope that "one day..."

In worship we are reminded of the message that a fallen world is being recreated, that it is moving towards becoming a new heaven and a new earth (Rev. 21:1). When we live our lives as an act of worship, we are able to enter the flow of this new creation. There is a word which breathes through this life of recreated discipleship; it is the word of faith, hope and love: "Maranatha – Lord come!"

The people of God are called to worship. There they meet God and reshape their lives for the present and future of his coming. There they give themselves to service, which is their worship in the world. There they come to know themselves as the community of God. And when that worship is engaged in through ecumenical settings, and with a respect for each other's expressions of worship, the worship of the larger community before the triune God can be a major factor in the search for Christian unity in the midst of recognized diversity.

Worship and the State Church

A Norwegian Perspective

ØYSTEIN BJØRDAL

• LUTHERAN •

The background to our topic

Until 1842 it was forbidden by Norwegian law *(Konventikkel-plakaten)* for persons other than the state-ordained Lutheran pastors to gather people for preaching, religious meetings and worship services. Before this time Hans Nielsen Hauge had became a very influential lay preacher and reformer of church life in Norway. He was at the same time an industrial entrepreneur and spiritual leader at the beginning of the 19th century. His preaching and religious meetings caused Hauge to be imprisoned for more than ten years, but his followers only increased in numbers and became stronger. The lay peoples' movement in the Church of Norway resulted in a strong mission movement, both within Norway and abroad, with certain worship characteristics. The distinctive effect of this on the Church of Norway is that the various mission organizations have remained within the state church structures, where they have served both as a challenge, supplement and enrichment of spiritual life in Norway and also as a popular counter-movement to the ecclesial establishment. That is, unlike revival movements of many other post-Reformation churches, they did not break away and form new churches.

There is in many cases a certain relationship between the self-understanding of a church and its worship traditions. In theological language, this means that ecclesiology and liturgy are mutually interwoven. Which one of the two is first and foremost is in this context irrelevant. In the Orthodox tradition the connection between the church and its liturgy is obvious; likewise, the Roman Catholic Church. With many nuances, the Baptist and Pentecostal traditions have similar profiles. In some churches, however, one can have the impression that the relationship between ecclesiology and liturgy is more vague, or open. In the Anglican tradition, for example, one may ask whether it is the "high church" or the "low church" form of worship which is closest to the heart of Anglicanism. Some would say that it is the very tension and togetherness of these two – or more – traditions side-by-side which is the very core of Anglicanism.

In the Lutheran state church of Norway, the situation is in some respects not so different from the Anglican scene. Awakenings during the 1800s and early 1900s were very influential for the spiritual life of the country, forming many mission movements and many so-called "prayer houses" with a freer form of worship than found in the conventional church establishment. Unlike in the Church of England, these mission groups and their spiritual "meetings" are organizations independent from the official church, but still an important part of that same church structure. While the "low church" traditions have their own churches and worship services within the Church of England, the lay people's movements in Norway invite persons to *non*-liturgical meetings with preaching, prayers and singing, and often with choirs or music of different kinds. Normally they do not celebrate the sacraments. Even though history and spiritual life has changed much over the past two centuries, the mission movements and their spiritual meetings are still a peculiar role and influence within the Church of Norway today. In some cases, to be sure, the "mission-people" have a very low degree of loyalty to the official church and its worship services; but in many cases they are the most faithful and dedicated worshippers in the congregations.

A state church with old roots
Let us remind ourselves that the early Constantinian state church inherited or imitated symbols and forms of the imperial court and cult. This pertains both to the church building as such, especially the basilica-structure, and to liturgical expressions such as processions, vestments, the use of candles, the seating (*cathedra*) of the bishop, and so on. Thus we realize that the interconnections between state and church – and the expressions of worship that come with them – have very old roots. Within a few centuries the early church developed from a persecuted minority to a privileged seat of authority within the Roman empire. And in the Middle Ages worship practice became a very important and effective way of unifying and uniting the church. This is the basic idea of Gregorianism, a church policy innovated by Pope Gregory the Great (540-604 CE) to unite the Christian church worldwide through unified orders of worship and rubrics. The newly privileged state church thus developed (to put it in the words of Anton Baumstark in his work *Comparative Liturgy*) from austerity to richness, and from variety to uniformity.

The state-church relationship is grounded in Norwegian history through St Olav and other kings, and through the powerful archdiocese of Nidaros (established 1152) in the Middle Ages. Kings were crowned by the church – and in other situations revolted against the see of Rome. At the time of the Reformation the political-religious empire described as *unum corpus christianum*, with the pope and the emperor as leading entities, was coming to an end. But the peace of Augsburg in 1555 introduced a new principle of church-state relations: *cuius regio eius religio* – as the ruler is, so is the religion [of both state and people]. This is the background of Danish-Norwegian state-church traditions. Norway was subject to the Danish king during the first centuries after the Reformation; and already in 1537 the first order of worship for the Danish-Norwegian church was published *(Kirkeordinansen)*. In 1689 this was further developed into *Danmark og Norges Kirkeritual*, a ritual of worship often described as the "hymn-mass", where hymns are substituted for many of the traditional liturgical elements of the mass. After Norway declared its independence from Denmark on 17 May 1814 the country was in union with Sweden until 1905, when the king of Norway was solemnly crowned in the national shrine, the cathedral of Nidaros in Trondheim. Since 1814 the new parliament has governed the country, not only in political but also in religious matters and even in the regulation of church policies.

The nature and purpose of worship

In 1884 parliamentarianism was introduced in the Norwegian political system, and this also had certain effects on church-state relations. The constitution of 1814 makes clear that "the king orders all public church – and worship, all meetings and gatherings in matters of religion..." (§16). This is still the public order of religion in Norway, and paragraph 2 leaves no doubt as to what confession we are speaking of: "The Evangelical-Lutheran religion remains the public religion of the state." Since 1884 this church order has been administered by the government, but in 1988 questions related to liturgy and worship were delegated from the department of church affairs to the national church synod, which today (together with the bishops conference) is the supreme authority of the Church of Norway.

The altarbook of 1889 represents a significant renewal of worship, a liturgical reorientation which was confirmed in the Norwegian altarbook of 1920. This period broke new ground for worship practice in the Norwegian tradition, leading up to the liturgical commission of the 1960s, with a new hymnal, lectionary and worship books in 1984-92. Dean Gustav Jensen was the principal reformer of the Altarbook of 1889/1920. One of his main ideas was to involve the congregation in a more active worship practice, so that they would not be only "Amen-responders" to the clergy of God – and the state. A more dynamic and spiritual way of involving the people in expressing their faith, responding to God in fellowship, praise and thanksgiving, gave new dimensions to worship life.

A general impression of the latest liturgical development – about one hundred years later – would indicate a greater openness to ecumenical and Anglo-American worship practice; but the Germanic-Danish Lutheran tradition is still a fundamental source of spiritual life. In this perspective the nature and purpose of worship can be characterized as women and men's response, in faith and life, to God's salvific initiative in sending Jesus Christ to this world. The Bible as the living word of God is the most fundamenal source of inspiration for Christian faith and life, and the word of God is the norm *(norma normans)* of faith and life in the church. This is the Word which "became flesh" and "raised its tent among us", to speak with St John (1:14). God's entrance into this world in Jesus Christ has had the greatest influence on the interaction of worship and culture in the Christian church. The reality of the incarnation has clear liturgical implications for the vital interaction between spiritual and physical reality, heaven and earth, God and humankind. Thus we confirm nature and creation as the gift of God and source of life and blessings, but also for an occasion for responsible stewardship and protection of the environment. This is also a fundamental worship perspective.

Distinctive aspects and qualities of worship

Hymn-singing is an important heritage in the worship life of Lutheranism. The Danish-Norwegian tradition has had a particular impact on the previously mentioned "hymn-mass" mentioned above. Hymn writers such as Kingo, Brorson, Grundvig, Dass, Landstad and Blix have contributed greatly to the worship caracteristics of our tradition. Today the Church of Norway probably has one of the richest variety of hymns and melodies as seen in the two official hymnals, *Norsk Salmebok* and *Salmer 1997*. The hymnals contain 1041 hymns, and 192 liturgical songs and prayers for different use in the holy services. Six new books with liturgical music for choir and congregation are also available (*Kantoribok* I-VI) offering a broad variety of church music, from Gregorian chant, Anglican and Orthodox music, and the rich Lutheran heritage of our own composers like Egil Hovland, Trond Kverno, Knut Nystedt, to newer forms like those from Taizé, Andre Gouze and church music influenced by popular musical forms.

A description of the characteristics of Norwegian worship life must include the place of the sermon and of preaching in general. Lay preachers have had a strong position in Christian communities in Norway. The state church and its prescribed worship life was the background for the lay people's movement, and for mission work and preaching in smaller gatherings, which have had a significant impact on spiritual life especially in the first three-quarters of this century. And it has influenced the understanding of the sermon as the centre and heart of the worship service. This is the heritage of the hymn-mass which characterized the service not as "Høy-messe" (high mass) but as "Høy-prediken" (high-sermon/preaching). However, at the very end of the 20th century there were many signs that preaching has become an increasingly difficult part of the worship service. In a time of liturgical renewal, pastors in preparing the sermon seem to be more focused on the congregation and the liturgy than before. Rather than preaching exegetically, the tendency is to focus on the three prescribed biblical texts as a unit, within the context of the church year, and in view of the situation in the congregation and the secular world.

With almost 84 percent of the babies born in Norway being baptized, it is obvious that baptism is a normal and frequent part of Norwegian worship life! This is certainly one of the main effects of being a state church. It gives a major part of the people in this country a feeling of "belonging to" the church, although the great majority seldom worship in the same church – except, of course, at major events such as Christmas, confirmation, independence day, baptisms, weddings and funerals. Thus during most of the 20th century there has been a liturgical tension between the celebration of baptism and holy communion. Until the 1980s, it was common not to celebrate communion regularly. Today many congregations try to adjust to the needs in the congregation for both a frequent administration of the baptismal sacrament, and a more frequent and regular eucharistic celebration. That there is a clear link between the two sacraments is obvious, and all parents and sponsors of baptismal candidates are now reminded of this in the words of "holy responsibility" within the baptismal liturgy: "...to pray for the child, teach her/him to pray and help her/him to use the word of God and the Lord's supper that she/he may remain in Christ when she/he grows up..."

The creed, either said or sung, is always included in our main worship services and it follows as a response to the word, either after the second reading or after the sermon. Intercessory prayers have their normal position after the sermon. There are six or more to choose from, according to the time and situation. These prayers are pre-established, but all of them have openings for silent, private prayer and for contextualization according to special needs and situations in the congregation, the worldwide church and pressing social, ethical and political issues, both far away and near at hand, in this world. In the first part of the worship service, scripture reading is a predominant part of the liturgy. Normally there are three readings, one from the Old Testament, the New Testament and the gospels. The Church of Norway lectionary is the old "ecumenical" order, which was, more or less, the order of the Roman Catholic Church before Vatican II. Together with other denominations we have brought the Old Testament back to the service, and on five to seven Sundays a year the prescribed text for the sermon is that from the Old Testament.

Statistics

Although statistics are often inadequate, they may give a picture of the relation of the state church to worship in Norway. In 1997, 83.9 percent of all babies born in the country were baptized in the Church of Norway, and this number has increased continuously since 1987 (when it was only 79.4 percent). In the same period, confirmation attendance has decreased from 83.6 percent in 1987 to 74 percent in 1997 (though, remarkably, these are percentages of *all* youths 14 years of age as of 1 January). The average worship attendance in all congregations is 98 persons (in 1996, 99 persons). In addition to these are all the worship services in institutions (hospitals, prisons, kindergartens, schools and so on) and the "occasional" services: wedding-services (60 percent), funerals (95 percent).

It is important to observe that these figures represent only the Church of Norway, not the many other denominations and free churches. Certainly these figures indicate an active and alive folk church with a broad influence on the lives of people in Norway. But it also tells an important story about the necessary inter-relation between a smaller community of faith in the worship service, and the broader membership in the folk church *(folkekirken)*. It is simply a necessity for a state-ordered "folk church" to have a community of faith that feels responsible for the inner life of the church. This vital relation between the folk church and the community of faith is documented recently in a research report by Harald Hegstad of the research institute, Church of Norway.[1]

Significant ceremonies in the state church

When King Olav V of Norway died in January 1991 people immediately began to express their gratitude, sorrow and fellowship. Within hours the open space in front of the royal palace was filled with thousands of people, with candles, flowers, poems, crosses, prayers, singing and so on. Memorial services and the funeral service united a people with their king, who had openly confessed his Christian faith in an active worship practice. The blessing of the new king and queen in the summer of 1991 was a major new event, with liturgical and musical expressions that made a deep impact on the people. King Harald V and Queen Sonja very much wanted this worship service, and clearly expressed their need for prayer and blessing over their mission as king and queen of Norway. Worship experiences like these become very important as a symbol for the people, and as an expression of their belonging to someone, and something, bigger than oneself. The responsibility of the church in this matter is obvious. Among the duties of the king is to be present at the ordination of a bishop. During the last year King Harald V has participated in no less than four ordinations for new bishops in the Church of Norway. It is also noteworthy that the royal chapel of the palace in Oslo today houses the student congregation of Oslo university for regular worship services every Sunday morning.

The state church issue is a very hot one today. Church politics is a burning theme, and in recent years several cases have made current questions even more intense. A commission is at work to study the many cultural, theological and ecclesiological aspects of the theme. Norway is also aware of the fact that the Church of Sweden loosened its formal ties to the state in the year 2000. One of the many paradoxes of the state church situation in Norway today is the fact that the previous prime minister from the Labour party – who is not a member of any church – expresses, together with the Labour union, strong opinions and even demands as to how he expects the church to think and act in certain matters. On the other hand, the prime minister at the time of this writing, representing the Christian Democratic Union, is an ordained pastor in Church of Norway.

A special challenge for the church today is how to integrate homosexuals into the life of the congregations. From media and political parties comes tremendous pressure to accept persons living in a homosexual partnership as pastors in a congregation. Some have been blessed by pastors as a couple, against the explicit order of the church. Against the unanimous agreement in the bishops conference and the general synod of the church, a lesbian pastor, living in partnership with another woman, and blessed against the ruling of the church, was accepted and welcomed by one of the bishops to serve as a pastor. One justification given for this decision was the legal "rights to work" which a state church pastor enjoys according to the rules of the state.

The influence of the ecumenical movement

As already mentioned, the Church of Norway has a strong tradition of mission work. Some years ago I was informed that Norway has the most Christian missionaries *per capita*; this may have changed, but I would not be surprised if it is still the case. Traditionally the mission groups have not been very eager about ecumenical relations, and their interest in worship and liturgical questions has also been rather superfluous, and in some cases even antagonistic. The lay person's focus on preaching, however, is very strong – as is often their critique of the ecumenical movement of the past two or three decades.

The lack of contextualization, and the need for inculturation of the worship, is a perspective that has come more to the fore in the same period. The concrete, practical dimensions of worship which arise from the theology of the incarnation are important, and they have come much more into focus through the ecumenical and the liturgical renewal movements. The Church of Norway is involved in the Lutheran World Federation's international ecumenical study project on worship and culture, and is about to implement this project in dioceses and deaneries of the church.

The WCC's Faith and Order Lima text *(Baptism, Eucharist and Ministry)* and the Lima liturgy have inspired a way of thinking and doing worship. There is a great difference between discussing professionally the question of Christian unity, and the actual sharing and celebration of visible unity in worship. In Trondheim, both inside and outside the cathedral of Nidaros, ecumenical fellowship has developed regularly since the papal visit in 1989. At at least one of the annual St Olav festivals, an ecumenical seminar and liturgical celebration has taken place. Roman Catholics, Baptists, Methodists and Pentecostals have been involved in the planning for this, together with the Lutheran host of the cathedral, the bishop of Nidaros.

In the national celebration of Norway 2000, the Christian churches were well represented. The Church of Norway is a member of the national committee. The churches received 18 million kroner to prepare and administer *Jubileum 2000*, an ecumenical entity under the Christian Council of Norway. Under this umbrella the liturgical centre of the Church of Norway is commissioned to prepare ecumenical worship material to inspire the celebration of the incarnation, the birth of Jesus Christ.

New developments in worship traditions which promote or hinder Christian unity

An important renewal of worship traditions in Norway has taken place in the last twenty or thirty years of the 20th century. New ecumenical garments have been substituted for the black gowns of earlier centuries. The German-Danish choral tradition has been supplemented by a somewhat more joyful Anglo-American music, and by hymns and rhythms of other traditions and cultures. Prayers have been developed which are closer to people's lives and experience. The many newer hymns also document this development. The dogmatic approach to liturgy and prayer has been augmented by spiritual experiences. These are all elements that will inspire a "liturgy for living" and will open up a broader variety of worship expressions, thus inspiring the need for greater Christian unity.

On the other hand, the tendencies to privatize and individualize spiritual experience go against both the meaning of liturgy and the spirit of ecumenism. The integrity of ecumenism may well be endangered when not only grassroots persons, but also church leaders, promote an individualistic approach to the life of the church. In the Lutheran tradition we are especially vulnerable to this situation – and even more so in a state church situation. Some would say this is just the strength and positive side of the state church. Others are inclined to evaluate the great openness to many forms and norms, all under one and the same state "umbrella", as a paradox, related to biblical and liturgical realities in a complicated (and sometimes difficult) way.

NOTE

[1] See KIFO Perspektiv no. 1, *Folkekirke og Trosfellesskap*, Trondheim/Oslo, 1996.

The Nature and Purpose of Worship
A Local South African Anglican Perspective

CYNTHIA BOTHA

• ANGLICAN •

My context

Who am I, and how can I contribute to this survey of worship in various Christian confessions? I am an Anglican priest serving as a self-supporting assistant in the parish of St Francis of Assisi in Parkview, Johannesburg, South Africa. I was ordained in 1997 and, before that, belonged to the parish of Christ the King in the suburb of Coronationville. The latter was my home parish for the most part of my life, and it is from that experience that I would like to write.

I belong to the so-called "coloured" population group in South Africa, which during the apartheid era in our country formed part of the oppressed people and was discriminated against. Coronationville is a so-called "coloured" area, and most of its congregations belong to this population group. We are a people caught between a strongly Western tradition on the one side and an African tradition on the other, though in Coronationville, I believe, the Western tradition is stronger. This being "between two worlds" is reflected in our life and worship.

The [Anglican] Church of the Province of Southern Africa (CPSA) has 23 dioceses spread over South Africa and also includes the countries of Lesotho, Swaziland, Namibia, Angola, Mozambique and the Island of St Helena. This represents a very diverse group of people with diverse habits, cultures, traditions and characteristics. The whole country, of course, is going through a period of change from the apartheid era to one of democracy and this is reflected in the life of the church as well. How the church can exist in this changed society, and transform its liturgy to suit this evolving context, is high on its agenda.

The diocese of Johannesburg is one of the more populous urban dioceses, racially well-represented and the most affluent of all the dioceses. It is also one of the dioceses which, over a number of years, has shown a willingness to change and be transformed and to experiment with new ideas both in worship and other matters. In the past ten years or so it has decreased in size, as it has given rise to three new dioceses. Change is seen in many ways, one of which is the way it conducts its diocesan synods, allowing for more lay participation and for the laity to help set the agenda on which the diocese plans to work and move in the future. The diocese is taking democracy and transformation seriously in all its structures and the bishop has been quoted as saying, "In the process of doing this, we are allowing the people of God to run the church."[1] Concern for the clergy, and their training and well-being, is also at the top of the agenda.

Another important development is the use of diocesan resource teams to focus on the areas of concern arising from the diocesan synods. The task of the liturgy resource team, to which I belong, is to keep the whole agenda of liturgy, and the possibilities which can be achieved in worship, ever before the eyes of the clergy. Our aim is that our worship does not become monotonous, boring and a thing of habit, but is alive and challenging to the people of God in their changing context. One of the ways the group is achieving this is by providing ideas of how the liturgy can be expressed during the different seasons of the church year. The newsletters prepared by the group give ideas for the services for the various festivals of the church's year.

Diocesan events also show signs of integrating the Western and African experiences; during these services, for example, there is much wider use of the different languages of the diocese, as well as the singing of African choruses. The marimbas, an African xylophone, is also used by a number of parishes. The participation of all races – both men and women – is also striven for, but not always achieved.

Distinctive aspects and qualities of worship in my context

The worship of the English missionaries had a marked influence on the liturgy of this area, and provided the basis for our worship today. This is evident in the Coronationville community, which was formed and influenced largely by the Community of the Resurrection, an English religious order for men. This accounts for the church "operating" in a very Anglo-Catholic, high-church manner and this is still very much evident in the worship.

Worship is understood to be a time when God is honoured for all that God has done for the people; as such, worship forms a very significant part of the community and its life. Of importance is the sacrament of holy communion, in which most members would take part at least once a week. Also of importance is the listening to the word of God and the sermon which follows.

The distinctive aspect of worship, therefore, is the expectation that members would attend the Sunday eucharistic service. This is true also for the other denominations in the community. The Sunday service is the focus of the week, as it is also a time for the community to come together and to share with each other events that have happened during the past week. This sharing is done in a very informal manner, over coffee after the service. During worship this also comes with the sharing of the peace – even though this was not the original intention of this part of the service. ("The peace" is the time when we greet one another by shaking hands, or hugging each other.)

The communion service follows rather rigidly what is provided in *An Anglican Prayer Book 1989*. This new prayer book offers much flexibility in its format and the use of modern English, yet is still seen by many to be rather "traditional" in style. It provides for four different eucharistic prayers, and for four different forms in which to lead the "prayers of the church". It allows for lay participation in the reading of the word and leading the prayers of the people, and this is usually experimented with at Christ the King. Anglicans are often accused of being a people of the book – and indeed they are, at Christ the King church at any rate. The *Prayer Book* is important and copies are provided in the pews, although most families possess their own. In this way they identify much more closely with the "white" population group and the Western tradition. The *English Hymnal* has been the main hymn book for the past twenty years and more. African worship, which is much more spontaneous, is "allowed" for on certain occasions, for example, at a family mass once a month; then the worship is freer, involves children and choruses are sung.

The different seasons in the church's year are followed very carefully, and during the season of Lent, for example, there are special devotional services, such as "the stations of the cross" which are led by lay people. The observance of Lent is taken very seriously, and most people make a point of going to the week-day eucharist and belonging to the special home Bible study groups formed for the duration of the Lenten period. *An Anglican Prayer Book 1989* also provides liturgies for the major festivals of the year and, for example, the Maundy Thursday service of the "washing of the feet" and the "stripping of the altar" will be carefully observed. The Easter liturgy, which includes the vigil, the lighting of candles, the liturgy of the word and the renewal of baptismal promises, will also be carefully followed during a midnight service leading into Easter day.

Essential to the celebration of a Sunday eucharist is the priest who leads and preaches. The usual Anglican vestments, and the use of incense and the ringing of bells, will be part of the service. Other essential elements within the service are times for adoration, confession, thanksgiving (the great thanksgiving/communion) and intercession. The sharing of the peace has become an important community event – to the extent that some of the more traditional in the congregation find it intrusive and point out, as I said before, that that was not the original intention behind its introduction into the service. Yet, as noted, it is an important time to express a sense of belonging to a community, and to greet each other.

Lay people become involved in the preaching during the weekday services, that is, at the weekday eucharists and on other occasions such as funerals. Funerals are community events, and occasions when the Western and African traditions mix very well. There is always a service at the home of the family of the deceased person – a time for the community to share in their grief. These home services are most times led by lay people and are of a much freer style. The *Anglican Prayer Book* provides an outline to follow, but this is used or not used depending on the leader of the service. Most funerals end at the local cemetery for the burial; cremation is not yet the order of the day – although it does happen.

The influence of the ecumenical and liturgical renewal movements

Our worship has been influenced to a great extent by the ecumenical movement and the liturgical renewal movement. The CPSA has followed the Anglican church worldwide in this respect. Liturgical renewal has called for services to be more intelligible, for greater lay participation, more simplicity and the need to experiment. In all of these areas the CPSA has participated – though I do not think that the people in the pew realize the extent of this sharing.

The old *South African Book of Common Prayer* was slightly different from the Church of England prayer book but was, in most respects, still a traditional Anglican prayer book. The first real breakaway from the *South African Book of Common Prayer* was the use of *Liturgy 75*. The CPSA was involved in experimentation during the 1960s leading up to *Liturgy 75*; this was the first collection of modern services in the CPSA. It broke away from the traditional prayer book and was authorized for use until the publication of the new prayer book in 1989. During this period much experimentation took place and this brought onto the agenda the consideration of "ecumenical liturgy". I serve on the provincial liturgical committee and remember that a number of parishes were involved in experimenting with the various new services being produced. From time to time the clergy were also asked to comment on the changes suggested; many comments were received and were seriously considered at the meetings of the liturgical committee. The end result, we believe, is a prayer book with which the people of the CPSA can identify and which they can use, since they participated in its production. There are some, though, who felt that we did not go far enough towards producing a more indigenous prayer book.

This prayer book was simultaneously published in six of the languages used in the CPSA and has since been produced in two more languages, with others in preparation. The missal, containing the eucharistic prayers, was produced in no fewer than fourteen languages. There is a fifth eucharistic prayer in the prayer book which is ecumenical and included in a freer form of worship – to be used for special occasions and with permission. This allows for a freer form of worship with other denominations. The lectionary followed is the ecumenical one.

Renewal is also seen in the understanding of the sacraments. Rites of passage are all marked and are important in the community's expression of itself. Different services have been produced to mark these rites of passage, and these are used and appreciated in Coronationville. Examples include the service for the "thanksgiving of the birth of a child", the service for the "blessing of a home", and the "unveiling of a tombstone"; many of these services reflect the African influence. Participating in vigils, for example at funerals, is also very much in line with the African church experience. In addition, as mentioned earlier, are the services surrounding great festivals in the church – Maundy Thursday, Good Friday, and Easter.

New developments in worship: helping – or hindering – the search for Christian unity

Ecumenically, the churches have continued to work together; a recent production by the Church Unity Commission (CUC) is the booklet *Unity in Worship*, which illustrates well this search for unity as expressed in the churches' worship life. This booklet of services from the CUC is approved for use by the five uniting churches of the CUC, that is, the CPSA, the Methodist Church of Southern Africa, the Uniting Presbyterian Church in Southern Africa and the United Congregational Church of Southern Africa. The services in this booklet are designed for use on Sundays (there are three different eucharistic prayers), and for major festivals of the year, namely Christmas, Lent and Easter. Liturgies for baptism and confirmation, and for the induction of a minister, are also included. Again, some feel that these services are still too close to the traditional format and that not enough indigenous material has been used. The agenda, however, is open to discovering appropriate forms of African worship. This kind of production can only help further the search for Christian unity; the problem, though, is that it is not widely used or known on a local level.

A further development was the passing of a resolution at the CPSA provincial synod in 1995, which asked for the CPSA to permit the ministers of the other CUC churches to exercise such ministry within the CPSA when duly appointed to do so. This has taken the church a step further than just the recognition of sharing at the altar. This was widely appreciated by the people in the pews, since in a small community like Coronationville it now meant that families whose members belonged to different denominations felt more able to worship together. If the various ministers were recognized by all, then members of different churches were happier visiting each other and participating in others' services of worship. This had happened before, of course, but not with the same sense of freedom.

Other new developments which have helped include the admission of children to communion, a step that has taken us closer to the Roman Catholic Church. Exciting too is the encouraging of the development of small home groups within parishes. This allows for laity to meet and worship together in informal surroundings. Here the diocese of Johannesburg has used the American-based Catholic programme known as Renew and, more recently, the English programme called Alpha.

It has to be said, though, that on the parish level there is little else that helps promote Christian unity. The yearly Week of Prayer for Christian Unity is noted, and sharing does take place amongst the local ministers in Coronationville. These services are, however, not always well supported. And where work is done together, the different denominations do identify strongly with their own tradition – we are very much aware that we are Anglicans visiting another denomination. Still our prayer is always, and will continue to be, for Christian unity.

I have not yet indicated the style of worship in the parish to which I now belong. As I mentioned, I am now serving in the parish of St Francis of Assisi in Parkview, a northern-suburb white congregation. This is a middle-class, affluent congregation where the style of worship is very different from that of Coronationville. As also noted it had its origins as an Anglo Catholic "high" church; but then it experienced a period of charismatic worship and is now very much a "low" church where worship remains very important, but there is little emphasis on vestments, incense, ringing of bells and so on. There is much focus on developing and maintaining small home groups, and in experimenting with different styles of worship, especially at the later 9.30 morning service and the Sunday evening service, which follows a very informal format. At both of these services choruses are sung, guitars are used and the laity have a major role in conducting the service. The earlier morning service at 7.30 is more oriented towards keeping to the rubrics of the prayer book. I found it difficult at first to fit in, but now feel very much at home at these services. On occasion, I do miss wearing my vestments and the use of incense. But that is part of the wonder of the Anglican liturgy – it is adaptable yet very recognizable as being "Anglican", and one soon feels at home in the new surroundings.

NOTE

[1] Quoted in New *Life*, an ad hoc publication of the CPSA.

The Mosaic of Mennonite Worship in North America

REBECCA SLOUGH

• MENNONITE •

Worship practice among North American Mennonites has never been denominationally regulated. Congregational worship has always been locally controlled. Hymnals, songbooks and ministers' manuals offer possibilities for some uniformity for congregations and pastors using these sources. Increasingly congregations are influenced by a wide range of practices and strategies that prevail in the North American religious scene, with differing theological emphases and views of how Christians are formed as disciples.

This paper must of necessity be a sweeping overview of worship practices of the General Conference Mennonite Church, the Mennonite Church of North America, and (to a lesser degree) the Mennonite Brethren Church. Their different denominational histories offer clues for determining how tradition is interpreted, and how Anabaptist identity is created in the present. Additionally, all three churches have significant numbers of members of non-European descent including Native peoples, African-Americans, Hispanics and Asians – all of whom influence the forms and styles of worship as actually practised in a given local church.

These three primary Mennonite denominations in North America share membership in the Mennonite Central Committee (a relief and service agency) and the Mennonite World Conference. They work collaboratively on numerous projects and influence each other on various fronts in addition to worship. (At present the General Conference Mennonite Church and the Mennonite Church of North America are working towards integrating their structures and ministries to become one denomination, recognizing their diverse constituencies in Canada and the United States.)

Major influences on Mennonite worship

The major influences on Mennonite worship in North American are: (1) traditional patterns of the past with heavy emphasis on preaching; (2) liturgical renewal opened up by the Second Vatican Council; (3) contemporary praise and worship styles that reflect evangelical revivalism in America as well as the charismatic movement; (4) a "church growth" and evangelism emphasis characterized by "seeker" services; and (5) blended worship that seeks to integrate so-called "liturgical" and "non-liturgical" styles into a coherent worship practice.

The traditional pattern of Mennonite worship in North America, with the sermon as the centre or focal point of the service, includes singing and prayer. It is perhaps the simplest worship form, reflecting times with fewer print resources, less need for direct congregational involvement, and a view of worship and preaching which served primarily didactic purposes.

The liturgical renewal movement reintroduced the lectionary to North American Mennonites, brought greater emphasis on the church (or liturgical) year, gave greater attention to the patterns and rites of worship that shape a life of discipleship, engages bodily senses more fully, and opened spaces for silence, and meditative prayer, that had been lost from the past. The contemporary praise and worship movement offers an active and emotive medium of expression (frequently including uplifted arms) through long periods of singing, using songs with tempos and other musical features taken from rock, folk and some blues genres. One primary means of freedom is found in having words and occasionally music projected with an overhead screen, doing away with the necessity of hymnals or song sheets in hand. Praise, instruction and prayer characterize the service done in this manner. Many large – or so-called "mega" – churches have popularized this style, and the hope of church growth has led some Mennonites to embrace it.

"Seeker services" heighten congregational awareness that North America is, in many respects, a post-Christian society. Attention to reaching the unchurched requires a different approach to structuring worship. Retelling the biblical stories using contemporary terms and images, as well as musical forms familiar from popular culture, characterize seeker worship. In this format, inviting rather than exhorting conversion is the dominant tone in preaching.

In many respects Mennonites have been doing blended worship for generations, borrowing from other Protestant traditions in their hymnody, formation of choirs, including musical instruments in worship, in their use of worship material written by others, and in using various preaching styles. The increased awareness of this long history of borrowing has opened congregations to the possibilities offered for integrating forms arising from both the liturgical renewal, and the praise and worship, movements. Rather than viewing these movements as antagonistic, congregational leaders are beginning to see points at which they are complementary.

Basic patterns – and options – in Mennonite worship

According to our ecclesiology, each congregation orders and reorders its worship in relation to local needs and stylistic preferences. Yet certain acts appear to persist among us, giving a basic pattern or structure to much Mennonite worship. These include:

1. A gathering of the people with word, song, instrumental or choral prelude, or combination of all of these mediums.
2. Congregational singing at various points in the service.
3. Scripture readings of one to four passages.
4. An offering, most often in the form of a monetary collection.
5. Extended prayer (often a pastoral prayer), possibly with other prayers interspersed throughout the service.
6. A closing with word, song, instrumental response or postlude, or a combination of these mediums.

Two other actions connected to these primary acts of worship are increasingly present, if not already ubiquitous among us.

First, sharing joys and concerns may precede the extended, or pastoral, prayer. In some African-American congregations, or congregations influenced by the Pentecostal or charismatic movements, this may be called the "testimony" period. Second, the children's story or children's time is, ideally, an extended application of the biblical text, or of the sermonic themes. This addition began appearing in Mennonite congregations in the late 1970s or early 1980s, aiming to engage children more directly in the service.

Music in Mennonite worship

Music for Mennonite worship in North America covers a wide range of styles, and comes from a variety of sources. As with many North American denominations, Mennonites produced new hymnals in the last decade to reflect the changing face of the church, and the styles that reflect our new members. *The Hymnal: A Worship Book* (1992) was produced by the General Conference and Mennonite churches (along with the Church of the Brethren); *Worship Together* (1995) was produced by the Mennonite Brethren Church. These books draw, in differing degrees, from the traditional hymnody of the Christian church, and from the body of contemporary styles of hymnody.

In no other place than in their beloved hymns and songs is it so evident how much Mennonites have borrowed from others. Hymnic styles (strophic hymns often sung in parts) are broadly ecumenical; they are usually bound in books, sung *a capella* or with some type of keyboard accompaniment (usually organ or piano). Words and music of integrity, with some theological sophistication, are valued. Hymnic styles found in

Mennonite collections range from Latin hymns, metrical psalms, chorales and gospel songs to contemporary hymns, with musical styles appropriate to the style of the text.

Contemporary praise and worship songs (including choruses, scripture songs, some black and white gospel songs) tend to be repetitive, and require music leaders to set several songs in a medley format. Usually sung in unison with "praise band" accompaniment (guitars, electronic keyboard, drums), these songs are projected upward so worshippers can raise their heads and look outward.

The Mennonite World Conference songbooks (1978, 1990) opened North American Mennonites to the rhythms, melodies and harmonies of Mennonites on other continents. African, South American and Asian styles in particular have become accessible to many congregations. The music of Taizé has influenced Mennonites, if not in their local congregations, then in the regions where Taizé services are planned. The contemplative and meditative aspects of this music has opened busy and, at times, sceptical Mennonites to deeper levels of prayer and spirituality.

Music has been a significant point of tension for many congregations. One of the tensions arising in music comes from the characteristics and values of text-based, written culture (as expressed in standard hymnody) as they encounter a sound-based, oral culture (as expressed in praise and worship and international songs). A second tension centres around views of singing as a primarily emotive, or a primarily rational, activity. It is often difficult to achieve agreement about how these two aspects of the "singing experience" balance each other.

Mennonite practice: passage rites and ordination

Mennonites continue to practise the primary rites of the Christian church. Baptism for believers is still normative; the average age of baptism fluctuates widely, from late childhood to young adulthood. Communion is generally practised twice a year, though some congregations observe the bread and cup service more frequently. Some congregations still practise foot-washing on Maundy Thursday, but on the whole less and less. Weddings are performed in the church, in some cases with greater awareness of the congregational role in witnessing and supporting the marriage and some slight movement away from the "traditional" style of wedding promoted by commercial bridal shops and florists. "Irregularities" in marital configurations (e.g. divorce, remarriage, unchurched people asking for a church wedding, marriage of people who have lived together before the wedding) have required new processes of preparation. A small number of congregations have faced questions of covenant ceremonies for gay and lesbian partners.

Funerals reflect local custom and, increasingly, are times for introducing unchurched family members to the Christian faith or for providing means of reconciliation among family members. In the last decade numerous congregations have introduced – or reintroduced – services of anointing, either as special services or during the regular Sunday service.

Ordination is carried out by the local conferences at the request of the congregation. General Conference and Mennonite Church congregations may ordain woman to pastoral leadership; Mennonite Brethren congregations do not ordain women. There is increasing understanding of all believers as ministers of the church, with the ordained pastors or leaders exercising a particular role in the congregation. In North America generally there is awareness of the need for a stronger ritual life in the church in order to ground persons in forms of ongoing discipline. Many congregations, often influenced by women, are more attentive to the normative rituals in church life, either strengthening ritual that already exists, or creating new patterns of practice in areas of need.

Conclusion: foci of Mennonite worship

Several theological and spiritual *foci* are prevalent in Mennonite worship in North America today:

1. The trinitarian nature of God is affirmed, though each congregation may give greater or lesser attention to each *persona* of the Trinity. Concern for dominantly masculine images and names for God have some times exacerbated the tendency to focus on one *persona* of God's revealed self more than the other two. An incipient modalism exists in most congregational worship practices; Jesus remains central for Mennonite belief and practice, even if different aspects of his person, life, ethic and atoning work receive emphasis.
2. A deep concern for personal righteousness (discipleship) exists and, increasingly, gives rise to confession – though, again, differing beliefs about what constitutes righteousness persist.
3. The nature and character of the church are central foci in discussions about church membership, discipleship and evangelism.
4. Peace and justice are still held to be important aspects of the gospel. Some Mennonite congregations have backed away from these characteristics in their public witness, due to the ways in which peace and justice have been linked to other church and political agendas in North America.
5. Deep commitment to scripture is evident in worship. Questions about how the Bible should be read and interpreted persist, particularly with regard to church leadership, issues of sexuality, engaging culture, the life of peace, and materialism.

This mosaic of worship among North American Mennonites demonstrates many of the same opportunities, stresses, strains and joys of other
North American denominations. The picture is not complete (it never has
been complete) and it is constantly changing. Worship for Mennonites –
for all Christians – grows out of the life circumstances of its people, people in particular places responding to specific events in and around them.
Forms and styles of worship change because life itself is always moving
towards the unknown, yet trusting in God's promise of final fulfilment.
What remains constant is our desire to serve God in Christ Jesus empowered by the Holy Spirit, the One God who is over all, through all and in
all.

The Jamaican Baptist Worship Tradition

BURCHEL TAYLOR

• BAPTIST •

The centrality of worship

Free church, Non-conformist ideas, as well as tradition bequeathed by British Baptist missionaries and reinforced by continuing association with the British Baptists over the years, have been the dominant influences on Jamaican Baptists. The centrality of worship to the life of the church and its individual members has always been maintained. This is so to the extent that a person's Christian commitment may well be judged by the regularity of their attendance at worship services. Usually this is expected to be twice on Sunday and once in midweek. It hardly matters that changes in conditions and circumstances may make such a pattern of attendance difficult, or even impossible; the general expectation tends to remain the same. For the most part the importance of worship is taken for granted, being considered self-evident. There is, therefore, no self-conscious effort to articulate a theology of worship, or offer a theological rationale for all or any aspect of it.

Patterns in our worship life

In keeping with the inherited tradition there has always been mistrust of fixed forms or orders of worship that are officially predetermined, or which suggest any semblance of ritualism. Rather there is high regard for freedom, displayed in spontaneity and extemporaneity in self-expression. Even if not always openly stated, it is felt that such qualities are essential characteristics of the inspiration of the Spirit in worship. What is strange, however, is that in practice there is to be discerned an order that is followed – and is, in many cases, predictable. Furthermore, the order itself is influenced by specimen examples and suggestions found in service books or worship manuals published especially by British Baptists. The order used, it must be noted, is not necessarily that found in the most recently published service books, or manuals that would have been influenced by more recent liturgical thinking and considerations.

The use of hymnals in worship has been standard practice. These too are published by British Baptists but are, again, not necessarily the latest versions. Even in some rural congregations, where the literacy level may be low, there is use of a hymnal. A literate individual will "track" the hymn from the hymnal. This means that the individual will read the lines that the congregation will then sing. Great expertise is often developed in this practice so that there is hardly any break between the reading of the words and the singing in response.

The organ and, to a lesser extent, the piano are the musical instruments that are generally associated with worship. Even congregations with limited resources, or with no persons adequately trained to play these instruments, would nevertheless seek to possess one of them, preferably an organ. Of course, in relatively recent times, the keyboard, guitar and drum set have become increasingly popular; yet these have not replaced the organ as the preferred musical instrument for worship.

A fairly basic pattern of our worship tradition is as follows:

- call to worship made up of sentences of scripture
- hymn of praise
- prayer of invocation and thanksgiving
- psalm with the verses read responsively between the leader and the rest of the congregation
- scripture lesson(s)
- prayer of confession and intercession
- hymn
- welcome and announcements
- offertory
- hymn
- special musical item by the choir (a group or soloist)
- sermon
- hymn of response
- the Lord's supper (at least once per month)
- closing prayer or benediction

There may be variations concerning the inclusion, omission and/or ordering of specific items, influenced especially by local congregational practice or the choice of individual leaders.

Conviction, passion and enthusiasm generally characterize the worshipper's participation. However, this is invariably *not* of the stereotypical vibrancy and vitality that some elsewhere often associate with worship in the Caribbean. The rhythmic swaying of bodies, foot-stomping, hand-clapping to singing; music of a pulsating beat and high noise level; and the unrestrained show of emotion and response are not typical.

Influences and challenges

The current ferment being experienced in relation to worship forms, content and practice among Christians throughout the world has had its influence in our midst. There are also factors peculiar to our setting which have had their influence in this regard. At present, then, the traditional approach to worship as already outlined has not been unaffected. By far the greatest source of influence and challenge has been the neo-Pentecostal or charismatic renewal movement. This has influenced most aspects of worship – its concept, form, content and practice. People's individual interests and tastes in relation to worship and its elements, less formal and structured arrangements of services, distinctive musical preferences, special gestures indicative of praise and emotional intensity, and focus on the manifestation of spiritual gifts in worship – these are some of the noticeable features reflecting these influences. To a greater or lesser degree, some of these factors have found their way into the worship tradition. There are now greater variations in the original pattern, with some embodying a large number of the charismatic features and others less so, but hardly any remain entirely unaffected.

A particular form of North American evangelicalism has had its own influence on the tradition. It has the effect of reducing the worship almost exclusively to an exercise in "saving souls". In this regard, most things done in the worship service are expressive of the intention to challenge and convince worshippers to commit themselves to Christ. An appeal that is made to achieve this end is an important component of the worship service. Without this, worship would be considered to be incomplete and not true to its purpose. Worshippers who are Christians are, in their participation, facilitators and supporters of this purpose. A great sense of fulfilment comes when decisions are made. Sometimes charismatic elements already mentioned are combined with this to shape the worship exercise. This combination is itself a growing tradition.

There is another trend which is much less widespread, but is assuming increasing significance amongst those who are open to it. This trend has a distinctive theological bias. The emergence of a distinctive Caribbean theological project has had its influence on thinking about, and participation in, worship. This project emphasizes reflection on engagement, in the light of the word, under the guidance of the Spirit. This engagement is with the realities of the Caribbean context which include poverty, infrastructural deficiencies, social and economic needs and injustice. Against this background there is greater sensitivity to the nature and character of the God who is honoured in worship. The experience of the people, shaped and formed by the realities of the context and taken into worship, becomes a critical factor both for their responses and their affirmation of faith.

The relevance and usefulness of cultural elements such as poetry, dance, musical forms and instruments (for example African drums), story-telling and testimonies are duly emphasized. It is felt that worship is enriched by honouring a God who relates more directly to the people's experience. It is more liberating, in that it is more in line with their day-to-day experience. There is also a greater sense of community experienced in a shared response to a God who means so much more to them in their common life.

Conclusion: a look ahead

At the moment greater diversity is being displayed in the manner in which worship takes place but, generally, an ordered pattern is maintained. There is more active and self-conscious thinking concerning the nature, meaning and purpose of worship; in fact, this has put worship at the centre of our thinking as it never has been before. There have been internal tensions in some congregations, but at the same time there has been shared understanding across denominational lines on this most important subject. There are signs in some instances of growing appreciation of the worship traditions of others, which also holds out the possibility for openness to them in other ways. There is even the case of more notice being paid to the Christian year, quite apart from Good Friday, Easter day and Christmas. The Lenten season, Pentecost and Advent are more and more being mentioned and observed in the worship tradition. The freedom cherished by the tradition is taking new and interesting forms, which seem to promise more positive than negative results in the days to come.

The Nature and Purpose of the Worship Service at Yoido Full Gospel Church

YOUNG-HOON LEE

• "MEGA-CHURCH" •

Worship is the essential element of the church. The living church is to worship God; and the church is the community of God's people who have been called by God to worship him. Furthermore, the people of God experience renewal and revival through the true worship in Spirit and truth.

Among the various works and responsibilities of the church, Yoido Full Gospel Church (YFGC) in Seoul, South Korea, considers worship as the most important. Attending worship services and having spiritual passion for worship are the first priority of the YFGC. The senior pastor of the YFGC, Pastor Yonggi Cho, takes every opportunity to emphasize that the foundation of church growth in any and all things begins with a successful worship service. Along with individual fellowship with God through prayer and Bible study, participating in the worship service is the greatest expression of devotion to God.

Worship means to praise, revere, adore and give thanks to the sovereign God of creation and salvation. Simply put, it means to acknowledge the Trinity of God and to adore him. The reasons for this are simple: first, God is deserving of all our praise, reverence, glory and obedience; and second, God has commanded us to worship him.

Accordingly the congregation, rather than being mere observers of a worship ceremony conducted by the clergy, become themselves worshippers and individually experience personal fellowship with the living God. When a person glorifies the Lord, then he or she can receive true joy and happiness from God.

The YFGC provides various worship services in order for church members from various classes to attend. The following services are offered at the YFGC:
- early morning prayer meetings – twice daily
- evening worship services – daily
- all-night prayer meetings – daily
- Saturday afternoon worship service
- Wednesday worship services – three services

- seven Sunday worship services
- cell group meetings (Fridays)

The distinctive aspects of worship services at the YFGC

Worship as celebration

The worship service at the YFGC is a dynamic celebration rather than a ceremony. A worship service is not limited to mere words or some formalities; a worship service must be brought to life. The enthusiastic participation in the worship services at the YFGC makes all services like Easter celebrations; this is why the worship service is to celebrate Jesus' resurrection, the beginning of new creation. Such dynamic services result from (1) the presence of the living God, (2) the joy which the congregation feels through God's presence, and (3) a supernatural manifestation resulting from the living Word and faith in God. For all these reasons, the worship services at the YFGC are very dynamic and full of life.

The worship service as participating in the kingdom of God

The worship service at the YFGC leads the worshippers to experience God's kingdom. In other words the worship service helps the members to come face to face with the living God, and to find solutions to problems and suffering in their lives. For in an individual's life there is nothing more important than having a spiritual relationship with God, and also experiencing the kingdom of God.

Although the congregation have not entered the eternal kingdom of God yet, they should experience it already through worship services; thus the church must be the place for experiencing the kingdom of God. All of the church's traditions, organizations and doctrines have this very purpose at their core. They are the portals through which human beings on earth can come to face God, and experience the kingdom of God. The spiritual renewal of believers begins with this experience of the kingdom of heaven.

The YFGC gives enough time for all worshippers to experience the goodness and the abundance of God, doing its best to lead people on the road to the natural outflow of praise and prayer.

A blessing which accompanies such an experience of the kingdom of God during a worship service is healing, and finding solutions to the health problems of the worshippers. Through the YFGC many have been healed of their illnesses. Many of the poor and the alienated come to the YFGC to be comforted by the Holy Spirit and to be encouraged by the word of God. As the Holy Spirit fills them and leads them to sing, clap their hands, call out, cry and pray, they will experience what it means to be joined to Christ and become one with him. Through such bonding one can be freed from the restraints of a wounded heart from the past, freed to be healed in body, soul and spirit, to be forgiven and to forgive through the help of the Holy Spirit, to experience truly the "miracle of the new creation", to experience truly the kingdom of God on earth. The worship services at the YFGC can be said to be a reappearance of the Spirit-filled worship services of the early church.

Worship services of divine healing and exorcism

One important aspect of the worship service at the YFGC is divine healing and exorcism. The senior pastor of the YFGC, and all church members, believe and emphasize the fact that healing of the sick and casting out of demons are, by the power of God, still occurring today. That is, all the members of the YFGC believe that divine healing is one of the works of salvation on the cross. They believe that as Jesus Christ was crucified, he not only carried our sins but also our bodily ills and curses. More important is the fact that when Christ commanded his disciples to spread the kingdom of God, he also commanded them to heal the sick and drive out demons from the possessed (Luke 9:1-2, 10:8-9; Matt. 10:7-8; Mark 6:12-13). At the YFGC, every worship service contains a prayer time for divine healing and casting out demons. It is during this prayer time that many church members experience the supernatural work of the Holy Spirit. The experience of the kingdom of God through divine healing and exorcism which results from the supernatural ministry of the Holy Spirit can be the gateway through which many non-believers are brought to God. It also serves as a mechanism of spiritual revival for church members.

The Holy Spirit is the Spirit of witness and renewal. When one is filled with the Holy Spirit he himself becomes a new person, and a desire to witness and share his joy with others springs up. Many members of the YFGC have witnessed such supernatural work of the Holy Spirit in the YFGC, and have been brought to Christ.

Sunday worship service

The following is the outline of a Sunday worship service at the YFGC:

– invocation
– opening hymn
– confession (Apostles' Creed)
– hymn
– prayer
– scripture reading
– anthem (choir)
– sermon

- prayer and altar call
- prayer for the sick
- offering
- announcements
- closing hymn (Lord's prayer)
- benediction

The influences of the ecumenical and liturgical renewal movements

The worship service at the YFGC is in line with the traditional worship service of the Assemblies of God. However, the YFGC has adopted a worship service outline which is quite similar to that of the majority of churches in Korea. Thus any member from a church of a different denomination attending the YFGC will not feel uneasy, as the worship service is closely in line with that of other churches in the country. In addition, the Bible used in the YFGC is the widely used Korean Revised Version. In this respect, all the members of the YFGC feel that their worship service has as much affinity to the worship services of the majority of Korean churches as it has differences from them. The YFGC regards these two aspects of its worship as evidence that, in its services, it is participating in the Korean ecumenical movement.

However, while the YFGC worship shares such affinities, there are certain characteristics and alterations unique to it. These characteristics include: there is an almost natural smoothness to the flow of the worship service (much like water flows); the worship service is longer than that of other churches; there is a greater emphasis on praise and prayer; there is a manifestation of divine healing and exorcism during the worship service; and, towards the end of the service, there is a testimony.

In the area of alterations, each worship service has its own unique quality. Some worship services emphasize the message, others emphasize prayer, yet others emphasize praise and divine healing. In particular, the worship service held for young men and women has adopted a form which has broken the mould of the traditional service; it fosters an atmosphere of freedom through praise and drama. Such freedom in a worship service has been greatly welcomed by the young men and women, and is very effective in preaching the gospel to non-believing young persons. All the members of the YFGC anticipate that such modification of the worship service will become increasingly important in the future.

As for the influence of the liturgical renewal movement on the worship service at the YFGC, there are certain aspects of our worship which I feel have been affected. The services at the YFGC contain both the Pentecostal and traditional Korean worship elements. However – uniquely among Korean churches – the YFGC shares in communion on a monthly basis, on the first Sunday of each month (other Korean denominations, such as Presbyterian, Baptist and Methodist currently share in communion three to four times a year). Although the YFGC feels sharing in communion has tremendous spiritual value, it does not practise it on a weekly basis since we believe this may lead to formalization of the ceremony. The YFGC also has water baptism by immersion on a monthly basis for new Christians. The YFGC encourages all church members to be baptized once so that they can be sure of their salvation through Jesus Christ.

From this perspective it can be said that the worship services at the YFGC have been indirectly influenced by the ecumenical movement and that, in the area of liturgical renewal, the YFGC has adopted an attitude of openness towards change.

New developments in the worship service

The YFGC is currently devising new developments in the worship service in two areas. First, it will continue to seek such developments in its dynamic Pentecostal worship service tradition, for it believes that this tradition has boundless possibilities and potential. The worship service at the YFGC, which is presided over by the Holy Spirit who fills the worshippers and provides the experience of divine healing and other miracles, will continue to offer healing of the body, soul and spirit for the worshippers. Through continued growth and change, the YFGC is confident that its worship service will become one which can provide healing for those who suffer from spiritual thirst and hunger, as well as from other burdens of the heart and body, well into the new millennium. In order for the Holy Spirit to preside and take the reins of its services, all worshippers at the YFGC will pray in earnest for the Holy Spirit as the church makes every effort towards fresh developments in the message of healing, and the greater promotion of praise.

Such dynamic Pentecostal worship services can bring about beneficial changes to the traditional worship service and become a source of spiritual vitality. The YFGC believes that its own worship service can provide a positive influence, providing diversity and vitality to the ecumenical movement.

Second, the YFGC will endeavour to develop an "open worship service" which can cater to the needs of the younger generation. As mentioned earlier, the YFGC feels a great need to develop a service with emphasis on praise and drama for the younger generation of church members, one through which they can fully experience communion with God. It believes that the "open worship service" for the young will lead a new trend in and for the ecumenical movement, incorporating various characteristics from diverse Christian traditions and thus becoming a focal point of Christian unity.

Christian Worship
from a Feminist Perspective

GAIL RAMSHAW

• FEMINIST •

It is helpful to begin by clarifying some terms. This paper defines feminism as the world-view positing equality between men and women and, in consequence, the activism required to effect this world-view in the society. Feminism seeks changes in language, rituals, behavioural patterns and social structures in order to bring to an end millennia of preference for males.

Like many Christian traditions and perspectives, the feminist Christian perspective is not univocal. Although in both church and society an early naiveté suggested that all feminist voices would concur on significant issues, this has not been the case. For example, African-American Christian women use the term "womanist" to distinguish their concerns from those of the dominant white feminist movement, which womanists view as racist; and Hispanic women, calling themselves Mujeristas, judge feminism to be classist. Reflection by lesbian Christians has worked to destabilize traditional categories about female and male, feminine and masculine. It is important to say that women do not agree on the meaning or usefulness of the term "woman's experience", and some in the movement are no longer citing this controversial category in their deliberations. However, even among the persons who call themselves feminists there are several distinct, and sometimes antagonistic, groupings.

We can suggest some of the diversity within feminist Christianity by delineating four types of feminist Christian worship:
1. Feminist Christians who are fully engaged in the worship life of their historic tradition, making the accommodations, often silently, that they deem necessary for themselves, and continuing to work within denominational structures to make worship more congruent with feminist ideals.
2. Feminist Christians who have already made substantial changes in the language and ritual of Christian worship within their communities.

3. Feminist Christians who worship only within separatist women-church groups and who, consequently, do not participate in many of the historically important and denominationally mandated Christian rituals.
4. Feminist Christians who have despaired of change in their situation, cannot locate or do not feel free to join with any local feminist expression, and so no longer participate in Christian public worship.

Even within each group feminists do not necessarily agree on what the major issues are and how the problems might be solved. For example, some feminists adapt and adopt as unisex historically male patterns, such as the use of a chasuble or ordination itself, while others judge that traditionally male symbols and status cannot be reformed but must be rejected. Some women are in two or more groupings, depending on the specific situation. For example, they may participate with their parish on Sunday morning, but meet with a women-church group in the afternoon. It is not surprising that women who come from those church structures that are perceived as impervious to change are more likely to disregard the liturgical tradition of their parent church, and to be creating innovative liturgical forms. In extreme cases liturgy such as the eucharist, which has constituted the church's self-identity, is abandoned and new forms, constructed by contemporary women, take precedence. This has happened particularly within Roman Catholicism. Some women define as "feminist" only those liturgical expressions which stand in critical tension over against the established worship patterns of the parent church body.

Two more groupings need to be distinguished. Some thoughtful feminist Christians see no difficulties with their traditional worship, and some even defend it. This is especially evident in Orthodoxy. But women in another group no longer identify themselves as Christian, having judged that the church's androcentrism cannot be eliminated so as to produce an authentic religious expression. Many of these post-Christian feminists participate regularly in feminist rituals which lie outside the purview of this report, but which do influence the development of feminist Christian ritual patterns. Finally, it is important to note that while feminists include both women and men, many Christian women are not feminist and do not intend to become so.

Granting the great diversity within the feminist Christian movement, and remembering that any single feminist ideal – for example, inclusive language – is being sought in a wide variety of ways, both small and great, some generalized remarks can be made.

The fundamental understanding of the nature of worship

While many feminist Christians would follow Christian tradition by asserting that the nature and purpose of worship is the praise of God, most feminist Christians would add as a distinctive emphasis that worship ought to be communal, in creation, in design and in execution. Hierarchy as expressed in language, ritual and organization is criticized. Feminist Christians are more or less critical, some highly so, of the church's inherited forms and the language of worship, for they see these as maintaining and even sanctifying male dominance, and as having been mandated by males in the past.

Feminist Christians seek to develop new language and rituals that are both inclusive of the entire present community and attuned to women's experiences. Some claim self-authorization for the development of new materials which may look more – or less – like historic Christian worship. Many feminist Christians claim that the church originally stood counter-cultural to patriarchy, and that contemporary changes represent a retrieval of primitive Christianity. The changes may be relatively non-controversial, such as eliminating masculine references to humankind. Some changes are influenced by a feminist biblical hermeneutic. Other changes may be church-dividing, such as changing trinitarian language or replacing eucharistic imagery with an innovative Christology and ritual. (To be sure, church authorities do not themselves agree on which changes are potentially church-dividing.) While some feminists have laboured to produce feminist-friendly worship materials for their parent church, other feminists resist the publication of these materials, having been influenced by non-Christian feminist rituals to value the uniqueness and spontaneity of each group and to resist participation in the authority of the published text.

Many feminists agree that one of the purposes of Christian worship is the nurturing of a community of justice. This emphasis is usually marked by some or all of the following: support for women's ordination; attention to the suffering of the world's women; story-telling from personal experience; focus on sin not as personal selfishness, but as the structures of social injustice. Again, feminist interest in hearing women's voices may show itself on many levels. When this interest is practised to a lesser degree, the ritual will be characterized by welcoming the voices of all participating women. Many feminists include in worship women's stories from the Bible and church history. When exercised to the fullest degree, this feminist interest rejects the biblical canon itself as sexist, and seeks its expansion. The purpose of these changes is to find a vehicle more open to women's experiences within which to find strength for a life of justice.

On the theological level, considerable conversation is occurring among feminist Christians as to appropriate theology. In seeking to lessen the male focus within the church, many feminists challenge the language of God's fatherhood. Some advocate a low Christology. Some feminists have explored the image of Sophia as female language for Christ, and some have designed liturgies in which Sophia is the dominant – if not sole – divine image. Other feminist theologians urge a creative approach to the Trinity as the best antidote to androcentrism. The amount of theological criticism or creativity, biblical knowledge and hermeneutical sophistication in feminist Christian worship varies greatly. Indeed, some ask to what degree these historic values should remain in the forefront in designing contemporary Christian worship.

Some feminist Christians view as an important component of the purpose of worship the conversion, rapid or gradual, of the entire Christian community to feminism. Other feminists are content within, or even defensive of, separatist worshipping communities. Naturally, these attitudes affect women's political decisions in relationship to their parent churches and the speed with which they advocate or inaugurate change.

The distinctive aspects of the feminist perspective on worship

Here is a list of some aspects of feminist Christian worship which, to a greater or lesser degree, one might find: (1) a removal of language that casts the human person as male, or refers to stereotypically male traits as preferable to female traits; (2) a removal of language that suggests that God is male; (3) an enhancing of each woman's self-esteem; (4) the valuing of the female body; (5) the incorporation of dance; (6) a ritual which is as broadly participatory as possible; (7) a creative approach to sacramental practice; (8) a selective approach to traditional Christian doctrine; (9) a critical stance over against the church's authority structure, leadership in the church, and historical theology; (10) use of non-hierarchical space. It is important to realize that in some communities, these goals will be sought with considerable respect to the inherited worship patterns, and in other communities far more innovative latitude will be present.

Take, for example, the current issue of the name for God used at Christian baptism: some feminist Christians will baptize using the traditional words, judging for one reason or another that this is not a controversial issue; others continue to use the words while lobbying for denominational change; others authorize themselves to use a different name for God, often with minimal fanfare. A second example is in the use of the title "Lord". Some feminists, especially womanists, are glad to call God (rather than a white male) their Lord. Others are searching for a replacement for this term as being too sexist, archaic or hierarchical. Some feminists refuse to use the term, editing it out of worship texts whenever the situation allows, while attending more or less (as the case

may be) to the Christological issues inherent in the title. A further com-
plication arises across languages, for each linguistic system presents a
unique situation in regard to gender issues.

The influence of the ecumenical movement
The feminist Christian movement has been exceedingly ecumenical
in nature, largely because the participants' identity as women has been
viewed as more foundational than their denominational or ethnic background. Feminist theology is read with practically no regard to denominational distinctiveness. Ritual books are widely shared across historic
boundaries. Conferences and retreats, formative for many women in the
movement, are often ecumenical in design and participation. In the
extreme, denominationally distinctive teachings are purposefully devalued, for they are seen as representing an obsolete male development of
churchmanship. Protestant women in particular join easily with any
group of feminist Christians for worship.

Much of what the 20th-century liturgical movement advocates corresponds to feminist concerns. Both movements value many of the same
goals: circular rather than rectangular space; participatory rituals rather
than passive attention to leaders; a re-evaluation of the role of the clergy;
multiplicity of voices in the assembly; the use of silence; a connection
between church symbols and calendar, and the cycles of the natural
world; and the valuing of culturally appropriate and locally applicable
texts. In fact it can be argued, not that feminists have been influenced by
the liturgical renewal movement, but the opposite: that the ecumenical
liturgical renewal movement is yet another demonstration of the rise of
feminist consciousness in the religious expression of the 20th century.

New developments
There is considerable evidence of the feminist-inspired reforms in
many denominations' structures, publications and priorities. For example, recent church hymnals include many innovative images for God,
and some denominations are producing new liturgical texts that incorporate some of the feminist concerns. The widely used *Revised Common
Lectionary* attempted to heed feminist critique. Thus some observers
conclude that feminism is slowly becoming the norm, at least in first-
world areas of the church.

However, it is difficult to judge to what degree feminism is reshap-
ing the church. There is considerable evidence of a backlash, as some
church leaders believe that a few changes "ought to satisfy the ladies".
Many seminaries have reformed their androcentric worship practices
and liturgical curriculums, only to find more conservative students

matriculating who question the new forms. It is clear that many people accept small changes, for example, adding "and sisters" to the address "brothers", but far fewer are ready for the serious and thoroughgoing reform of divine imagery, theological language and denominational structure envisioned by feminists. Thus while some women are able to effect change within their churches, some are moving away from connection with traditional Christian churches. Particularly younger women in first-world countries around the world cite as a major reason they no longer attend Christian liturgy the androcentrism which they encounter in worship.

It is crucial that church authorities, including those not identified with feminism, take seriously the challenge that the women's movement presents to an historically androcentric religion. Similar feminist critiques are heard now in Judaism and Islam, as women in all three monotheistic world religions seek a re-examination of traditional language, ritual, sexual ethics and church order. Many feminists are devout believers who wish to remain within their reformed parent churches. These feminist Christians have already shown themselves as a force for ecumenical unity. The task ahead is to keep this lively reform movement within the churches. Perhaps the WCC's Faith and Order Commission can take onto its agenda the advocacy of meetings of such feminist Christians, as a sign of the church's attention to this massive challenge for world Christianity.

The Worship Life
of the Community of Grandchamp

THE COMMUNITY OF GRANDCHAMP

• RELIGIOUS COMMUNITIES •

The basic understanding of the nature and goal of our worship

The Community of Grandchamp is ecumenical, of monastic inspiration and issuing from the Reformed churches. It is recognized by the Evangelical Reformed Church of the canton of Neuchatel, Switzerland, and, through it, belongs to the Swiss Protestant Federation and the World Council of Churches.

An ecumenical community

We are an "ecumenical" community due simply, in the first place, to the diverse origins of the sisters. They are, for the most part, Reformed but are also Lutheran and Methodist, and come from different countries in Europe, as well as from Indonesia. Catholics (and, more rarely, Orthodox) share our life for shorter or longer periods. The origins of the guests whom we welcome are also quite varied, with regard both to their nationalities and their faiths. Sometimes we receive Jewish, sometimes Muslim women.

At this writing there are about sixty sisters within our Community, most living at Grandchamp (which is located near the city of Neuchatel in French-speaking Switzerland), but with others living in German-speaking Switzerland, Algeria, Jerusalem, the Tessin (Italian-speaking Switzerland), France and the Netherlands.

From the Community's inception at the end of the 1930s, Christ's prayer "that all may be one that the world might believe" (John 17:21) has been at the centre of our prayers and of our life. Conscious that their particular vocation could benefit greatly from the experience of other confessions, the first sisters were from the outset open, in all confidence and simplicity, to the reality of the universal church. Contact with the brothers of Taizé, whose rule we adopted, assisted, confirmed and

---

• See also the paper by Sœur Minke in *Liturgie in Bewegung/en mouvement*, Bruno Bürki and Martin Klöckener eds, Fribourg/Geneva, Universitätsverlag and Labor et Fides, 2000.

strengthened us in this direction, while the Community remained profoundly rooted in our Protestant origins.

Since the World Council of Churches assembly at Vancouver in 1983, we have been aware that our prayer and work for Christian unity concerns the whole of suffering humanity and the whole creation, and we know that we are engaged in the struggle for justice, peace and the integrity of creation.

Of monastic inspiration

The Community was born in the 1930s, as one result of the rediscovery of spiritual retreats within the Reformed churches of French-speaking Switzerland by a group of women seeking a deeper life of faith. From the beginning these retreats, based on listening and meditating in silence on the word of God, gave the nascent community its monastic flavour. Long stays in Anglican, Catholic and Orthodox monasteries allowed further experience of this calling, which had given such an impulse to the early church. Numerous contacts with the Orthodox (especially Paul Evdokimov, but also Fr Boris Bobrinskoy, Fr Sophrony from England...), and with Eastern monasticism (in Lebanon), nourished and shaped our monastically-inspired vocation.

The direction and goal of our worship life

We have been set aside by the Holy Spirit in the cause of Christ and the gospel to celebrate and show forth together, within the universal church and in the world, the love of God the Thrice-Holy, to proclaim – and allow ourselves to be transformed by – the mystery of faith: the Christ who died and was raised again, and whose return we await.

We have come together in order to be "a house of prayer for all nations" (Mark 11:17; Isa. 56:7). As we say,

> Yearning towards the kingdom where God will be all in all, let us welcome at each dawn the presence of the Risen One who opens us, in confidence and in freedom, to God's new day.

Since the spring of 1936, a bell has called the sisters together for prayer. Our common life of prayer and hospitality is given its rhythm by the prayer of the hours, like the life of the Jews and the first Christians (Acts 2:42,46a), and as it still is today in monasteries and religious communities: in the evening (vespers and compline), in the morning and at midday, and at times during the night (Ps. 119:62).

This common worship culminates in the celebration of the Lord's supper, the eucharist, at least twice a week: on Sunday morning and Thursday evening. For the reality of Easter is central to our life. Through this reality we are enabled ever anew to pass from death to life, dying with Christ to everything within us which leads to death and separation, and to rise with him to a new life, by receiving newness of life through the Spirit. When we receive his body and his blood, we become a *koinonia,* a communion renewed by joy and by forgiveness. Easter is our great feast day and each Sunday, from Saturday evening onwards, is a little celebration of Easter.

> Will you, from now on, together with your sisters, celebrate the newness of life which Christ gives you by his Holy Spirit; will you let this new life live in you, among us, in the church and in the world, in the whole creation, thus carrying out the service of God in our community?[1]

The eucharist, memorial of the death and resurrection of Christ, centre of our faith, renewing the grace of our baptism, brings us together as the people of God. Here we take root as members of the body of the risen Christ, strengthening our communion; it "builds us together spiritually into a dwelling place for God" (Eph. 2:22).

Our common worship, the very breath of our community life, culminating in the celebration of the eucharist, constantly brings us back together into the harmony with God which encompasses the reality of all humanity and of the creation. This reality is found in the communion of saints in heaven and on earth, thus anticipating the worship expressed in Revelation, when God will be "all in all" (Rev. 4:1-11, cf. 1 Cor. 15:28).

The Community takes shape, grows, and becomes more receptive to the work which God wishes to accomplish in the world through the faithfulness of each sister to the word. She reads, studies and meditates on it in silence; hears, sings and proclaims it in common worship; and puts it into practice in daily life, with its tasks and relations with others. The more actively each sister participates, the greater the communion among them, each opening up in adoration to a larger reality than her own experience: to love, to forgiveness, to solidarity. In praising God together we are enabled to receive others and ourselves, and what is happening in the world, all in the light of the Holy Spirit.

Sharing in worship together engages not only our heads, our minds, but the whole body and all the senses through our different postures, through song... The moments of silence during worship, but also the beauty of the worship space and the way it is arranged, including the placement of the various symbols (the cross, the Bible, communion table, lights, icons, flowers...), all invite us to meditation and prayer – and we are very attentive to that.

In conclusion, our worship life is absolutely central to the life of our Community. Without worship there would be no Community of Grandchamp for it is that which sustains, nourishes and cements the communion among us, which enlivens us and directs our path.

A brief history of liturgical development within the Community of Grandchamp

All of the earliest sisters, and many of us today, come from Reformed churches where the liturgical life is genuine but fairly austere in comparison with that of other traditions. That varied, of course, depending on the region in question. The first sister who came at the beginning of the 1960s from a high Lutheran church in Germany had to give up several of the expressions of her piety (crossing herself, candles on the altar – except for Saturday evening and Sunday...). Nevertheless the sisters were already trying more "objective" and biblical forms of worship, thanks to the biblical and liturgical renewal of the 1940s and 1950s.

From its publication in 1943, the sisters had used *L'office divin* (the divine office), elaborated by the pastors of the movement "Eglise et Liturgie" (Church and Liturgy) in the French-speaking area of Switzerland[2] (a result of the 1927 first world conference on Faith and Order in Lausanne!). Taizé had reworked this for use in a more monastic context. We used it first of all with the brothers in draft form; since 1964 we have used the *Office* of Taizé, *La Louange des Jours* (Daily Praise) – having adapted it to our own situation as women, and in accordance with what we have discovered and experienced through our encounters with others and within our own sisterhood. In Algeria we have experienced a very simple way of life; in Lebanon, direct contact with the monastic renewal of the Syrian Orthodox Church, and the discovery of icon painting; and, in Israel, our Jewish roots... We have been more attentive to the use of inclusive language (with regard to women and to the Jewish people), and our singing is greatly inspired by Byzantine melodies. We have also learned to arrange our chapels in a simpler manner, with Rublev's icon of the Trinity in the centre, the low altar during the Prayer of the Hours in order to allow more space...

We would say that our liturgical life had reached a certain stability by the end of the 1970s and 1980s – but it is a stability which is open, flexible, always seeking greater simplicity, more silence, more inwardness.

Some essential elements in our liturgical life (that which is constant, that which varies)

It is fundamental that the sharing of worship, and especially the eucharist, did not originate with us – it is a gift which was made to the universal church. It is important that each sister learns to enter into this worship which belongs to all the ages: the psalms, certain biblical hymns, liturgical texts, the readings given in the lectionary, the stages of the liturgical year, a certain basic sequence – especially, for the eucharist... We cannot do just anything at any time according to our own ideas, or needs of the moment. The same texts repeated each year enter into us ever more deeply. This discipline is, in itself, already an ecumenical act! Our worships together allows us to enter into the worship practice of the Jewish people with its psalms, and into that of the whole church, on earth and in heaven. And within this pattern of prayer, there are plenty of spaces for innovation and creativity: composing or choosing hymns, songs, certain responses; and, in each *office* (service), free intercessions are important.

We regularly review our whole liturgical life, attentive to the sensitivities and insights of our times (for example, with regard to outdated language, the need for participation, gestures... see below).

Our shared worship must remain lively, simple, open to the Holy Spirit. But we always seek to be faithful to the mystery of the Christian faith, respecting the main lines of the tradition, always seeking to know more about that which is essential, and precious, for other confessions (for example, making sure to consume – within the celebration itself – the unused bread and eucharistic wine...).

Our whole liturgical life is the fruit of biblical and liturgical renewal. Our liturgical life is closely linked to the ecumenical movement, and contributes to it more and more (as is clear from this account!)

New developments within our liturgical life

Towards an ecumenical spirituality

It is not always easy to find balance and stability while still moving forward. We are called to live an ecumenical spirituality, without which we cannot grow in true unity among ourselves and within the church. Our shared worship leads us there. Sisters who come from a more "Catholic" or more "free" ("evangelical") tradition, or those who are not particularly familiar with any tradition – we are all on the way together towards the church of tomorrow and, above all, towards... the kingdom of God! This ecumenical spirituality teaches us not to look back, hang on to confessional principles, and seek security by clinging to liturgical habits. We must open ourselves to a greater reality and consequently must know how to live with a certain provisional character in our worship. But it is essential that our worship is, and remains, a source of nourishment, of communion, of unconditional welcome for ourselves and our guests.

As we have seen in our account above, the Community has seen many liturgical developments in the course of its history, thanks to contact with the different churches: these include prayer which is more "objective" than subjective, the singing of psalms, the singing of litanies, icons, evening prayers, and more emphasis on the unfolding of the liturgical year... Other forms of prayer have enriched our liturgical life, such as the way of the cross, praying around the cross, and pilgrimages (particularly for the feast of the Transfiguration, which offers the opportunity to make a strong link with today's world by remembering the bombing of Hiroshima, also on 6 August).

Holy week

The liturgy of holy week has also been greatly developed and enriched. In particular:

– *Maundy Thursday (evening)*: we try to place the eucharist, and its institution, in the context of Christ's last supper. In the first part of the celebration we share the meal, recalling the *seder,* in the chapel which is furnished with twelve low tables; then we experience again the institution and the Lord's supper.

– *Good Friday*: we pay great attention to what we are saying in respect of the Jewish people, and have reviewed the formulation of our prayers. For example, the ancient prayer for this *office* which was formulated thus:

> O Lord, we pray thee, look upon on this family which is thine, for which Jesus Christ, our Lord, did not refuse to be handed over to the wicked, nor to endure the cross, He who reigns with thee and the Holy Spirit, now and for ever.

has become:

> Lord God, for our sake your beloved Son endured accusation, abandonment, suffering and death on the cross. Grant us, through your Holy Spirit, understanding of what he did for us. May your grace rest upon the Jews, your people whom you love with an eternal love, upon the church and upon all the families on earth. We ask this in the name of Jesus, our Lord.

On Good Friday evening, during the *office* of the burial of Christ, we have the opportunity to place flowers upon the altar, which symbolizes the tomb into which Christ was placed after being taken down from the cross.

– Holy Saturday is observed by a deep silence, which is gradually penetrated by the hope and joy of Easter (Ps. 27:13, 14)!

– The celebration of Easter day starts early in the morning around a large fire in the courtyard. Then we go up together into the chapel, singing the resurrection – with material from the canon of St John of Damascus, and a series of *troparia* sung in different languages...

The most recent developments

The lectionary: We wanted to preserve, for example, a pre-Lenten period (formerly Septuagesima, in memory of the Exile, so appropriate in our world today), and we have introduced a pre-Advent period.

The two central cycles of the liturgical year are very important in helping us to enter ever more deeply into the mystery of the faith, letting it enter more and more into our daily lives. Associated with Christmas and with Easter, these are:

a) the cycle of Christ's incarnation, of his nativity (Christmas until the baptism of Christ) preceded by the long preparation of the chosen people in the first Testament; and

b) the cycle of redemption, with Christ's passion, death and resurrection and the forty days until Ascension, Pentecost and Trinity Sunday.

The time of the church[3] (the periods of the liturgical year associated with neither of the two central cycles above) has its own rhythm; it is punctuated by the remembrance days of the saints – mostly "biblical" , but we have also included St Francis, St Silouane, Dietrich Bonhoeffer, Mgr Romero, Edith Stein... Other aspects include the following:

a) The feast of the Transfiguration (see above) also begins, for us, a special period of forty days leading up to 14 September, the day for remembrance of the life-giving cross.

b) We have revived the tradition of the rogations in the seventh week of Easter, to ask a blessing – in a service which takes place in the garden – upon the little patch of ground given into our care, our own garden, with all that has been sown in it. And in the autumn, at harvest time, we bring some of our produce to a festive eucharist and share it with all who are present. The celebration is followed by an *agape*.

Anointing with oil: On Ash Wednesday evening, having received the ashes that morning at the eucharist, we can receive unction, as a sign of the "strength and gentleness" of the Spirit who strengthens us on our way towards Easter. On holy Saturday evening, unction is also offered to mark our entry with Christ into new life.

The Bible placed on the communion table: After much study we have found its rightful place... to the great joy of those of us from the Protestant tradition!

Liturgy: the basis of our life... unto eternity

The liturgy permeates the whole of our life... and our whole life is liturgy... until its end. As far as possible, we watch with and accompany right to the last a sister who is approaching the end of her life's path. And when she has "passed over" we gather around her to pray and to sing. The coffin is carried from the bedroom to the chapel and during this little procession we sing Psalm 91 and the *Trisagion*. Then after each *office* we pass by the chapel where the coffin, still open, is placed. Gradually the grief we express in our songs is transformed into confidence, to faith in the resurrection in the light of the communion of saints. In a last gesture of farewell, we place flowers in the coffin before closing it, just as we do at the *office* of burial on Good Friday. The resurrection service which follows allows the joy of Easter to break forth, even in the midst of our pain. The eucharist celebrated around the coffin strengthens us in our faith and hope. Again at the cemetery we affirm our faith, and sing the *Troparion* of Easter as we walk around the cemetery, placing flowers on the tombs of the sisters who have gone before. This long procession all around the cemetery, with the paschal candle, is a heritage from the Orthodox tradition.

Concluding reflection

In general, our visitors enter into our liturgy very well and react positively to it. But we must take the trouble to explain what is going to happen – and why. People today feel more and more strongly the need to participate, to express themselves with words and gestures...

We are careful to borrow from the liturgies of other confessions (and for us this applies especially to the Orthodox liturgy) only that which is appropriate, respecting the place in the liturgy where one finds a particular gesture, song, prayer... (a certain "popularizing" and an unsuitable use of hymns and liturgical elements can be disturbing).

Some Protestants no longer feel at ease in our chapel and in our liturgy – "it's Catholic" , or "all these icons", they say. This is a pity, because often Reformed persons find a dimension of adoration, simplicity, universality in our worship which they have not known before. And we have noticed – at Grandchamp (in the cantonal church of Neuchatel), as well as at our Community of Sonnenhof (in the cantonal church of Basle-Land) – that, through our guests, and especially through the pastors who come to celebrate the eucharist, another dimension of the prayer of the church can shine forth.

NOTES

[1] From the second commitment made at a sister's profession.
[2] See André Bardet, "Le mouvement liturgique dans l'Église réformée du Pays de Vaud", in Bruno Bürki and Martin Klöckener, *Liturgie in Bewegung/en mouvement*, Fribourg/Geneva, Universitätsverlag und Labor et Fides, 2000, pp.152-54.
[3] Also sometimes referred to as the cycle (or season) of the year or, less happily, as *ordinary time*.

The Worship of the Iona Community

KATHY GALLOWAY

• RELIGIOUS COMMUNITIES •

Worship has been fundamental to the life of the Iona Community since it began in 1938. It was with the intention of breaking down the barriers between our everyday lives and language, and the life of the worshipping community, that the first members of the Community – Presbyterian ministers and craftsmen – engaged together in the rebuilding of the ruins of the medieval abbey of Iona. They began and ended each day with common worship. Work and recreation were encompassed within the pattern of worship, because they are not to be held apart. Each informs the other. The worship of the Iona Community is the backbone of an embodied and integrated spirituality.

Our pattern of worship – and life

On Iona and Mull

On Iona, the pattern still remains the same. The continuing group on whose life the daily worship is based is the resident community living in the abbey and the MacLeod centre (the Community's youth and family centre). Their work, and that of the guests who week by week form community with the residents and volunteers, is rooted in worship. We are accountable in all things to God. We make account as a community, we give testimony (that is, tell the common *story* that directs our common *task* and shapes our common *life)* in our worship.

Morning worship is the daily office of the Iona Community, which follows a set form of prayers, songs and readings, and during which every member of the community is prayed for, by name, in a monthly cycle. This prayer by name is also done by the individual members scattered throughout the world in their own daily prayer – though divided by distance, we are united in prayer.

Evening worship reflects the concerns of the Iona Community (which are, of course, concerns of the whole Christian community) for justice and peace, for personal and political healing, for the integrity of creation, for economic justice and personal accountability, for the celebration of human community. The liturgy for these services is prepared each day by residents, volunteers and guests, and may vary widely in style, although there are outline orders which may be used. On Friday evenings, the sacrament of holy communion is celebrated informally round long tables carried into the abbey church. Sunday morning is also a eucharistic celebration of a more formal nature, and includes the preaching of a sermon. On Sunday evening, worship takes the form of an extended period of corporate silence, followed by extempore prayer from the congregation. During the summer months, when many day visitors come to Iona who otherwise could not share in worship, there are afternoon prayers for justice and peace, a particular concern of the Iona Community. Each day is encompassed by worship – no benediction is said until the end of the evening service, and at the end of the morning service, worshippers immediately rise to go to the day's activities.

At Camas, the Iona Community's smaller and much more isolated adventure centre on the nearby Ross (island) of Mull, the day is encompassed by worship also, held either in the Chapel of the Nets, or outside on the rocks by the sea. Camas worship, in the remote and intimate setting of interdependence and dependence on nature, offers unique opportunities for creative worship and contemplation.

On the mainland

But the worship of the Iona Community does not take place only on Iona and Mull. There are many occasions when the Community gathers on the mainland – in the family groups which are its base communities, in plenary session in different places, for special events and acts of witness. And each individual member is committed to working out the rule of the Community in her or his own context of place, work, people, and within their own worshipping community. Therefore, there are many occasions and situations in which the Community is engaged in finding, as our prayer puts it, "new ways to touch the hearts of all" in worship on the mainland. Because the membership of the Community (and its associate members, friends and staff) come from such a diversity of backgrounds, nationalities, faith traditions and experiences, the kinds of worship they are involved in is enormously varied. The life and service of the local church, the work of community and campaigning groups, ecumenical and international events, small groups and house churches, are all part of the engagement of Community members. And all of these are proper places for worship.

Constant features of our worship

But whether on Iona or at Camas or on the mainland, whether it is the Community gathered or the Community dispersed in small groups, there are some features of our worship which are constant.

Our worship is *incarnational*. At its heart is the belief that God in Jesus Christ became a human being like us, sharing fully in all the hopes and fears, joys and sorrows of our lives, to let us know that God loves us, forgives us, frees us, makes us whole, desires to give us life in all its fullness. An incarnational spirituality is the profoundest motivation of the Iona Community; it cannot be properly understood without knowing this. Thus Ron Ferguson, then leader of the Community, writing its history in 1988:

> The doctrine most emphasized by the Community was that of the incarnation – the coming of God to humanity in the shape of Jesus Christ. God, in love, had entered the human situation in all its mess and glory. Humanity had thus been dignified and ennobled. The spiritual had been joined to the material in Jesus Christ, and the material could therefore never be despised. Since the face of Jesus was to be discerned in the poor, the hungry, the prisoners and the victims, social and political action could never be divorced from spirituality.[1]

This incarnational emphasis was set from the Community's inception by its founder, George MacLeod, who in the 1940s wrote,

> The gospel claims the key to all material issues is to be found in the mystery that Christ came in a body: and healed bodies and fed bodies: and that he died bodily and himself rose in his body, to save man body and soul.[2]

As a Community, therefore, we believe that there is no part of life that is beyond the reach or outside the scope of our faith. The word of life, which we attend to and seek to discern and interpret in worship, is as much for our politics as for our prayers.

Our worship is *historical*. It draws on the experience and creativity of our mothers and fathers in the faith. On Iona, the Community inherits three traditions. The Celtic church of Columba had a strong and deep sense of the incarnation and, partly through its close Orthodox links, of the glory of God in creation, of God as Creator as well as Redeemer. As we share in these beliefs they find expression in our worship, in liturgies for justice and peace, in creation liturgies, and in the weekly pilgrimage round Iona. The Benedictine monks who built the abbey of Iona in the Middle Ages had values of hospitality and the centrality of prayer which we share in our life as a community today. And we drink deeply from the well of the biblical faith, and the belief in the priesthood of all believers of our Reformed forebears in Scotland. Sometimes we use the orders and creeds and liturgies which have come down through the ages. They are part of the great drama of worship; they remind us that we are part of the communion of saints.

Our catholicity is contemporary as well as historical. Our worship is *ecumenical,* because we are an ecumenical community and part of a worldwide oikoumene. Though in its origins the community was Presbyterian, and its worship reflected this, as the membership has grown far beyond the Church of Scotland, so we are constantly receiving gifts from the various traditions represented in it: from Quaker and Anglican, from Methodist and Baptist and Brethren and Congregational, from Presbyterian and Roman Catholic. We cannot but be ecumenical. We are not "interdenominational". Many members of the Community do not actually know what denomination others are, unless they ask specifically. We are simply members of one another. We do not believe this condemns us to the blandness of the lowest common denominator. We believe this challenges us to be open, honest and creative. This is, of course, a constant struggle, and sometimes a source of conflict and pain. But these are the places where we grow.

To be ecumenical in its true sense demands that we be *inclusive.* We believe that God welcomes everyone who seeks to worship in spirit and in truth. So it is a matter of faithfulness to God's purposes that people do not feel unwelcome, or devalued by the use of language which excludes on account of gender, race or culture. Nor should it be the case that our worship is an arcane activity, understandable only by people who have degrees in theology, or have grown up in the church. It also means that the planning and leadership of worship is not confined to the clergy. In fact in all our worship leadership they are always in the minority, though they may play a significant enabling role, and services in the abbey are as likely to be led by a 20-year-old volunteer cook as by the warden. This has always been the case for us, since the time when ministers laboured for the craftsmen in rebuilding the abbey and the masons and carpenters, in turn, led the daily worship.

Thus the priesthood of all believers extends for us to our worship, and we have been greatly assisted in this by the outstanding theologians of the people of God, such as T. Ralph Morton and Ian Fraser, in our membership. Since liturgy is literally "the work of the people", we do not want to take this merely as a pious phrase but to make it live, so that the people are fully and actively engaged in worship in songs, responses and open prayer, in symbolic acts, and in the many ways in which it is possible to "break the word" in order that it might be shared. The only exception to this pattern at present is in the celebration of the sacraments, which may be done only by those who are ordained persons or recognized celebrants in their own denominations. This is an open question within the Community, however, and there are family groups where, without prejudice, all members share in celebrating communion.

And our worship is *creaturely*. We are whole people, God's creation, and we seek to respond with our bodies, through our senses as well as our intellects. In movement and stillness, through touch and sight and sound, through smell and taste, we pray and worship in many ways. Reformed worship has been characterized as being overly intellectual and "wordy", and in this sacramental and sensory emphasis in our worship we are drawing on an older tradition, that of the Columban church.

Our inspiration: the Columban church

The Iona Community and its worship have often been described as "Celtic", and in recent years we have seen an explosion of interest in all things considered Celtic. But this is not an accurate description of our community. Our membership is not primarily composed of Gaels (Irish or Highland Scots); and what can, with any legitimacy, today be termed Celtic is held in the Celtic languages: Scots and Irish Gaelic, Welsh, Breton. We do not worship in any of these languages. Our community is Lowland more than Highland Scottish, and has many non-Scottish members. It started in Glasgow, not Iona. But we share with the Columban church[3] an incarnational and creaturely spirituality, and in fact it is this which people see and name incorrectly as Celtic.

Based on Iona, we cannot help but be influenced by the Columban church with its strong sense of Christ as Creator as well as Redeemer, and its emphasis on the Trinity; and the community has always stressed the work of the Holy Spirit. Our founder, George MacLeod, was himself a Highland Gael,

> an imaginative poet whose Celtic imagery and language pushed the parameters of orthodoxy. As early as 1942 the memorable themes of his sermons and prayers in Iona abbey were prefiguring the themes of process and liberation theology, which were not to come to the fore for another twenty or thirty years.[4]

The use of poetry and song, of art and symbol and ceremony, the metaphors of pilgrimage and presence and encompassing, have been and continue to be important for us in our worship, as they were for the Celts – not because we are Celts, but because we are human.

But we seek to incarnate our faith in inner cities, and to discover appropriate and creaturely worship not just in churches but on demonstrations and picket-lines, outside embassies and military bases, in homes and community centres, in schools and hospitals and in the market-place. It is our engagement with these places, where people struggle on the knife-edge, and we among them, that drives us to worship and prayer. In such contexts, we must inculturate while remaining firmly part of the universal church, as Columba did, and as George MacLeod intended when he founded the Community.

Contributions from musicians and liturgists

Faith changes people; worship changes people. This we believe. Therefore, we wish to be *open to change,* to the new, to the movement of the Holy Spirit. God meets with us out on the borders, on the margins, as much as in what is familiar and reassuring. The Iona Community has been blessed by the contribution of a number of gifted musicians and liturgists. Apart from the unparalleled beauty and integrity of the prayers and writings of George MacLeod himself, the work of Tom Colvin in introducing the Community in the 1960s and 1970s to the praise offered in Africa, and of Ian Fraser in telling the faith stories of ordinary people in communities across the world, planted seeds that are still bearing fruit today. More recently, the Community has had within its membership a number of gifted women liturgists and song writers such as Kate McIlhagga, Jan Sutch Pickard, Ruth Burgess and Anna Briggs who, encountering the challenge of inclusiveness within our own body, sought to find "new ways to touch the heart" that included the experience and insights of women.

But the worship of the Iona Community has become best-known through the work of the Wild Goose worship and resource groups. The liturgical pieces, drama and meditations of John Bell and Graham Maule and their colleagues, and in particular the songs of John Bell, have found recognition, acceptance and widespread gratitude. This wealth of new work has given many people and churches in Scotland (where John has also been the convener of the Church of Scotland's panel on worship and of the committees to produce both the new Church of Scotland hymnbook and the new ecumenical hymnbook, *Common Ground)* "a new song to sing", and has introduced us to the many ways in which the church throughout the world sings its faith, especially the church in the poorest countries of the world.

In addition, the groups' work in training, facilitating and encouraging local churches throughout Britain has been instrumental in opening up liturgical expression and renewal. The annual school of music and worship on Iona is in its fifth year, and is so over-subscribed that a similar school now takes place in England also. Its work is, above all, accessible. Its language is the spoken language of today; it has encouraged congregations to find their own unaccompanied voice as liberating and exciting in song; it uses ways of teaching that do not depend on choirs, organs, or even being able to read music. It has drawn on the indigenous and folk traditions of Britain. And it has done this without sacrificing quality, beauty or relevance. It is material that connects with people's lives and faith.

Worship, the ecumenical movement, and engagement in the world

The Iona Community has not found its liturgical work and emphasis to be a problem or hindrance ecumenically – rather the reverse. We have found that it tends to break down barriers of history and dogma, especially among ordinary church members. However, it has not always found approval within the Church of Scotland at an official level. Though this may reflect some liturgical resistance to the new, my perception is that this is more related to the Community's theological and political stance than to its liturgy. A great many people like to sing good songs. Somewhat fewer are keen to sing them outside the South African embassy every week, as used to happen, or in anti-poll-tax protests. The Community's desire for intercommunion evokes a large silence in some hierarchies. But generally speaking, within Britain at least, it seems that the Iona Community's worship is seen as a positive force towards Christian unity. This may not always be the case in international contexts, where issues such as inclusivity in language, new images of God, new ways of sharing the word, and high levels of lay participation may be seen as more problematic than they are in Britain.

Ultimately, however, for the members of the Iona Community, our worship sustains most, refreshes most, and has the greatest integrity not when our words are most beautiful, our liturgies most reverent or innovative, and our music most heavenly, but when our lives are most fully engaged. In the words of George MacLeod,

> I simply argue that the cross be raised again at the centre of the market-place as well as on the steeple of the church. I am recovering the claim that Jesus was not crucified in a cathedral between two candles, but on a cross between two thieves; on the town garbage heap; at a crossroad so cosmopolitan that they had to write his title in Hebrew and in Latin and in Greek (or shall we say in English, in Xhosa and in Afrikaans?); at the kind of place where cynics talk smut, and thieves curse, and soldiers gamble. Because that is where He died, and that is what He died about. And that is where the church should be, and what the church should be about.[5]

NOTES

[1] Ron Ferguson, *Chasing the Wild Goose: The Story of the Iona Community*, Collins, Fount, 1988; Glasgow, Wild Goose, 1998, p.72.
[2] *Ibid.*, pp.72-73.
[3] St Columba (ca. 521-597 CE) was founder and abbot of the monastery on Iona.
[4] *Chasing the Wild Goose*, p.74.
[5] *Ibid.*, pp.73-74.

Reflections on
Worship in
Ecumenical Contexts

Ecumenical Worship – Experiences, Problems, Possibilities
Some Basic Considerations

DAGMAR HELLER

What is ecumenical worship?

The concept of "ecumenical worship"[1] raises some questions. Is it even possible to worship "ecumenically"? Does this not simply lead to a new form of worship, in addition to the confessional forms of worship which already exist? Or, if this is not the case, does ecumenical worship perhaps claim to be Christian worship per se, a sort of super-worship? How, then, does "ecumenical worship" relate to worship according to confessional traditions?

The following reflections will examine these basic problems of ecumenical worship and point out possible ways of conceiving and shaping ecumenical worship which take us further in the search for Christian unity. Thinking about what makes worship "ecumenical" will show what basic considerations should be kept in mind in planning ecumenical worship services. It cannot be denied that these reflections are written from a Protestant background, from which I have tried to understand others and to bring different attitudes closer together.

These introductory lines have already pointed towards a particular understanding of "ecumenical worship", by contrasting it with "confessional worship". But I would like to go back a step and begin with a wider, more open concept of "ecumenical worship", presupposing only that we are talking about Christian worship. That is to say, ecumenical worship is all worship in which Christians from different traditions join together in celebrating, praying and praising God. There have been such worship services at least as long as the ecumenical movement has existed, at different levels: in local communities, where Christians of various traditions who live in the same town or region pray together, and at international ecumenical conferences, where Christians of different confessional and cultural backgrounds, from all over the world, work together and call upon God. In each case there are basically two possibilities: either a worship service is held according to the liturgical order of one of the traditions represented, and everyone participates; or an attempt is made to bring the various traditions together by combining different liturgical elements, so that everyone can find something of his or her own in the resulting worship service.

A look at the history of ecumenical worship

A tradition of common worship

The history of common prayer and celebration shows a certain development taking place. Since local ecumenical worship services around the world present an infinitely vast field that would be impossible to cover, this historical overview will take the examples of worship services at international ecumenical conferences of the 20th century.

The richness and variety of worship life to which we are accustomed at ecumenical conferences today was not a matter of course from the beginning. But starting with the earliest international conferences of the ecumenical movement, there has been common worship, both according to confessional forms and in new forms which participants planned together.

Early steps: sharing our traditions in worship

At the first universal Christian conference on Life and Work in Stockholm in 1925, for example, a prayer service or reflection was conducted each morning by one of the participants in the manner of his or her own confessional background. It is interesting that the first of these morning prayer services concluded with a benediction spoken by the patriarch and pope of Alexandria. On Sunday the participants went their separate ways to worship services in local congregations.

There were also the earliest beginnings of a common liturgy. The festive opening worship service had the following sequence: hymn, an antiphon (*Domine, labia mea aperies...* "O Lord, open thou my lips") from the Latin prayers for the canonical hours (the worship bulletin carried a note that this was a 4th century litany), scripture reading, Te Deum, sermon, hymn, collect for Rogation Sunday (introduced by a *salutatio*), Lord's prayer, Benedicamus, benediction, hymn. Clearly this was a bringing together of liturgical elements from the ancient church (antiphon and Te Deum) which are still in use in the Western church, arranged in an order of worship with the sermon in central position as in the Protestant tradition. The criteria used in preparing this liturgy were unfortunately not recorded.

The closing celebration, in contrast, was a Swedish Lutheran "Högmässa" (high mass) which included as a "special addition" the Nicene Creed spoken in Greek by Archbishop Photios of Alexandria.[2]

Towards common planning of worship

Things were somewhat different at the first world conference on Faith and Order in Lausanne in 1927.[3] Here, each session was opened with devotions, but the reports do not describe the order of worship followed. Each time the leader was a participant from a different church, but conspicuously none of these was Orthodox. However, there were more jointly planned worship services than in Stockholm. The opening worship service united in a very simple and straightforward way the liturgical elements common to the churches represented. A hymn from an ecumenical hymnal was sung, then the Apostles' Creed was spoken by all, followed by silent prayer. Then came the sermon by Bishop Brent. A second hymn was followed by the Lord's prayer, spoken by each participant in his or her own language, and the benediction.

The closing worship was similar in form. Interestingly enough, it included three sermons (in English, French and German) from different confessional perspectives (Moravian, Anglican, Reformed) on the theme "Jesus Christ, the same yesterday and today and for ever".

In addition, the conference programme included a common service of repentance and prayer. On the Sunday, many of the participants attended a communion service at the local Reformed church, while the Orthodox participants attended a liturgy at the Greek Orthodox church.[4]

Here again no indication is given of the criteria used in planning the joint services. From analysis of the orders of worship one can only conclude that the concern was to find something like the lowest common denominator. It is striking that, despite the presence of Orthodox participants, the Apostles' Creed was chosen instead of the Nicene-Constantinopolitan, and no Orthodox took part in leading these worship services.

According to the agenda of this first world conference, no further thought was given to the issue of common worship. But it set up a model for the planning of common worship, which was developed further at succeeding conferences. Thereafter, there was always a combination of confessional worship open to others and new, jointly planned forms of worship.

At the second world conference on Faith and Order in Edinburgh in 1937, the morning prayers were conducted according to the tradition of the person leading them. Some were held in the assembly hall, some in the cathedral. The evening prayers for each day were planned by a small committee in simple form and assembled in a prayer book, which also contained a collection of psalms and prayers in English, French and German. This time there was an Orthodox among the leaders of these worship services.

The opening worship service began with the singing of a psalm, followed by a prayer, the Lord's prayer and another psalm. Then came two scripture readings (by Metropolitan Germanos and Dean Yngve Brilioth), the Apostles' Creed and another prayer. Then a text was read from the work of the previous world conference in Lausanne, followed by a hymn and then the sermon by the archbishop of York. The service ended with another hymn and the benediction.

There was no conference worship service on either Sunday; the participants were free to attend local worship services. The closing worship was a brief act of thanksgiving immediately following the final plenary session, consisting mainly of a litany of thanks, hymn, scripture reading, silent closing prayer and benediction.[5]

A similar model was followed at the founding assembly of the WCC in 1948 in Amsterdam: here too there was a careful mixture of confessional worship services and services combining material from various traditions. The morning worship services were confessional in character; the other services had combined liturgies.[6] The opening worship service began with a hymn, then came a penitential section introduced by words from scripture, then the Apostles' Creed, followed by two readings from scripture, and finally two sermons, separated by a hymn sung by a soloist from India. The closing benediction was spoken in Greek by the Orthodox Archbishop Germanos.[7]

H. Herklots says in his report, "The World Council of Churches is not itself a church: it cannot therefore hold services of holy communion."[8] This was the reason why local churches were asked to offer eucharistic worship services which the assembly participants might attend. Thus in the second week, instead of the morning worship services there were eucharistic services in the Anglican, Orthodox and Lutheran traditions. On the Sunday, the Netherlands Reformed Church invited the participants to a communion service.

As far as I know, the Amsterdam assembly was the first to hold on the Saturday evening a so-called service of preparation for the celebration of the eucharist, which was attended the next day in the different confessional traditions. Liturgically speaking this was an innovation. It began with an entrance prayer, followed by a hymn, then by a scripture reading. Then came another hymn, then Psalm 51, and finally a confession of sin with absolution according to the Old Catholic rite. Everyone responded with the Lord's prayer and a hymn. Hendrik Kraemer gave a sermon, ending with a prayer and silence. There followed a prayer from the Orthodox tradition, a hymn and the benediction. Here it was very clear that a careful attempt had been made to gather elements from the various traditions, yet the structure could not clearly be attributed to any one tradition.

Each evening the session ended with a brief evening prayer, whether the assembly was in committee meetings or plenary session.

Another high point was the closing worship service, which had the following form: hymn, scripture reading, psalm (sung by an Orthodox choir), prayers (litany of thanks and intercessions), Lord's prayer, hymn, homily in French, homily in German, homily in English, Te Deum, collect, benediction. Here too, care was taken to see that representatives of all traditions took part in leading the service.

In Lund at the third world conference on Faith and Order in 1952, we again find this proven model. Besides the daily prayer services, the opening worship again is interesting as a jointly planned service. It began with a hymn, followed by two scripture readings (in French and German). The Gloria Patri and the Apostles' Creed were recited by the congregation together. There followed prayers of repentance, thanksgiving and intercession. The two sermons were preceded and followed by hymns, and then the service ended with a benediction.

Here too there was a common service of preparation for the celebration of the eucharist, following the example of Amsterdam in its form.

On the first Sunday the Church of Sweden invited all participants to a mass in the cathedral, at which anyone who wished could also receive communion. On the second Sunday of the conference people went to various local churches, but in the evening there was common conference worship with a hymn, praise and confession of sins, hymn, psalm, hymn, scripture reading, Nicene Creed, sermon, hymn, intercessions, Lord's prayer, benediction. As far as I can tell, this was the first time the Nicene Creed was used at a conference on Faith and Order.

The closing worship had this form: hymn, sermon, collect, Lord's prayer, scripture reading; thereafter it followed the form of a Methodist covenant service (as printed in *Venite Adoremus I*).[9]

At the fourth world conference on Faith and Order in Montreal in 1963, for the first time Bible studies were held at the beginning of section meetings. Days when plenary sessions were held began with morning prayers. The evening services again followed a prayer book prepared for the conference. The closing worship had the following simple structure: hymn, prayer, sermon, hymn, litany (from the tradition of the Syrian Oriental Orthodox Church), hymn, benediction.[10]

The experience of worship at Santiago de Compostela

In comparison, the fifth world conference on Faith and Order in Santiago de Compostela in 1993 probably had the richest worship programme. The daily morning devotions were prepared this time by a planning committee and assembled in a worship book. They followed a simple liturgical model with an introductory part (silence, greeting, prayer), a confession of sin with absolution, scripture reading, Bible study, silence, confession of faith (texts from different contexts and traditions were used), prayer of thanksgiving, Lord's prayer, benediction. These elements were interspersed with hymns from various cultural contexts. The basic pattern was chosen because it is found, structurally, in most Christian traditions.[11] The scripture readings were a systematic reading of the whole of Galatians and the Bible studies were given by a Methodist woman theologian from England. On four of the days the service was also followed by Bible study in groups on these texts.

The evening devotions included times of silence and followed a simple scheme, also familiar in most traditions: blessing, hymn, response ("God, open my lips..."), hymn, prayer, reading, silence, Magnificat (spoken responsively and introduced by a Taizé chant), intercessions, Lord's prayer, blessing, final song (Nunc Dimittis). The texts and songs were fixed this time, so that these evening services had the same *form* and also the same *content* (except for the readings, which varied) on four evenings. This was an idea taken from the traditional prayers for the canonical hours, as known in both Eastern and Western churches; a fixed form with fixed texts (which might change with the seasons) used for worship at a certain point in the day. This idea was here put into practice with the help of traditional elements such as the Magnificat and with hymns from various traditions. On two other evenings a Roman Catholic and an Orthodox vespers service, respectively, were held.

For the celebration of the eucharist, the earlier practice was again taken up and a local church was asked to invite the conference participants to a service of the Lord's supper. Two churches together, the Spanish Evangelical Church (Reformed) and the Spanish Reformed Episcopal Church (Anglican), organized a communion service which, for practical rather than theological reasons, was held in a Roman Catholic church.

A new element, which had already appeared at the WCC assembly in Canberra in 1991, was also part of this conference – a night-time prayer vigil for the victims of injustice throughout the world.

Not to be forgotten was the festive opening worship service in Santiago cathedral, held on the evening of the first day, after a brief opening act of worship in the assembly hall that morning. The liturgical order of service was as follows: prelude, silence, entrance of the icons, hymn ("Hagios O Theos"), entrance of the Bible, hymn, entrance of the cross, hymn (traditional hymn to St James the Apostle from the pilgrim tradition of Santiago de Compostela, accompanied by the swinging of the *Botafumeiro*, the great censer in Santiago cathedral); then a greeting, opening prayer, litany of thanksgiving and confession of sin, words of forgiveness, gloria, readings from Old Testament, epistle and gospel, sermon, silence, Nicene-Constantinopolitan Creed, hymn; then the recollection of Faith and Order history with words from Lausanne, Edinburgh, Lund and Montreal; then the prayer of intercession, Lord's prayer, sharing of the peace, closing prayer, benediction and closing hymn.[12]

There was clearly a will here to let various traditions be expressed, including local tradition. At the same time the historical context of the worship service was plainly taken into account in its liturgical form.

The closing worship service was somewhat simpler: silence, invocation of the Holy Spirit, opening prayer, gloria, litany, Old Testament and gospel readings, sermon, silence, hymn, intercessions, Lord's prayer, litany of commitment, exchange of greetings, hymn, Nicene-Constantinopolitan Creed, blessing, hymn.

Joint planning of worship: a sign of deepening fellowship and commitment

Overall, these examples show that the tendency in the course of time was increasingly towards joint planning of worship services. The first steps in Stockholm and Lausanne were still very hesitant, but in Santiago great creativity developed in this regard. It is striking that, from the beginning, the high points to be celebrated in a conference, the opening and closing worship services, were always jointly planned liturgies. The morning prayers, which earlier had followed confessional traditions, gradually came to be jointly planned also. In recent years only the occasional service and – still, today – the celebration of the eucharist have followed confessional traditions.

Over the years, much more time and care came to be taken in preparing conference worship services. There has clearly been an increasing concern to include a variety of traditions, including local traditions of the place where the conference is held. Forms have been found uniting the different confessional and cultural traditions. There is a clear movement away from the strictly Protestant emphasis on the word. This is shown by amongst other things the fact that in recent years it has no longer been felt necessary to have more than one sermon in a service, as used to happen frequently in the early days. As the number of member churches in the South increased, there has also been stronger use of elements from a variety of cultures in these worship services. More space was given to free prayer, and to Orthodox elements. In this way, over time, the aspect of common worship in singing and prayer came to be emphasized more strongly. Elements which emphasize community, such as the exchange of a peace greeting, or elements which create a reverential atmosphere, such as a procession with icons, are more frequently included.

The eucharist: an enduring issue

This is why the fact that it is still impossible to celebrate the eucharist together is increasingly experienced as a serious problem in ecumenical worship. But even here there has been some development. The assertion mentioned above that the WCC as such cannot celebrate the eucharist does not seem to have been discussed further. In any case, at the assembly in Vancouver in 1983 a common celebration of the Lord's supper was held for the first time. Although not all those present were able to receive communion, a large part of them did take part in the liturgy. It was based on the so-called Lima liturgy, which since then has been repeated at the 1991 assembly in Canberra[13] and on other occasions. It is striking, however, that the world conference on Faith and Order in 1993 returned to the former practice and did not offer any official communion service within the conference programme. This decision had to do with the observation that even the Lima liturgy did not solve the problem of the separation of the Christian churches at the Lord's table. A significant part of the delegates at Vancouver and at Canberra could not take part in the communion. In 1993 it was felt, therefore, that separate eucharistic services held in different ritual traditions would be more appropriate to the ecumenical situation.

Problems of ecumenical worship

The Orthodox especially (but not only they) have expressed strong criticism in recent years of the kind of ecumenical worship described above, in the form of new, jointly planned liturgical orders of worship. For Orthodox Christians these are very Protestant in character and give hardly any consideration to Orthodox forms of worship (apart from the singing of a kyrie or an alleluia, and now and then a litany). Orthodox Christians find hardly anything of their own in these worship services,[14] and for them even an appropriately prayerful atmosphere is often lacking. They feel extremely insecure, especially when new elements are introduced, such as new symbolic acts which do not clearly fit in with the Orthodox understanding of the sacramental character of acts of worship.

Many Protestants also experience such worship services as a "mixed cocktail" with which they do not really feel at home. They miss the familiar which helps them to concentrate on the essential. Such worship services may be an exotic experience, but a number of people have wondered whether, in many cases, the doxological aspect has been displaced in favour of the "big event" and the feeling of community.

This criticism is based on three factors. One is a psychological phenomenon: the human need to feel secure, particularly in worship, a need which finds expression in the repetition of liturgical forms. In a newly created liturgy it is hard to get one's bearings, to let oneself be carried along the way one does when the structure is familiar. Secondly, from a liturgical point of view, jointly planned ecumenical liturgies are sometimes in danger of becoming simply a succession of different elements which are insufficiently related to one another. Such worship services are inconsistent in themselves and have no unifying thread of meaning. They do not give the worshipper space for inner calm and concentration on the essential; thus it can easily happen that people find them unauthentic. The planning shows a lack of liturgical sensitivity, so that the worst of these worship services give the impression of an empty ritual, doing something together for the sake of the community, but not to the glory of God.

A third point must be considered, especially in the dialogue with the Orthodox tradition. This concerns the basic understanding of liturgy and the fundamental differences which exist. Protestant churches generally deal more freely with liturgy and allow the possibility for orders of worship to be freely created, while the Orthodox tradition maintains the forms which have been handed down.[15] These include many kinds of symbolic acts, some of which have a sacramental character. Worship is centred on the mystery of God and serves to unite human beings with God. Thus it has a deeply mystical component. Furthermore, for the Orthodox, in contrast to Protestantism, the centre of a worship service is the divine liturgy, that is, the celebration of the eucharist.[16] Protestants regard a service of the word as a complete and fully valid worship service; when such a service is conducted jointly with others, they can find in it the essentials of worship. For Orthodox Christians, however, it is not possible to hold a true worship service, namely the celebration of the eucharist, in common with others. Thus there is a fundamental imbalance here in the way in which ecumenical worship is experienced and in the ability to share in worship with others.[17]

Because of these difficulties, a stronger call for confessional worship services which are clear and authentic in themselves has again been heard in ecumenical circles. When such services are open to members of other confessions, everyone knows "where they are" and can join in common prayer with these others and learn to know and understand a tradition other than one's own. To "old ecumenical hands" this is a step backward. But can we speak of forward or backward movement in relation to forms of worship? There are various possibilities for worship in common, each of which has advantages and disadvantages. As seems meanwhile to be accepted, the ecumenical movement is not about one unified church, so neither can there be one unified form of worship.

But this does not answer the main problem in ecumenical worship, that of shared celebration of the eucharist. As long as the question of mutual recognition of ministries, and hence the ecclesiology question, has not been resolved, common celebration of the eucharist will not be possible. Thus there will be no common worship in the fullest sense.

The basic question that now arises more sharply than ever is: Can we pray together, in spite of the differences which divide us? If we say yes, there are various possibilities. The most important consideration is what is appropriate to the specific situation. But thought must also be given to how our differing conceptions of worship can be brought together.

How can we worship together ecumenically?

The question of ecumenical worship goes back to the beginning of the ecumenical movement. But surprisingly enough it was not on the agenda from the beginning; the second world conference on Faith and Order in Edinburgh was the first to give more attention to it. Section IV dealt with the topic "The Church's Unity in Life and Worship", recommending a study of the different models of worship which are characteristic of the different churches. This led to studies on "Ways of Worship", and on "Intercommunion", which both appeared in 1951.

Diversity as richness

One of the most important findings of the first-named study was that "the different ways of worship... need not be regarded as incompatible".[18] The diversity of worship as richness, and as a common heritage, was also acknowledged at the 1961 World Council assembly in New Delhi. The report of the section which worked on unity said:

> God is to be praised in every tongue and in the setting of every culture and age, in an inexhaustible diversity of expression. Yet there are certain factors in Christian worship such as adoration, penitence, intercession, petition and thanksgiving which are grounded inevitably in the unique acts of God in Christ, discernible still in our divided traditions. As we learn more of each other, we shall more clearly discern this *common heritage* and express it more fully.[19]

The next step can be seen at the fourth world conference on Faith and Order in 1963, in Montreal, where one section had as its theme "Worship and the Oneness of Christ's Church". There was discussion of "The Nature of Christian Worship" in general, but also of specific questions like "Baptism and Holy Communion", "Christian Worship in the World

Today", and "Worship, Mission and Indigenization". The section report said,

> It is of crucial importance that we should investigate (worship's) forms and structures, its language and spirit, in the expectation that this process may throw new light upon various theological positions and affirmations, perhaps even lend new meaning to them, and thus open new possibilities in ecumenical dialogue.[20]

It stated further,

> There is no point at which the inherent difficulties of the worldwide ecumenical movement are felt more acutely than in worship, because there is no point at which one is usually more dependent upon the use of the language and the tradition to which one is accustomed. So difficult indeed is this cluster of problems that the technique of worship in ecumenical gatherings has not yet received the attention it deserves. It should be recorded therefore that the arrangements made at Montreal and the way in which they were carried out indicated that, if there is so much yet to be done in this delicate and complex field, some progress has nevertheless been made.[21]

This progress was not described in detail.

However, comparison of the various conference worship services makes clear that common worship services with a jointly planned liturgy have increased. These are no longer confined to the use of elements which are common to all, but rather bring elements together from different traditions in a structure which is in some way common to most traditions. This is true for services of the word as well as eucharistic services.

Services of the word: discovering a common structure

These joint services of the word have greatly differing structures if one considers the sequence of the liturgical elements. If these elements are considered according to their function, however, these orders of service can be reduced to three fundamental parts which are common to all of them, though they are constructed in differing ways and the individual elements used vary.

– Opening: greeting, prayer, psalm(s), litanies, confession of sin, hymns
– The word of God: readings, sermon, silence
– Response: confession of faith, intercessions, Lord's prayer, hymns, dismissal/sending

The individual elements which are used in these three parts do not always occur in a specific order, and are not always together in a block. But they can be assigned to the three fundamental parts on the basis of their function. So what makes these worship services "ecumenical", besides common liturgical elements and texts, seems above all to be this common basic structure.

It is striking that this basic structural division can also be found in all confessional services of the word. Thus there is a basic commonality among Christian traditions not only at the level of liturgical elements, but also at the structural level. This is also the line of thought in a newer Faith and Order study, which took up these issues at a consultation at Ditchingham, England, in 1994. Here the concept of the *ordo* of worship was introduced, meaning the basic form of worship. The attempt was made to filter out a basic structure common to all Christian traditions, which draws all churches together and is the framework within which inculturation and adaptation to each of their contexts must take place.[22]

Celebrations of the eucharist: the Lima liturgy

With regard to celebrations of the eucharist, similar observations can be made. Common celebration of the eucharist first became possible at an international ecumenical level when the Commission on Faith and Order, meeting in Lima, Peru, in 1982, adopted the convergence document on *Baptism, Eucharist and Ministry*. In Lima, Max Thurian, a Taizé brother, was asked to put the insights of this paper into the form of a liturgy.[23] In doing this, he tried also to take into consideration the liturgical tradition of the church through the centuries. So he looked for traditional liturgical elements which corresponded to the main points of BEM, and included all the elements of a eucharistic worship service which are named in the Lima document,[24] as they had developed over the course of time in the various traditions.

The liturgy has three main parts: (1) liturgy of entrance, consisting of a confession with absolution (texts from the North American Lutheran liturgy), a Kyrie litany (newly written for Lima), and a gloria (traditional elements from the Western tradition); (2) liturgy of the word, with three readings and a homily at its heart, followed by the Nicene-Constantinopolitan Creed as a response to the word; the intercessions (structure and style following Pope Gelasius's litany from the 5th century) lead into (3) liturgy of the eucharist, which begins with the preparation of the elements; then come blessings from the Jewish liturgy and a prayer from the Didache; thanksgiving is expressed in the preface (composed on BEM themes), the words of institution, an anamnesis and two epicleses (inspired by the liturgy of St James from the 3rd century); then come commemorations, the Lord's prayer, the peace, the breaking of the bread, communion, word of mission and blessing. An important element is the participation throughout of the congregation, by sung responses or verses.

In summary, this liturgy could be said to be "ecumenical" because:
1) all the elements named in BEM as belonging to the celebration of the eucharist are here;
2) texts from various traditions are used;
3) the congregation participates actively as much as possible;
4) Christians from different traditions can participate fully in large parts of the liturgy.

This liturgy has been highly regarded and found wide acceptance, but has also met with criticism – particularly that it is too long and too wordy. This criticism was discussed during a seminar in 1995 at the Ecumenical Institute in Bossey. On the basis of the idea at Ditchingham of the *ordo*, it was suggested that a common, basic model for ecumenical eucharistic worship be proposed,[25] which could then be developed according to the needs of each situation. A worship service planned using this model would thus be ecumenical by virtue of its basic structure which is common to all traditions.

In summary it can be said that, building on the basic insight that differences in liturgies need not make them mutually exclusive and that there is a common foundation, the most recent discussions have strongly emphasized the shape of worship and pointed out the common structure that exists – while texts, music and so on are open to choice. Here again, however, we must note that in the Orthodox tradition there is no such distinction between form and content as is found in the Western church. Recognizing the fundamental common structure still does not help to bring us nearer to worshipping together. Reflection on jointly planned worship services in which Orthodox Christians are to participate must therefore also take content into account, in a way that places the worship in a continuity and consistency with the whole of Christian tradition.

Considerations in planning ecumenical worship

I would like to summarize the conclusions of these reflections on ecumenical worship in the form of theses, as follows:
- Ecumenical worship is not an additional, new form of worship. Ecumenical worship is not a "super form" of worship.
- Every form of Christian worship must be ecumenical at its core, in the sense that it is adoration of the God who is revealed to everyone in Jesus Christ, and in the sense that it is open to other Christians, stands in relation to them, stands in relation to the whole tradition and aims to create community.
- Ecumenical worship is worship in situations where Christians of different traditions come together.

- Therefore criteria must be found which help the whole worshipping group to feel that the worship service is their own. It should be "worship which expresses the confessional, cultural and regional diversity which is intrinsic to that community".[26]
- The criteria chosen must also help such a worship service to be a consistent whole and not an arbitrary mixture of components.

These basic theses could be put into practice by using the following check-list when preparing an ecumenical worship service, whether it is to be confessional in character or to have a new form:

- The planning group should include representatives of the different traditions whose members are present.
- Are we truly ready to worship *together*?
- The setting, including the traditions represented, must be considered.
- What needs to be considered with regard to the different conceptions of worship in the traditions of those present?
- What are the known common liturgical elements?
- Are there common structures?
- Are there common conceptions of worship? If not, what aspects are important to the various traditions? How can they be respected appropriately?
- What do we want to do in this worship service (for instance, are we to pray for a successful meeting, to share in an "office", with prayers for a certain time of day, and so on)?
- What possibilities are there for leadership of the worship service?
- What are appropriate liturgical elements for the setting/context in which worship will take place (elements from the traditions represented, new elements)?
- Which elements can help those present from each tradition to recognize something familiar in the service? Which elements help those of various traditions to find the right atmosphere for prayer?
- Are symbolic acts adequately explained, so that they are understandable for those of all traditions?
- Is there a sufficient balance between doxological elements and elements which emphasize community?
- Is there a common thread of meaning in the worship service, in relation to the setting, context, conference theme, and so on?
- Which texts are appropriate here?

NOTES

[1] Since this article was written the central committee of the WCC, at its meeting in Aug.-Sept. 2002, proposed – based upon the recommendations of the Special Commission on

Orthodox Participation in the WCC – that we should no longer use the notion of ecumenical worship but rather talk about either confessional common prayer or interconfessional common prayer. Since this terminology is still under discussion and since, from a Protestant perspective, there is no fundamental difference between "worship" and "prayer", I will use the terminology of "ecumenical worship" in this article. This may make it easier for Protestants to understand some of the difficulties expressed by Orthodox about ecumenical worship.

[2] See *The Stockholm Conference 1925: The Official Report of the Universal Christian Conference on Life and Work Held in Stockholm, 19-30 August 1925*, G.K.A. Bell ed., London, Oxford UP, 1926.

[3] For a review of Faith and Order work in relation to worship see Janet Crawford, "Faith and Order Work on Worship: An Historical Survey", in *Minutes of the Meeting of the Faith and Order Standing Commission 4-11 January 1994, Crêt-Bérard, Switzerland*, Faith and Order Paper no. 167, WCC/Commission on Faith and Order, 1994, pp.45-52. For a review of worship at Faith and Order world conferences see Janet Crawford, "Worship at Previous Faith and Order World Conferences", in *Minutes, Crêt-Bérard*, pp.53-59.

[4] Information taken from *Faith and Order: Proceedings of the World Conference, Lausanne, August 3-21, 1927*, H.N. Bate ed., London, SCM, 1927.

[5] See *The Second World Conference on Faith and Order held at Edinburgh, August 3-18, 1937*, Leonard Hodgson ed., London, MacMillan, 1938, esp. pp.15-23. See also Janet Crawford and Thomas Best, "Praise the Lord with the Lyre... and the Gamelan? Towards Koinonia in Worship", in *The Ecumenical Review*, 46, 1, 1994, pp.78-96.

[6] See Crawford and Best, "Praise the Lord with the Lyre...", p.82.

[7] See the report by H.G.G. Herklots, *Amsterdam 1948: An Account of the First Assembly of the World Council of Churches*, London, SCM Press, 1948, pp.13ff.

[8] *Ibid.*, p.16.

[9] *The Third World Conference on Faith and Order held at Lund, August 15-28, 1952*, Oliver S. Tomkins ed., London, SCM Press, 1953.

[10] *The Fourth World Conference on Faith and Order: The Report from Montreal 1963*, P.C. Rodger and L. Vischer eds, Faith and Order Paper no. 42, London, SCM Press, 1964.

[11] Cf. the report in English, *On the Way to Fuller Koinonia: Santiago de Compostela 1993, Official Report of the Fifth World Conference on Faith and Order*, Thomas F. Best and Günther Gassmann eds, Faith and Order Paper no. 166, WCC Publications 1994, p.xvi.

[12] See *Worship Book: Fifth World Conference on Faith and Order, Santiago de Compostela 1993*, WCC/Commission on Faith and Order, 1993 (in four languages), and *Celebrating Community*, Janet Crawford, Terry MacArthur and Thomas F. Best compilers, WCC Publications, 1993 (in four languages). The opening and closing worship services are available only in photocopied form in the archives of Faith and Order.

[13] See *Signs of the Spirit: Official Report, Seventh Assembly*, Michael Kinnamon ed., WCC Publications, 1991, p.21.

[14] This was formulated in the report of the Orthodox pre-assembly meeting, held in Damascus 7-13 May 1998, to prepare for the Harare assembly, as follows: "Yet the issue of common prayer has increasingly become a topic of discussion... Non-eucharistic common prayer... has also become an increasing area of tension in Orthodox discussion. Two *pastoral* factors make common prayer more difficult now than ever before: the increased tension in our churches on this issue, and the changing character of what we experience as 'ecumenical worship' in recent years and assemblies. In ecumenical worship services there is a marked decrease in the sensitivity to the different traditions, their liturgical sensibilities and liturgical ethos" (p.9).

[15] Cf. Georges Florovsky in *Ways of Worship: The Report of a Theological Commission of Faith and Order*, Pehr Edwall, Eric Hayman, William D. Maxwell eds, London, SCM Press, 1951, pp.64ff.: "The main distinctive mark of the Eastern Orthodox worship is its traditional character. Devotional forms and manners of the early church are preserved, or rather have been continuously used for centuries, without any major changes... in the process of its continuous use the rite has been kept alive, and is still a natural means of a spontaneous expression of the religious life. It is felt, within the tradition, to be the most adequate vehicle of the spiritual experience... The ultimate aim of the whole worship is to establish and to perpetuate an intimate communion with God, in Christ Jesus, and in the

community of his church. The ultimate emphasis is spiritual: the aim of the Christian life is the acquisition of the Holy Spirit, the Comforter, by whom believers are established in the fellowship of the church."

[16] Cf. Alexander Schmemann, *Introduction to Liturgical Theology,* trans. Asheleigh E. Moorhouse, Crestwood NY, St Vladimir's Seminary Press, 1986, p.24: "...the eucharist is not only the 'most important' of all the offices, it is also source and goal of the entire liturgical life of the church".

[17] The Catholic attitude towards ecumenical worship is not mentioned for the reason that there is not so much material available in this respect. The Catholic church is not a member of the World Council of Churches, and has only been a member of the Commission on Faith and Order since 1968. In principle its attitude towards the celebration of the eucharist is comparable to the Orthodox attitude. Towards ecumenical, jointly planned services of the word, the Catholic attitude is generally more open, since these worship services are based on the Western tradition.

[18] Florovsky, *Ways of Worship,* p.36.

[19] *The New Delhi Report: The Third Assembly of the World Council of Churches 1961,* W.A. Visser 't Hooft ed., London, SCM Press, 1962, pp.120ff.

[20] *The Fourth World Conference on Faith and Order,* p.70.

[21] *Ibid.,* pp.15ff.

[22] The report is published as *So We Believe, So We Pray: Towards Koinonia in Worship,* Thomas F. Best and Dagmar Heller eds, Faith and Order Paper no. 171, WCC Publications, 1995.

[23] See *Eucharistic Worship in Ecumenical Contexts: The Lima Liturgy – and Beyond,* Thomas F. Best and Dagmar Heller eds, WCC Publications, 1998, pp.14-21.

[24] See *Baptism, Eucharist and Ministry,* Faith and Order Paper no. 111, WCC, 1982, para. 27.

[25] See "Celebrations of the Eucharist in Ecumenical Contexts: A Proposal", in *Eucharistic Worship in Ecumenical Contexts,* p.29-35.

[26] Crawford and Best, "Praise the Lord with the Lyre...", p.91.

Ecumenical Prayer: An Orthodox Perspective

PAUL MEYENDORFF

Few issues cause the Orthodox as much consternation as those concerning ecumenical worship. They rarely complain about meetings to hammer out theological differences, or about common efforts among Christians in peace-making or relief efforts. They happily participate in academic symposia and workshops. But put them in the context of an ecumenical service, and they instantly become uneasy. Yet the reasons for this are rarely articulated. Other than occasional, and anachronistic, appeals to ancient canonical literature – "No one shall join in prayers with heretics or schismatics", Laodicea Canon 33 (4th century), and compare also Apostolic Canon 45 – very little of substance has been said on the subject. At the same time, ecumenical worship serves as a kind of lightning rod, drawing the wrath of those who would see the Orthodox withdraw completely from the ecumenical movement. It might be worthwhile, therefore, to take a closer look at some of the factors, cultural as well as theological, which are at play.

Differences of ethos in worship

That the Orthodox are uncomfortable in ecumenical worship is a fact. This discomfort is shared by persons across the whole spectrum of Orthodoxy, whatever their position on Orthodox participation in the ecumenical movement. Often the reason is simply cultural, due to the fact that ecumenical services are generally Western in style and content, conducted either in some sterile meeting room or in a Western church, which to Eastern eyes often seems equally sterile. Like the legates of Prince Vladimir who reported in the 10th century on worship among the "Germans" (that is, Western Christians), they perceive "no glory".[1] Eastern Christians worship with their entire body and all their senses, and this is reflected in a worship environment that engages the entire person, and not just the mind. Icons, iconostasis, incense, vestments – all are integral elements of Eastern worship. So too are inherited patterns and structures of worship which are clearly distinct from those which developed in the medieval West or later in the Reformation traditions.

In short, there is a basic difference of ethos which is immediately apparent to any Easterner attending a typical ecumenical worship service. And if the tables were turned, Western Christians would be equally uncomfortable attending Eastern services, which to them seem overly long, repetitive, overladen with symbols and rituals, and at times shocking: what good Calvinist or Lutheran does not cringe at hearing, at the conclusion of most Byzantine offices, the exclamation "Most holy Theotokos, save us!"?

But the discomfort goes deeper. The Orthodox always identified their worship with their theology. In recent centuries, however, this has been taken in a literal sense, so that even the word "Orthodox" has come to be understood as "right worship". This is particularly the case among the Slavs, whose conversion in the Middle Ages essentially consisted of the reception of a ready-made liturgical tradition from the Greeks, without the rich theological synthesis that lay behind it.[2] As a result, one often sees a kind of fundamentalism vis-à-vis the liturgy among the Orthodox – a sense that Orthodox liturgy has remained unchanged since apostolic times. This approach can extend to every minute detail of Orthodox worship. Since the 17th century, there have been several schisms in reaction to liturgical changes, such as the Old-Believer schism in 17th-century Russia, or the more recent divisions over the adoption of the Gregorian calendar by some Orthodox churches. And it is largely liturgical differences today that prevent Eastern and Oriental churches from restoring communion, despite their theological agreement on Christological issues.

Diversity and unity in liturgical practice

The irony, of course, is that unity in liturgical practice was never the norm in Christian history, and Orthodox liturgy, particularly in the Byzantine tradition, has been more changeable, more adaptable, than that of any other Christian tradition.[3] Recent biblical and historical scholarship has clearly shown the diversity of the early church. Within the Byzantine tradition, diverse monastic and cathedral practices coexisted at least until the 15th century, and it was only in the 16th century that the printing press served to codify existing liturgical practices and to make further changes more difficult, if not impossible. Unfortunately, a broad, historical perspective is as absent among contemporary Orthodox as among many Protestants today.

How, then, did Christians move from openness to, and tolerance of, diverse liturgical practices to greater uniformity? It can be demonstrated that the hardening of positions was the result of schisms. Schisms, particularly those resulting from the Christological and trinitarian debates of the 4th to 6th centuries, led to the dominance of the Byzantine rite in the East, the Roman in the West. The earlier liturgical traditions and families were either absorbed into the Byzantine and Roman, or were preserved only in churches that were in schism from the imperial church. "Orthodox" minorities in regions dominated by schism eventually adopted either the Roman or Byzantine rites. After several centuries, liturgical differences came to be identified with differences of faith. Witness the acute debate between East and West in the 11-12th centuries over the use of leavened versus unleavened bread in the eucharist. Both sides accused the other of heresy: Easterners, for example, accused the West of rejecting Christ's divinity, symbolized by the leaven of the eucharistic bread. This was the burning issue, and the *filioque* was hardly mentioned![4] In later centuries, the Old Believers in Russia would explain differences between Greek and Russian liturgical practices by the fact that Greeks had fallen into heresy as a result of their betrayal of the faith at the council of Ferrara-Florence in 1438-39.[5] In short, differences in worship also often imply that the other group lacks ecclesial status!

Worship: an act of the church

This brings us to the real issue. For the Orthodox, liturgy is the fullest expression of the church.[6] This is particularly so with the eucharist, in which the church is fully realized and manifested, but it extends also to all other forms of worship, which themselves find their fulfilment in the eucharist. Liturgy, therefore, is by definition an action of the church. Thus only the church can celebrate the liturgy. The implications of this for ecumenical worship are obvious. The World Council of Churches (or a national council, or any other ecumenical body) is not a church as such, and therefore the Council cannot celebrate the eucharist. This is what lay behind the decision not to have an official eucharist at the WCC assembly in Harare in 1998. The eucharist, and therefore communion, is possible only in a visibly united church.

With regard to non-eucharistic services, the Orthodox approach is more ambiguous, but the same general principle applies. Precisely because ecumenical bodies are not churches, the Orthodox always feel more comfortable attending the worship of a particular church, in a particular tradition. For a tradition implies a community, an ecclesial reality. And the worship of that community is the fullest expression of its faith, according to the principle first articulated in the 5th century by Prosper of Aquitaine: *lex credendi lex statuat supplicandi*.[7] In this, the Orthodox are not alone, and I have heard many others complain about the generic, bland worship that consists of a patchwork of elements from diverse traditions, but speaking to none of them. That, of course, is a question of taste, but beneath it does lie an often unarticulated ecclesial sense.

Ecumenical worship: possibilities – and concerns

So is any form of ecumenical worship possible? As we saw at the beginning, the Orthodox are not of one mind. There are some, and they represent a vocal minority, who would answer in the negative. Basing themselves on a strict Cyprianic ecclesiology, they identify the church with the canonical limits of Orthodoxy, and affirm that non-Orthodox Christians are no different from pagans, that their sacraments, including baptism, have no validity. Obviously, common prayer with them is an impossibility, and the reception of converts always involves (re)baptism. But such an approach clearly flies in the face of both reality and the tradition of the church.

Christians who are not Orthodox are not simple pagans, and ecumenical organizations are not merely secular institutions. Some degree of unity clearly does exist, and the basis for this unity is explicitly affirmed in the constitutions of councils of churches, whether national or international, and is expressed in our common baptism. And if some degree of unity does exist, then ought it not to find some expression in common worship, which can affirm both the limited unity that already exists and contain prayers that full unity may be achieved, in fulfilment of the Lord's command that all may be one?

Most Orthodox would answer in the affirmative, despite the discomfort this may cause. But it is a cautious yes, and they would express a number of concerns:

1. Common worship must not confuse participants or observers into believing that full visible unity has already been achieved. Hence a common eucharist, which is the fullest expression of the unity of the church, is at present an impossibility. For the same reason, Orthodox participating in ecumenical worship do not wear full liturgical vestments (a distinction often lost on Western observers).
2. Common worship must not violate basic Orthodox teaching. This may seem self-evident, but the Orthodox are increasingly disturbed about a recent tendency, in some circles, to avoid the traditional, biblical, trinitarian names, Father, Son and Holy Spirit. While most Orthodox have no difficulty accepting inclusive language referring to human beings,[8] they see a danger of modalism, or worse, in substituting attributes for names, such as "Creator, Redeemer, Sanctifier".
3. Common worship must be trinitarian and must be centred on prayer for Christian unity. It cannot be used as the platform for various social or political agendas, which may be incompatible with the gospel and only lead to further divisions.[9]
4. Common worship must be sensitive to cultural, political and religious sensibilities, as well as to how reports (or images) will be received back home. In this age of the Internet and instant communication, provocative images, often presented totally out of context, can often do great damage to the ecumenical movement.

Conclusion

In conclusion, it must be stated that ecumenical worship poses a real challenge for the Orthodox. While they may legitimately complain about a certain Western hegemony that has prevailed during the first fifty years of the conciliar ecumenical movement, or about certain perceived abuses, these are not the real problem. The ecumenical movement in the 20th century has brought the Orthodox face to face with other Christians. Whereas for centuries East and West lived either in a state of confrontation (in areas such as Poland, the Austro-Hungarian empire, Ukraine...), or more commonly in virtual isolation, that is no longer possible in a globalized world, in which Christianity is rapidly losing its privileged position.

The central question, I repeat, is ecclesiological. If the Orthodox are able to see in other Christians something that is essentially true, good, and beautiful, if they are able to recognize the validity of their baptism,[10] then a degree of unity already exists. And when separated Christians assemble, should they not express that degree of unity, however partial, which already exists among them?

NOTES

[1] *The Primary Chronicle*, trans. F. L. Cross, in Serge A. Zenkovsky ed., *Medieval Russia's Epics, Chronicles, and Tales,* New York, E. P. Dutton, 1963, p.67.
[2] This was similar in many respects to the conversion of Barbarian Germanic tribes by Roman missionaries in the West. See the study of Jean Delumeau, *Catholicism Between Luther and Voltaire*, Philadelphia, Westminster, 1977. See also my article, "Reflections on Russian Liturgy", *St Vladimir's Theological Quarterly,* 33, 1989, pp.21-34.
[3] See, for example, R. Taft, *The Byzantine Rite: A Short History*, Collegeville, Liturgical Press, 1992.
[4] On this issue see John Erickson, "Leavened and Unleavened: Some Theological Implications of the Schism of 1054", *St Vladimir's Theological Quarterly,* 14, 1970, pp.155-76.
[5] On the Old-Believers, see my *Russia, Ritual, and Reform*, Crestwood NY, St Vladimir's Seminary Press, 1991. The council of Florence was the last of a series of failed councils that sought to reunite East and West.
[6] See the classic work of J. Zizioulas, *Being as Communion*, Crestwood NY, St Vladimir's Seminary Press, 1985.
[7] "Liturgy is a norm of faith".
[8] In most traditional Orthodox languages, including Greek and Slavic, different terms are used for humanity, on the one hand, and male and female individuals on the other. As a result, when the Orthodox hear the discussion about inclusive language, they understand it as referring exclusively to trinitarian names. Hence the condemnation of "the heresy of inclusive language" in Harare by a delegate of the Russian Orthodox Church. There is here a clear hermeneutical problem.
[9] This principle was spelled out in the statement, "Orthodox Liturgical Renewal and Visible Unity", in *Orthodox Reflections on the Way to Harare*, T. FitzGerald and P. Bouteneff eds, WCC, 1998, par. 27, p.145.
[10] This was the subject of the June 1999 meeting of the North American Orthodox-Catholic Theological consultation, which issued an important statement, "Baptism and 'Sacramental Economy'".

Overviews and Analyses

Seeds of Hope: A Reflection on Accounts of Worship from Varied Traditions

RUTH C. DUCK

Diversity is a gift of the worldwide church. The authors whom I have been asked to review have provided a beautiful mosaic of the theology and practice of Christian worship as experienced in varied traditions and in many places around the world. Justo González has written that, just as the four gospels complement one another to witness to Jesus Christ, so the global church, in all its diversity, bears witness to the gospel in more completeness than any one church in any one culture:

> It is necessary that believers from all the four corners of the earth bring the richness of their experience and perception of the gospel, so that we may all come to a fuller, more "catholic" – "according to the whole" – understanding of the gospel.[1]

While the authors I have been asked to review demonstrate profound differences among, and within, particular communions, this collection of texts offers the hope that churches may enrich one another in understanding and shaping worship so that its witness to the gospel may be fuller and more complete.

Shared foundations and concerns

The good news is that writers from many of the churches share a basic theological perspective concerning worship: namely, that worship is an encounter between God and the church. This encounter begins with

---

• It is appropriate to identify my own location as I begin this paper. As a member of a federated church, I am a member of both the United Methodist Church and the United Church of Christ (UCC). I am ordained in the UCC, and for ten years I was a member of the Presbyterian Church, USA. I am also ecumenically influenced by my Southern Baptist mother, by an Assemblies of God youth group, by my commitment to Christian feminism, by my master's work in liturgical studies at the University of Notre Dame, by my service on the Disciples of Christ hymnal committee, by my associate membership in the Iona Community, and by many experiences of worshipping in African American churches of varied denominations. My ancestors have lived in the US for at least 200 years; they are from Scottish, English and Cherokee backgrounds. I find that, as I read and respond to these papers, I am particularly influenced by my academic studies based in the liturgical renewal movement and my varied experiences in churches that encourage spontaneity and freedom in worship.

God's initiative in Christ through the Spirit, which inspires human responses of praise and thanksgiving. Many of the writers also affirm that worship is not an end in itself, for it leads to mission and service in daily life, and it contributes to an ongoing process of sanctification and/or liberation.

This theological consensus is more striking than it might seem. Some who write about worship often emphasize divine self-revelation almost to the exclusion of human response; others characterize worship as human response to God and are reserved about claiming that any human actions (such as preaching or sacraments) necessarily reveal God. Still others speak of worship as a human ritual activity, or an enactment or rehearsal of the reign of God (so that, for example, our eucharistic meal enacts and rehearses the open sharing of food and community).[2] So it is heartening to notice how many of the writers in this collection hold together the divine self-revelation and human response, understanding worship as a divine-human encounter leading to mission and service in daily life.

Armenian Orthodox writer Nareg Alemezian has said, "The end purpose of worship is to meet God, and to enter into union with him." Daniel Albrecht calls Pentecostal worship a conversation or communion between worshippers and God. Several authors (from Lutheran and Reformed backgrounds) speak of the expectation that the church will meet the risen Christ in worship. Quaker worship centres on waiting for, and responding to, a word from God given by the Spirit. As Lawrence Stookey argues, worship holds together our offering of praise to God and God's gift of blessing to us; and for United Methodists, this understanding takes place within a theology of covenant initiated by God. The congregation of Yoido Full Gospel Church in Korea eagerly expects God to be powerfully present among them, and so it is ready to respond with joy, praise and love.

It might be said that since the scholastic theologians, the Roman Catholic Church has emphasized God's self-revelation in worship more than the human response (for example, in the *ex opere operato* understanding of the sacraments). But the documents of Vatican II also hold the two poles together, so that worship is dedicated to both the glorification of God and the sanctification of humanity. Patrick Lyons highlights the need for a right relationship "between these two elements of sanctification and glorification, the receptive and active roles in the church's worship". In this understanding, worship as encounter with God is part of the Spirit's work of transforming the whole creation through the grace of God.

Another recurring theme, expressed in different ways by persons from varied traditions, is the connection of worship with daily life. Some writers (Caribbean Baptist, African American, the Iona Community, Quakers, a feminist perspective) reflect on the relation of worship to the work of liberation and justice in social and economic life, while others (Orthodox, Pentecostal) speak more generally of worship as an impulse to mission, service and ethical living. The representative of the Church of Norway speaks of prayers and hymns being developed "which are closer to peoples' lives and experience".

In these ways worship is seen to have a transformative effect on human life – for, as Dimitrios Passakos explains, worship is a *liminal* mode of being which subverts our lives and our world as they are. This emphasis on the way worship inspires and informs just and righteous living is a commonality among many of the confessional statements which should not be taken for granted; for even today some would keep worship "pure" and abstracted from the real world, while others are so intent on social action that worship seems a distraction. As the Mar Thoma representative observes, the search for unity in worship is "inextricably linked" with the challenge to common mission in the post-modern world – although churches may be reluctant to hear that call.

Liturgical inculturation also keeps worship and life in close relation, as Christian communities take seriously the incarnation, the affirmation that "God, in love, ha[s] entered the human situation in all its mess and glory. Humanity ha[s] thus been dignified and ennobled."[3] The principle of incarnation means that expressions of worship call on local cultural languages (music, symbol, visual arts, movement, architecture and so on) to give voice to praise, proclamation and prayer and to address the "mess and glory" of life as it is in a concrete time and place. In general, where the authors gathered here mention inculturation, they lament that movement towards genuine cultural expressions in worship comes so slowly. Examples are the use of the *English Hymnal* as the main song-book and the *Anglican Service Book* as the main worship resource in Johannesburg, or the slow movement towards incorporating cultural elements in the liturgy of the Church of South India. Another "growing edge" of churches, demonstrated most clearly in recent hymnals, is the need to address the multicultural realities of congregations and the world. Connecting worship and life through the integration of cultural elements is a subject for further theological reflection and liturgical revision by the churches.

Several of the churches, from varied parts of the globe, are concerned to reach out with new forms of worship appropriate to the culture of younger generations. At Yoido Full Gospel Church, young men and women welcome worship which "has broken the mould of the traditional service" through "an atmosphere of freedom through praise and drama".

Some Jamaican Baptists are making use of the keyboard, guitar and drum, while others are adopting evangelistic forms of worship aimed at "saving souls". In the Church of Scotland, which is facing decline in church membership, some seek to make worship "appealing, accessible, attractive" through "the adoption of new music and media such as video"; the Iona Community has also been seeking (in words used in the Community's daily prayer) "to find new ways to touch the hearts of all" through the use of more lively and relevant music and worship. New forms of worship designed to reach young people are also found among Lutherans and Mennonites in Germany and Disciples, Mennonites and United Methodists in the United States.

Several commentators express reservations about these outreach attempts; for example, Lawrence Stookey fears that these services neglect the sacraments and diminish the biblical content of worship. Nevertheless, I believe it would be better to develop these services with as much theological and liturgical integrity as possible, than to abandon such attempts to invite younger people into encounter with God through worship by including their cultural expressions.

Word, sacrament and song contribute to the church's unity *and* diversity

There is much divergence in how churches understand the role of scripture in worship, from Pentecostals who "take the words of scripture at face value" to Quakers who subordinate the Bible to the "Spirit which gave it forth". Still, scripture is central to worship across traditions, with the use of lectionaries growing even in churches that traditionally have chosen texts for preaching locally, week by week. (I worshipped on Trinity Sunday one year at an Assemblies of God church in Chicago with a predominantly African American congregation; the preacher used the week's common lectionary text, though never referring to the lectionary or Trinity Sunday as such!)

Despite great divergence in sacramental theology, some signs point towards greater unity in practice and understanding in this area. Some churches (Yoido church in Korea, United Methodists in the US, German Lutherans) witness to a somewhat more frequent celebration of the eucharist than before. A new appreciation of ritual, symbol and sacramentality in worship and life also leads towards mutual understanding. For example, Roman Catholics, who now discern the presence of Christ not only in consecrated elements but also in the gathered community, can enter into a new dialogue with Quakers who, without outward sacraments, can nevertheless now speak of the "eucharistic real presence" of Christ in their gatherings. Many churches are recovering a richer eucharistic theology; Stookey writes that United Methodists in the US are coming to realize that "the sacrament is a corporate and eschatological feast, and not merely a historical re-creation of the Upper Room meal for the benefit of individual believers". The influence of ancient texts such as the 3rd-century eucharistic prayer attributed to Hippolytus, or contemporary eucharistic prayers, is another source of convergence. As churches move towards deeper understanding, and more meaningful practice, of the sacraments (often drawing on ancient roots to do so) they move closer to one another, despite their differences.

Churches are influencing one another deeply in regard to baptismal practice. The Roman [Catholic] Rite of Christian Initiation for Adults is a model for baptismal preparation which has inspired Episcopalians, Methodists and Lutherans. Disciples of Christ churches, which traditionally practise baptism of those who confess faith for themselves, are increasingly recognizing the validity of infant baptism. The *Baptism, Eucharist and Ministry* document carefully presented the perspectives both of denominations which baptize at any age and those which wait for a personal confession of faith, highlighting the strengths and dangers of each approach. When we are able to express divergent views in a way that each party involved can recognize, mutual understanding is more possible.

The songs of the worldwide church are divergent in style and – quite literally – "without number", but the papers collected here testify to the centrality of song in all Christian worship. Indian churches developing local song, Iona Community members collecting songs from around the world, Syrian Orthodox Christians gladly singing ancient songs, Mennonites in the US and Germany singing songs from Taizé, American Methodist Episcopal Christians voicing songs of liberation, and United Methodists and Disciples finding new songs for seekers – all testify to the power of music in their worship.

Tensions: both creative and challenging

Despite a common love for song and scripture, small movements towards rapprochement in sacramental thinking, and shared theological affirmations, striking tensions also exist in the worship of churches worldwide. Among the many sources of these tensions are the churches' varied inclinations towards structure or spontaneity, towards textuality or orality, towards continuity or change, local or denominational design of liturgy, and experience or dogma.

One tension is between structure and spontaneity. Churches that emphasize structure follow the same sequence Sunday after Sunday, seldom changing it in response to happenings among the congregation, creative inspirations by worship leaders, or the leading of the Spirit. In extreme form, churches which value structure are like the Chicago church that continued worship without interruption while someone had a heart attack, an ambulance was called, and the person was carried away. Structure in worship, however, provides familiarity and comfort that may create space for wholehearted participation in worship, and connect worshippers with Christians of other times and places. The great majority of churches in this survey appear to value structure over spontaneity.

Pentecostal and charismatic Christians, including the Yoido congregation in Korea, as well as Quaker Christians, encounter God in worship particularly through the guiding of the Spirit in the present moment. Other churches, such as the African Methodist Episcopal and Disciples of Christ congregations, have important elements of spontaneity in otherwise structured worship. There is a range between spontaneity and structure in denominations such as the United Methodist Church, which provides liturgical resources in the hymnal and book of worship, yet which allows congregations to adapt or abandon printed liturgies as local tradition allows and the Spirit leads.

Spontaneous worship has an improvisational character as, for example, preacher and musician interact with one another while the congregation sings, hums or says "Amen!" in response. It is not, of course, structureless: charismatic churches may follow a basic order more or less predictably, and hold unspoken understandings about when it is appropriate to be silent, to speak or to move. When high technology instrumentation and visual displays support singing, significant preparation may undergird seemingly "spontaneous" worship. In extreme form, preference for spontaneity may be an excuse for not caring for the worship life of the congregation (as when worship leaders are deciding who will do what next while the congregation sings a hymn). But with spontaneity there is freedom to create with the moment, as various elements and persons interact with the living Spirit of God in their midst.

In his book *¡Alabadle!* Justo González argues that when Hispanic Christians worship in a spontaneous spirit of fiesta, a particular kind of preparation is required.[4] When we give a party, we prepare the house with festive decorations. We prepare food and drink in abundance and invite people we think will enjoy being together. We seek to be hospitable to everyone, helping people feel comfortable and introducing those who do not know each other. We do not script the conversation or the exact order of events – but the song, the cake, the toasts, the gifts, will all appear in due time. So it is with worship: we prepare the place and the people, with openness to what may emerge.

The Mar Thoma church represents an emphasis on structure in contrast to spontaneity; in fact, Abraham Kuruvilla states that "rigidity in liturgical form has come to be equated with preserving the unity" of the church. As in some other Eastern churches, the liturgy of St James is primary, and the service proceeds through elements which have ancient forms and texts at their core. The African Methodist Episcopal Church, diverse as it is, proceeds through familiar opening words and music, through scripture readings and the decalogue to the sermon and then provides opportunities for response, including prayer at the altar rail and an invitation to Christian discipleship. Anglican, Lutheran and Roman Catholic liturgies have liturgical orders that have borne the test of time and guide the prayer of the faithful. Often preference for structure is a preference for continuity over change. This is clearly stated in the chapter on worship in the Armenian Orthodox church, which seeks to follow the "oldest order of worship", rejecting modernism and building unity through faithfulness to dogma and ritual inherited from apostolic times.

Closely related to the tension between spontaneity and structure is the tension between textuality – the quality of worship dependent on liturgical books, bulletins and hymnals – and orality – the quality of worship dependent on spontaneous, memorized and repeated words rather than print media. Pentecostal worship, for example, finds words for worship through the active participation of the congregation in prayers, testimonies and movement as the Spirit leads, whereas Episcopal worship draws many of its words from printed texts from the *Book of Common Prayer* and other denominationally approved sources.

Rebecca Slough, in her analysis of Mennonite worship in North America, says that local churches of her denomination experience tension between "the characteristics and values of text-based written culture (standard hymnody)" and "sound-based oral culture (as expressed in praise and worship and international songs)". This conflict is by no means unique to Mennonites among Christians in North America, where the culture increasingly favours visual communications and where fewer people are learning to read musical notes. Given this cultural context, it appears that churches which are print-dependent may need to enhance the oral and visual qualities of their liturgy.

Peter Donald notes that "in current church union discussions, the Reformed churches resist being obliged to use fixed liturgical forms". The distinction here is not between spontaneity and structure, for in Reformed churches the emphasis is not on words and actions emerging spontaneously at the time of worship, but on words prepared or selected by leaders at the local level. Nor are printed worship aids absent; there may be a bulletin prepared by the pastor or worship committee, or hymn

262   *Overviews and Analyses*

texts complicated enough to require print. The pastor as "teaching elder" in Reformed traditions bears responsibility, as a local theologian, for shaping the words of worship. So we identify another related tension, that between liturgy created locally and liturgy shaped by denominations or groups of denominations.

Another tension has to do with whether churches emphasize immediate experience or inherited dogma. Reading the chapters on Armenian Orthodox worship and Pentecostal worship one after the other created a stark contrast. Nareg Alemezian understands worship as a living encounter of creatures with the Creator, an encounter built on careful theological reflection: "Rich worship is founded on the clear theology and doctrine of the Armenian Orthodox Church." Although he advocates some change to make the liturgy more intelligible, beautiful and accessible, the primary task is to educate members to understand the theology and ritual of traditional orthodox worship. Daniel Albrecht, on the other hand, says that

> there is little doubt that the value that most informs and supports Pentecostal worship is experience... Personal experience of God by the Holy Spirit not only lays at the core of the worship service for Pentecostals, it is for them the realm of authentic and vital religion.

Dogma has its place, but it is secondary to the immediate experience of God in worship. Feminist worship actively questions and critiques inherited dogma, as it seeks to integrate women's experience (so varied and hard to define) into previously male-dominated liturgy.

The tension between dogma and experience comes into play in efforts to inculturate worship; for example, Thomas Thangaraj notes that efforts to bring Indian cultural elements into the worship of the Church of South India sometimes meet resistance because of the desire to maintain Christian identity. In consequence, Christians keep church architecture, art, music and worship distant from Indian cultural forms in order to keep their worship distinct from Muslim and Hindu expressions. Thangaraj argues that solidarity with Indian people requires movement towards inculturation of worship, but acknowledges that addressing the need for Christian identity will be complex and difficult. Surprisingly similar tensions exist between contemporary and traditional worship in the United States: when distinctively Christian symbols such as the cross and the sacraments are removed from worship in order to reach the unchurched, has Christian identity and theology been sacrificed in the name of contemporary experience? Or are traditionalists distancing themselves so much from culture that they are failing to witness the gospel to emerging generations?

Living with tension – a source of growth?

Tensions over the above issues – where the various churches stand on the spectrum between structure and spontaneity, between textuality and orality, continuity and change, local and denominational design of liturgy, and experience and dogma – are such that diverse groups may scarcely recognize one another's liturgies as genuine Christian worship. At Garrett-Evangelical Theological Seminary (ETS), for instance, persons from traditions which define true worship in terms of spontaneity, orality, and direct experience of God question chapel services that are highly structured and scripted; they do not sense the presence of the Spirit in such worship. When it is the time for persons from these "spontaneous" backgrounds to lead worship, community members who value structure and printed texts may feel inhibited, especially if spontaneous words seem not to reveal theological reflection, or if there is no bulletin to guide them. And when one considers that most Garrett-ETS community members come from US Protestant backgrounds, one can see how challenging it could be to recognize worship across international and ecumenical boundaries.

Tensions involved in recognizing one another's worship seem particularly poignant as Orthodox Christians evaluate attempts at ecumenical worship often crafted by Protestant and Catholic Christians without adequate Orthodox participation. Dagmar Heller notes that for the Orthodox, Christian worship is not itself if it lacks the celebration of the eucharist, is without a sense of the mystery of God, or is without continuity with liturgical tradition. Paul Meyendorff also notes that "Eastern Christians worship with their entire body and all their senses". He points out that theological differences sometimes even cause Christians to question one another's ecclesial status. To place his article alongside the one by Gail Ramshaw fully demonstrates the tension. For Paul Meyendorff, change in the traditional trinitarian naming of Father, Son and Holy Spirit violates basic Orthodox teaching; but according to Gail Ramshaw, feminists envision "thorough-going reform of divine imagery [and] theological language". Indeed, it is not uncommon in such debates for traditionalists and feminists to accuse each other of idolatry because they cling to, or change, language about God. How, then, could members of these conflicted groups recognize one another's worship as genuine Christian worship?

Ecumenical tensions around worship reflect not trivial concerns, but basic issues of theology and Christian identity. The question is whether we are willing to live, work and worship together in the midst of tension, ambiguity and even conflict, not expecting quick or easy solutions. My eleven years at Garrett-Evangelical Theological Seminary, for most of which I have been a member or chair of the worship committee and/or dean of the chapel, have taught me about living with tension as we seek to design worship in a community of great cultural and theological diversity. One learning is that all solutions must be considered provisional and temporary. For example, in order to include worship styles from various cultures, we have experimented both with having culturally mixed worship teams and with giving people from the same background the opportunity to work together. The question whether it is better to emphasize one approach or the other does not go away, but is visited again and again as new students come with new critiques and concerns. This is analogous to the Faith and Order Commission's variation between worship planned and led by members of one tradition, and worship planned by a group drawn from several traditions. Each generation of ecumenical leaders will need to revisit the question, sometimes devising new approaches that former commissions never imagined.

Another learning is that people working in situations of diversity must relinquish the fantasy that the "perfect" worship service acceptable to all Christians exists in the real world. We must expect, indeed invite, critique, in a process of continual learning and revision. Worship touches deep concerns of faith and life, so we may expect that ecumenical liturgies will bring profound joy to some, but also pain or anger to others; the great concern is if the same groups consistently feel distant or excluded from worship. Often the most serious critiques will concern issues the planning group never anticipated, a situation that can be alleviated (though not prevented) by securing truly diverse persons to serve on planning committees. A third learning is that those of us who worship in culturally and ecumenically diverse contexts must learn to look for the presence of God beyond our familiar landmarks. Paul Meyendorff raises this issue in terms of ecclesial identity: to worship together, we will need to recognize one another as Christians, affirming our common baptism. It follows that we will also need to be open to the presence of the triune God in styles of worship that are not familiar to us, in the spirit of this prayer by Thomas H. Troeger:

> Holy Spirit,
> help me to withhold judgment
> of what is strange and new to me.
> Use this service to deepen my belief in God,
> to expand my understanding of the gospel,
> to strengthen my bonds with all people,
> and to serve more faithfully Jesus Christ,
> in whose name I pray, Amen.[5]

Miriam Therese Winter has advised, "Do not be discouraged if it seems that our worship is a continual tug of war. Authentic worship is related to life, and life is continual tension."[6] Tensions are a given. Unity is also a gift; it is already given in the present, yet always to be pursued because it is not yet fulfilled.

Seeds of hope

Tensions abound, but there are signs of hope that fuller Christian unity can blossom, even on that most contentious ground of shared worship. One seed of hope is the way in which churches are influencing each other's practice. Some churches, of course, are not sure whether being significantly influenced by other worshipping traditions would be a good thing! Almost all name some ways in which the liturgical renewal movement and ecumenical dialogue have already influenced them. More widespread use of shared or similar lectionaries, growing commonality in eucharistic prayers, fuller lay participation, and sharing of congregational song across national and denominational boundaries are elements of movement towards common practice.

Although the average lay person may or may not be familiar with ecumenically produced documents, these changes *are* felt at the local level. For example, the United Church of Christ congregation I served in Hartford, Wisconsin, was literally next door to a Roman Catholic parish. Not only could Protestant-Catholic couples drive to church together; over lunch they could often discuss sermons on the same lectionary text, used at both churches. As Christian communions influence one another in their worship practices, their members can attend Sunday services, marriages and funerals conducted in other churches with more comfort, even in cases where eucharistic sharing is prohibited. There is no doubt that we are learning more about one another. This seed of hope sometimes blossoms in changed practice, and almost always brings fruits of increased understanding and appreciation.

Interaction provokes questions which, in turn, may cause the breaking open of the seed without which growth cannot occur. Learning about the practice and theology of worship across ecumenical boundaries has opened new areas for exploration in the various denominations. (For example, Keith Watkins of the Disciples of Christ notes that learning about the worship practices of others raises questions about the vitality of Disciples' worship, the role of laity and clergy at the table, and the admission of unbaptized children to communion.) Questions about worship growing out of ecumenical encounter include the role of women and children, methods of inculturation, the frequency of the eucharist, and the involvement of the senses.

Engaging the tension between orality and textuality could help some congregations raise their heads, and worship more freely, than they can with their heads always buried in a hymn or worship book, or service bulletin. Engaging the tension between change and continuity could enrich "contemporary" congregations with resources from the saints of previous times. Although our differences are often fraught with tension, there is no doubt that we have much to learn from one another, much that could cultivate new life in our liturgies.

Another seed of hope is the communities which are deliberately seeking to draw on the riches of the worldwide church as they shape their worship life. The Community of Grandchamp seeks to live out Christ's prayer that all may be one by weaving together worship traditions from Reformed, Catholic and Orthodox sources, in ways that respect the original sources. The Iona Community also seeks to draw on ecumenical and global sources in its song and prayer as an expression of the rule of the Community, which calls members to work for justice and peace, and to pray for all people. These communities, both growing from Reformed roots and both structures which are complementary to the churches, are a witness to others that gifts from the worldwide church's diversity can enhance the worship of all.

We may plant and water the seed through dialogue and experiments of shared worship, but it is God who gives the growth (1 Cor. 3:5). Christians will be most able to accept the validity of one another's worship, and of ecumenical worship, when they are able to discern God's presence at work in worship. Unity is a gift of the Spirit, not something we can manipulate through liturgical technologies. Our best attempts to "engineer" ecumenical worship will come to naught unless we are open to the Spirit in whom all Christians are baptized into one body (1 Cor. 12:13). Encounter with the triune God is the distinctive mark of Christian worship, as most of our theologies affirm. Through this encounter we receive God's self-giving, we offer our praise and our lives, and we continue the journey of living out our baptisms.

Janet Scott, from a Quaker perspective, writes,

> We may from time to time worship with other Christians in their way, but the motivation is from fellowship rather than from the expectation of depth and power. We can, or course, be surprised by what we experience in the worship of other Christians. But we can also be irritated by what seems to be "busyness" in liturgy and ritual.

Dagmar Heller notes that Orthodox Christians consider that "an appropriately prayerful atmosphere is often lacking" in ecumenical services. It is true that Quakers miss silence in worship designed by other

Christians, just as Orthodox Christians feel they have not worshipped if the eucharist has not been celebrated. But these statements can be read not as statements of being comfortable with particular gardens, but as warnings about a storm that could destroy the harvest of all. Heller writes that "worship is centred on the mystery of God and serves to unite human beings with God". What if this centre is lost through our commendable efforts to bring in elements and leaders from as many traditions as possible? What if our purpose subtly shifts so that ecumenical worship becomes an end in itself, with the mystery of God no longer at the centre?

If people from varied Christian traditions are to worship together, a common attitude of praise and discipleship, more than focus on the mechanics of balancing elements of different traditions, is most likely to bear fruit. Obviously, worship across cultures, nations and denominations will only be effective if it includes the traditions and leadership of diverse people – but always as means to the ends of glorifying God and sanctifying humanity.

Diversity is a gift of God that can lead to fuller, deeper praise and a broader understanding of, and commitment to, Christian mission. Unity is also a gift of God, bestowed on the church through one baptism into Jesus Christ through the Spirit. It is clear that at times our diversity is divisive, and our "unity" is really the imposition of the perspectives of one group on another. As the Faith and Order Commission of the World Council of Churches, along with many other Christian groupings, seeks to move towards genuine unity, the challenges are great. We must learn more deeply how to celebrate diversity and to discern the presence of God in practices which are unfamiliar to us, without ever seeking to mix the rich colours of the global church into a drab sameness. We must learn the unity that comes from respect so deep that we expect to learn from one another, while holding deeply to the patterns and convictions that matter to us. Each tile of the mosaic, with its different hue and texture, contributes to the whole. Our hope is in the Spirit of God, the Artist who brings out the design in what seems to be fragments of broken stone.

NOTES

[1] Justo González, *Out of Every Tribe and Nation*, Nashville, Abindgon, 1992, p.28.
[2] John Burkhart, *Worship*, Philadelphia, Westminster, 1982, pp.31-33.
[3] Ron Ferguson, *Chasing the Wild Goose: The Iona Community*, London, Harper Collins, 1988, p.85.
[4] Justo González, "Hispanic Christian Worship", in J. González ed., *¡Alabadle!*, Nashville, Abingdon, 1996, pp.19-24.
[5] In Carol Doran and Thomas H. Troeger, *Trouble at the Table*, Nashville, Abingdon, 1992, p.148.
[6] Miriam Therese Winter, *Prepare the Way of the Lord*, Nashville, Abingdon, 1978, p.43.

Worship and the Search for Christian Unity

A Response

ROBERT GRIBBEN

The scope – and limitations – of the papers reviewed

From many of the papers which I have been asked to review I have learned a great deal. Some have inspired and encouraged me. There are inevitably omissions, of varying significance, among the churches covered and of course regional variations within confessions cannot be covered sufficiently when the focus is on one particular church.[1]

Contributors were asked about the "essential" and the "optional" in worship, and the status of *ex tempore* or "pre-established" prayer, but few very informative answers are to be found. The paper of Hans Krech on the Evangelical Lutheran Church in Germany lists as essential "the preaching of the word, celebration of the sacraments and common prayer" but there is no detail about the elements of these services. I do not recall any reference to Eucharist §27 of *Baptism, Eucharist and Ministry* which lists the possible elements in the Lord's supper. We do not learn whether the prayers which animate a Church of Scotland service ever or always consist of (for instance) adoration, confession, thanksgiving and intercession. The most detail is probably found in the "basic pattern of worship" of the United Methodist Church, and the outline of Church of South India worship requirements. But given the specificity of the request for information, it is surprising that the answers are so general, and so taken over by statements of "high" liturgical theology. Perhaps theologians do not believe in the significance of ritual detail!

Another question put to contributors asked about new developments and their relevance to the search for Christian unity, and again the answers are insufficient. The replies sometimes combine this question with another, about the influences of the ecumenical/liturgical renewal movements on the worship of the confession in question. Here there is a good deal of evidence of "cross-pollination". Some of this has come about through careful theological examination or modification, others are mere borrowings. (There is also evidence of resistance, for example the Yoido Korean Pentecostal church does not accept the otherwise almost universal preference for a weekly eucharist – see also the Mennonite essays.) If Gail Ramshaw is right that "the ecumenical liturgical renewal movement is yet another demonstration of the rise of feminist consciousness in the religious expression of the 20th century", there is very little appreciation – or critique – of the influence of the surrounding culture, especially the all-pervasive Western forms; in a few places where "seeker services" are spoken of, there is no hint that there are theological (or liturgical, or missiological) questions to be raised about them. In short, the "new developments" are not, it would seem, indicative of any serious change across the board in liturgical theology or practice.

Given these omissions, and the varying styles and quality of the responses, I do not believe we have the material to draw significant sweeping conclusions from them. My only suggestion is that a review of the literature on worship across the whole spectrum may give some more clues: studies within traditions may help us see what is enduring, or fundamental, and what is changing or currently emerging as new directions. Studies in dogmatic or sacramental theology might also assist, though in my experience there is a significant gap between the scholars and the *plebs sancta Dei* on many matters of worship and belief. A study of liturgical texts confines us to a few (if large) traditions, but that is equally partial. Few churches have undertaken anything like the worship and culture study[2] of the Lutheran World Federation, or work in which anything like a basic *ordo,* or pattern of worship, is even imagined.

The ecumenical questions

Dagmar Heller's fine paper "Ecumenical Worship – Experiences, Problems, Possibilities: Some Basic Considerations" seems to me to sum the matter up, and to state the actual deep and difficult issues well. As it says, there have been two approaches to "ecumenical worship": first, the opportunity to experience together the prayers of a particular tradition ("confessional worship services") and, second, the composition of "new" liturgies made up of representative elements in which all may share. This has applied both to prayer-offices (and/or "services of the word") and to the eucharist – though actual communion is governed by other factors such as recognition of ministries.

Theoretically, one could assume that there was no objection to confessional worship. After all, every church may celebrate its own liturgy with integrity. There is real value in this, because it allows a certain measure of "entering into the spirit" of another tradition's worship. This may move one to admiration or criticism, it may stimulate theological or pastoral thought, and, in the churches which have this freedom, a desire to adapt or borrow. Faith and Order began its explorations of worship in this way in the 1940s and 1950s, an approach generally known as "comparative liturgy". Its limitations soon became apparent (as in other areas, such as theology), not least because everything remains discrete; there is discovery only at the "scientific" level of observation. Ecumenism requires a deeper commitment, a genuine dialogue.

"Permission" to alter liturgies: a Reformation gift?

I suspect that this latter desire, for something beyond comparative liturgy, gave rise to the second mode of "ecumenical prayer": namely, the putting together of elements from diverse traditions for an ecumenical occasion. For many member churches this was theologically possible because of the nature of their understanding of worship; and it was attractive. It builds, indeed, on both the fundamental methods of liturgical reform practised in the 16th century.

Luther (and Cranmer) proceeded by excising or replacing those elements in the received liturgy (that is, the mediaeval Western mass) which offended against the theological principles of the Reformers. Thus Luther removed from the mass "all that smacked of oblation", and Lutheranism was left with a seriously truncated (by modern standards) eucharistic canon. Cranmer in England moved with a similar dogmatic agenda, but also with caution (in their own time, the Mar Thoma Church founders used the same method in reforming their received liturgy of the Syrian Orthodox Church in India – see Abraham Kuruvilla's paper on Mar Thoma worship).

The other method was Calvin's: to begin with "first principles". If the scriptures record a commandment of the Lord, or commend particular forms of worship, then these – and none other – are to be used in Christian worship. Thus scriptural warrant is found for the two gospel sacraments of baptism and the Lord's supper, and for preaching, for prayers of intercession and thanksgiving and so on. There were debates about certain forms which were driven by a great deal more than theological principle, and this reliance on scripture as a book of precedents led to some absurd conclusions in the century following the Reformers' deaths.

Both these fundamental approaches, though different, allow pastors and other authorities to change or create liturgies on agreed "theological principles". My own church, the Uniting Church in Australia, both authorizes a book of worship with complete liturgies, and gives permission to substitute, for almost any prayer, a prayer in similar words, *ex tempore* or borrowed from another source, provided the theological content and intention is the same. (The exceptions are those words which need to be guaranteed for the purposes of law, that is, the marriage vows, or for ecumenical relationships, that is, the baptismal formula.)

From the 1950s, it became clear that one of the debts to the ecumenical movement was the borrowing of liturgical material. I suspect that the use, at the Amsterdam inaugural WCC assembly, of a "service of preparation" for the eucharist was a borrowing from a practice in the newly-formed Church of South India, whose founders were also leaders of the nascent WCC (for example, Lesslie Newbigin. The Church of South India liturgy could be regarded in some ways as the first "Lima liturgy"; the methodology is the same.) From there, the borrowing and creating of liturgies – which, with due attention to theology, assisted Christians of divers traditions to worship together – grew. For these WCC member churches this kind of worship was an experience of the oikoumene, of the ecumenical church. In the variety of words and customs (and not least vestments) they saw the diversity of the world church.

Many of the papers express their gratitude for this "ecumenical permission" to borrow good things. (In addition, it is also the basis for what is offered for the Week of Christian Unity prayer services.) Hans Krech, writing on the Lutheran church in Germany, acknowledges the importance of the baptism, eucharist and ministry studies. It even attributes to them a recovery of dimensions of God the Father and the Holy Spirit in a Lutheran tradition which was "largely Christocentric", as well as a greater sensitivity to other churches in, for example, the treatment of "consecrated" elements after the eucharist, a recovery of a fuller "Christian year", and the daily office. Peter Donald's description of the Church of Scotland, Lawrence Stookey's of Methodism, Rebecca Slough (and, more cautiously, Corinna Schmidt) of the Mennonites acknowledge similar debts. According to Keith Watkins, the Disciples are asking questions about the efficacy of *ex tempore* prayer, about their practice of baptism, and about American culture, because of ecumenical experience of worship. Several papers also mention the influence of Pentecostal worship – something which is "ecumenical", if not central to the WCC member churches (Jamaican Baptist, Mennonite), and Daniel Albrecht's paper on Pentecostal worship is of particular interest on this. Some churches (Orthodox of various families, Quakers, perhaps the Yoido Full Gospel Church of Korea) seem to resist such cross-pollination, lest they compromise their distinctiveness. Perhaps Thomas Thangaraj's paper on the Church of South India may be read as one church stepping back from an earlier ecumenical searching?

Early Orthodox participation in ecumenical services

Dagmar Heller points out rightly that for the Orthodox participants this diversity – at least as it has developed in recent assemblies – is no longer welcomed. I do not know whether the sources exist to discover what the earliest Orthodox participants actually thought of the liturgical diversity they experienced in ecumenical gatherings. Archbishop Germanos and other hierarchs did take part in these interconfessional services. Did he feel compromised? I doubt it.

I think it is important to recognize that we are at a later stage of church history, and that we are dealing with the fallout of the collapse of communism (followed by the revival of earlier established churches, e.g. Greek Catholics in the Ukraine or Methodists in Russia, and the arrival of new "missions"), and the rise of Islam, as new non-theological factors in ecumenism. Thus there are new sensitivities which have given rise to new assessments of the past and the present. These particularly affect liturgical issues (notably, eucharistic hospitality) amongst the plethora of other issues within the WCC today, and they may halt our progress, at least for the moment. I wish that the Orthodox papers had addressed these issues directly.

The churches of the Radical Reformation

But Dagmar Heller draws attention to another group for whom the liturgical issues in the ecumenical movement are equally as sharp. I wrote earlier of the theological principles of reform of Luther, Calvin and Cranmer, but these are representatives of the "mainstream" Reformation. In each case they were highly educated and privileged men, and they carried through their reforms (or failed to do so) in direct relationship with the powers that be – electors and municipal councils and kings respectively. The significant changes in 17th-century England – the source of the legacy of a major portion of Protestant churches in the world, including Anglican, Presbyterian and Congregational – were created through the historical exigencies of civil authority, monarch or commonwealth. In each of these cases there were other groups of Christians who agreed neither with monarch nor new civil governor, with neither Catholic nor Reformer, and who consciously remained separate, and paid with their lives and freedom. In the ecumenical movement, the witness of the Radical Reformation needs to be clearly identified and honoured. In the debate between mainstream Western churches, Catholic and Evangelical, and Eastern Orthodox, their witness must be guarded and heard. They are represented amongst our papers by Baptists, Disciples, Mennonites, Quakers and churches of Pentecostal inspiration.

Is there an elitist form of ecumenism?

I underline this because I think there is a tendency to regard the larger churches, the churches of influence in the WCC, as a kind of aristocracy, an elite. In liturgical studies, contemporary developments are often judged by the measure of Roman Catholic or classical Reformation theology and practice. The Orthodox are easily respected for their antiquity; but as for the Radical Reformation, the less formal, folk-centred, anti-establishment voices of this important Protestant family are ignored. Particularly in the Western churches, where reform and renewal are positively regarded, conservative groups with seemingly "strange" ways are disregarded. What if they are right? They point us to human values which are often lost in the large organization. If we need to value concepts like koinonia, or the local, or the care of minorities and their cultures, if we seek the movement of the Spirit in our day, we need to listen to these churches.

It will not do, however, to value them merely as phenomena in the ecclesiastical scene. There is need of genuine dialogue, and allowing the possibility that change may occur on both sides because of the dialogue. These churches represent, for instance, a challenge to some central presuppositions in liturgy and theology.

The existence of the tag *lex orandi, lex credendi* has allowed many churches to talk to each other on the basis of written evidence. The main doctrines of the Trinity, of Christology, ecclesiology, soteriology and the rest may be demonstrated by reference to texts. This is the way in which universities have dealt with issues of truth for many centuries – and the universities are the creatures of the mainstream churches. But what if your tradition has no texts, and was excluded from the universities (by law or by the dictates of conscience)? Burchel Taylor's paper on the Baptists in Jamaica says,

> For the most part the importance of worship is taken for granted, being considered self-evident. There is therefore no self-conscious effort to articulate a theology of worship, or offer a theological rationale for all or any aspect of it.

Does this exclude this tradition from the debate? Does our very method of pursuing this project militate against our obtaining answers in some cases?

How does one weigh the fact that for centuries Baptist pastors, and many others, have prayed *ex tempore* in language which is (deeply biblical and) trinitarian, and expressed their church's Christology in Chalcedonian (!) terms – to choose just two central matters – when many are poorly trained by academic standards, never recite the creeds in church, and have no liturgy books and no hymnbooks issued by any authority other than the local? The fact that many of these churches have moved towards the mainstream, "become respectable", and can now enter into dialogue on the majority's terms, is no great gain. Equally, the argument from "exceptional circumstances" dissolves in the face of the circumstances in which *many* Christians live their lives normally (say in Central American countries, or the Australian outback).

The effect of sheer, grinding poverty on what some churches may achieve (for example, the inability to staff a full faculty of theology in Thailand or Bulgaria) must be taken into account by those who have everything and may be able to meet all of their own high standards. We need new ways of discerning Christian authenticity. It is clear that Christian faith has been maintained for a long time in situations where none of the usual criteria for guaranteeing it exist.

These are dramatic instances, but real ones. They raise questions which also apply in situations much closer to the mainstream ecumenical debate. Many member churches will never meet the criteria which have governed ecumenical discussions for half a century – we need, then, to revise the criteria.

Yet we are not speaking of watertight compartments. There is the possibility of dialogue. It is interesting to read Dimitrios Passakos of the Orthodox tradition on the relationship of worship and mission. This uses the image of the heart-beat, diastole and systole, an image which I met first in the writings of the Swiss Reformed liturgical theologian Jean-Jacques von Allmen. Several papers (Hans Krech's, and Kathy Galloway on the Iona Community) mention the confusion, or lack of connection, between worship and mission. Some – too few – offer a critique of the use of worship as an evangelical tool (Lawrence Stookey on the United Methodist Church; perhaps surprisingly, Burchel Taylor, from the Jamaican Baptist context; uncritically, the Mennonite papers, and Yong-Hoon Lee from Yoido; with important distinctions, Daniel Albrecht on the Pentecostal churches).

Liturgy and the struggle for unity: the "Lima liturgy"

I wish to return to the tension between confessional and "multi-confessional" liturgies in ecumenical contexts. It does not matter how far we have come in mutual liturgical understanding; other issues prevent us from gaining any benefit.

For instance, if at a eucharist in an ecumenical context an Anglican presides, doing so with the appropriate approvals of his or her church and finding the particular rite acceptable under those rules, then it is, to the guest participating in the service, an Anglican eucharist. This, almost alone, is what has made the Lima liturgy possible. An Orthodox or a Quaker knows to what degree they may participate in such a service. If there is a Disciples presider it may be (as Keith Watkins's paper points out) a lay person, yet duly authorized and working within the canons of his or her church; in that case there will be another set of personal and ecclesial decisions. But on each occasion it is (more or less) clear for each person present what they may choose to do. In short, we are still working under the rules of confessionalism.

Dagmar Heller points out clearly the difficulties in regard to a – what is it? – "non-confessional", a "multi-confessional" eucharistic rite. The World Council has meticulously avoided any act which suggests that it is a church, or even a "council" as the churches of the first millennium understood a council; it has no eucharist to celebrate. It cannot baptize. It is a council of *churches* which celebrate baptism and eucharist (and much else). The conciliar process allows the WCC assemblies and other meetings to make suggestions to the member churches about these things – that, for example, in order to underline baptism as a sacrament of unity there ought to be witnesses from other churches at any baptism in a local place. So from the beginning the Lima liturgy was a dangerous exercise for those sensitive to such ecclesial issues, and especially (but not only) to the Eastern churches. The report of a study seminar I chaired at the Faith and Order worship consultation at Ditchingham in 1994 summarizes the issues.[3]

Nevertheless, the composing of a liturgy at the end of the BEM process was a creative move, and its good intentions must not be doubted. This applied to the eucharist what had been applied regularly to other forms of prayer in ecumenical contexts. Because of the studies on the eucharist reflected in BEM, it was able, with real theological integrity, to attempt such an exercise seriously. It is not merely assorted texts (and music) cobbled together – rather, it draws on the most widely accepted liturgical structures and theological intent available to the churches at this time. Western churches, on the whole, have readily recognized the Lima liturgy's integrity (as well as its limitations) from their own positions and experience; the canons of apostolicity of the *liturgy* (leaving aside questions of ministry) are largely accepted: that is, the supreme basis of holy scripture, and faithfulness to the living tradition. This is in keeping with contemporary studies and ecumenical documents. Of course it does not, and cannot, solve the more difficult issues.

The future of agreed texts

The Roman Catholic Church recognizes as authentic eucharistic liturgies only those texts for which there is a duly authorized *editio typica* in Latin in Rome. The only acceptable presider is a bishop or priest in communion with the bishop of Rome. Nevertheless, until fairly recently, it was possible for Rome to approve new liturgical texts, and one might have hoped for the acceptability of a text which was also accepted for use by a number of other churches. This would not, of course, solve all the problems, but it would allow some fruitful convergence of practice and experience.

The Orthodox and Oriental Orthodox churches recognize both a number of distinct liturgies (e.g. Chrysostom, Basil, James) and a number of centres of authority (the patriarchates); but this variety does not stretch to authorizing other than historic texts, or presiders not in communion with one of their hierarchs. The apostolicity, and the acceptability, of particular rites is guaranteed by their historic association with the apostles or apostolic sees. There may have been expansions, or even changes, over the centuries so that the present rites are not precisely those of the earliest times (I think of the multiplication of litanies, or the effect of the invention of the tall *iconostasis*), but these are not seen as significant changes; they do not affect the substance. But no rite is authorized which does not have ancient roots as defined by tradition. By definition, then, we may say that there is no way forward in offering new texts to the Orthodox for approval. Even if major problems lie elsewhere, this is an ecumenical problem of huge dimensions.

Other churches which normally proceed by authorizing texts could presumably follow the method mentioned above for the Roman Catholic hierarchy. My own church shares a eucharistic prayer with the Anglican Church in Australia; it is printed in both our liturgical books, and is intended to be used on ecumenical occasions. The English Language Liturgical Consultation (ELLC) has been seeking such mutually acceptable texts for some years,[4] and continues to share its discoveries with its ecumenical member consultations.

For many churches represented in our papers, this is a plodding and absurdly hierarchical process. As I have said above, such churches object to set liturgies, and to liturgies imposed from on high, with the same vigour as Orthodox hold to the opposite. The position of these churches reflects their historical experience of persecution: they have martyrs to prove it. They hold a distinct view of church and state relationships forged in the heat of *Realpolitik*. As the papers indicate, they do not recognize the activity of the Spirit as easily in prepared prayer texts as they do in *ex tempore* (or *ex corde*) prayer. They have to be taken seriously, as seriously as are their critics, who may be more powerful and (by a doubtful view of history) more ancient. There is evidence in texts before the 4th century of the practices they value, and New Testament and patristic evidence points to a wider view of acceptable ways of governing churches (presbyteral, congregational, different modes of *episcope*)[5] than emerged from later controversy. These results of studies lying in Faith and Order's files must be taken seriously also.

The breakdown of former liturgical disciplines

But there is another significant development. Even in the so-called "liturgical churches" – those with authorized books – it is increasingly the case that local pastors and other worship leaders vary a set text, or add to it, sometimes with serious theological implications. Lawrence Stookey's paper notes this breakdown in the United Methodist Church's discipline on baptism. In vain do the ecclesial authorities complain or attempt to stop it. This is one of the clear effects (mentioned almost nowhere in our papers) of the breakdown of old disciplines and protocols, the major and profoundly significant changes in culture which the West is experiencing to different degrees. The implications for ecumenical cooperation are vast.

If, as Gail Ramshaw reports, ministers of churches whose official position is the use of the name of the Trinity at baptism – and this is the basis for the mutual acceptance of baptism between these churches – now alter that ancient and ecumenical formula in the name of feminist conviction or something else, where do our mutual agreements stand? They don't. Liturgical authority is breaking down.

For a long time, some churches have admitted members of other churches in good standing to communion at their eucharist on the basis of the visitor affirming a belief in the "real presence" of Christ, and/or other doctrines which accord with those of the host church. It is not possible to insist on such precision of conscience, let alone understanding, in many believers today. Some canonists, some theologians, some clergy, may see these matters as important; for many, many others, it no longer matters. One acts on one's conscience, one offers one's personal integrity to another Christian brother or sister – and that is sufficient. Amongst the young of the present generation, this is a matter of high morality, and many of their elders share it. They do not even see it as "holy disobedience". This is anathema to Orthodox hierarchs (but not to them alone). Unfortunately it adds fuel to their mounting suspicion of the West; but it is a fact.

It may well be true that the WCC has proceeded, in its liturgical life, on grounds which are not acceptable to the Orthodox. Certainly that needs to be addressed; but the answer is not to deny the positive contributions which member churches (not, by the way, neatly categorized as "Western"; for many are African, Asian or Hispanic, and perhaps debtors in some way to Western missionaries) have made and can make. The Orthodox have found their voice, and I welcome it, but others are not required to withdraw from the conversation. The question must be pursued in its full complexity and untidiness.

A personal note

Let me put this more personally. I have held a "high" view of liturgy from my earliest days, and I have found it in forms of worship of a classical kind. I have attempted to "raise the standards" in liturgical theology and practice for both my own and other churches in Australia and beyond. I have a concern for the good use of language, for faithful doctrine, for intelligent, spiritually sensitive, pastoral liturgical leadership, for worthy music, for the recovery of symbol, for worship which uses the body and all its senses.

I have realized insufficiently how culturally biased my views have been. Over recent years, through experience of a wide variety of worship (from Quaker to Russian Orthodox), through consultations such as those at Ditchingham in 1994 and Bossey in 1995,[6] and through contact with such projects as the Lutheran World Federation's worship and culture study, I have seen new perspectives, and above all I have come to appreciate *difference*. I love my own (fast disintegrating!) culture, but I have had numerous demonstrations of the authenticity of Christian worship in cultural forms and languages vastly different from my own. Separated from the familiar or the approved, I have nevertheless found myself truly and deeply at worship. For this, I thank the ecumenical movement from the bottom of my heart.

Some of the papers acknowledge a similar influence from the ecumenical and liturgical movements. It is interesting to see how often the reforms of the Second Vatican Council are acknowledged by churches with a long-held anti-Catholic bias! Within my Western tradition, I have welcomed the biblical and theological bases which were then opened up by Roman Catholic scholars; with occasional adjustments, they translate very well into Reformed and Evangelical arguments. The Reformation churches are gathering to themselves again things which they had lost – the accidental fall-out of the historical Reformation. On the other hand, many of us are also debtors to the Orthodox, again for a rich theology and spirituality, for the ability of their "timeless" liturgies to recreate a sense of the sacred, to rediscover the numinous which is largely absent from current Western worship.

But, as I have argued, I am also learning to respect the experience and the theology of the other end of the spectrum, of the Radical Reformation, whose history was certainly neglected in my own theological education (history is taught by the victors!). I find myself at a point of *metanoia*. I stand in awe of the commitment to Bible study, to prayer, to community-formation, to breaking the eucharistic bread together, and to costly social justice, of people whom I have met through the ecumenical movement, and who could not stand in greater contrast to a middle-aged, educated and apparently sophisticated, ordained, white Anglo-Australian male. Amongst their treasures is no Bach, no icons, no books, but Christian *martyria* of the highest order. The miracle (from my former perspective) is that fidelity to the faith can be maintained and lived not only in fixed liturgies, or creeds and ancient hymns, or through an authorized hierarchy and an approved teaching ministry, but also through the continuity and discipleship of a Christian community.

I say this without rejecting my own Reformed and Evangelical inheritance, or my debt to contemporary Roman Catholic scholarship, or my friendship with many Orthodox congregations and their priests; nor am I uncritical of these, or of what I have called the inheritors of the Radical Reformation. In this search for ways for the world's churches, the whole spectrum, to worship together, I want *all* partners to be respected.

Maybe there have to be two ways of worship at any WCC conference, maybe twenty-two – the whole spectrum sensitively and respectfully offered for the oikoumene to "taste and see" how good the Lord is. We may just have to wait. I expect that some illumination will come from other places, perhaps, pray God, from the reception of the work of the Special Commission on the relation of the Orthodox to the WCC.

An emerging *ordo*?

The remaining question is the continuation of our explorations at the Ditchingham and Bossey consultations. What has emerged that is fruitfully common or converging in the areas we addressed there such as the developing notion of an *ordo* (or common structure) of worship, and the whole range of questions about inculturation, and the relation of the church and worship, to culture?

From these perspectives, I think the papers presented here reflect the present situation rather than taking us very far beyond it. Each contributor clearly regards worship as a high point in the life of their church; that is very important, but does not break new ground. It is not even true to say that all agree that the eucharist is the summit of our worship – even here, the churches seem largely to remain where they have been. Few are as genuinely thoughtful and creative in their devising of contemporary worship forms as the (Swiss Reformed) Community of Grandchamp – the issue of the formation of a nurturing *community* is vital. I am concerned that so few are critical of their own forms of worship and their relationship to the church's mission: reading these papers one would hardly suspect the massive decline in church attendance, or the church's public influence, in the West. Modification to traditional forms in order to respond to this crisis seem weak (see the experience of the Church of

Scotland); and, as I noted above, where such things as "seeker services" – a distortion of worship, in my view – are mentioned (the Methodist, Mennonite papers) they are not critiqued. Children are hardly mentioned at all, despite the complex questions faced by many churches today about children in relation to worship.

Nor is there evidence of many churches facing the issues of cultural change (Patrick Lyons, Hans Krech, Kathy Galloway, Cynthia Botha and Thomas Thangaraj are exceptions, but all too brief). Is this not an absolutely *critical* issue for worship? It is worth recalling that the storm over gospel and culture at the WCC's Canberra assembly in 1991 was caused by the reaction to what appeared to be a worship service devised by a Korean woman theologian. I regret that there seems to be no engagement with the philosophical and cultural changes in the West through the collapse of modernism and the inadequacies of post-modernism (see, for example, the literature from Jacques Ellul on the influence of technology; the writers summarized in, say, Marva J. Dawn's recent books). It is disappointing to find little evidence of the struggle for authentic worship translated into present cultural forms as represented in Fr Vincent Donovan, C.S.Sp.'s letter from the Masai, *Christianity Rediscovered*,[7] or the work of the LWF's worship and culture studies, or of Faith and Order's recent work.

We need more confirmation of the elements which regularly appear (though not necessarily in a consistent order) in the worship of the world's churches (note the list in BEM, Eucharist §27, mentioned above). My own view is that Faith and Order must continue its exploration of the possibility of an underlying *ordo* or pattern of worship. I believe this to be a fruitful pursuit, and best done by scholars and pastors representing the churches. It is clearly going to take some time before study of this question becomes widespread, or the literature thus far produced is recognized. It is important that this exploration be regularly reported to WCC member churches, and introduced in a wide variety of other consultations and contexts.

As I have hinted several times, I think the issue of ecumenical worship is far from being the central one concerning the churches at the moment, and therefore the resolution of the key question – the ways in which one church may recognize in another church true or "orthodox" worship (as Dimitrios Passakos defines it, the giving of "right glory" to God) – must await its *kairos*. It will indeed be closely allied with the ecclesiological question of how one church recognizes another church as true church. It will take some time before the members of the WCC will be able to give these important ecumenical problems the serious consideration they deserve.

NOTES

[1] For example, African indigenous churches and Hispanic churches in the US.
[2] See *Worship and Culture in Dialogue*, S. Anita Stauffer ed., LWF Studies, Geneva, Department for Theology and Studies, Lutheran World Federation, 1994; *Christian Worship: Unity in Cultural Diversity*, S. Anita Stauffer ed., LWF Studies, Geneva, Department for Theology and Studies, Lutheran World Federation, 1996; *Baptism, Rites of Passage, and Culture*, S. Anita Stauffer ed., LWF Studies, Geneva, Department for Theology and Studies, Lutheran World Federation, 1998.
[3] Thomas F. Best and Dagmar Heller eds., *So We Believe, So We Pray*, Faith and Order paper no. 117, WCC, 1995, appendix 1, pp.22ff.
[4] See for example *Praying Together*, Nashville, Abingdon, 1988.
[5] Cf. Ernst Käsemann "& co.", for example Käsemann's famous presentation to the fourth Faith and Order world conference in Montreal, 1963.
[6] See note 3 above, and *Eucharistic Worship in Ecumenical Contexts: The Lima Liturgy – and Beyond*, Thomas F. Best and Dagmar Heller eds, WCC, 1998.
[7] Revised, Maryknoll, Orbis Press, 1994.

Christian Perspectives on Worship

PAUL MEYENDORFF

Some time ago, a group of authors together representative of the broad Christian tradition were asked to submit brief papers describing the worship of their respective traditions. They were instructed to address the following questions in their responses:
1) the fundamental understanding of worship in your tradition;
2) the distinctive aspects of worship in your tradition;
3) how your worship tradition has been influenced by the ecumenical and liturgical renewal movements;
4) new developments in worship in your tradition, and their effect on the search for Christian unity.

In my brief analysis of the papers submitted to me for review, I shall follow closely the following outline which was suggested by Faith and Order staff:
1) fundamental understandings of worship;
2) lines of convergence;
3) differences, particularly those which reflect fundamental differences in theology or ecclesiology, and whether these can be overcome;
4) implications for worship in ecumenical contexts;
5) ways in which worship can nurture the unity of the church.

In offering my comments, I make no claim to represent any of the authors who have contributed to this project. Rather I am offering my own personal reaction to what I have read. Of course, I try to speak out of my own Eastern Orthodox tradition, and I am aware that others may have an entirely different "take" on the papers. My only aim, therefore, is to stimulate further discussion. And if I have mis-stated anyone's position, the responsibility is entirely mine.

Fundamental understandings of worship

In reviewing the papers, I was struck by the different ways in which authors articulated their perception of the fundamental meaning and nature of worship. Some began with a "classical" definition of worship as the essential task of the church. Not surprisingly, this was the approach of the Roman Catholic and Orthodox respondents, as well as of the mainstream Reformation churches (that is, Lutheran, Anglican, Methodist...). Somewhat more surprisingly for me, this tack was also taken by the respondent from the Yoido Full Gospel Church in Korea, a Pentecostal community affiliated with the Assemblies of God: "Worship is the essential element of the church. The living church is to worship God; and the church is the community of God's people who have been called by God to worship him." The paper from this community continues by describing a daily cycle of services that would be the envy of any medieval monastery, Eastern or Western! For other traditions, chiefly Western "free" churches, this question seemed to have little resonance, and the respondents found it difficult to articulate an answer, or simply ignored the question altogether.

In every case, however, worship lies at the heart of each tradition. Gathering for worship is understood as essential, even if the understanding of worship (whether indicated explicitly or not), and particularly its content, vary widely. There is a clear sense in *every* response that a community's worship is its primary, if not chief, expression. Whether the respondents articulate this or not, a community's worship is therefore constitutive. The church realizes itself in each local gathering for worship, and no tradition represented in the responses would say that its worship was optional or insignificant. This is just as true of those churches with a clearly defined order of worship and prescribed liturgical texts, as of those whose *ordo* is more spontaneous. It is precisely this centrality of worship which makes it such an important ecumenical question.

Lines of convergence

The latter half of the 20th century has witnessed a remarkable process of convergence in liturgical practice within a broad spectrum of Christian traditions. This is due largely to a liturgical movement tracing its roots to 19th-century Anglican and Roman Catholic scholarship, chiefly in Western Europe, but also to unexpected places such as Russia. This began as a rediscovery of the early sources of Christian worship, such as early church orders (the *Didache,* 2nd century; *Apostolic Tradition,* 3rd century; *Didascalia Apostolorum,* 3rd century; *Apostolic Constitutions,* 4th century, and more), as well as 4th-century commentaries on baptism and the eucharist by such great figures as Cyril of Jerusalem, Ambrose of Milan, John Chrysostom and others. This movement led to a rediscovery of the centrality of baptism and the eucharist in several Christian traditions, both Western (Anglican, Roman Catholic) and Eastern (Eastern Orthodox) already in the late 19th and early 20th centuries. It was this movement that set the stage for further developments, notably Vatican II in the Roman Catholic communion and the document *Baptism, Eucharist and Ministry* (BEM) produced by the Faith and Order Commission of the WCC.

Perhaps the most significant result has been a strong emphasis on the eucharist as the central act of Christian worship. Within the Roman Catholic and Eastern and Oriental Orthodox traditions, this has led to a strong eucharistic revival. In churches where the regular, frequent reception of communion had long been forgotten, now it is being restored. Needless to say, the restoration has taken place very gradually, and the various churches are at very different stages in this process. Among the churches issuing from the Reformation, the process has been similar. Churches which once celebrated the eucharist only quarterly or monthly are moving towards a regular, often weekly celebration. This is evident from the papers submitted for this project, and is a clear indication of the influence of the ecumenical movement on the lives of ordinary Christians.

Accompanying this increased emphasis on regular eucharistic celebration has been a heightened perception of its ecclesiological ramifications. There has been an increasing awareness of the connection between eucharist and *koinonia* (communion). In a conceptual framework of a "eucharistic ecclesiology", the eucharist *makes* the church: in other words, the church is fully realized precisely when it gathers for the celebration of the eucharist in a particular time and in a particular place. And the unity of the worldwide churches exists only as the unity, in communion, of all the various local eucharistic communities. Different churches may use diverse terms in expressing this understanding, but the underlying concept has certainly been a hallmark of the ecumenical movement in recent years. Indeed, it has resulted in several cases of restored communion in North America and Europe within the last decade.

The responses further indicated the large degree of mutual influence, particularly among the Western churches. Much material is shared, including hymns and prayers, as well as a common lectionary. This is made possible largely by the fact that all the Western churches actually share a common (Western) liturgical tradition. Indeed, among the more "liturgical" churches, visitors often cannot tell whether they are in a Roman Catholic, Lutheran, Anglican, Presbyterian or Methodist eucharistic liturgy. That this is so is largely the result of the liturgical movement of the late 19th and early 20th centuries, of Vatican II, and of ecumenical convergence statements such as BEM. In addition, Western liturgical scholarship has discovered the treasures of Western liturgy, and thus many contemporary liturgical books and hymnals contain materials drawn from Western sources. Such resources as WCC assembly worship books are widely available, and contain elements drawn from across the entire spectrum of Christian worship.

The liturgical practices of the Eastern churches, because they derive from quite distinct liturgical families, have been much less influenced by these Western liturgical developments. Western hymns and prayers sound much too foreign to their ears. Nevertheless, these churches have not remained completely isolated. Thus they share with many Western churches a eucharistic revival. In most Eastern churches, although the eucharist is celebrated weekly only a few of the laity actually receive communion. Increasingly, the practice of regular, frequent communion is being restored, thanks to the influence of persons such as Alexander Schmemann, an Orthodox theologian who grew up and lived in the West during the peak of the Roman Catholic liturgical movement in Paris of the 1940s and 1950s and who was influenced by the work of scholars such as Jean Daniélou and Louis Bouyer (who are themselves the "liturgical fathers" of Vatican II). Another example of Western influence on Eastern practice has been, in many churches, the restoration of the centrality of preaching. This has largely been the result of the Protestant stress on the importance, indeed the centrality, of the word.

An important result of these modern developments in liturgical scholarship, liturgical reforms, and cross-fertilization in liturgical practice has been the increased attention paid to various "lost" aspects of worship. I was struck, for example, by the statement that the Jamaican Baptists are rediscovering the importance of the church year. In my personal experience as a member of the worship committee for the WCC assembly in Harare in 1998, I noted the thirst of mainline Protestants for a more holistic worship that engages all the senses through the use of material symbols, symbolic gestures, and other non-verbal means. While the evidence here is largely anecdotal, and the number of essays submitted for this project is limited, nevertheless it manifests a new and notable trend within the Western communions.

Differences

Despite the high degree of convergence described above, significant differences remain. In fact, similarities in worship often conceal significant theological and ecclesiological differences; while divergent liturgical practices can prevent us from seeing fundamental agreements. To give just one example, Roman Catholic ecclesiology and eucharistic theology is far closer to the Eastern Orthodox understanding than, say, to the Presbyterian. Yet, until the mention of the pope in the intercessions, visitors would be hard-pressed to decide if they were attending a Roman Catholic mass or a Presbyterian Lord's supper.

This is one reason why the universal acceptance of a liturgical text such as the Lima liturgy cannot, of itself, bring about the unity of the church. In speaking of differences, therefore, one must approach the topic on several levels: first, liturgical differences themselves and the degree to which these differences create obstacles to unity; and second, fundamental theological and ecclesiological differences which stand in the way of unity, and which cannot be "papered over" by creating a kind of liturgical uniformity. These distinctions, however, are not always clear, and what is a dogmatic issue for some may seem trivial to others.

The role of the eucharist

One clear difference is the role of the eucharist. While in an increasing number of churches the eucharist plays an important, indeed central, role, in others it remains marginalized. And whereas in many churches the eucharistic celebration takes place weekly, in others it is performed monthly (Yoido Full Gospel Church), quarterly (Mennonites, Church of Scotland), or even more rarely. Similarly, though some form of baptism is practised in nearly every tradition, it is optional in some. Underlying these differences, of course, are divergent theologies. If the eucharist is seen primarily as a memorial of a past event, performed chiefly because of the Lord's command – a command that said nothing about frequency – then it makes perfect sense to limit its celebration and to focus on the proclamation of the word. If, however, the eucharist is a remembrance *(anamnesis)* of the once-for-all sacrifice of Christ, making it real, present, and effective for the gathered assembly in every time and place, then its celebration every Lord's day is clearly normative. This is particularly so when the eucharist is understood to be the primary locus of the church, when a local community gathers to *become* the church, the body of Christ.

These differences in eucharistic practice and understanding exist not only among the churches, but also within them. Within several Protestant churches, eucharistic practice varies widely as individual communities have been influenced by the liturgical and ecumenical movements in varying degrees. Even among the Eastern and Oriental Orthodox churches, who claim to have a strong eucharistic ecclesiology, the regular, frequent communion implied by this ecclesiology is far from the rule. The very fact that these differences can exist within communions raises the question as to how divisive these issues, in fact, are. Perhaps what is needed is greater sensitivity on all sides regarding the historical factors which have led to these developments.

The variety of liturgical practices

One sign of the richness of the Christian traditions is the degree to which worship practices become inculturated. One has but to attend a

WCC assembly to see the colour and breadth of Christian life across the world. Here one sees, perhaps for the first time, the worship of the East and West Syrian traditions, as well as the Armenian, Coptic or Ethiopian – many of which trace their history back to the apostolic age, and whose liturgies contain what are perhaps the most ancient Christian liturgical texts. Even the sober liturgies of the Western churches take on more colour as they are transplanted into Africa, Asia or South America.

But this diversity also poses some challenges, particularly in an ecumenical context. Persons attending worship in a tradition different from their own can feel alienated and excluded.

Differences can easily lead to misunderstanding and become issues of contention, as happened so often between East and West during the Middle Ages. In fact, the variety that existed in the early church – and then caused no problems for the unity of the church – did cause problems once the church began to split over Christological and trinitarian issues. Liturgical differences became issues of contention, such as the dispute between the Latins and the Byzantines over the kind of bread (leavened or unleavened) used for the eucharist. Even in our day, one of the sticking points in the discussions between Oriental and Eastern Orthodox churches involves liturgical differences between the two families.

A further difficulty is raised when liturgical worship comes to be used as a vehicle for preserving ethnic heritage. This is often an issue for those churches with the most ancient traditions. A good example here is the Orthodox church in Greece, which still uses the original Greek text of scripture, as well as a hymnography composed in a Byzantine Greek, both of which are all but incomprehensible to the vast majority of believers. This is also the case for Christians who find themselves living in a minority situation, where they often face persecution. And it is particularly the case for Christians living in diaspora, such as the ethnic communities of Eastern Christians in Western countries.

This is not, however, a uniquely Eastern phenomenon. Inculturation has been a typical aspect of Christian worship, and there is no worship which is not, to some extent, culturally conditioned. Western Protestant or Roman Catholic worship is also very much influenced by its cultural setting, though this may not be perceived in a situation of cultural dominance. Lutheran Swedes attending a service in Stockholm are certainly not aware that their particular style of worship reflects a very particular culture; for them it simply expresses who they are. And unless they travel abroad, or attend an ecumenical gathering, they may not even realize that theirs is not the sole form of worship. It is hardly surprising, therefore, that when people migrate to other parts of the world, they cre-

288 Overviews and Analyses

ate communities of Swedish or German Lutherans, or Russian, Greek, Serbian, Romanian, Armenian or Coptic Orthodox, and so on.

In an ecumenical setting, therefore, it should come as no surprise that the patterns and style of worship should follow those of the dominant group. Most often, ecumenical worship is of a Western, Protestant, European/North American stripe. A few "foreign" elements coming from Africa, Asia or Eastern Christianity may be inserted in token fashion. But the basic ethos remains that of the dominant Protestant culture. This explains, at least partially, the discomfort so many Eastern Christians have with "ecumenical worship".

Liturgy and dogma

This is an area that most of the confessional papers submitted for this project do not really address. Nevertheless, to the extent that worship touches on essential Christian teaching, this is an issue that must be dealt with. It is evident that some liturgical traditions, particularly those of the East, tie their worship very closely to dogma. Their services often contain creeds, anathemas or particular dogmatic formulations. The various cycles of feasts, particularly the paschal (centred on the resurrection) and the incarnational (anchored on Christmas), have at their base essential Christological, trinitarian and soteriological truths. These dimensions are emphasized particularly in the Eastern traditions for historical reasons, since the theological debates over such issues took place primarily in the Christian East. Just as the worship of the Eastern churches was strongly coloured by the debates of that era, so the worship of the Western churches, which were less directly affected by these earlier disputes, was coloured by the Reformation debates of the 16th century and beyond. These historical differences are compounded by centuries of mutual isolation, and it is only in the recent past that we have begun to overcome them.

As an example of the difference between the Western and Eastern approaches, one might consider their trinitarian and pneumatological emphases. Western churches tend to use the earlier, and briefer, Apostles' Creed in their worship – if, indeed, they use any creed at all (and some churches explicitly reject the use of any creed!). The Eastern churches tend to use the Nicene Creed, elaborated at Nicea (325) and Constantinople (381), with its much more clearly articulated trinitarian definitions. Prayers of the Eastern churches often contain explicit epicleses invoking the Holy Spirit, thus making clear the active and distinct roles of all three persons of the Trinity. Western prayers generally lack such invocations, or make them exclusively Christ-centred. From the Eastern perspective, Western Christians often seem in danger of falling into a kind of Modalism (as is mentioned, for example, in the paper on Mennonite worship). This suspicion is further heightened when some churches or individuals begin to abandon traditional (and biblical) trinitarian names (Father, Son, Holy Spirit) in favour of functional titles (such as Creator, Redeemer, Sanctifier...). For Eastern Christians in particular, but certainly not for them alone, such innovations represent a departure from the apostolic faith and from tradition. This is not to say these are not important issues, or that they should not be discussed, but when they enter the realm of the *lex orandi* they also touch upon the *lex credendi*, in the oft-repeated 5th-century aphorism of Prosper of Aquitaine.

Worship – objective or subjective?

One further distinction, and a highly significant one, is the differing emphasis in various communions on the "objective" or "subjective" character of worship. In some traditions, the Roman Catholic or Orthodox, for example, subjectivity is considered to be an abuse. For these traditions, liturgical texts and actions follow fixed forms which are not subject to the whims of the celebrant or the congregation. Worship is understood primarily as a corporate act in which the worshipping members are expected "to lay aside all earthly cares" and, as a united body, to meet the risen Lord and to be incorporated into a greater whole: the body of Christ, that is, the church. Roles in the assembly are typically highly structured, with each individual having his or her proper place and function within it. Churches following this approach typically place a strong emphasis on the sacraments, baptism and the eucharist in particular, as well as on festal and sanctoral cycles.

In other traditions, typically coming out of the free-church movements, the emphasis is on the subjective. In the Pentecostal churches, for example, the primary focus is on individual experience. The worship allows for moments of personal testimony. Liturgical texts and hymns, if they are written down, typically stress individual conversion, in an emotional vein. Worship is typically much less structured, and leaders and worship committees are given a free hand to shape it according to the needs of the moment. Roles in the assembly are much more flexible. The Lord's supper tends to be less frequent, and there is little or no emphasis on feasts and calendars.

Of course, reality is more complex than the caricatures depicted above. The line between objective and subjective is not very clear, especially when one speaks to the ordinary person in a typical congregation. Every church (including the Eastern churches!) in the first group has been affected by pietism during the 18th and 19th centuries, and the faithful often experience the worship of their communities primarily as subjective, private and emotional. There is thus often a disjuncture between official church teaching on worship, and how the faithful understand and experience it. And worship in the free churches can often be highly structured, objective and corporate in nature. Most communions find themselves somewhere along a spectrum between worship as subjective and focused on the individual on the one hand and, on the other, worship as objective, with its focus on the community.

The difference between the two approaches is more than just superficial, for it touches on questions of ecclesiology and anthropology. Is the church primarily a collection of individuals who share a basic set of beliefs, or is it a corporate body? Does membership in the church create a new relationship to God, as well as to fellow human beings? And what is the nature of this relationship? Is the human person simply an autonomous creature, or does being truly human imply being in communion with the other? Worship is precisely the medium in which this reality is realized and played out! Thus the classical faith and order issues – ecclesiology, Christian anthropology, soteriology and so on – find their expression in Christian worship.

Possibilities for ecumenical worship

Precisely because worship lies at the heart of every Christian tradition, it has become a neuralgic point in the search for Christian unity. The chief reason for this is that communities find and express their own identity – ecclesial, theological, as well as cultural – primarily through worship. We all feel comfortable and at home within our own traditions, and we all feel some discomfort in stretching our horizons, be they ecclesial, theological or cultural. And it is often precisely in ecumenical worship that the opportunity to broaden our horizons has been given to us. The very notion of "ecumenical worship", however, raises some important theological questions, questions that are all too often ignored.

The essential theological question is ecclesiological. Liturgy is, by definition, an action of the church. It is through the liturgy that the church is realized and manifested. And the central liturgical act of the church is the eucharist, by which the gathered assembly becomes the corporate body of Christ. This ecclesiological perspective, I am well aware, is not shared by all. In some Western churches, worship, including the Lord's supper, does not carry the same ecclesiological weight. It is precisely these different perspectives, often not articulated, that lie behind the controversy over communion or intercommunion, as well as over ecumenical worship in general.

If one accepts the premise that liturgy or worship is an act of the church, then only the church can celebrate "liturgy" in the technical sense of that term, as the common action of the people of God, the church. The World Council of Churches, the various national councils, and other ecumenical organizations are not "the church". The WCC as such, therefore, cannot celebrate the eucharist. This is what lay behind the decision at the 1998 WCC assembly in Harare not to have an official eucharist. The eucharist, and therefore full communion, is possible only in a visibly united church. To celebrate the eucharist together and then to return to our former (and continuing!) divisions would, in the words of St Paul, be a failure to "discern the body" (1 Cor. 11:29).

This last point, however, does raise the question of just how much unity is required before eucharistic communion is possible. Here the answer is not simple. Does it mean full agreement on the essentials of the faith? But just what *is* essential? Does it mean structural unity, with clearly-defined and common decision-making bodies? Does it mean liturgical uniformity? The answers to these questions are as varied as the churches that comprise the contemporary ecumenical movement, and these questions will keep the Faith and Order mavens busy for generations to come. In addition, as we have already mentioned, divisions exist not for theological reasons only, or else the Eastern and Oriental Orthodox churches would have restored communion as soon as agreement was reached on Christology – the one theological issue that divided them.

It would be a mistake, however, to limit the discussion of ecumenical worship to the eucharist. In fact one of the unfortunate consequences of the eucharistic revival in many churches, Western and Eastern alike, has been the reduction of liturgical life to the eucharist alone. The discipline of daily prayer, both communal and private, has diminished greatly and is in danger of being totally abandoned. Yet it is precisely in the daily cycle of prayer that Christians have traditionally offered praise and thanksgiving to God, have interceded for one another, and have sought forgiveness from the sins committed in their daily lives. And since sin is the primary cause of our divisions, is it not here that we ought to begin? One of the strengths of the worship at the WCC assembly in Harare in 1998 was its emphasis on repentance. The primary worship event at the assembly, designed precisely to replace the eucharist, was the vigil of the cross, during which participants followed the cross around the worship space, listened to the proclamation of the passion narrative, and repented of their inability to come together around the Lord's table. The worship during the entire assembly centred on that beautiful carved, African cross, symbol both of brokenness and of hope.

While the goal of full visible unity has yet to be achieved, it is evident that progress towards this goal has indeed been made over the last fifty years. A degree of unity does already exist. It is this recognition of partial unity, and the desire for greater unity, which served as the impetus for the creation of conciliar ecumenism. With the exception of a minority who hold to a rigidly exclusive ecclesiology, most WCC member churches, to a greater or lesser degree, recognize in one another marks of the apostolic faith. Ultimately, what unites us is greater than what divides. Ought not this partial unity that already exists find its expression in common prayer? Is it not possible to celebrate this partial unity and to pray together for the goal of full unity? While there are those who would answer in the negative, a majority would certainly answer these questions in the affirmative.

If one accepts the possibility of ecumenical prayer, then the question arises as to its style and content. Since (with rare exceptions) the responses gathered in this volume did not address this issue, I take the liberty here of proposing some basic guidelines; some of these points I have noted in my earlier contribution to this volume.

1. Common worship must be honest. It must not confuse participants or observers into believing that full visible unity has already been achieved. For many communions, the fact that it has not yet been achieved makes a common eucharist impossible at present.
2. Common worship must not violate the apostolic faith. This may seem self-evident, but many Christians are increasingly disturbed, for example, about the recent tendency in some circles to avoid using the traditional, biblical, trinitarian names, Father, Son and Holy Spirit. The Orthodox, in particular, while they have little difficulty in accepting inclusive language referring to human persons, see a danger of Modalism, or worse, in substituting attributes, such as "Creator, Redeemer, Sanctifier", for names.[1]
3. Common worship must be trinitarian and must be centred on prayer for Christian unity. Visible unity is, or should be, the primary goal of the ecumenical movement. Ecumenical worship should not be used as the platform for various social or political agendas which, however worthy, only divide us further.
4. Common worship must be sensitive to cultural, political and religious sensibilities, as well as to how reports (or images) will be received back home. In this age of the Internet and instant communications, provocative images, often taken out of context or deliberately misinterpreted, can do great harm to the ecumenical movement.

Worship and the unity of the church
Many of the responses here gathered mentioned the high degree of mutual influence and borrowing that has taken place over the last fifty

years. The liturgical reforms of Vatican II, the *Baptism, Eucharist and Ministry* document produced by Faith and Order, the common lectionary used by a number of Western churches – all have left their marks. A greater emphasis on the eucharist is evident in a number of traditions, as well as renewed attention to the church year. And as churches become more open to the practices and experiences of others, they also seem to move closer together. The experience of the Church of South India is a striking example. This church came into being as a union of Anglican, Presbyterian, British Methodist and Congregational churches, just weeks after Indian independence. One of the first priorities of this church was the creation of common forms of worship, particularly for the eucharist. Although slow to be accepted and facing linguistic, cultural and denominational obstacles, these common forms of worship have proven to be the glue that holds this church together and expresses its unity. At the same time, a group originating from the Anglican tradition recently left this church to form the Anglican Church of India: the reasons for this split were largely, though not exclusively, connected with worship and liturgy.

This example, and others like it, raise some serious questions about the relationship between worship and Christian unity. Worship functions very much like language: to take away the French language from the people of France, for example, would be to take away their identity. This language allows them both to communicate with one another, and to distinguish themselves from all those who do not have French as their mother tongue. French speakers feel comfortable around their French-speaking compatriots, and ill-at-ease when surrounded by persons speaking other tongues, or even other French dialects. They naturally see their language (read also: culture, cuisine and so on) as the best; the implication, generally left unsaid, is that all others are inferior. Such an approach is often taken also with respect to the liturgy, and this is true whether one is Coptic Orthodox, high-church Anglican, Lutheran, Pentecostal or Quaker.

Does this imply that unity is possible only if the churches adopt a common form of worship? The historical evidence is ambiguous. Certainly the church has never known absolute uniformity. Recent biblical scholarship has shown that pluriformity existed even in the apostolic church. But the liturgical families which arose in the early centuries (that is, Rome, Alexandria, Antioch, Edessa, and later Constantinople) did create a strong degree of uniformity within geographical areas, and this uniformity was important in maintaining ecclesial unity. The basic historical pattern, then, seems to be uniformity within a geographical region and variety among the regions. As the churches split over Christological issues in the 5th-6th centuries, differences in liturgical practice came to be seen as evidence of difference in faith as well. Byzantines condemned the Latins for using unleavened bread in the eucharist, anabaptists condemned paedo-baptists for baptizing children... The style and content of one's worship, therefore, became a confessional label.

Until the modern period churches remained for the most part territorial; this is true for the East as for the West. The imperial Roman church survived in the Byzantine empire until the latter's fall in 1453, and in the Russian empire until 1917. In the West, the imperial Roman church survived to some extent in Roman Catholicism, but also in the state churches of Western Europe. In recent centuries, however, the situation has grown much more confused with the gradual disestablishment of state churches and the massive migrations of people, particularly to the Americas. The American situation is particularly striking, with churches of different tradition on nearly every street corner. Here, living side by side, one finds Copts, Lutherans, Eastern Orthodox, Reformed, Armenians, Swedenborgians, Syrian Orthodox, Roman Catholics, Quakers – all with their distinct worship practices. In much of the rest of the world, a pluralistic model has also emerged as the result of missionary efforts, chiefly of Western churches. As a result, there is no more liturgical uniformity within geographical areas, as there was throughout much of Christian history.

This raises some serious questions. For a majority of Christian traditions, their worship life is the glue that holds them together. This is as true of the Anglican communion, with its *Book of Common Prayer*, as of the Eastern Orthodox churches, with their common *Typikon* and service books, or the Roman Catholics, with their centrally regulated liturgical texts. Even those traditions without standard liturgical structures or texts have a particularly ethos which clearly defines them. So, in the search for visible unity, is liturgical unity necessary – if not at the global, then on the local and regional level? Is not a local church an entity that speaks a particular "language" or "dialect"? It is certainly true, in the words of St Paul, that in the church there is "neither Jew nor Greek" (Gal. 3:28), that all cultures are welcome. But what are the implications of this radical claim for the worship life of the churches?

No doubt, the present diversity has made possible a great amount of cross-fertilization. Christians today are more likely to have been exposed to people of other traditions, and to see them in a less negative perspective. Especially among Western Protestant churches, recent years have brought about remarkable convergence and serious attempts at unity, including a shared eucharist and a shared ministry among a number of churches. From a liturgical perspective, this is hardly surprising, as these churches belong to the same liturgical family and therefore speak much the same "language". One could say the same about reunion attempts between the Eastern churches of the Chalcedonian (Eastern Orthodox) and the pre-Chalcedonian (Oriental Orthodox) families. These churches, too, though they belong to different liturgical families, nevertheless share the same ethos. It is likely that we will see a restoration of communion between these churches in the coming years.

But there has been less success in bridging the gap between East and West. Part of the reason, I would argue, has been a kind of Western hegemony in the conciliar ecumenical movement. The agenda of the WCC (and most national councils of churches) has been driven largely by Western concerns and issues. This problem has been raised increasingly vocally by the Orthodox (both Eastern and Oriental), and is on the agenda of the Special Commission established at the Harare assembly. This Western hegemony is also evident in the worship conducted at WCC meetings. The structure and content of ecumenical worship services is typically Western and Protestant, reflecting the majority membership of these churches. Such an approach clearly fails to increase mutual understanding, as Western Christians are exposed to the Eastern ethos only in token fashion, often through the insertion of an Eastern element (such as the *Trisagion*) into what is essentially a generic Western service. As a result, Eastern Christians attending ecumenical meetings often feel alienated. But it must also be stated that a number of Western Christians are similarly uncomfortable with the bland, generic style of much ecumenical worship.

The first and obvious solution is to achieve greater variety in ecumenical worship by incorporating not only isolated elements, but also the structure and content, of Eastern worship, at least on occasion. This can pose quite a challenge, as Eastern worship typically engages all the senses and requires a particular setting, both architectural and artistic. The space for worship is of critical importance for Eastern Christians, and the worship spaces typically available at ecumenical gatherings are less than optimal. On the other hand, the fact that Eastern liturgy is typically conducted in ancient languages – Greek, Old Slavonic, Ge'ez, Syriac, and so on – is less of an obstacle today, since 20th-century migrations have led to an increased presence of these communities in the West, and thus made available modern translations of liturgical texts, particularly into English.

Ideally, meetings could be held at a site which includes a church from a particular tradition. In that way, participants could immerse themselves for a time in that tradition, and thus gain a greater knowledge and appreciation of it. Just as the best way to learn a foreign language and culture is through an immersion experience, so too with worship and liturgy. Christians can achieve greater unity only by gaining greater knowledge of one another. This is true because worship lies at the heart of every ecclesial body and is, to great extent, the bearer of the tradition. Whether at the international, regional, national or local level, Christians can learn about one another by attending and, to the extent possible, participating in one another's worship. Needless to say, respect for each other demands that guests observe "the rules of the house" and not impose their own presuppositions and rules.[2] Not violating one's own conscience also means not violating the conscience of the other.

***

So far, ecumenical discussion has centred primarily on issues of dogma. Indeed, remarkable progress has been made in this area, and few would argue that agreement in essential elements of the faith is not important. But churches do not live by dogma alone. The daily, ongoing life of a community and of individual Christians depends largely on shared experiences and activities. Here, worship holds primacy of honour. Through worship, the assembly realizes itself as the body of Christ. Through worship, individuals affirm their own membership and participation in this corporate body. It is in worship that God is praised (this is, after all the meaning of the word), that dogma is transmitted, that scripture is read, that the word is proclaimed through preaching, that Christians are taught how to live. The very essence of Christian living is, therefore, the worship of God the Father, through the Son, in the Holy Spirit. And, of course, our worship itself calls us all to unity: Jesus himself prays that we may be one (cf. John 17:20-21), as the Trinity is united in the Godhead.

The challenge is great. In fact, it may be more difficult than reaching agreement on technical, dogmatic definitions which, though necessary, are one step removed from the actual life and experience of Christians. Worship touches the very heart of the self-identity of any given group. In worship, individual Christians, as well as Christian communities, celebrate their intimate relationship with God and with one another. These relationships are developed within the life of local communities, as well as within regional, national or global communions. The healing of Christian divisions, therefore, requires not just theological agreement, but the healing of broken relationships – or, in many cases, the creating of new relationships. The first step is simply getting to know one another as we really are; and the most direct way in which this can be accomplished is by experiencing one another's worship. This requires great sensitivity in order to avoid offending one another. It requires respect for one another's traditions. It requires humility and a non-judgmental attitude, so that we do not impose our own pre-conceived views on the other.

This proposal may seem much too modest, particularly for those churches, primarily Western Protestant communions, which have gone far beyond this in their recent union agreements. Yet these churches in fact represent only a small minority of Christians worldwide. For most Christians, visible unity remains an abstract dream. Even many churches that participate in the conciliar ecumenical movement – not to mention the many churches that do not – in fact continue to live in virtual isolation. This is the case in most areas of the world outside North America and Western Europe, where Roman Catholics, Eastern Orthodox, Evangelicals, Oriental Orthodox, Pentecostals live in situations of either mutual ignorance or outright hostility. In areas such as this the proposal is not too timid, but extremely daring and, indeed, perhaps impossible. But, as we read in the gospel, what is impossible for us is possible for God (Matt. 19:26).

NOTES

[1] As noted in my earlier paper in this volume, in the traditional languages of most Orthodox, including Greek and Slavic, different words are used to refer to humanity on the one hand, and male or female individuals on the other. As a result, when the Orthodox hear the discussion about inclusive language they understand it as referring exclusively to trinitarian names. Hence the condemnation of "the heresy of inclusive language" in Harare by a delegate of the Russian Orthodox Church.

[2] This applies particularly, though not exclusively, to questions of communion and "intercommunion".

Leitourgia – the "Work" of the People and the Unity of God's People

JIM PUGLISI, SA

The project undertaken by the Faith and Order Commission to look more deeply at worship in the churches, and the role that worship has played in the ecumenical movement, is a challenging and ambitious one. It is challenging because of the diverse ways in which the Christian churches understand the meaning of worship, and ambitious because it attempts to bring this rich diversity together in a synthesis that might be able to be presented to the churches for further reflection and possible action. I believe that after the long process which produced the convergence document on *Baptism, Eucharist and Ministry* – which, in turn, has influenced many churches in their thinking and practice – the time is ripe for moving forward together on the path to Christian unity. Surely worship will be an important aspect of that moving forward.

Our analysis of the papers submitted to us for review will consider the following points: the understanding of "worship" according to the different traditions; the relationship between theory and practice in the various traditions; points of convergence and divergence in the understanding of the relation of worship to the question of Christian unity; the liturgy as theological locus – the relationship between scripture, worship and ethics; elements held in common; and, finally, where do we go from here? What is the work of the people in the service of the unity of the people of God?

It is obvious that in such a review and reflection as this, one must make choices and establish criteria for analysis. I would like to lay out briefly those which have influenced my reflection, so that the reader will have a frame of reference for understanding what follows.

In his book *Liturgical Literacy*, Dennis Smolarski defined worship as follows:

> ...the expression of our love, reverence, honour, and adoration of a good and gracious God through various communal and private activities. In general, in Christian tradition, the worshipping assembly prays to God (the Father), through Christ, empowered by (or in the unity of) the Spirit of God... Expressions of public worship are not normally directed to Christ, and, in fact, the

council of Hippo in 393 forbade the direct addressing of Christ in public prayer.[1]

I begin with this definition of "worship" because, in the past, that has been the term most used to speak of the cultic action of the Christian assembly when describing the relationship of the faithful to God. This definition reflects the trinitarian nature of the activity of the Godhead, as well as the relationship of the people to God. However for at least the past two centuries another word, liturgy, has been used with increasing frequency to designate this central aspect of the Christian mystery. In the following definition of liturgy we can see the same elements as cited above, with a more precise articulation between them:

> The liturgy can be defined also from the angle of encounter between the faithful and God. This implies that through the church's worship the faithful both as a body and as individual members enter into the presence of the triune God. Such encounter is personal on the part of the faithful as well as on the part of God. In the liturgy the church offers worship to the Father, through Jesus Christ, in the unity of the Holy Spirit... The Father is the origin and hence the end of all creation and salvation; Jesus Christ is the sacrament who reveals the Father and the mediator who reconciles humankind with God; the Holy Spirit is the power whereby Christ lifts up the fallen and leads them to the Father...

Thus the definition of the liturgy as encounter with God involves the ad extra working of the Trinity in salvation history. The trinitarian dimension is expressed by the liturgy through its basic components of anamnesis and epiclesis, whereby the different roles of the three persons are recalled and their saving presence is invoked.[2]

The end purpose of this "work of the people" is to give glory to God. St Paul reminds the Romans of this when he writes, "May the God of steadfastness and encouragement grant you to live in harmony with one another, in accordance with Christ Jesus, so that together you may with one voice glorify the God and Father of our Lord Jesus Christ."[3] Obviously, being Christian means being in the world in a certain way. As members of the mystical body of Christ, we need to have the same mind as Jesus Christ and therefore live in the world as he lived in the world, namely directing all to the Father. Hence as long as Christians live in the world in a condition of division, they do not render that witness that Jesus would have his followers give. On the eve of his passion, Jesus prayed for the unity of his followers "so that the world might believe".[4] In this unity they glorify the Father as Christ has glorified God's name and shown forth the depth of God's love for creation. In order for Christian liturgy to be true doxology, therefore, it needs to witness to the unity of God's people. And this brings us to the heart of the ecumenical issue which the Faith and Order Commission has asked me to reflect upon.

The issues of faith and order are the issues at the heart of the search for Christian unity. It will not be sufficient for Christians simply to collaborate with one another; if they are to be obedient to the will of Jesus, they must indeed be truly united to one another. This is why I have opted to use the word "liturgy", rather than "worship", to express the work of the people in communion with the desire and will of Christ to render glory to God. With this in mind, let us now turn our attention to the papers I have been asked to review.[5]

The understanding of worship/liturgy according to the different traditions

It is amazing to see that there is an overwhelming consistency in the understanding of worship among the various traditions represented in the papers I have reviewed. This is all the more remarkable given that they come not only from Orthodox/Roman Catholic but also from Protestant, Pentecostal and United church traditions, as well as from the ecumenical context.

There appears to be general agreement in seeing a relationship between worship and service. For example, "Worship is... God's redeeming act in Christ through the Spirit. At the same time, it is the way the community understands its nature and its purpose in the world" (Orthodox). "Worship is first of all service of God through the means of word and sacrament in the communion of saints. ... The community is thus prepared for acceptance, prayer and praise as well as for loving deeds in the world" (Lutheran). "Worship and service are essentially one. Through service expectation, encounter and response overflow to penetrate all aspects of a community's daily life, and devotion to God extends into commitment to serve. Therefore, the worshipping and serving community become one body..." (Armenian Orthodox). Forms of worship may change, but "what remains constant is our desire to serve God in Christ Jesus empowered by the Holy Spirit, the One God who is over all, through all, and in all" (Mennonite).

Theologically speaking, all of the traditions speak of worship as being "the heart of Christianity" (Armenian) and giving access to the life of the Trinity (Lutheran, Catholic, Orthodox), as well as granting "fellowship with the living God" (Yoido). This dimension represents an important point of convergence. In the past, the liturgies of many traditions were highly Christocentric, often leaving the trinitarian dimension in obscurity. What biblical, patristic and liturgical scholarship has shown is that fully Christian prayer is always trinitarian, being addressed to

God through Jesus Christ in the power of the Holy Spirit. The studies considered here represent a very strong convergence on this point, and hence a fundamental building block towards the re-establishment of a common liturgical tradition.

This does not mean a monolithic tradition, rather a convergence among traditions which all pray in some way with the same theological mind-set. Diversity is possible, and indeed illustrated by the many instances of eucharistic prayers that have come down to us through the centuries. These represent a rich source of differing ways to present a eucharistic theology which is both diverse, and recognized as authentically expressing the faith of the church through the ages. The same is true not only for eucharistic prayers but also for other prayer forms within the Christian tradition, such as the liturgy of the hours, divine office or lauds, vespers and so on; and these prayer forms can be seen to represent this trinitarian understanding of prayer. Here it should be noted that the annual celebration of the Week of Prayer for Christian Unity represents a long-standing tradition of ecumenical prayer.

Lastly, and more specifically in relation to ecumenical worship, the paper by Dagmar Heller attempts to put into relief the progress in Faith and Order in developing ecumenical instances of prayer. An important distinction is made between "ecumenical worship" and "confessional worship" in order to arrive at two possibilities:

> Either a worship service is held according to the liturgical order of one of the traditions represented, and everyone participates; or an attempt is made to bring the various traditions together by combining different liturgical elements, so that everyone can find something of his or her own in the resulting worship service.

What is finally suggested, after a survey of past worship in an ecumenical setting, is finding those elements which are common to many traditions and then structuring a worship service using these elements. This may be the solution for non-eucharistic liturgies, but probably will not be accepted for a eucharistic celebration. Personally I feel that nothing can substitute for an eventual mutual recognition of the eucharistic celebration of other churches, whereby we see the "faith of the church through the ages" present and celebrated in their liturgies. This would be in keeping with the practice of the "catholica", that is, the united church of the first millennium. Underlying this approach is a profound ecclesiology which will take into consideration the unicity of the catholic faith, and the legitimate diversity of the same. What is understood as underlying this ecclesiology is a real, profound and continual exchange between churches, a synodality that spreads from local situations to regions, nations and beyond. This type of ecclesiology will not only be concerned with liturgical matters but with matters of the very unity of the church of Christ, all the while respecting the diversity within the same body because all will have "put on the mind of Christ".[6]

The relationship between theory and practice in the various traditions

My second set of observations touches upon the relationship between the various accounts given here of worship, and how the respective churches actually live the reality of their worship. This is what I would like to call the "reality check": every theory needs to be tested against the background of actual practice, to verify the theory itself. While we are not talking about scientific experiments, we are talking about the possibility of conflict of interpretation, intellectual dissonance and an eventual discontinuity between word and deed. It is this type of situation which causes difficulty in the ecumenical dialogue and the search for Christian unity.

We have seen that churches will make statements in ecumenical dialogues – and even agreed statements – that are, at times, difficult to verify in their actual day-to-day living in the world. Another situation may exist: a church may have a particular theology in its confessional documents but practice its faith in a way which is different from the declared theological position – or vice versa, with the practice of a church expressing a reality different, or far beyond, its theological position. What I have discovered in my research on ordained ministry is that, in many cases, there is a higher degree of convergence on the level of practice than on the level of theory or theology.[7] Here we are obviously in the context of the famous dictum *lex orandi, lex credendi*.[8]

The majority of the papers demonstrate that there has been a cross-fertilization in the field of liturgical revision, and especially in practice. The sample of papers which I have surveyed has emphasized the Orthodox/Catholic tradition (to use a stereotype from the past!). In spite of this, the other traditions – which tend to be on the free church end of the spectrum – show a high level of convergence in the areas of forms of worship and liturgical principles.

First, there is the overwhelming affirmation of the use of the scriptures as a central point of all worship. Hence the word of God is central in any liturgical form of prayer. We have already noted the accent placed on the centrality of the life-giving Trinity on the context of worship. It is likewise interesting that the Oriental churches seek to explain how this trinitarian dimension of the worship is played out in the aspect of witnessing and service to the world. The Armenian Orthodox paper says it most clearly: "Worship and service are essentially one... the worshipping and serving community becomes one body (1 Cor. 12:12ff.) as branches of a living tree (John 15:1ff.)". Both the Mennonite paper and the Church of South India paper speak of the role the liturgy plays in witnessing to the culture in which they live, and in the fundamental task of evangelism. The Catholic paper says the same, in a more technical or theological way, when it talks about the two dimensions of the liturgy (the vertical/horizontal and transcendent/immanent). It speaks of "... the liturgy's transcendent yet participatory character", and how the "commemoration of the mystery of Christ in all its aspects, historical and eschatological, [is brought] into greater prominence". We see the dynamic impact of this as the liturgy enters into dialogue with the various cultures where the church finds itself.

While the relationship between liturgy and justice has not been specifically mentioned, this has been a growing concern among the churches. The awareness of celebrating the eucharist in a world where grave injustices reign has pricked the consciousness of many Christians who attempt to see that their liturgical life flows over into the world, where the "spirit of the beatitudes" will condemn the "spirit of the world". This dimension is likewise indicated in *Baptism, Eucharist and Ministry* when it speaks about the relationship of the eucharist to the world (Eucharist, §§19-21).

Lastly, the influence of the charismatic renewal has been mentioned (Yoido, Mennonite) as an important element in the renewal of these churches' worship, helping it to conform more to their task in the world. In short, all of the churches need to make a reality check to be sure of the integrity of their witness to the world, and to escape from the pitfall of a narcissistic closing in on themselves. This will enable the principal goal entrusted to the church to go forward, namely proclaiming the gospel to the world by being ambassadors of God's reconciliation.

Worship and Christian unity: points of convergence and divergence

The central point of convergence seems to be that all of the churches see the liturgy as an essential part of what it means to be church. If there is an awareness on this level then it means that there can also be an awareness that, although we might do things differently, we are still all striving to be the body of Christ in the world – and that in God's house there are many mansions. This means that we can be one, and indeed, we need to be one if we are to fulfill that mission entrusted to us as the church of God.

Further convergence is seen in the fact that certain elements have become (or are becoming) the central elements of the churches' worship life: I refer to the centrality of the word of God, the eucharist as the heart of Christian worship, a trinitarian form of praying and a greater place (in theology and in the life of the churches) given to the Holy Spirit, and a clearer relationship between personal piety and the liturgical life of the community. These elements, I believe, are leading to an awareness that it is in and through authentic prayer that we are being transformed into that unity that God wants. In other words, each of our churches is learning, in obedience to the Spirit, how to empty itself that it might learn how to be one in the Spirit in accordance with the will of Christ. The Groupe des Dombes, in its document *For the Conversion of the Churches*, talks about the conversion which needs to take place on three different levels in the life of the churches[9] – the most difficult level being the structural level. This means that, due to the convergence taking place on the theological level, all of our churches will need to make changes in the way they do things and the way in which they are in the world.

The statement from the Groupe des Dombes also speaks about three types of conversion which correspond to three identities: Christian, ecclesial and confessional. At first hearing we might find the correlation "identity-conversion" a bit odd; but in reality they are opposite sides of the same coin. What makes this discovery so relevant is the fact that the social sciences are used as an aid for theologizing, and hence enable a discovery of new relationships.

Identity is seen as a "living reality: it is a concrete expression of continuity and change".[10] Identity refers back to a history which precedes us; it makes us what we are, in advance of ourselves. This identity is like a "construction" or a "pilgrimage" in that it is always building on a foundation, moving from one reality to another reality, and hence combines a stable, unchangeable part with new elements. Therefore our identity is progressively being built, while respecting its essential core. Anthropology and sociology teach us that there is a collective identity as well. The Groupe des Dombes expresses its conviction that "conversion is an essential constituent of an identity which seeks to remain alive and, quite plainly, faithful to itself".[11] This is the link which can be proposed between the two realities of identity and conversion. I would use the expression of the philosopher Gabriel Marcel, who talks about "creative fidelity" being at the heart of this dynamic.

We can briefly describe the distinctions made by the document in this way: at the heart of each of the three identities (Christian, ecclesial and confessional) is a corresponding conversion which gives each identity its foundation and form.

Christian identity consists in the mystery of "God's fatherly initiative in communicating himself to human beings by sending his Son Jesus

Christ and bestowing his Holy Spirit".[12] The conversion that gives foundation and form is the appropriation by faith, and implementation, of that mystery which baptism inaugurates and celebrates.[13]

Ecclesial identity means that the church is the body of Christ, where "by reason of the gift of the Spirit... the irreversible and unfailing presence of the gift God has given of himself to human beings in Jesus Christ"[14] is made manifest. "Ecclesial conversion is the constant effort of the church community as such to strive towards its Christian identity";[15] for example, *ecclesia semper reformanda*. Ecclesial identity therefore is at the service of Christian identity.[16]

The third element in this triad is confessional identity, which relates to the particular form and mode each church has of confessing its faith. Conversion at this level is the most difficult. Hence

> Confessional conversion is first of all conversion to the God of Jesus Christ and consequently a fraternal reconciliation among the churches as they seek full communion and full mutual ecclesial recognition – not to the detriment of confessional identity, but for purification and deepening in line with the gospel.[17]

I have chosen the document by the Groupe des Dombes to illustrate the thesis that, while the dialogue process is important and has produced some significant, clarifying statements and agreements, these words alone are insufficient for achieving Christian unity. What is needed is a radical conversion – a change in the way of thinking and acting towards oneself and towards the other. Unless changes are made in our structures, in our modes of thinking, in our witnessing, we can produce all the words and statements we want but we will not arrive at our goal of Christian unity!

In the papers surveyed, much liturgical reform has been noted in almost all of the churches. On this level, too, there has been much cross-fertilization and sharing of experiences. For example, the Mennonite paper by Rebecca Slough identified five influences on Mennonite worship:

> (1) traditional patterns of the past with heavy emphasis on preaching; (2) liturgical renewal opened by the Second Vatican Council; (3) contemporary praise and worship styles that reflect evangelical revivalism in America as well as the charismatic movement; (4) a "church growth" and evangelism emphasis characterized by "seeker" services; (5) blended worship that seeks to integrate so-called "liturgical" and "non-liturgical" styles into coherent practice.

Not all of the churches spoke to the ecumenical dimension of their worship. Judging from those that did, it was apparent that this question was understood differently by different churches. The Lutheran paper talks about the relationship between engagement in the ecumenical movement and the impact this has had on its liturgy:

> This [enrichment of its worship] is reflected amongst other things in a new diversity in prayer and gesture, in the restoration of the eucharistic prayer in the celebration of the Lord's supper, in the inclusion of the creation in the composition of worship as such. Traditionally, Lutheran worship is largely Christocentric in character. Nowadays, through the influence of the ecumenical fellowship and also movements of a charismatic nature, the confession of God the Creator and God the Holy Spirit comes much more clearly to expression as well and has gained new creative force.

With the Lutheran position it is interesting to note that other instances of worship have been discovered and have been well received, such as the service for the sick. While such forms of worship are not often called sacraments, there is a recognition that worship goes beyond the two sacraments of Christ (baptism and eucharist) to other key moments in the life of the community such as forgiveness, healing, establishing members in the service of the church, and others (see also Mennonite, Yoido, Catholic).

Divergence appears in relationship to the admission to the eucharist, rather than on how the eucharist is celebrated or its liturgical shape. It is obviously here that work still has to be done. My personal reflection is that there is a pressing need for significant work which will make explicit the ecclesiologies underlying our diverse forms of worship. It is clear from the various arguments for and against intercommunion that there is here a fundamental ecclesiological issue relating to worship in general and the eucharist in particular. It was suggested in the Catholic paper that inter-ecclesial marriages are a valid place for carrying out more reflection along this line. This brings me to my next point.

The liturgy as theological locus – the relationship between scripture, worship and ethics

While the mutual relationship between the three realities of scripture, worship and ethics was not made explicit, it seems to me that this is an implicit theme underlying the positions taken in the various papers here. In his research, Louis-Marie Chauvet has presented much grist for the mill of our thinking about this triad.[18] The papers surveyed have spoken about the importance of the word and its centrality for worship, as well as the sacramental or mystery dimension of liturgy and the necessity of a coherent Christian witness in the world today. When these were spoken about, they were most often mentioned in the context of the urgent need for a new evangelism by the churches. It is my supposition that the more the churches use the liturgy as a locus of theological reflection, the more we will converge on the path to Christian unity. The fact that Faith and Order has, practically from the beginning, been including reflections on worship as part of its method is important here. I remember talking to some members of the Faith and Order Commission when it was beginning its work on confessing the apostolic faith today. The creeds as the form of confession were being looked at. I noted that it was important to realize that it was not the creeds that the early church used on a weekly basis to confess its faith, but rather the eucharistic anaphora – this was the confession of faith par excellence of the worshipping church.

Likewise we note with pleasure that, from the beginning, liturgical or worship themes have been an intimate part of the work of Faith and Order. *Baptism, Eucharist and Ministry* represents a long journey initiated at the start of the last century. The importance of this document is reflected in the fact that it appears as "a given" in the stances on worship taken in the papers surveyed here. The "ecumenical" papers reflect on the use of worship at key meetings as a way of accompanying the work of the WCC and Faith and Order. When worship is used in theological reflection, it needs to be taken together with two other poles – scripture and ethics – so that a certain "checks and balances" system is built in. For any worship which does not relate to the word of God does not flow from the depths of the wellspring of our faith, and can be perverted or misused or manipulated. Likewise, any worship that does not find itself relating to how the Christian community actually lives in the world is not authentic. This is why I see the liturgy as a real focus for our ecumenical work and theological reflection.

Elements held in common

The common elements for ecumenical worship have been summarized clearly in the list given in the ecumenical paper prepared by Dagmar Heller. It seems to me, however, that we would need to go beyond creating ecumenical worship which might or might not look like worship in one or another of the traditions. The anthropologist Margaret Mead once said that good worship is made up of "a lot of the old and a little of the new". This is obviously due to the fact that if we cannot find ourselves within the form of worship, then it will be impossible for us to let go of the earthly and be caught up in the contemplation of the divine mysteries, to be able to see the daily realities that surround us in a different light and to find meaning in them.

Many of these papers have presented elements of their liturgies, and we can rightfully say that there are indeed many common elements. The difficulty arises from the fact that not all were speaking about the same realities. In the Orthodox position papers the eucharistic liturgy was often used as the paradigm for worship – which would be natural for an Orthodox. With the exception of some papers (including the Yoido and Mennonite), it seems that the eucharist or Lord's supper or communion is – or is becoming – a central part of the churches' weekly worship tradition. This trend obviously reflects the recommendations of *Baptism, Eucharist and Ministry* for a more regular celebration of the eucharist. However reasons are not always given for the frequent, or infrequent, celebration of the eucharist. If one aim of the movement for Christian unity is the celebration of a common eucharist, one could indeed ask that we take seriously the disparity in practice found here.

For all of the traditions represented in these papers, the Bible or word of God figures as a central part of the worship experience of the churches. This factor is a positive one. One of the principal aspects of rediscovering our unity in Christ begins from our being gathered together by his word, and discovering together that our ecclesial lives are intertwined in the very history or story of Christ.

Almost all of the positions presented here show an awareness of the need to celebrate God's loving mercy, and the gift of repentance and admission of our sinfulness. This is another common element in our worship practices. In addition, rendering praise to God plays an important role in the liturgical traditions represented. Several have likewise mentioned sanctification as an important part of the church's liturgical life. After the recent Catholic-Lutheran agreement on justification, we need to understand that when we speak of sanctification in one tradition the corresponding reality in the Protestant tradition is expressed with the term "justification", or by "deification" in the Orthodox tradition. Hence we are speaking about the same reality by using a different vocabulary. I am personally encouraged by the level of agreement found in the common elements noted by each of the traditions.

Where do we go from here? The "work" of the people in the service of the unity of God's people

From a solid base we can progress together on the path of Christian unity – but with a caveat. The warning flag needs to be raised over the fact that we have seen a coalescing at two poles: one which might be identified as a more traditional, mainline form of worship, while the other is around the free or charismatic pole. We can therefore ask whether there is a possibility to reconcile these two tendencies. It must be noted, however, that on the whole the more Pentecostal, free church traditions seem to be growing at a very rapid pace while mainline churches are declining. This trend should tell the churches something about the way they worship, and where people find meaning in their prayer life. The risk here is that if we are not careful we can find ourselves at odds, pitting tradition against tradition. This factor could cause greater division among churches.

Another factor is that we need to be able to do something about the issue of the eucharist, from its celebration to its sharing. This means that deeper ecclesiological studies (both theoretical and practical) need to be carried out, to see exactly how the churches understand what they do when they celebrate the eucharist; what they do when they invite persons to – or exclude them from – its reception; and lastly, what would happen if we recognized the eucharist of another church as having all the elements that our church believes are required by the apostolic faith.

What might become a great risk here is that what was called at the second European ecumenical assembly at Graz (1997) "an ecumenism of the people" should be considered as being in opposition to an "official" ecumenism, that is, an ecumenism of the theologians and ecclesiastics alone. The Spirit will move where, and when, and how the Spirit desires. The churches need to be attentive to this reality, not only in theory but also in practice. This means that we need to move towards greater, and better, communication of the results of the dialogues, as well as a more profound liturgical catechesis in each of the churches, so that our faithful will understand the necessity of common prayer, of knowing about other Christian traditions besides their own. What goes hand in hand with this is that each ecclesial tradition needs to verify in its own life the relationship of theory to practice (or, if you prefer, of orthodoxy to orthopraxis). This will be the real litmus test of whether or not the work of the people in praising God with their lips is also the work of the people in glorifying God through their witness to being God's one people.

NOTES

[1] D. C. Smolarski, *Liturgical Literacy: From Anamnesis to Worship*, Mahwah NY, Paulist, 1990, pp.205f.
[2] A. J. Chupungco, "A Definition of Liturgy", in *Handbook for Liturgical Studies, vol. 1: Introduction to the Liturgy*, A. J. Chupungco ed., Collegeville, Liturgical Press, 1997, pp.6f,8; see also P.-M. Gy, "Liturgie", in J. Y. Lacoste ed., *Dictionnaire critique de theologie*, Paris, Presses universitaires de France, 1998, pp.662f.
[3] Rom. 15:5f.
[4] Cf. John 17:1-24.
[5] The 11 papers I have been asked to review are those by Nareg Alemezian, Dagmar Heller, Aphrem Karim, Hans Krech, Abraham Kuruvilla, Young-Hun Lee, Patrick Lyons, Dimitrios Passakos, Corinna Schmidt, Rebecca Slough, Thomas Thangaraj.
[6] J.-M. A. Tillard, *Church of Churches: The Ecclesiology of Communion*, Collegeville, Liturgical Press, 1987, especially chapters 2 and 3; see also his *L'Eglise locale. Eccle-*

siologie de communion et catholicité, Cogitatio Fidei, 191, Paris, Cerf, 1995, especially part 3.

[7] See J. F. Puglisi, S.A., *The Process of Admission to Ordained Ministry: A Comparative Study*, 4 vol, Collegeville, Liturgical Press, 1996-2000.

[8] See the work of G. Wainwright, *Doxology: The Praise of God in Worship, Doctrine and Life. A Systematic Theology*, London/New York, Epworth Press/Oxford UP, 1980, in which the Methodist exegete and liturgist has studied the relationship between the these two principles and their application to liturgical theology with this observations: "They [Catholicism and Protestantism] tend to differ on the question of which of the two, doctrine or worship, should set the pace, and they differ profoundly on the question of whether either or both – the church's worship or its doctrine – may fall into error" (p.252). This critical analysis does not impede the same author from seeing a convergence towards an authentic liturgical tradition in the revisions that Protestant churches have made in their worship services; cf. G. Wainwright, "The Understanding of Liturgy in Light of Its History", in C. Jones, G. Wainwright and E. Yarnold eds, *The Study of Liturgy*, London, SPCK, 1978, p.506. See also the works of P. De Clerck, "'Lex orandi, lex credendi': The Original Sense and Historical Avatars of an Equivocal Adage", *Studia Liturgica* 24, 2, 1994, pp.178-200, and K. W. Irwin, *Context and Text: Method in Liturgical Theology,* Collegeville, Liturgical Press, 1994, pp.265-310, and the recent work of D.N. Power, *Sacrament: The Language of God's Giving*, New York, Crossroad, 1999, who takes an innovative look at the same issues from the point of view of the human sciences and especially linguistics.

[9] Groupe des Dombes, *Pour la conversion des Églises*, Paris, Centurion, 1991; English translation, *For the Conversion of the Churches*, WCC, 1993.

[10] *Ibid.*, §10.

[11] *Ibid.*, §14.

[12] *Ibid.*, §17.

[13] Cf. *ibid.*, §19.

[14] *Ibid.*, §22.

[15] *Ibid.*, §41.

[16] *Ibid.*, §25.

[17] *Ibid.*, §51.

[18] L. M. Chauvet, *Symbol and Sacrament: A Sacramental Representation of Christian Existence*, Collegeville, Liturgical Press, 1995. Another very important work is done by the Lutheran canonist H. Dombois, *Das Recht der Gnade. Ökumenisches Kirchenrecht*, I; 2nd ed., Forschungen und Berichte der evangelischen Studiengemeinschaft, 20, Wittenburg, Luther Verlag, 1969.

Worship and Ecumenism

PAUL P. J. SHEPPY

This essay forms a response to the confessional papers which I have been asked to review, and which describe how worship is practised and understood within various traditions, and how those traditions understand their specific practice of worship within the ecumenical whole. It does not seek to offer detailed comment on the individual papers. In my view, readers will be better able to make their own judgments without an "official line" being suggested. My intention, rather, is to address two main questions arising from the collection:

1. What are the common patterns in worship which emerge from the confessional statements, and how do the differences reveal and/or impede those common patterns?

2. How does the ecumenical perspective influence emerging patterns of worship?

A third question I wish to address is not widely raised by the individual papers, but ought not to be allowed to escape our attention. The purpose of our enquiry into what is happening in worship ought not simply to be an account of the past, or even of the present where it is shaped predominantly by the past. We need to ask about the *future*, and to enquire how the present changes in our world are being reflected in worship. Gail Ramshaw's paper on feminist approaches to worship describes one example of how change in social thought impinges on worship, and I want to widen that issue. In doing so I do not want to evade the challenge of the particular, but to show how the feminist experience raises a more general question:

3. Are the theologies which underlie our worship adequate to express the changing demographic nature of the church, and how does the tag *lex orandi, lex credendi* imprison – or liberate – our worship?

Perversely, it is with this third question that I wish to begin; and I shall wish to return to it at the end.

Changes in demography and ideology

Much contemporary discussion among liturgists addresses the question of inculturation: How far can local culture and custom shape worship, and how far does Christian theology and worship have to be counter-cultural? Such a discussion gains particular force and focus in the experience of a church no longer bound by one Christianized culture, and no longer inhabiting a world where the modernist consensus holds unchallenged sway.

Demography: North to South, West to East

Throughout the 20th century a huge demographic shift has been taking place in the life of the Christian church. In 1900 more than half the membership of the Christian church was to be found in the northern hemisphere and in the west (that is, Europe and the North American landmass); now, in 1999, more than two-thirds are to be found in the southern hemisphere and in the east. In this paper I shall refer to these two manifestations of the church's locatedness in the world as "the old church" and "the new church".

Ideology: modernism to post-modernism

In the same period we have seen the ideological shift from modernism to post-modernism, from a number of coherent meta-narratives to an extreme form of relativistic pluralism which rejects meta-narrative (though it is itself at least a type of meta-narrative). For many Christians this shift is extremely serious and one to be resisted, since the Judaeo-Christian witness to God is a meta-narrative giving coherence and meaning to all our living.

For many Orthodox this issue is addressed quite differently. Modernism has been regarded as a departure from the vision of God. On such a view modernism has meant humanism, and humanism has obscured our creatureliness and dependence upon God. And post-modernism is simply a further step on a godless journey.

Such a root-and-branch rejection of modernism (and, by extension, post-modernism) has meant that Orthodox worship has maintained an historical "otherness" which remains profoundly attractive to many whose acceptance of modernism and post-modernism is not uncritical. For many of those who find modernism and post-modernism spiritually unsustaining, there is an appeal in the holistic vision of Orthodox worship. But not for all.

For those who welcome the modernist and post-modernist projects, a return to a pre-modern worship would be impossible, whatever its glories, for it would mean that split between spirituality and daily life which the Orthodox, from a different perspective, also reject. For such modernist and post-modernist Christians, worship has to be expressed precisely in the *new* context.

Worship and mission

Each of these issues has either missiological and/or euchological-liturgical implications. What we say, read and sing in worship is shaped by, and itself shapes, what we say and do in mission. The instinctive response of worshippers towards liturgy (written or unwritten) is conservative, no matter how radical the missionary imperative may be. Even when worship "modernizes" itself, it usually simply adopts and adapts existing cultural practices. As contemporary examples of this we may cite the use of country music in much of the charismatic worship scene, and house, garage and rap music in the rave worship scene.

If we are to take the demographic shift from North to South seriously, we in the old church will have to learn from the new church something of how they worship. Unlike the old church in the West (with the recent exception of those in Eastern Europe), the new church in many places experiences persecution, torture and oppression. While the teaching of the old church is predominantly about finding forgiveness from sin and the patient bearing of our sufferings (however unjust), the new church talks of freedom and the struggle to overcome. And the worship of the new church is characterized by active hope – even in suffering.

Context and tradition

That sociological and demographic issues are extremely important is evidenced by the fact that the writers of the confessional papers in this volume have wanted to set what they have to say about worship in a wider context – whether ecclesiological, historical or theological. Context is all. However, in selecting contributions the demographic issue seems to have been largely ignored; certainly it has been overlooked. The 20th century shift in the church's locatedness might almost not have occurred.

In such a silence, theological and ecclesiological explorations pursue the traditional categories of the old church, and ecumenism becomes a question of how to work together without losing sight of the old distinctions. Of course, this is quite comprehensible; the past which has shaped the old church has been costly and often bitter. For many, ecumenism involves a call to embrace a future in which identity shaped by the past will be significantly changed, and perhaps even lost. Since that identity has nearly always been bought at the cost of martyrdom, the call to change can appear, to some, to be a call to betrayal.

When we ask whether ecumenical worship is a new worship, or whether the ecumenical church is a new church, the answer nearly always seeks to allay the fears and suspicions of those who see the past as something which must not be betrayed. Tradition becomes a monolithic system which must be preserved intact.

The marginalization of the new church

But in many of the base communities of the new church, the traditional answers do not fit the experiential questions. Old ways of reading and interpreting the scripture by reference to the tradition are being challenged – and sometimes abandoned. Where there is no access to theological libraries and to biblical commentaries, or to those accustomed to the use of such resources, a communitarian exegesis has arisen. Where there is no regular clerical presence, the priesthood is expressed by the congregation both in word and sacrament.

By and large, in the essays we have received in this collection this experience of the new church is marginalized. As suggested above, at one level this is not surprising: the overwhelming response to the new is the attempt to regularize it by means of the hierarchical authority of the old. It is not surprising but it is, perhaps, deeply disturbing that the contracting old church feels that it has a competence, a right and a responsibility to direct the expanding new church in the conduct of its life, worship and witness.

I shall have more to say about this at the end of the essay. For now we need to consider what patterns can be discerned in the confessional papers.

Signs of convergence and divergence

Initially, as we read these articles, we gain a strong sense of convergence. There is wide agreement that the activity of the church in worship reflects the high priestly ministry of Christ.

There is an increasing (though not unanimous) impression of forms of worship which share a common liturgical shape. In services or liturgies of the word, the growing influence of the *Revised Common Lectionary* (RCL; see below)[1] creates a powerful perception of the scriptures we hold in common. Yet in other areas divergence remains. There is still no agreed understanding of the nature of the sacraments, or of who may preside at the eucharist. The priesthood of all believers is variously understood, and the nature and location of authority in the church is still a contentious issue.

Whatever *Baptism, Eucharist and Ministry* (BEM) may have suggested in terms of agreement, the confessional papers reveal that much of the ecumenical journey remains to be made. This is more than simply the difficulty of recognizing one another's forms of ordained ministry. There is still an unresolved problem about how authority and ministry are *expressed* within different traditions; and this arises from distinct understandings of the nature of the church. Apparently convergent language may yet conceal divergent theology and ecclesiology.

Worship as a reflection of Christ's high priesthood

As an example of such divergence within convergence, it may be helpful to consider the central theme of the paper from the Evangelical

Lutheran Church in Germany. Hans Krech offers a masterly theological account of how the worship of the Christian church expresses the high priestly ministry of its head, Jesus Christ. Reading other papers might lead one to conceive that there is a high degree of convergence here. However on deeper reflection, and when we consider how others express in their liturgies the same doctrine, Krech's analysis raises as many problems as it solves.

In few traditions is the priesthood of all believers expressed in lay presidency at the eucharist. Yet some communities – for example, some feminists, some Pentecostalists, some Baptists, some members of the Iona Community – will permit, and even encourage, the priesthood of all believers to mean that the eucharist can, and should, be celebrated even when no ordained person is present. Not all communities permitting lay presidency see it as the norm, though some do. Some do not have ordained ministry. Very few, however, would allow just anyone to preside; the task is normally reserved to persons approved by the congregation or other authorizing body. Most seem to consider the lay presidency as exceptional – but there is here a fault-line of *praxis* which indicates a deep fault-line in the apparent solidity of the doctrinal *terra firma*.

Worship as eucharistic

The majority of papers adopt the position that eucharistic worship is the norm. This is not universally the case, however, and there are several ways in which the Sunday celebration of the eucharist is either not a common experience, or is in some way expressed less than fully by the congregation.

In a number of traditions (mostly among the Reformation churches) there is a far less frequent celebration of the eucharist. For such congregations, the normal Sunday service is a service of the word. Eucharist may occur twice or once a month, or even once a quarter. In part, this reflects a high view of the eucharist: too frequent an observance, it is felt, would diminish its sacred nature. In part, it may be said to show a low view: the eucharist has no saving effect in the sanctification of the believer.

However, the distinction is not quite as easy as this. Even where the eucharist is celebrated every Sunday, there may be very few who receive the elements. Among the Orthodox, it is clear that many may present themselves for communion only once a year. This infrequent reception has nothing to do with a "low" or "high" view of the eucharist, objectively considered. It is far more complex and arises from what appear to be custom and practice, which are derived, in turn, from what we might now call psychological and sociological factors. Here, then, is another case where some degree of apparent convergence (regular weekly eucharistic celebration) obscures divergence (the frequency – or lack of it – of congregational reception).

Nor is it easier to argue a case for convergence when, for example, the Quaker paper describes their worship as "eucharistic". Clearly, as Janet Scott observes, this use of the word – in a tradition where the outward sign of the sacrament is rejected – has a different reference and weight from that accorded to it by, for example, Roman Catholics. Yet again we have an instance where convergent language is used in a situation where considerable divergence of *praxis* remains. Scott herself is quite clear about the divergence, yet a convergent word "eucharistic" is used. There is no dishonesty here, but we do need to be clear how words change meaning and weight when set within their given context.

A common liturgical "shape"?

Both in services of the word and of the eucharist there is an apparently increasing convergence of liturgical shape. In part this may be a result of the response, in the liturgical renewal of the 1960s and 1970s, to Dom Gregory Dix's *The Shape of the Liturgy*. Whether such a consensus will survive the current round of liturgical revision (with the challenge to Dix's monolithic structuralism posed by the English liturgist Paul Bradshaw and others) is less clear. Certainly the suggestion that the early church had considerable variety in its liturgical practice from one centre to another may be said to legitimate the current interest in the diversity which local and regional inculturation offers.

Nonetheless in the traditional free churches – and particularly those springing from the Anabaptist and Independent Congregational trajectories – a quite distinct liturgical shape remains. In the services of the word there is little use of the office canticles, and the main liturgical shape is given by hymnody rather than by service books. In these traditions, the eucharistic prayers are frequently uttered by appointed lay members of the congregation, and in many cases separate prayers are spoken before the breaking of the bread and the administration of the cup (or cups).

Those who follow such a line point to 1 Corinthians 11 as the earliest New Testament evidence for a eucharistic service, and understand that a blessing was pronounced for bread and wine. Notice that the blessing is "for" the bread and wine, not "of" them. In the confessional papers, where the weight of eucharistic understanding presumes a consecration of the elements, this dissenting witness is obscured. For congregations in these traditions, the eucharistic blessing is a blessing of God; and while this may lead to a so-called "Zwinglian" memorialism, it is far from clear that Zwingli was as reductionist as is often claimed.

If earlier I was constrained (*pace* BEM) to point to a divergence over understandings of ministry, here we see that there is continued divergence over the understanding of eucharist. Once again, we must not allow ourselves to believe that convergent language necessarily means convergent thought.

The liturgical year

One area where there does appear to be some convergence in thought as well as in language is in an increasing observance of the liturgical year. For many traditions the liturgical year provides the essential shape of the liturgy. The paper from the sisters at Grandchamp describes this; but they are not alone. Groups as apparently diverse as the Orthodox and Reformed churches express the paschal mystery in worship through the cycle of the liturgical seasons.

Perhaps one reason this is so is because there is less controversial theological history about the liturgical year. Even the least liturgically minded congregation will scarcely refuse to observe Christmas and Easter (although it must be admitted that some keep these feasts in quite a minimalist fashion). Increasingly the season of Advent is being recovered, and the charismatic movement did much among non-Pentecostals to restore the celebration of Pentecost as more than a doctrinal event. Lenten study groups, and the fresh post-Vatican II focus on penitential seasons, have strengthened this recovery of the liturgical year in the Western church.

I would have welcomed some further exposition of this topic from the Syrian Orthodox tradition, not least because of their way of looking at the period beyond Pentecost. The description of Sundays as belonging to "ordinary time" is often more depressing in tone than need be, simply because the *ordo* of the liturgical year in the West is so lopsided. In my own work I have experimented with a Pentecost season lasting until 6 August which I celebrate as the feast of the Transfiguration (not least because of Hiroshima in 1945, and despite the move to return that feast to Lent). I have then tried to inaugurate a season of Transfiguration lasting until 29 September, when I propose a final season of Michaelmas leading to Advent.

I do not expect instant acclaim for my clumsy efforts to give a more balanced shape to the liturgical year; but I am encouraged to think that among the Orthodox there exist more equally divided seasons. With such a provision, the wider experience of becoming the new humanity (Transfiguration), and the struggle against evil (Michaelmas) – which are missiological presumptions of what I earlier called "the new church" – can begin to deepen what is gradually becoming a far more common way of thinking about our Christian living, a way in which the worship of the year, attuned to Christian seasons, deepens our understanding of God's creative and redemptive work.

We may find more opportunity for convergence in this more liturgically driven milieu than in more traditional theological debate, where we are tempted to reiterate our set positions.

The Revised Common Lectionary

Among English-speaking churches there is an increasing use of the *Revised Common Lectionary* (RCL), a close sibling of the Roman Catholic *Ordo Lectionum Missae*. This has produced an extraordinary and unforeseen benefit. As more and more churches use the same scriptures each Sunday, there has been a growth of ecumenical Bible study dealing with the scripture being used in the liturgical assembly.

At present, the RCL is confined to English-speaking churches, but there is no reason why this should necessarily be so. Other language groups might equally use the lectionary, since it simply lists the readings for the main service of Sundays and the great feasts. The lectionary assumes a eucharistic pattern of worship with Old Testament, Psalter, epistle and gospel lections, but it can equally be used for services of the word.

The English Language Liturgical Consultation (ELLC – see note 6 on p. 68 of this volume) is responsible for the publication and promotion of the RCL; it is engaged in a programme of discussion with other language groups, with a view to wider adoption of this common pattern for reading the scriptures in worship.

The influence of ecumenism

The confessional papers brought together here nearly all show some awareness of what is occurring in other traditions. Some instinctively seek to respond to wider trends – while others see their contribution to ecumenical debate as an unchanging witness to what they have always held.

Lex orandi, lex credendi

Here we can begin to return to my earlier question about the influence of the tag *lex orandi, lex credendi*. At the beginning of this essay I suggested that this saying might be either liberating or imprisoning. If we allow it to mean that the prayers of the people will show how faith develops, the saying may become intensely liberating. Where we use it as a regulatory refusal to change praying simply because doing so will mean a shift (not to be borne!) in what we believe, it may well lead to a stifling of the Spirit and an imprisonment of the congregation.

Of course, this is to put the matter quite partially. Several of the confessional papers (particularly the Orthodox contributions, but not exclusively so) remind us that one of the huge strengths of set liturgies is that they prevent the tyranny of individualism. In the liturgical act we are not dominated by our subjective feelings and personal preferences; rather, we rely on the common mind of the church arrived at in councils and in the experience of the centuries.

While as a working liturgist I am strongly sympathetic to such a view, I am still uncertain that it is a complete answer. In a divided world church, can the answer of any one tradition – however venerable – be adequate for all? From those who express the priesthood of all believers in more democratic terms, the question may be posed more sharply: how far is the use of liturgy as a means of preventing individualism actually a means of exercising central, clerical control, of stifling the holy people of God? How does such a centralizing, clerical use of liturgy accord with the emergence of a literate, enfranchised laity?

Ecumenism as a word of the church and of the world

At this point we return to the demographic questions I raised above. "Ecumenism" has become a church word, a word to describe the church, but it was not always so. *Oikoumene* was not, in the first place, a word about the church. The founders of the modern ecumenical movement knew this; their agenda sprang from missionary concerns, and they knew that *oikoumene* is primarily a word about the world, meaning "the inhabited (earth)". It later came to mean "the known world", and in Christian thought became part of the belief in the fullness of Christ's eternal reign – "the world to come" (*ē oikoumene ē mellousa*, cf. Heb. 2:5).

It is this deeper sense of ecumenism, of the church's place within the world made and redeemed by God in Christ, that is so muted in the confessional essays. Many of our concerns about the ordering and enacting of worship are about ecclesiology rather than mission. Hans Krech reminds us that liturgy is *public* worship, "and that is why the bells are rung". Perhaps we need to address this "demographic" sense of *oikoumene before* seeing it in its churchly context.

Demographic ecumenism and inculturation

If we are to take seriously this primary sense of *oikoumene*, then we are constrained to be engaged in questions of the church's place in the world, and of how worship is inculturated.

St Paul's classic exposition of the church's relationship to the world is that we are in it, but not of it; this is an uneasy tension, but the tension has to be maintained. In his own missionary journeys the apostle knew that there were times to use the culture (for example, at the Areopagus in Athens), and times to resist it (for example, the Diana *cultus* at Ephesus). Outright dismissal of the existing culture is as counter-productive as uncritical espousal of it.

While several of the papers address the issue of inculturation – and in particular the paper from the Church of South India, to which I shall return – the question of how people's experience of daily life is expressed in worship is less clearly articulated. At the same time, we need to ask how Christ is manifested in worship. Do the formal liturgical texts reflect the same Christ as indigenous hymns and songs? Where there is a mismatch, does the difference itself have a moderating effect on both the tradition and the local expression? Or do the two reveal and exemplify an unresolved difficulty?

The old church has been very successful at inculturation. When we look at icons, the tradition is very strong and coherent. Equally, when we walk into St Peter's in Rome we see an extraordinarily successful example of inculturation. Around us are the huge statues of the apostles, casting the twelve in the role of entrants in some *Il Signor del Risorgimento* contest – great, muscle-bound figures twisting their bodies to display pectorals, biceps, triceps, quadriceps, trapezoids, deltoids and the rest.

"We" (those of us in the old church) scarcely notice the inculturation of the biblical figures until we see the peoples of the new church – Africans, or South Americans, or Indians, or Asians, or Polynesians – beginning their own programme of inculturation. Then we begin to ask whether the disciples really did wear grass skirts, or whether Mary of Magdala really did have twelve brass rings around her neck and a wooden disc in her lower lip. Why does the older form of inculturation pass largely without comment? Is it simply that age has dulled our critical wits? Is it the shock of the new that excites anxiety – and even condemnation?

Church ecumenism in worship: goal or reality

Time and again the confessional papers demonstrate an awareness of the churchly nature of ecumenism. Yet they seem to suggest that its impact on our worship is still more a goal than a current reality. This is not as depressing as some may find it. The task of recovering an ecumenism of the church is not simply one of unravelling ecclesiastical history. We cannot return to an imagined *status quo ante*. The *ante* (*pace* the Orthodox rejection of modernism) is not recoverable; clocks cannot be wound back. The worldwide expansion of the church cannot, it seems to me, be contained within some "pressure cooker" type of central control. The New Testament story of the missionary expansion into the gentile world – into the *oikoumene* – demonstrates that, while there was collegial unity among the apostles, there was also freedom of development in order to meet the missionary task. Gentiles did not need to be circumcised, and a life of prayer and worship had to be developed beyond the Temple and the synagogue.

The changes in our world will not be as quickly addressed – particularly from within a divided church. But the realization that the task needs enterprising is welcome, so long as we allow a freedom of voices equivalent to that which prevailed at the council of Jerusalem. The language of dominance has to be resisted if the church is to grow, and if its worship to become truly the work of the priesthood which is that of all believers.

Thomas Thangaraj's paper describing the Church of South India's worship makes very specific some of the questions I have just raised. For many Indian Christians, inculturation is a two-edged sword. CSI congregations are emerging from a worship shaped by their missionary founders, but they are hesitant about an inculturation which would render them indistinct from Hindus and Muslims. There may be a danger that the current enthusiasm about inculturation is being distorted by a Western paternalism. If inculturation is to occur it must be indigenous, but it must also be a *Christian* inculturation. The likelihood is that local new church Christian leaders and congregations are more able to see what must be resisted and what may be adopted, than old church authorities in the distant theological and liturgical redoubts!

Along with liturgical change, the CSI is experiencing the challenge of what it means to have a strong *praxis* of the priesthood of all believers. Dalits can no longer be kept outside (one might ask how they ever were): surely there can be no support for such an apartheid from the New Testament. Time after time, the gospel writers tell us of Jesus keeping table and company with the untouchables of his day. Now the church of South India – a new church with old church foundations – is making the difficult change to a new church life which is more inclusive of all its people. We must watch and pray with them.

Old church and new church: the future

While the *churchly* nature of ecumenism is at least present on the agenda, it is less clear that the *worldly* nature of ecumenism is. What I have called the old church is increasingly seen as irrelevant by the world in which it is placed. Our worship struggles to engage with a global culture which lives in a "pick-and-mix" market place. To see all over India – and not just in the big cities, but in the tiniest villages as well – kiosks offering international telephone connections with subscriber trunk dialling and facilities for faxing and electronic mailing, is to be reminded that Marshall McLuhan's "global village" is more than ever a reality.

For the old church to attempt to dictate or dominate the agenda as it did in the past is no longer a serious option. In the global village, different families have different ways of doing things, but (*pace* the post-modernists) there are village patterns. The question is whether the village consents to be ruled by the elders any longer.

In such a world, the church needs to read the signs of the times and to discern the spirits. That church does not have the same demographic shape that it did a century ago, and in many places its worship is changing. One of the difficulties presented by the papers I have been asked to review is that we are unable to discern clearly the underlying nature of that change. In part, this is because we are still dominated by old church ways of thinking about the theory and practice of worship, and the ways in which we order and regulate it. In part, it is because the change is still in process and we cannot see the end.

As I have read these papers, I have been encouraged that there is a widespread sense of the importance of the ecumenical movement in the developing liturgical story. My hope is that we will widen both our churchly and the worldly understandings of the *oikoumene* so that the worship of the whole church – in heaven and on earth – will reveal Christ, who fills the whole universe in all its parts (Eph. 1:23), and all creation may be filled with the glory of God as the waters cover the sea. Then we shall truly know an *ecumenical* worship.

NOTE

[1] For further information on the *Revised Common Lectionary* see the web site of the Consultation on Common Texts at http://www.commontexts.org/.

Contributors

Rev. Dr Daniel Albrecht is professor of church history and Christian spirituality at Bethany College of the Assemblies of God, Santa Cruz, California, USA.

Bishop Nareg Alemezian is ecumenical officer in the department for ecumenical relations, Armenian Catholicosate of Cilicia. He is a member of the Faith and Order Plenary Commission.

Presiding Bishop Vinton A. Anderson is bishop of the 2nd episcopal district, American Methodist Episcopal Church, Washington, DC, USA.

Rev. Dr Thomas F. Best (Christian Church (Disciples of Christ)) is executive secretary in Faith and Order, World Council of Churches.

Rev. Dr Øystein Bjørdal was, at the time of writing, the director of the liturgical centre, Church of Norway.

Rev. Cynthia Botha is a pastor in the [Anglican] Parish of St Francis of Assissi, Parkview, Johannesburg, South Africa, and coordinating secretary of the Church of the Province of South Africa publishing committee.

Rev. Jeff Carter is pastor of the Manassas Church of the Brethren, Manassas, Virginia, USA, and chair of the denominational name study committee.

Rev. Dr Peter Donald (Church of Scotland) is minister at Crown Church, Inverness, Scotland. He is a member of the Faith and Order Plenary Commission.

Rev. Dr Ruth C. Duck is professor of worship, dean of the chapel, and coordinator of the theology and arts programme at Garrett-Evangelical Theological Seminary, Evanston, Illinois, USA.

Dr Denis Fortin is professor of theology and associate dean at the Seventh-day Adventist Theological Seminary of Andrews University, Berrien Springs, Michigan, USA.

Rev. Kathy Galloway is leader of the Iona Community, Iona and Glasgow, Scotland.

Dr Michael Ghattas is lecturer at the Centre for Patristic Studies in Cairo, Egypt, and head of the department for Coptic music in the Institute in Coptic Studies, Cairo.

The Community of Grandchamp is a religious community of sisters, ecumenical in character and issuing from the Reformed churches. Its home is in Areuse, near Neuchâtel, Switzerland.

Rev. Dr Robert W. Gribben (Uniting Church of Australia) teaches liturgy, missiology and ecumenics and is head of the department of practical theology, United Faculty of Theology, Melbourne, Australia.

Rev. Dr Dagmar Heller (Evangelical Church in Germany), a former executive secretary in Faith and Order, is now executive secretary for ecumenical relations, and for bilateral dialogues with Orthodox churches, of the Protestant Church in Germany (EKD).

Rev. Dr David R. Holeton (Anglican) is professor of liturgy at Charles University, Prague, Czech Republic.

H.E. Archbishop Mor Cyril Aphrem Karim is patriarchal vicar for the Eastern USA of the Syrian Orthodox Church of Antioch.

Rt Rev. Dr Sigisbert Kraft is bishop emeritus of the Catholic Diocese of the Old Catholics in Germany, and chairman of its liturgical commission.

Rev. Dr Hans H. Krech is executive secretary in the office of the United Evangelical Lutheran Church of Germany. His responsibilities include the areas of worship and liturgical questions.

Rev. Dr Abraham Kuruvilla (Mar Thoma Syrian Church of Malabar) is director, TMA, Counselling Centre, Kottyam, India.

Rev. Dr Young-Hoon Lee is president of the International Theological Institute, Yoido Full Gospel Church, Seoul, South Korea.

Fr Patrick Lyons OSB (Roman Catholic), a monk of Glenstol Abbey, is professor of liturgy at Mary Immaculate College, Ireland.

Dr Paul Meyendorff (Orthodox Church in America) is Father Alexander Schmemann professor of liturgical theology at St Vladimir's Orthodox Theological Seminary, Crestwood, New York, USA.

Rev. Nathan Nettleton (Baptist) is lecturer in liturgical studies at Whitley College (affiliated with the University of Melbourne), Melbourne, Australia.

Dr Dimitrios Passakos (Church of Greece) is a teacher of religious education in Athens and a member of the "Artos Zoes" educational and philanthropic institute.

Rev. Dr Jim Puglisi, SA (Roman Catholic), is director of the Centro Pro Unione, Rome.

Dr Gail Ramshaw (Lutheran) is professor in the graduate programme in theology and ministry, LaSalle University, Philadelphia, Pennsylvania, USA.

Colonel Earl Robinson is secretary for spiritual life development and international external relations of The Salvation Army.

Rev. Corinna Schmidt is pastor of Mennonite churches in Lübeck and Hamburg, Germany.

Janet Scott is a member of Britain Yearly Meeting of the Religious Society of Friends (Quakers) and clerk of the committee on Christian and interfaith relationships. She lectures in religious studies and religious education in the faculty of education of the University of Cambridge, and is a member of the Faith and Order Plenary Commission.

Rev. Paul P.J. Sheppy, BD, former secretary of the Joint Liturgical Group, is minister of Abbey Baptist Church, Reading, UK.

Dr Rebecca Slough is associate professor of worship and the arts at Associated Mennonite Biblical Seminary, Elkhart, Indiana, USA.

Rev. Dr Laurence Hull Stookey (Methodist) is Hugh Latimer Elderice professor of preaching and worship at Wesley Theological Seminary, Washington, DC, USA.

Rev. Dr Burchel Taylor is pastor of Bethel Baptist Church, Kingston, Jamaica, and a member of the Baptist World Alliance commission on ethics and communication.

Prof. M. Thomas Thangeraj (Church of South India) is D.W. and Ruth Brooks associate professor of world Christianity at Candler School of Theology, Emory University, Atlanta, Georgia, USA.

Rev. Dr Keith Watkins (Christian Church (Disciples of Christ)) is professor of worship (emeritus) of Christian Theological Seminary, Indianapolis, Indiana, USA.